COLUMNS 4

2016 — 2018

Murphy Givens

COLUMNS 4

2016 — 2018

Murphy Givens

www.nuecespress.com

Corpus Christi, Texas

Library of Congress Control Number 2018962281

Givens, Murphy

COLUMNS 4   2016 — 2018

Includes index.

1. South Texas — History.
2. Nueces County — History.
3. Corpus Christi — History.

ISBN   978-0-9832565-9-5

Published by Nueces Press, Corpus Christi, Texas.

Cover design by Jeff Chilcoat

Cover photo: Fishing on the Don Patricio Causeway; see page 222.

www.nuecespress.com

PUBLISHER'S NOTE

For 20 years Murphy Givens wrote a weekly column on a subject of South Texas history. Over the years he wrote about nearly every person, place and incident in our history. From Murphy we have learned about diverse figures such as Cabeza de Vaca, Henry Kinney, Richard King, Daniel P. Whiting and Roy Miller. We were intoduced to Camp Scurry, the Reef Road, Nuecestown, the Cotton Road and Fort Lipantitlan. Events such as the Mexican War, Black Land Express, the Civil War battles in South Texas, the Ropes boom (and bust) and building the seawall were brought to us.

Writing is hard. Writing history to make it interesting adds another layer of difficulty to the process. The demands of meeting a deadline creates another problem. After many years the topics of our history were all recorded and finding new and different subjects became more difficult. I have long been amazed that, week after week and year after year for 20 years, Murphy Givens was able to write a weekly column on South Texas history — and to do so in a way that makes history, which can sometimes be a dull subject, entertaining and enjoyable.

I am always surprised by a new subject or photograph that Murphy has discovered. He has read virtually every book and article in the local history archives of the public library and, more impressively, remembers their contents. Whenever I need information or an answer to a question about local history, I email Murphy and invariably he knows the answer or knows where to look. I will miss Murphy's unique view on our past, since he retired from writing a column each week.

This volume is our fourth and the last collection of Givens' columns from the Corpus Christi Caller-Times. This will be the tenth book, since 2009, published by the Nueces Press. I believe that each book offers insights into the fascinating history of South Texas. I am pleased to bring you this, our latest volume.

Jim Moloney
Nueces Press

Table of Contents

Mr. Bascule caused a few problems

"Corpus Christi is a fine, beautiful city, but that bridge I
don't like." —Capt. O. Nillson from Oslo

Corpus Christi residents got to know the bascule bridge very
well before they were done with it. Bill Walraven, the late
longtime columnist, described it as "a dark, dingy affair, painted
black and covered with a heavy coat of grease to protect it from
the salt air. Sirens sounded mightily when it was about to be
raised and barriers with flashing lights barred both vehicular and
pedestrian traffic."

It was a great day when the bascule bridge was opened to
traffic on July 30, 1926. Riding across in the first car, a new
Buick sedan, were Mayor P. G. Lovenskiold and Navigation
District Chairman Robert Driscoll. Two months later, on Sept.
14, 1926, the port was opened with a momentous celebration.
The new turning basin must have looked gigantic to the residents
and the new bridge was a massive structure compared to the little
wooden bridge that had spanned Hall's Bayou.

It was not given a formal name but was known as the bascule
bridge. People asked — Who was this Mr. Bascule? But the
name referred to the type of counterbalanced lift bridge that was
called "bascule," French for seesaw. This unfamiliar term
became a very familiar one in South Texas.

The bridge weighed 1,500 tons. It was 121 feet long and 52
feet wide. It was so finely balanced that two small electric motors
could raise it 141 feet into the air in a minute. It had a walkway
on one side, streetcar tracks in the middle, and railroad tracks on

the port side. It was built by the Wisconsin Bridge & Iron and cost the city $406,000.

People were pleased with the new bridge spanning the port entrance. The siren that signaled an approaching ship would bring out the curious, who would park their cars and watch as the bridge began to swing up and out of the way for a ship coming in or going out to sea. Doc McGregor, the ubiquitous photographer, would ride it up, to get bird's-eye photos. Bill Walraven was going to ride it up but backed out. He didn't want to get his clothes greasy.

People gathered at the bascule got a close look at passing vessels. As Walraven wrote, "You could almost reach out and touch the ships. People waved to the seamen on deck as they scurried about, preparing to dock the ship." There has always been something intriguing about great ships coming in from the sea, some mystique about the nearness of shipping, the smell of salt air and perhaps that imagined smell of tar and hemp and distant ports of call.

But the bascule soon lost its mystique as it became outdated. It was built for smaller ships, a smaller port, and a smaller town. In five years it came to be seen as a bottleneck to traffic, a menace to navigation, and a hindrance to progress.

It could take 12 to 30 minutes for a ship to clear and while that was happening motorists were stalled on both sides of the bridge. They became impatient and watched as a ship moved slowly across the bay — "like a painted ship upon a painted ocean."

Day after day the siren would sound, the red lights flash, and the bascule would rise to the occasion. Children liked this interlude. They could play beside the cars and watch the arriving and departing ships. Some adults found the experience exciting but for others it seemed that going anywhere from anywhere meant a long delay because of Mr. Bascule.

As ship traffic increased so did the necessity for raising the bridge. Drivers would get angry and frustrated. The insults they yelled at bridge tenders could get technical and they would tell them what they could do to themselves. One tender — Leon Kirksey — said drivers called them "things that aren't in the Sunday school books."

The bascule bridge is up as a ship passes through the entrance to the port turning basin in 1935. The bridge served the city for more than 33 years, after it was erected in 1926 to span the port entrance. The 97-foot opening was a tight squeeze for larger ships. Photo by Doc McGregor.

If the bridge was an annoying nuisance for motorists, it was an outright danger for ships. The 97-foot opening was a tight squeeze for vessels with a beam of 70 to 80 feet. Originally, the U.S. Corps of Engineers opposed building the bascule because they felt that the 97-foot opening would prove to be inadequate for the larger ships being built. But the city, which was paying for the bridge, said $400,000 was all it could afford. It was a mistake for which the city would pay.

The Port of Corpus Christi became notorious in shipping circles for what pilots and captains called threading the needle. Capt. O. Nillson, from Oslo, Norway, skipper of the ship Fernland, said, "Corpus Christi is a fine, beautiful city, but that bridge I don't like." Another captain, John Peter Dekker, of the

Dutch freighter SS Almdyk, said of the tight squeeze, "It scared hell out of me."

One local pilot who made a living threading the needle said it was really tough in the winter, with a choppy sea, trying to bring in an empty ship. "It bounces around like a bubble, and it's a pretty bad business; you can't see the bridge piling when the empty ship is riding so high."

Newspaper archives contain stories about ships that collided with the bridge or brushed against the sides of the protective fenders. The bridge was closed for 10 days after it was hit by the SS Youngstown in 1931. Part of the wooden hull of the Constitution, Old Ironsides, was scraped off when it smashed into the bascule in 1932.

In 1933 the city tried, and failed, to get the Public Works Administration to finance building a new lift bridge. It tried and failed again in 1936, asking the PWA to fund digging a toll tunnel. The city revived the effort to dig a tunnel in 1941 but dropped the idea with the start of World War II. After the war, an idea was discussed to reroute the ship channel around North Beach, but it was too costly and the obstacles were insurmountable.

When raised to its full height, the bascule was like some great black albatross hanging over the port entrance. And the city, like the bascule itself, was poised with its own devilish balance. It couldn't afford to replace it but, if the port and city were to prosper, it couldn't afford to keep it.

—Jan. 6, 2016

Replacing the bascule sparked a fight

"Too many half-truths and misstatements are being
bandied about. I hereby resign as mayor." —Albert
Lichtenstein

The question of how to replace the bascule bridge must have
given officials some sleepless nights and led to one of those
hammer-and-tong fights for which Corpus Christi is famous.

The bascule was built in 1925-1926 over Hall's Bayou. As it
turned out, the 97-foot opening under the bridge was a tight fit
for ships, which often scraped the sides of the bridge and
sometimes knocked it out of commission. Getting into the port's
turning basin through this narrow channel was a dicey maneuver
called threading the needle.

The bascule was also a nuisance for motorists. When the siren
sounded that a ship was approaching, the bridge was raised,
stopping traffic. Drivers fumed because the ship was so far out in
the bay. But ships had to signal when they were a mile away and
the bridge tender had to raise the bridge.

It would stay up 20 minutes or so (less for a barge or small
vessel) but the wait seemed endless. The record said the bridge
would usually stay up 10 to 12 minutes, or five minutes for a
barge, but many believed it was much longer. Of course, people
measure time differently.

As the bascule became increasingly inadequate, as the volume
of ship traffic grew, it became a symbol of the city's original
mistake. But how to replace it? In the early 1950s the town
debated whether to dig a tunnel under the port entrance or build a

bridge over it. Tunnel supporters argued that a high bridge would tower over the city like a big ugly bird cage, depicting it as a larger version of the bascule. They argued that a historic part of town would have to be leveled to build the network of bridge approaches.

The town was divided. At one heated session of the City Council in the tunnel vs. bridge debate, Mayor Albert Lichtenstein, leader of the tunnel faction, got into an argument with Mayor Pro Tem Ellroy King. "Too many half-truths and misstatements are being bandied about," said Lichtenstein. "I hereby resign as mayor." Lichtenstein walked down and sat in the audience. It was a dramatic incident that is still recounted.

The issue was decided when the Department of Highways offered $9 million to build a bridge over the port entrance, but not a nickel for a tunnel. The chairman of the highway department, E.H. Thornton, cited problems with tunnels around Houston and said that he wouldn't build another toll tunnel, not for Corpus Christi or for Christ.

Studies put the cost of a tunnel at about $22 million. The high bridge would cost roughly the same — with the related costs of acquiring rights of way and moving rail facilities — but the state would pay almost half. That ended the debate.

Work began on the high bridge in June 1956. At the time, it was the largest single project ever undertaken by the State Highway Department.

Building the bridge was dangerous. The wind could knock a worker off his feet. Four workers were killed in falls from the structure, one of them an especially tragic story. A 16-year-old painter from Dallas, Clarence Whitehead, was working beside his father when he lost his footing and plunged to his death. His father watched helplessly as his son fell. The other three men killed were James Sutton, Samuel Tyson and Jesus Maldonado.

They started building it simultaneously from both sides. The north and south ends were joined on March 13, 1959, when steel workers put the first link in place. When the two met in the middle the spans were off a few inches, but that had been expected. One side was jacked up until the two fell perfectly into line, a fine piece of engineering.

A photo taken from the top of the Driscoll Hotel shows the Harbor Bridge and the network of roadways that would funnel traffic to the bridge under construction in 1958. The bridge was opened to traffic on Oct. 23, 1959.

It took three years and four months to build the Harbor Bridge. The finished structure included 21.5 million pounds of steel and 134.4 million pounds of concrete, for a total weight of 155 million pounds. It was 5,818 feet long, 250 feet above the water at its highest point, with 138 feet of vertical clearance. It quickly gained a nickname. Sailors called it Napoleon's Hat for its distinctive shape.

The new Harbor Bridge opened to traffic on Oct. 23, 1959. It was a big day for the city, after almost three decades of dreaming, planning, fighting and botched efforts. There was a parade of dignitaries and six bands played, from Naval Air Station Corpus Christi, Del Mar, Ray, Carroll, Miller and Solomon Coles schools.

One of the speakers at the ribbon-cutting was John Young, who would soon be elected to Congress, at least in part because of his leadership on the bridge issue as county judge. One wit said Harbor Bridge was the longest bridge in the world, stretching from Corpus Christi to Washington, D. C.

7

Cars in the official motorcade crossed over the bascule bridge and drove to North Beach so they could make the return trip, heading into the city over the new Harbor Bridge. In the lead car was Eleanor Tarrant, a 46-year-old housewife whose name was pulled in a drawing. After that, a steady stream of cars and trucks crossed over the bridge for the rest of the day and evening. Highway counters recorded 45,663 vehicles that drove over the bridge on that first day.

They were going nowhere, just back and forth across this wonderful new bridge, unhindered by any siren or flashing lights or endless waiting. The new bridge was more efficient, more striking, and yet more lifeless than the bascule. With the bascule one could almost reach out and touch passing ships, said Bill Walraven. But with the Harbor Bridge the sky was closer while the bay was far below. The closeness of ships and sense of the sea were gone.

A year later the wreckers went to work on the bascule. They used 50-pound charges of dynamite, delayed to explode five pounds at a time, for they dared not use greater charges because of the proximity of the new bridge. Nothing remains of the bascule except the memories; it was a bridge not easily forgotten. A bit of time has elapsed since then and now we are awaiting construction of a new bridge to replace the 57-year-old Napoleon's Hat.

—Jan. 13, 2016

The cabbage era and the Poenisch family

You can just about pinpoint when the farm era began because it coincided with the arrival of German immigrants from Sherman, the Poenisch family.

Before the town grew to spread over creation there were pastures where cows grazed and plowed fields where cabbages grew along Ocean Drive, where today a constant stream of traffic roars past.

Farming around Corpus Christi was always marginal. In the 1840s Hiram Riggs had a farm in the area later known as Blucherville. Henry Kinney grew cotton on his Oso ranch and Matthew Dunn grew cotton west of town. James McBride had a dairy farm and grew Irish potatoes three miles west of the city. Jean M. Priour planted cabbages and cauliflower at his farm by the Salt Lake. He sold vegetables in town before the Civil War.

These examples aside, there was not much agriculture around Corpus Christi. It was stock country, best suited as grazing land for cattle, sheep and horses.

E. H. Caldwell wondered about the lack of farming when he arrived in town in 1872. As he wrote in his memoirs, "Since I had been raised on a farm in a land flowing with milk and honey (Tennessee), I was aware of the lack of such things as butter (except for the Goshen brand, in tubs from New York, the very thought of which makes me sick). There were no eggs or chickens, no vegetables, and no feed except grass for the horses, mules and cattle."

There was no milk, no honey, and Caldwell wondered why. He asked a prominent rancher. The rancher said, " 'If I had two rolls

9

of silver dollars and buried one six inches in the ground, packing it down good and hard, and then laid the other roll on top of the ground, and you could take your choice, which roll would you pick?'

" 'Why, the top roll of course.'

" 'Yes,' the rancher said, 'a man would be a fool to do otherwise. And that's why we cattlemen take our money off the top of the ground. You see, this is dry country. To break the soil is hard work and as soon as you do it the moisture, if any, floats away. You can't raise crops on land without moisture. That's why.' "

That logic changed when artesian wells brought dependable water supplies to a drought-plagued land. With fencing and improved stock, cattlemen didn't need as much pastureland so they began to sell off excess acres. And what had been seen as stock country began to attract farmers who produced good crops from the fertile black soil. As the farmer came into prominence, old cattle ranges on the outskirts of the city were rooted up and plowed. Cowboys disdainfully called this process turning grass upside-down.

You can just about pinpoint when the cabbage era began because it coincided with the arrival of German immigrants from Sherman, the Poenisch family, who came to Corpus Christi in 1889. This was a turning point in the city's history, though they didn't recognize it as such at the time.

Lena Poenisch Pearse was 82 when she told a Caller-Times reporter, in 1962, about the Poenisch family's arrival shortly before Christmas in 1889. She was nine then. The whole family went to Flour Bluff to look at land, but Lena's father Friedrich didn't like the looks of the sun-scorched, white sandy soil at Flour Bluff. It was getting dark and too late for them to return to Corpus Christi so they spent a miserable night sleeping on the cold floor of an old butcher house.

hAfter more searching and sifting of the soil, Friedrich Poenisch bought land between where the Port Ayers shopping center and Del Mar College are today. (A Poenisch descendant, Harriet Tillman, has diligently recorded the family history, on which I have relied to write this narrative.)

A buggy traveling south on Ocean Drive drives past the intersection with Airline Road in 1910. On the right is the home and farm of W. A. "Farmer" Clark. The bay, unseen in this photo, is to the right. Farmer Clark's place was a little to the south of the Aberdeen community.

The sons of Friedrich Poenisch started their own farms. Ernest farmed in an area between Alameda and Ocean Drive. His brother Herman had a farm where the Country Club golf course is today. Another brother, Robert, had a farm along Alameda, from the vicinity of Airline to the Oso. A fourth son, Frank, lived with Robert.

They cleared the brush and discovered that the land was infested with rattlesnakes. Lena said they were everywhere and that it wasn't unusual to kill 15 in a day. When she was 10, she was bitten by a large rattler. The bite was doused with whisky and since there was no hospital a cot was set up in the back of a drugstore where she stayed to recuperate.

The Poenisches were thrifty and hard-working. They sold cabbages to produce brokers and the Poenisch wives ran egg and butter routes. Robert had a large orchard with figs, grapes and peaches. Herman's wife Bertha raised and sold turkeys and geese. Herman cut down trees, piled the stumps together and covered them with straw and dirt, as Harriet Tillman tells it. The

11

pile was set on fire and left to smolder for weeks. When the fire went out, charcoal remained and Herman sold bags of charcoal in the town.

Other farmers moved in. "Farmer" Clark brought his family in a covered wagon from Bell County in 1895. He began a farm in the area where Airline intersects with Ocean Drive.

The pages of the Corpus Christi Crony were filled with reports of cabbage shipments. On March 8, 1902, the Crony reported that six boxcars filled with cabbages — 168,950 pounds — were shipped out and on March 29, 486,361 pounds of cabbages were shipped to northern cities.

A mild winter helped make area row crops successful. They were planted in the fall and harvested in March, giving Corpus Christi an early monopoly on the market. This worked well until the area suffered several Arctic-like winters. In the frozen fields the cabbages were ice-covered and sparkling in the sun — and dead.

The life of a cabbage in freezing weather was a short one. And so was the cabbage era. Cabbages, onions and row crops gave way to cotton and grain sorghum and, well, concrete and asphalt.

—Jan. 20, 2016

Martha Rabb, the Cattle Queen

Martha had a formal portrait of her late husband, John
Rabb, dressed up in his Confederate uniform, hung in a
place of honor in the outhouse.

When John Rabb, one of Nueces County's leading cattlemen,
died in 1872 his widow Martha became known as the Cattle
Queen of Texas. We have no more than a peephole into the
world of John and Martha Rabb but let us peep.

John Rabb was born in 1825. He was related to the Rabbs
around LaGrange. His father, Andrew Rabb, was the first county
judge of Fayette County and his uncle, also named John, was one
of the founders of Rutersville College near LaGrange. The
younger John was a student at Rutersville in 1838, where he met
his future wife.

In March 1842, when John Rabb was 17, he joined volunteers
who were organized in response to the raid on San Antonio by
Mexican Gen. Rafael Vasquez. When he was 21 Rabb joined
Zachary Taylor's army and was wounded in the battle of
Monterrey. He was discharged on Oct. 2, 1846.

John met Martha Ann Reagan at Rutersville College when they
were students. She was considered striking, with brown hair and
gray eyes. Her friends called her Mattie. John and Martha were
married on May 23, 1848. They moved to Helena in Karnes
County.

In 1857 they moved again, with their four children, to
Banquete in Nueces County. John may have been encouraged to
move there by his cousin Sally Skull, who lived nearby. Rabb
bought 400 acres on Banquete Creek and began a cattle ranch.

He recorded his bow-and-arrow brand at Corpus Christi in November 1857. He built a home near Banquete and bought a house in Corpus Christi, originally built by Walter Merriman.

When the Civil War broke out, John Rabb was enrolling officer for local militia and mustered in 25 men on July 16, 1861. The 25 men included ranchers and ranch hands from around Banquete. Little is known of the activities of Rabb's company except that they served to protect remote border region ranches.

John Rabb died on April 15, 1872. His obituary in the Nueces Valley said he died at 2 a.m. at the ranch house. It did not list a cause of death, but he was 46. He was buried in Banquete Cemetery. A gloomy inscription on his tombstone reads: "Boast not thyself of tomorrow, for thou knowest not what a day may bring — for death is everywhere."

He was a rich man when he died. He left 10,000 cattle and 3,500 sheep on the open range. Only Richard King and Mifflin Kenedy could claim more cattle than John Rabb.

After her husband's death, Martha began to buy land, and it was cheap, because of the tumultuous times of the 1870s when rustlers and raiders kept South Texas in turmoil. She greatly increased the size of the ranch from the original 400 acres to 30,000 acres. In 1875, she had the ranch enclosed with a wooden fence. It was called Rabb's Ranch or Martha Rabb's Pasture or Rancho Flecha, for the bow-and-arrow brand.

Martha Rabb also built a home in Corpus Christi which she called Magnolia Mansion. It was built on the bluff with a fine view of the bay. The Southern plantation-style mansion was the most impressive house in town.

In July 1877 her youngest son Lee was shot to death at Petronila. He had taken a girl to a dance and while they were sipping coffee someone shot Rabb from an open window. The shooter escaped on Rabb's horse. John Dunn said in "Perilous Trails of Texas" that "some know-it-alls said he was never caught, however he was missing at all the elections since."

In 1879 Martha married the Rev. Curran M. Rogers, a Methodist minister in Corpus Christi. She was 53 and he was 38 and had recently buried his wife. He cut short the bereavement to court the wealthiest woman in town.

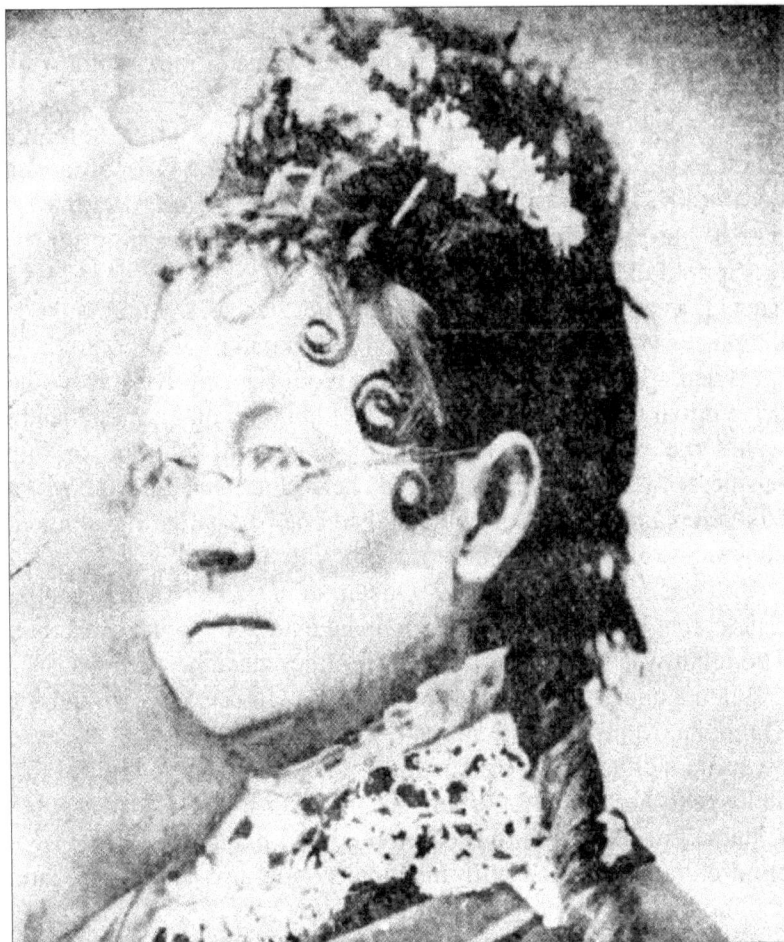

Martha Rabb, shown without her usual cigar, was called the Cattle Queen of Texas. She alienated her children when she moved her late husband's portrait from the parlor to the privy.

The Magnolia Mansion was taken over by the Rev. Rogers and his six children; the oldest was 14 and the youngest two. It must have been awkward for Martha's children, who did not approve of the marriage; they believed Rogers married her for her money.

Martha didn't help matters. She had a portrait of Capt. Rabb in his Confederate uniform moved from the front parlor and hung in a place of honor in the outhouse. Martha's sons — Green, named

for her brother, Dr. Green A. Reagan, and Frank, the youngest —
never forgave her. When she visited the ranch, Frank would stay
away until she was gone.

Five years after she married Rev. Rogers, Martha sold the
ranch to D. C. Rachal. (He later sold it to Robert Driscoll and it
became the source of Clara Driscoll's great fortune.) Martha, as
part of the sale agreement, was allowed to run her cattle on the
ranch until they were sold. Mrs. P. A. Hunter, a daughter of D. C.
Rachal, lived in the ranch house with her husband, who managed
the place. Mrs. Hunter left us a vivid portrayal of Martha Rabb.

"When she came to the ranch we would get in my surrey and
drive down to the cattle pens. She would climb up on the fence to
watch the branding and selling of stock, all the time talking
business to the buyers. I liked her. She was a woman of
education and refinement, but she had one bad habit. She smoked
cigars. She always had a box of them with her."

She was called the Cattle Queen of Texas in a newspaper
article that poked fun at her marriage to the young preacher.
Though it was used in derision, the epithet made her famous.

When Rogers was elected to the Texas House, Martha sold the
Magnolia Mansion and moved — bag and baggage and the
reverend's children — to Austin. Rev. Rogers dabbled in politics
and spent her money. When she died in 1901 she left what
remained of the estate to the reverend and his children. Her own
children contested the will and finally gave up. The cattle, land
and most of the money were gone anyway.

At the heart of this story, I suspect, is a mystery that would
explain John Rabb's sudden death, Martha's dishonoring of his
memory and the estrangement from her children. But it is
something may never know. You can see only the dim outlines
from history's small peephole.

—Jan. 27, 2016

Revival split town into hostile camps

"When it comes to rotten conditions, Pompei had
nothing on Corpus Christi. I have never before heard of a
man and four women sitting half a day at a beer table
together perfectly nude." —Rev. Mordecai Ham

Corpus Christi recorded 77 years of relatively uneventful
existence — except for that bombardment of the city during the
Civil War — before the arrival of the Rev. Mordecai Ham. But
when he brought his revival to town, 100 years ago, on Jan. 9,
1916, he shook things up.

The First Baptist Church invited the Rev. Ham to pitch his
revival tent in Corpus Christi. Ham was a Baptist evangelist who
was popular throughout the South and well-known to Texas. He
came from a long line of Kentucky preachers and could quote
Scripture by the yard.

Before he departed eight weeks later, the whole town was in a
state of intense excitement. Half the town would not speak to the
other half. Blows were exchanged in the street. Charges were
hurled and counter-charges hurled right back. Customers
threatened merchants with boycotts. Normally respectable
citizens were arrested and charged with assault. Children,
reflecting the views of their parents, fought in school. There were
mass meetings, parades, sermons, court hearings and editorials.
All were fueled by the combustible mixture of sex, alcohol and
religion courtesy of Reverend Ham. There was no
uncontroversial ground in the city.

The revival started peacefully enough. The Rev. Ham's crew
arrived and erected a huge tent at the edge of Lawrence and

Water Street. It was called a tabernacle. The first sermons were conducted on Jan. 9, 1916, a Sunday. Because of the Rev. Ham's fame, many churches cancelled their own services so their worshippers could attend the revival.

Given almost equal billing with Rev. Ham was his director of music, Rev. William J. Ramsay. The irreverent called them "Ham and Ram" and then it was just "Ham and" — much as a harried waitress would yell to the cook for "Ham and!"

In the early days of the revival some of Rev. Ham's sermons were reported in the Caller. But the newspaper quit reporting on the sermons when the evangelist began to preach about rampant sin and prevailing vice in Corpus Christi. Ham said the town was overrun with liquor houses, gambling dens and loose women or, in his Biblical description, whores of Babylon.

That January was intensely cold. But the tabernacle, with two stoves and hot sermons, stayed very warm. Rev. Ham and Rev. Ramsay stoked interest in the services by making enquiries about certain citizens and then making revelations at the meetings. Actual names were not used but the persons were so well described that people knew exactly who was being pilloried.

One day as the Rev. Ham returned to the Nueces Hotel where he was staying one of the men whose sins had been laid bare struck Ham across the face with a leaded quirt, knocking off his glasses. (This man exposed by the Ham-Ramsay revival later committed suicide.)

Some men in town who didn't know one end of a church from another took exception to the quirting of Rev. Ham and showed up at the evening service, carrying guns, to protect the evangelist. The whole city was fighting mad.

Rev. Ham thundered, "When it comes to rotten conditions, Pompei had nothing on Corpus Christi. I have traveled over Europe, North Africa, much of Asia, and many states of this Union, but I have never before heard of a man and four women sitting half a day at a beer table together perfectly nude."

In another sermon he preached: "Let me tell you fool sisters something. While you are chasing around after bridge parties and winning silk stockings . . . some of your husbands are flying around with other women whose names are linked with theirs in

A newspaper ad in the Caller and Daily Herald on Jan. 9, 1916 announced the revival of the Rev. Mordecai F. Ham (left) and his chorister, William J. Ramsay (right). Their eight-week revival set off one of the most contentious periods in Corpus Christi history. (Both photos taken from the advertisement; Corpus Christi Central Library.)

whispers in the street. I could produce evidence that would precipitate a riot before morning."

In another sermon he said: "This is not a fight of Ham and Ramsay for victory over the opposing gang. It is a crusade for the deliverance of Corpus Christi from conditions so iniquitous that it is stinking in the nostrils of all Texas." The Rev. Ham stated that one woman out of every five in Corpus Christi was a prostitute, that 300 gambling halls and 40 houses of prostitution were operating in the city, that public officials allowed such unlawful conditions because they were blind or corrupt.

The revivalists were subpoenaed to appear before Justice of the Peace E. H. Miles and were questioned about their assertions of lawless conditions and official corruption. They said the comments were based on hearsay or on confessions which, as ministers of the gospel, they could not reveal.

There were two newspapers in town. One, the Caller and Daily Herald, took a stand to oppose the Rev. Ham. Its competition, the Times, was a keen supporter of the evangelist and printed his sermons.

John W. Stayton, editor of the Caller, finally had enough. On Feb. 29, the newspaper printed a full-page editorial to answer Ham's charges that Corpus Christi was sunk in the depths of depravity. "Further silence would be treason to the people," the editorial said. "There is a limit to the merit of patience. The good name of Corpus Christi has been dragged in the dust and prostituted beyond precedent. Its officials have been defamed. Its citizenship rebuked.

"Rev. M. F. Ham and his man of all work, W. J. Ramsay, made their debut in Corpus Christi on January 9 . . . From the hour of their arrival they began their work splitting a quiet town into rival camps." The Caller editorial answered Ham's charges point by point. At the end of what must have been one of the longest editorials ever run in the newspaper, it said, "We believe such slander as that engaged in by these men, under the cloak of religion, is a menace to society. We cannot sit passively by while our city and its people are maligned."

The Rev. Ham said later that the editor of the Caller was too rotten to go to hell. The editor, Stayton, replied in the newspaper that that was fine with him, since it would mean that he wouldn't have to associate with "Ham and." The Ham-Ramsay revival became mixed up in the prohibition campaign and that led to a dirty and ugly fight.

—Feb. 3, 2016

Mordecai Ham joins prohibition campaign

The city, already split into rival camps, became even more bitterly divided over religion, politics, and prohibition.

As the revival led by the Rev. Mordecai F. Ham and his associate Rev. William J. Ramsay raged on, it became a big part of the wet-dry campaign of 1916.

The city was already split into rival camps. It became even more bitterly divided — over religion, over politics, and over prohibition. It was a community riven, said the Caller, by dark passions. That two-month period from the beginning the revival on Jan. 9 to the prohibition election on March 12 became the most contentious time in a generation.

The Denison Herald wrote that Rev. Ham so churned up the waters of Corpus Christi Bay that fishermen had to go 40 miles out into the Gulf to get a nibble.

The Nueces County Prohibition Club, organized in December 1915, was conducting a campaign to close 43 saloons in the county — three in Port Aransas, three outside the city limits of Corpus Christi, and the other 37 inside the city. The rest of Nueces County was dry, by local option.

The Prohibition Club circulated a petition to hold an election to decide whether the sale of liquor should be prohibited countywide. The people behind the campaign were called "Pros" for prohibitionists and those opposed were called "Antis".

The Pros were led by former Mayor Clark Pease, H. G. Sherman, who had lost a race for mayor, and prominent rancher

W. W. Jones, who was part owner of the Nueces Hotel. The Antis were led by Mayor Roy Miller, Nueces County Judge Walter Timon, and Walter Elmer Pope, soon to be elected to the Texas Legislature.

The Pros used Rev. Ham's revival as a fulcrum of their campaign. Rev. D. B. South, pastor of the First Baptist Church, said later that prohibition became identified with the revival but "the pastors had not planned it to be so. It was never clear as to how this came about."

The Ham tabernacle was usually filled with worshippers — with three services daily except for Monday — as the Rev. Ham fulminated against demon rum and the sinful conditions in Corpus Christi which, he said, was sunk in the depths of sin and depravity.

When the Rev. Ham wasn't preaching or investigating into the background of prominent sinners, he was leading auto caravans to outlying towns to bring back people to his revival.

Meanwhile, the Prohibition Club was holding mass meetings and parades and conducting their own caravans out into the county, traveling to Agua Dulce, Banquete and Robstown. The Pros hoped, the Caller reported, to overcome the strong Anti-vote in the city with a heavy Pro-vote in county precincts.

The petition for an election was presented to the County Commissioners. The names of 1,200 qualified voters (all men) were certified and the election set for Friday, March 10. The Caller said both sides were ready for the fray.

Tempers were running hot at a meeting of the prohibitionists outside the Nueces Hotel. As the Rev. Ham spoke from a wagon bed, there was a fistfight between R. P. (Dick) Blucher and Tom Cahill. A city policeman was arresting the two when Matthew Dunn stepped in and warned the policeman to let Blucher go. Dunn raised his cane as if to strike the officer and Sheriff Mike Wright slapped Dunn. Blucher, Cahill and Dunn were arrested. Blucher and Dunn were leaders of the prohibition movement; Cahill was on the other side.

The Caller reported that the revival's collection plates at one service on the previous Sunday contained $3,000 (over the course of the revival Rev. Ham conducted 156 services). These

Roy Miller (left), the mayor of Corpus Christi and former editor of the Caller, was strongly opposed to the Prohibition campaign of 1916. W. W. Jones (right), a wealthy rancher and part owner of the Nueces Hotel, was a staunch backer of the Ham-Ramsay revival and Prohibition movement.

were splendid returns, said the paper, and wondered how much good that money would have done for local pastors.

In another edition, the Caller noted that two Pro leaders — Clark Pease and H. G. Sherman — were "lined up with Ham and Ramsay and shouting prohibition from the housetops."

On the last Saturday night before the Friday election the Pros led a parade through downtown. There were floats decked with bunting and flowers, caravans of autos, and more than 3,000 people (a tremendous turnout in a city of 5,000.) On Thursday night before the election, the Antis held a rally at Artesian Park.

On the day of the election, the Rev. Ham left early that morning. The revival was over and the Rev. Ramsay had left some days earlier. There were many in the city who were not, we suspect, overly sad at their departure, and probably more unkind things than that were said of "Ham and."

At the polling places in the city, large crowds of women and children gathered and sang "Goodbye Booze" and "Nueces County Going Dry." They harangued male voters and some used small cameras to take photos of the men arriving to vote, just to make sure, they said, there were no irregularities. This spooked some men and they departed without voting.

A total of 3,377 men voted — 92 percent of those registered, which was probably the largest turnout, percentage-wise, in county history. The Pros won by 218 votes, a clear victory for the dry forces. The Caller was tactful. "That which is best prevails. Prohibition will become a fact in a few weeks. If it is salutary, it will outlive all agitations against it; if it is hurtful, it will be retired by the people."

The saloons were closed on April 21. Afterwards, Corpus Christi adjusted to life without beer and skittles, or beer anyway. The nearest place to buy a beer was in Rockport, 30 miles away. That put the lid on the saloon business in Corpus Christi for 16 years, until national prohibition was repealed in 1933.

The Rev. Ham and his sidekick Ramsay never returned to Corpus Christi. It took a long time for the ill feelings engendered by the revival and the prohibition campaign to die down. In the summer of 1916, a law school student at the University Texas came home for vacation and found that half the town was still not speaking to the other half. But on the whole the town was quieter and the news less sensational. Later that year, in August, Corpus Christi was struck by a major hurricane. It was the second bad storm of the year. The first one was Mordecai F. Ham.

—Feb. 10, 2016

I Remember . . . Sally Skull

"She came to our house bringing some of the finest
butter ever made, large yellow balls of butter packed
way down in a stone jar." —Eli Merriman

Eli Merriman was born in Hidalgo in 1852, the son of Dr.
and Mrs. E. T. Merriman. The family moved to Banquete in 1857
where Dr. Merriman bought a ranch and practiced medicine. Eli
became a newspaperman and was later one of the founders of the
Corpus Christi Caller.

Merriman once recalled the times when he was a boy growing
up on his father's ranch, about a mile from Banquete. He
remembered the quilting parties, where the women gossiped as
bad as the men folks, talking about their neighbors who weren't
there. "Some of the ladies dipped snuff, a custom among the best
at that time. I remember being sent down to the creek after
hackberry roots to make the snuff brushes for the quilters. There
were so many ladies around the frame that I had to crawl under
the quilt to distribute the brushes."

Perhaps topic number one was their notorious neighbor, Sally
Skull, who refused to ride side-saddle, who dressed like a man,
carried two guns and wasn't bashful about using them, having
killed more than one man. She was a strong-tempered woman
who commanded respect. "She had the eye of a hawk with
staring eyes," wrote Merriman. "While she may have had her
faults, she was jolly and joking with her friends. She came to our
house bringing some of the finest butter ever made, large yellow
balls of butter packed way down in a stone jar."

25

Eli Merriman, who grew up on a ranch at Banquete, remembered cutting hackberry roots by Banquete Creek for the women to use as snuff brushes.

When he was six his mother sent him and his younger brother John, who was five, to take lessons with his Aunt Mary, who had married his uncle, Marcus Fusselman.

Eli's Aunt Mary taught them to recite poems. Eli's was: "Twinkle, twinkle, little star; how I wonder what you are; Up above the world so high; Like a diamond in the sky; When the blazing sun is set; And the grass with dew is wet; Then you show your little light; Twinkle, twinkle, all the night."

26

His brother John's was: "How I like to see a little dog; And pat him on the head; So prettily he wags his tail; Whenever he is fed." (From the Caller, March 9, 1936; Times, April 16, 1936.)

Annie Schallert was born in the family home at Laguna and Water in 1862. Her father and mother were Mr. and Mrs. Charles Schallert. Three days after she turned 17, and after she had finished the eighth grade, she married Ernest Bagnall, who became one of the town's first undertakers. Bagnall was a fine carpenter who made his own caskets. When they were married they lived in a house on Starr Street.

In the hurricane that struck on Aug. 12, 1880, the sky was dark, the wind blowing hard, sea water filled the streets and slanting rain stung like nails.

"Mr. Bagnall carried many across the street," she said. "The water was up to his waist. We went to a higher place and stayed there for hours. When we got home there was part of a boat sticking into the house and all our stuff was washed into the street, like everybody else's. People got back what they could. We watched a tin tub full of clothes as it floated down the street." (From the Times, Aug. 29, 1952; interview, Nov. 25, 1939.)

Mrs. Frank Skidmore was born on May 7, 1855. Her father, R. H. Dickson, moved to Rockport when she was a child. At 16 she married Frank Skidmore, on Aug. 3, 1871. Frank Skidmore established a cattle ranch around the area that is now Skidmore. The Skidmore family built a 14-room, two-story house on the bank of the Aransas Creek, north of the coming town.

During the Nuecestown Raid, on Easter weekend 1875, Mrs. Skidmore and her brother William Dickson traveled to Corpus Christi to go shopping. They crossed the Nueces River on the Sharpsburg Ferry two hours before the raid.

She was in a millinery shop in Corpus Christi when the sheriff rode up and down the streets yelling a warning. Her brother borrowed a saddle and took one of the buggy horses to join a posse to chase the bandits. There wasn't much shopping done after that. "The raiders got off light. I think the posse killed only one member of the raiding party. We learned later that they robbed the Noakes store." (From the Caller-Times, May 7, 1950; May 6, 1951; May 4, 1952.)

Rejino Rodriguez, born in Tamaulipas in 1862, came to Texas as a small boy. His father worked on roads around San Antonio, San Diego and Kenedy. Rejino was interviewed in 1964 when he was 102 years old.

"When I first came to Mathis there was not even one house. An old Mexican put up a restaurant for the cattle workers. He was Pavlino. He died a long time ago. There was no lake at that time, but there was the Nueces River, where we watered the cattle. Lots of timber back then. People used to come from a long way to travel to San Antonio. When they came this way they got the lime they used in their tortillas. They stayed there sometimes for two weeks cooking the caliche for the lime. I lived in Mathis for 36 years, but I worked here long before there was a town." (From the Mathis News, Jan. 9, 1964.)

Alice Doughty was born across the Mission River from Refugio in 1861. She grew up in the town of St. Mary's and later Rockport before her family moved to a ranch near the present town Sinton.

They shopped in Corpus Christi, traveling by wagon on a pasture road and crossed the Nueces River on the ferry. They purchased in large quantities to keep the number of trips down, buying coffee by the 100 pounds and flour by the barrel.

Alice married J. L. Quinn who worked for her father, J. M. Doughty Sr. He later worked for the Coleman Fulton Pasture Company. When their kids reached school age they were taught at home by a governess. After a school was built at Sinton, her children rode to classes by horseback.

She remembered when Sinton had only a railroad section house and when it was necessary to flag a train if there was a need to stop it. (From the Caller, Dec. 23, 1949.)

—Feb. 17, 2016

I Remember . . . Ellis the drayman

"He would curry his horse and hitch him to a rubber-tired buggy and drive down Chaparral. He always led parades on horseback." —Carlyle Leonard

Carlyle Leonard's grandfather, Will Leonard, came to Corpus Christi as a free bondsman after the Civil War and opened one of the town's first barber shops. Carlyle Leonard once recalled that in the old days all the hauling was done by drays. These were flat bodies with two wheels and one horse.

"Most of the hauling of cotton, dry goods and other things was done by Ellis and Brown, two men from Jamaica. Ellis was quite a character. He would drive his horse to his dray every day but Sunday. Then he would curry his horse and hitch him to a rubber-tired buggy and drive down Chaparral. He always led parades on horseback."

Carlyle's grandfather, Will Leonard, was one of the city's first barbers. His shop was on Chaparral. He was known for an incident when Gen. William Tecumseh Sherman stopped in Corpus Christi for a visit. The mayor, J. B. Murphy, refused to meet the famous general because of his march through Georgia at the end of the war. There was to be no official welcome.

Will Leonard was at the depot. He jumped on a baggage cart, waved his hat, gave a rousing cheer, and made a short speech welcoming Gen. Sherman to Corpus Christi. (From the Caller-Times, Oct. 18, 1936; April 27, 1952.)

Carlyle Leonard. His grandfather, Will Leonard, a pioneer barber, made sure that William Techumseh Sherman received a proper welcome to Corpus Christi.

Nellie Musselman arrived in Corpus Christi from New Orleans in 1886. She brought with her the elegant dancing pumps that she had worn at Mardi Gras. Her twin brother Tom was already living in Corpus Christi and she had half-sisters in Rockport.

She married Thomas B. Dunn, chief of the city's volunteer fire department, and they built a 12-room home on North Carancahua. When the house was filled with flowers it was a sign that the firemen's parade was coming up since the Dunn home was headquarters for women who decorated the floats with flowers.

Early in the morning after the 1919 storm, volunteers brought survivors to the Dunn home, which became an emergency shelter. "It was awful to see them come in. They were all covered with oil and blood."

In the 1950s the Dunn home was razed to build the approaches to the Harbor Bridge. (From the Caller-Times, Oct. 30, 1955.)

Mrs. A. R. Yeargen, with her husband and children, moved to Corpus Christi from Georgetown in 1911. They came by railroad to start a grocery store on King Street. They brought their horse and buggy on the train.

"The horse and buggy were a necessity for the grocery business. My husband used to start out early in the morning going house to house taking orders. At the store he filled the orders and delivered them in the afternoon."

They sold vegetables, butter, eggs and meat. Sugar and lard came in barrels. Coffee was ground in the store. Coal oil for lamps came in large cans. (From the Caller-Times, June 2, 1963.)

Elizabeth (Freasier) David, born in Coleman County, moved with her family to Dinero in a covered wagon in the late 1880s. Her father, Ben Freasier, was a Confederate soldier in Robert E. Lee's Army of Northern Virginia. When the war was over her father came home and brought his gray horse with him. Bizlin was his name and, like her father, he had seen a lot in four years of war.

Three of the children would get on the back of the old warhorse and another would hang on to his tail, but Bizlin was always steady and polite, like the old soldier that he was. When Elizabeth began courting her future husband, they used a hollow tree as a post office for their love notes. She would write a letter and one of her brothers would ride to put it in the tree. Mr. David would pick up the mail and put an answering letter back in the tree. They were married in 1886 and lived on a ranch near Dinero. (From the Caller-Times, Nov. 13, 1960.)

Peter McBride, son of Mr. and Mrs. James McBride, was born on Aug. 3, 1863 in the family home on what is now Blucher Street. Growing up, the young McBride helped his father with chores and running the family dairy five miles out of town.

Peter's father and Matt Dunn bought a herd of wild horses at an auction. It was Peter's job to take them out to the open prairie and bring them home each night. When he was 17 he joined the delivery crew and began to make the daily milk run.

"We used horses and wagons to deliver the milk, which was taken to the homes of customers before daybreak. We began deliveries at 3 a.m. Milk was placed in 10-gallon cans at the dairy and loaded on milk wagons. Customers would leave their quart or gallon containers on doorsteps to be filled from the large cans." The days seemed longer then because they got up so early.

Peter McBride married Minnie Alice Priour on Aug. 18, 1890. They were married at St. Patrick's by Father Claude Jaillet.

They ranched near Corpus Christi until 1913 when they moved to San Diego and from there moved to Realitos. (From the Caller-Times, Aug. 21, 1955.)

Angie Westbrook arrived in Corpus Christi on Jan. 27, 1900. The wagon she and her family were riding in came down the bluff from Leopard Street. This was 15 years before the bluff balustrade was built. "We had to lock all four wheels of the wagon and then we could hardly hold the horses, the bluff was so steep." Mrs. Westbrook, her husband and three children arrived from Madison County. They had been traveling two months with three other wagons with families from East Texas.

Their first night in Corpus Christi was spent in a wagon yard where the Nueces Hotel was later built. Next morning it was drizzling rain when they got up to look for work.

Mrs. Westbrook found a job in a dairy, which paid 50 cents a day, and she washed and ironed the white clothes the dairymen wore for a quart of buttermilk every other day and a pound of butter once a week. She and her husband later operated their own dairy for 38 years. (From the Caller-Times, Jan. 22, 1961.)

—Feb. 24, 2016

I Remember . . . fist fights after school

"If you don't send Robert off to boarding school so you can get him off the streets, it is my prediction he will wind up in the penitentiary before he is 20." —Rachel Dougherty

Robert Bluntzer, son of Vincent and Kate (Dougherty) Bluntzer, once remembered when he and other boys hid a chicken in Sister Gertrude's desk at the convent school, resulting in considerable squawking from the chicken and teacher, both shaken by the experience.

He recalled the daily battles between convent boys and public-school boys. They would meet after class and conduct fist fights. One Sunday there was a violent melee between the combatants and Robert was wearing his father's favorite gray silk tie. He had borrowed it on the sly. He got his nose bloodied and his father's tie splotched with blood. He got another whipping at home.

Robert's grandmother, Rachel Dougherty, told his mother: "If you don't send Robert off to boarding school so you can get him off the streets, it is my prediction he will wind up in the penitentiary before he is 20." That made his mother so mad she wouldn't speak to her mother for a spell.

Contrary to his grandmother's expectation, the young hooligan, in the fullness of time, graduated from Georgetown University and became a respected oil man in Corpus Christi. (From the Caller-Times, March 12, 1961.)

Hattie Littles' mother was working for a family at Ingleside when she died. It was in the 1870s. On her deathbed she asked

Robert Bluntzer recalled the days when the convent school boys and the public school boys would meet after classes to have fistfights in the streets.

Malvina Moore to take care of her two little girls. Malvina wasted no time in going to the courthouse to file the adoption papers.

Not long afterwards the former employer of their mother came to claim them. Hattie remembered him standing there, wearing a white felt hat crushed down on top. He had a short gray mustache and a wooden leg. "He said that my mother had told him to take us and that he would give us a horse and saddle and a cow and a calf. But Malvina (we called her "Mama" later) told him that she had the papers of adoption, that we weren't slaves anymore, that we were free now, and that we were going to stay with her and go to school. And what could we do, just little girls, with a cow and a horse?"

Hattie and her sister were raised by Malvina Moore, who washed and ironed by the piece. "Mama" Moore was strict with

34

them, Hattie said, but a better woman never lived. (From the Caller, Aug. 28, 1955.)

Josephine Hill was born on Caney Creek, in Matagorda County, on April 6, 1855. During the Civil War her father was a Confederate officer, Capt. John Hill.

Josephine and her sister married in a double wedding on St. Joseph's Island on March 30, 1871. Guests came from Corpus Christi, St. Mary's, and Indianola. The dancing didn't end until the sun came out. The wedding guests ate breakfast and drank coffee made in large iron wash pots. Her sister became Mrs. Alexander Singer and Josephine became Mrs. William Petzel.

In 1874, Josephine and her husband moved to Corpus Christi to run a butcher shop. Her husband came home one day and said that Morris Lichtenstein had rented a room and moved in his store goods from Indianola. He was getting them arranged. Josephine and her mother-in-law went down to the new store. It was on Chaparral, where the Nueces Hotel was later built.

She bought some towels and stockings, which she didn't need, but you could always use towels and stockings. (From the Caller-Times, March 28, 1946.)

Marion Clemmer was the daughter of Mr. and Mrs. Eli Merriman. Merriman was the longtime editor of the Caller. Their house at the corner of Water and Schatzel was torn down and a new one built in 1900.

In the yard was a plant which produced lily-like blossoms that gave a narcotic effect. One of their chickens behaved as if it were intoxicated, caused, they believed, by the plant. The chicken followed a guest of the Merrimans as he was going downtown.

The chicken's drunken antics behind the unsuspecting visitor were a source of great merriment to the Merriman children. They would never forget the drunken chicken story for the rest of their lives. (From the Caller-Times, Feb. 12, 1958.)

William Gaines Blake and wife were living in Runge in 1905 when they decided to move to the Rio Grande Valley. Bill Blake took the "Brownie" Railroad and arrived in Brownsville, tired and dusty, at night. He asked the manager of the Miller Hotel, "Do you have a room with a bath?"

"No," the manager said.

"Do you have baths on any of the floors?"

"No."

"Is there a barbershop in town with a bath?"

"No."

"Well, are there any baths in Brownsville?"

"No," the manager said. "When we want to take a bath we go over to Mexico."

Bill Blake got back on the train and returned to Corpus Christi, which he said had better amenities. The hotels were filled when he arrived but a Capt. Allen opened his home to the traveler.

"I sat on the gallery and the salt spray blew over me and knew I wanted to live here." Blake's father-in-law bought the Sidbury Lumber Company and put Blake in charge. (From the Caller-Times, Aug. 8, 1947.)

Mamie Atkinson was born in a house on Tancahua Street in 1887. Her grandparents were early Corpus Christi settlers, Rachel and Thomas Parker. In 1904, when Mamie was 17, she married a city constable, M. K. Hawley.

After he died in 1914 she married Earl Jones, a fireman. In 1926 she was hired by the school district as the first woman truant officer. "Aunt Mamie" became feared by a generation of kids as the hooky cop.

It didn't take Mamie Hawley Jones long to learn that children stayed away from school because 1) they had no proper clothes or 2) they didn't have enough to eat. Over the years she helped to provide clothes and food for hundreds of students.

Long after she retired her former truants would come around to see her, bringing wives and children and they would talk about how scared they had been of Aunt Mamie. "I loved them all." (From the Times, Dec. 7, 1954.)

—March 2, 2016

I Remember . . . teaching school in Civil War

"The Confederate soldiers would go into someone's pen
and get the best beef they could find then the boys would
surround it and drive it to the Salt Lake for slaughter."
—Rosalie Hart Priour

Rosalie Bridget Hart's parents came to Texas in 1832. Her
mother ran a store in Corpus Christi. and Rosalie was sent to a
convent school in Mobile, where she married Jean M. Priour.
They returned to Corpus Christi in 1851. She taught school
during the Civil War in the house where her mother's store had
been.

"We moved our furniture down from our dwelling house,
intending to remain in town, but were glad before long to return
to the house we had built at the Salt Lake. The town was
sometimes occupied by one side and sometimes by the other.

"I used to watch my children as closely as possible, but just
when I would think they were asleep they would get out through
the window and join the other boys. Confederate soldiers would
see them in the day and appoint a place of rendezvous for the
night. When all of the town boys were assembled, the soldiers
would go into someone's pen and get the best beef they could
find then the boys would surround it and drive it to the Salt Lake
for slaughter. Next day, it would be hung up in the market and
those who wanted meat were invited to come and get a piece.

"This was the only way the Confederates could get meat.
Confederate soldiers received half rations and even with the meat
they killed they suffered from hunger. Mr. Priour went to Austin
for flour and sugar, but it took all he made to cover expenses."

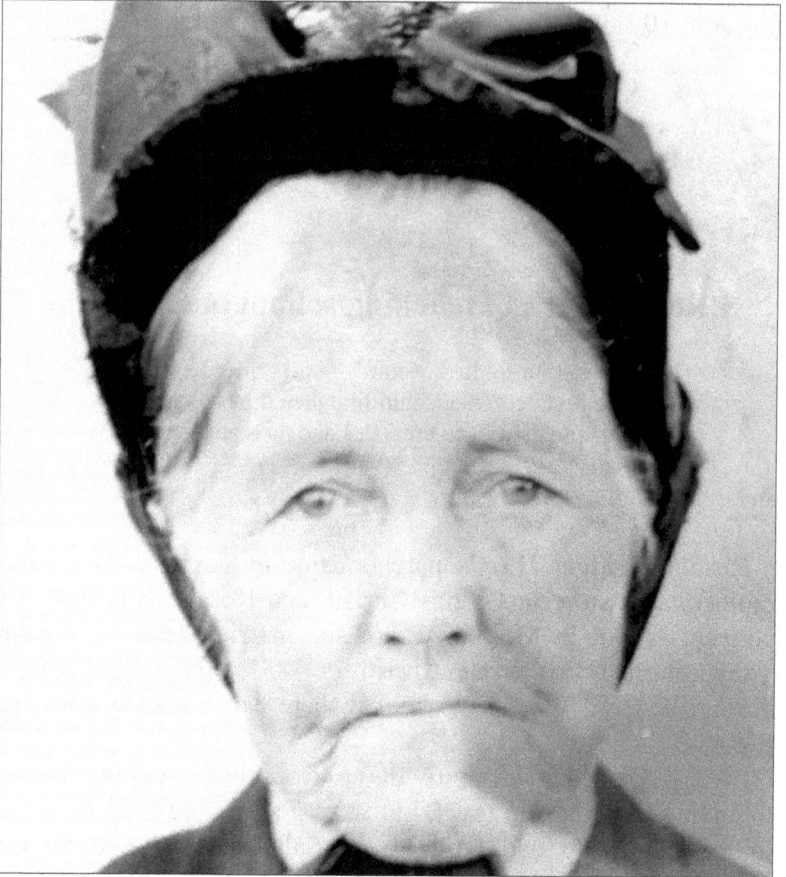

Rosalie Hart Priour taught school in her mother's store in Corpus Christi during the Civil War. Her family lived at the Salt Lake, where Confederate soldiers would butcher their stolen beeves.

When Rosalie's son Julian turned 18 he was conscripted into the Confederate militia. After his unit was transferred to Brownsville the officers threw a fancy-dress ball which angered the enlisted men and they lost some of their zeal for the Confederate cause.

"They threw bricks and broke all the windows of the ballroom. No one could blame them. They had been kept for months on half rations and no pay while their officers were feasting and giving balls." (From Rosalie Priour's memoirs.)

Mrs. Cheston L. Heath (the former Mary "Mollie" Smythe) arrived in Corpus Christi in 1875. She lived in the 100 block of South Chaparral. She recalled the bellowing of cows that came in from the pastures and fields to soothe their mosquito-bitten legs in the cool waters of the bay.

She recalled that ice was brought twice a week on the mail boat from Indianola and that fresh vegetables were scarce or not available. Fred Kaler grew some vegetables and had a few for sale. Mrs. Heath's mother would pay any price for these fresh vegetables. Later on, many families raised vegetables for their own use but few had any to sell. (From an interview, March 13, 1940.)

John Anderson, born in Kalmer, Sweden, was a sailor before he arrived in Corpus Christi on a lumber schooner in 1870. He stayed and got work as a carpenter and later became the foreman of a machine shop that built boxcars and flatcars for the Tex-Mex Railroad.

The shop was located on Railroad Avenue (now Kinney) and it included a blacksmith shop and brass foundry. They turned out a boxcar or gondola a day. The plant built more than 2,000 boxcars in its time.

Anderson didn't like cursing — except to say "By Josa!" — and he didn't like girls wearing pants like boys. When he married Mary Shoemaker his favorite song was, "When You and I Were Young, Maggie." (From the Caller, June 16, 1940.)

Agnes Kelley and her husband H. M. came to Corpus Christi in 1913. He ran the Alcove Confectionery and Chili Parlor on Mesquite Street, across from City Hall. The firemen would come over to get coffee and they called him "Alcove" Kelley. He became a partner with L. G. Collins in a North Beach bathhouse.

"We lived on Leopard and every afternoon I would take the children on a streetcar to the beach. My husband served wonderful sandwiches and we would stay until he came home with us." (From the Caller, Jan. 2, 1960.)

Porfidia "Nanita" Gonzalez remembered when her father Jesus Gonzalez joined the Confederate Army. He rode from Corpus Christi to Victoria to enlist while Porfidia and her mother Petra (Saures) sought work in a several places to stay near him.

After the war, she recalled a long and torturous four days' journey from the Rio Grande to Corpus Christi in a mule-drawn cart, with no seat, no springs, and only a quilt to ease the rough ride. Once back in Corpus Christi she kept house and did the exquisitely fine stitching known as Mexican drawn work.

She made her cigarettes of leaf tobacco wrapped in corn shucks, the way her grandmother taught her to relieve her asthma, with her fingers dark as the leaves of the tobacco. (From the Times, July 25, 1940.)

Clara (Gephart) Stroman grew up on a farm in Lavaca County, near the Hope community. She was one of seven girls and two boys. Because there were so many girls in the family, her father switched from cotton-farming to growing fruit. He thought it would be easier for his daughters to pick peaches instead of picking cotton.

When the peaches were ripe her father took them to Victoria to sell and on the way there he always spent the night in a cemetery. He figured that was one place where he wouldn't be robbed.

During the harvest season they spent a lot of time canning food. "My mother always tried to have one jar for every day of the year." (From the Caller-Times, March 19, 1961.)

—March 9, 2016

I Remember . . . the shivaree

"They hauled the bridegroom up the length of Chaparral
and back again. His new white hat was ruined." —
Andrew Anderson

Andrew Anderson was a year old when he arrived in Corpus Christi. It was in 1853 when his parents, Capt. John and Mrs. Anderson, moved from New Orleans. His family lived in the Anderson home on Water Street, where the Nueces Hotel was later built. Andrew, like his father, became a ship captain and bay pilot.

In an interview in 1940 he recalled a shivaree as "a very harsh method of getting some special favor from a married man. If the bridegroom didn't grant the request of the crowd, usually for refreshments all around, he was shivareed."

The biggest shivaree in Texas, at least that Anderson knew about, was given to a man in Corpus Christi. "This man was 65 years old and had lost his wife only six months before he married a girl of 16. He was not very popular at this time because he had refused to donate to a fund being raised to take care of the (Bayview) cemetery. The boys decided to make him suffer.

"After the wedding he disappeared. Although his bride was at her parents' home on Water Street, he was not there. He couldn't be found. He was finally discovered hiding in the old tumbled-down Cahill house on Chaparral, where he had made himself comfortable and was reading.

"He was brought out and put up on the seat of a street sprinkler, and hauled through the city, to the accompaniment of a

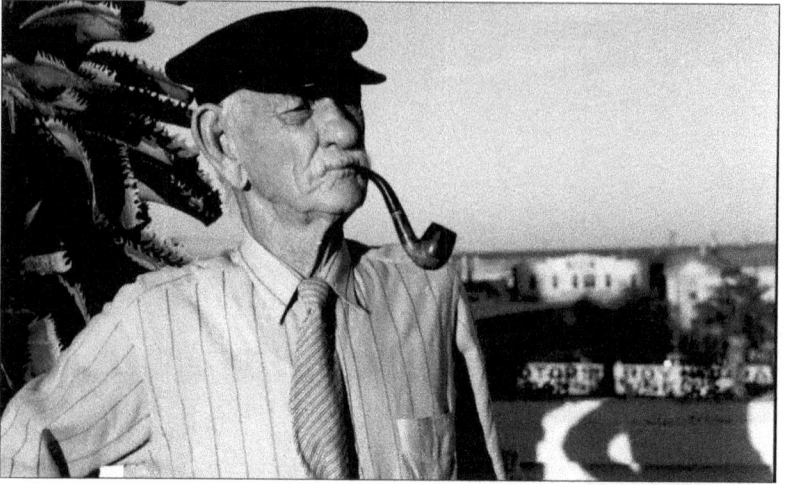

Capt. Andrew Anderson remembered when a stubborn bridegroom was "shivareed" until he agreed to make a donation to the cemetery fund.

Great din or noise from tin cans and bells. They asked him to give $100 to the cemetery fund, but he wouldn't.

"They hauled the bridegroom up the length of Chaparral and back again. His new white hat was ruined in the rough and tumble fun the boys were having, but he was as determined not to give as they were that he should.

"He finally said he would give $50. The boys, knowing he was pretty well fixed, refused to accept the offer. The celebration continued. The thoroughly angered victim offered $75, but that was not accepted either. He was finally released at the bride's home and the boys received $100 for the cemetery fund." (From an interview, 1940.)

Vicente Lozano, born in 1879 at Bagdad, Mexico, came to Corpus Christi in 1891. He worked in the fishing business and then in a grocery store selling charcoal for five cents a bucket and cleaning the oil lamps. When he was 20, in 1899, he married Elvira McCarthy and opened his own grocery store on Mesquite. He later built a new store at Agnes and Staples.

Lozano once recalled his early years as a fisherman. They would unload the day's catch at Blucher's Ice House. Some of the big fish would be sold to the chefs at the St. James Hotel. There were no ice boxes on the fishing boats back then. The fishermen kept their catches fresh by keeping them alive. They dumped their fish in skiffs rigged up like bait boxes. There were holes in the sides through which saltwater could flow. This kept the fish alive until they were towed to the fish house.

In those days, oysters brought 50 cents a barrel and Lozano could earn three cents a pint shucking oysters at Royall Givens Packing House. (From the Times, March 26, 1947.)

Mrs. Sam Rankin (born Lillie Mussett) recalled the first sewing machines and first dolls in town. Her mother and Mrs. Wrather "had the first sewing machines in Corpus Christi. They were sold by Uriah Lott, who had a little store north of where the Corpus Christi National Bank was built." This was when Uriah Lott was a young man before he started building the Tex-Mex railroad.

"These sewing machines were a great boon to the women. Up to that time women did all their sewing by hand. I don't remember them myself, but I do remember the one my mother got just after her first one. It was so far behind the present machines in every way but was still considered a big improvement over the first one. The original must have been a very simple thing indeed. My mother was just a young married woman when she got the machine, so it must have been about 1866.

"On the corner where the bank is now (Corpus Christi National Bank) was Dreyer's store, a little dingy shop, hardly more than a shack. Here the first dolls to appear in town were bought." (From an interview, Sept. 25, 1939.)

Kate Dougherty (later Mrs. Vincent Bluntzer) was the daughter of Robert Dougherty, who was teaching school in Ireland during the great famine.

"In 1848 he left Ireland," Kate said of her father, "and came to this country. Seven of the children of that family left home and their mother to come over here. But she stayed in her native land with relatives and they never saw her again.

"Father Gonnard conducted the Hidalgo Seminary in Corpus Christi until the yellow fever epidemic in 1867 cost him his life. My father was asked to take charge of the seminary. He came to Corpus Christi to become the head of the school. We lived in a cottage on Chaparral.

"The Hidalgo Seminary for boys stood at what is now the corner of Lipan and Tancahua. It was a plain two-story concrete building, with a little portico in front. Downstairs were several rooms while there was one big room upstairs. An outside stairway had at its foot a long white stone on which the boys would sharpen their pencils." She said the school had the agreeable smell of education: of chalk and ink and varnish.

"In the upstairs room, father taught the higher branches of learning while downstairs my mother taught the little boys their letters. There were about 90 boys enrolled. They were bad boys, good boys, big and little boys. But they were all good in father's school. Boys from all over the country, even Mexico, were sent to the Hidalgo Seminary. It was a famous school.

"The boys who lived there slept in two of the downstairs rooms. In 1874 father gave up this school and went to San Patricio for his health. Here he built St. Paul's Academy at Round Lake." (From an interview, Dec. 7, 1939.)

—March 16, 2016

44

I Remember . . . when city was bombarded

"It was the first time I had ever eaten cornbread and
buttermilk and the first time I drank coffee." —Anna
Moore Schwein

Anna Moore Schwien, a former slave, was the daughter of
Sam and Malvina Moore. In her memoirs, Anna recalled when
Corpus Christi was bombarded by Union ships during the Civil
War in 1862.

"After the warning had been received, Mrs. Britton came for us
with an ambulance and took us out to Judge Cody's in the Motts"
— Nuecestown (12 miles distant, up the river) where they lived
in the rough for three days. "People slept wherever they could,
out under the trees. A few had blankets spread on the ground. All
we had to eat was cornbread, with black coffee and buttermilk. It
was the first time I had ever eaten cornbread and buttermilk and
the first time I drank coffee."

Anna talked of the Blucher family. "I remember the colored
woman, Phyllis, toting Miss Julia Blucher. Busse was an old
German who lived on part of the Blucher place; he was a
gunsmith. He had a lovely garden, with plants of all kinds. My
mother's calves would stray over near Busse's place and when I
would go after them I would look through the gate at the
beautiful flowers. Mother taught me that it was all right to look at
other people's flowers through the fence, but that I must never
reach my hand through to pick one.

"There were no roses in this garden. At that time there was
only one rose bush in Corpus Christi and it was called the Rose

45

Anna Moore Schwein once recalled the time, in August 1862, when she and mother were evacuated to Nuecestown during the bombardment of Corpus Christi by Union warships.

of Castile. It was pale pink and very fragrant. It grew on a great big bush in the yard of a woman named Trinidad who lived where the Perkins Brothers store was later.

"The Lovenskiolds sent to Havana for roses for their garden. Col. Lovenskiold paid Pat Dooley $300 a year, plus board and lodging, to take care of his garden. This was about 1867."

Anna Moore Schwein was briefly married to a German immigrant who was run out of town for marrying a black woman. In later years, Anna Moore Schwein was not bitter over the unfair treatment of her husband. "You can't go to heaven with hate in your heart." (From her memoirs compiled from interviews, Nov. 8, 1938 to May 15, 1941.)

Kate Smith (later Mrs. Adolph Anderson) was born in Indianola in 1860. Her family moved to Corpus Christi when she was nine, but she remembered the big Morgan Line ships that docked at Indianola when she was a young girl.

She said Corpus Christi in 1869 looked like a cattle ranch. "There were not many houses then. On the way to the convent I would eat granjeno fruit from the bushes along the way. We would go up the hill from the Baldeschweiler corner, at Mesquite and William, but I couldn't cross the street until the wagons and mule teams passed by.

"I met Adolph Anderson here. He came on a lumber schooner about 1881 or 1882. I knew him for six years before I married him. My husband was an express messenger on the train. I lived next to Blucher's ice factory on the bay for 40 years. I would gather the bark that fell from the wood at the factory for my own use. I have seen many and many a cord of wood unloaded at Blucher's for the boilers of the factory." (From an interview, May 23, 1939.)

Frank Gay lived in a house at Antelope and North Carrizo. His father was the landscape gardener for Mifflin Kenedy's mansion on the bluff. Frank's father was planning to go to the New Orleans Exposition to select shrubs for the grounds of the Kenedy mansion. Kenedy wanted his yard, like his house, to be an ornament for the town.

"Capt. Kenedy asked him, 'Gay, how much you think it will cost?'

"Father had it all figured out, including his travel expenses, and he said, 'Three hundred dollars.'

"Capt. Kenedy turned to Major White, his bookkeeper, and told him to write out a check for $500 and said, 'Gay, if you need more, let me know and I'll furnish it.' "

When Gay's mother was expecting his father back from New Orleans, she pulled the lamp down from the ceiling by a chain and lit it so that Frank's father could find his way home from the depot late at night. There were no buildings near where the Gays lived and his father would have to cross the old arroyo, where it would be as dark as the inside of a cow. (From an interview, June 6, 1940.)

A. C. Kuehm's family traveled by wagon from Poth, Texas, to Robstown in 1901 when the railroad to Brownsville — the Brownie line — was being built.

Kuehm's father put up tents near the later site of the depot. Two served as a kitchen and mess hall, four had cots for railroad and construction workers, and one was for the Kuehm family. A.C.'s mother did the cooking. The Kuehm family lived in the tent until a two-story hotel was built in 1902. It was later moved and enlarged. It was called the Germania Hotel.

Kuehm recalled a smallpox scare in 1908. A peddler in a covered wagon stopped at the Germania Hotel. His mother noticed the sores on his face and recognized the signs of smallpox. She notified Dr. Connally who had the man isolated in a boxcar until he was taken to Corpus Christi. Only one person contracted the disease in Robstown, a woman who passed the peddler in the street. (From the Robstown Record, Nov. 18, 1982.)

Matt Pellegrino, the son if Italian immigrants, was born in a house on Starr Street in 1888. He attended both the convent and public schools and spent much of his time playing baseball.

Pellegrino earned extra cash by pulling the rope-operated fans in the Horne Barber Shop for $2 a month. Pellegrino drove a beer truck, worked in Joe Mireur's saddle shop and then joined the city's six-man police force in 1922. He later became a detective, a position he held until he retired. (From the Times, July 13, 1948.)

—March 23, 2016

The woman who saved the Alamo

Clara Driscoll grew up on the ranch where one of their favorite diversions was a South Texas version of fox-hunting. They kept greyhounds for chasing coyotes which, it was said, could run the pants off any fox.

Daniel O'Driscoll, a sergeant in the U.S. Army at Fort Jessup, La., left to join the Texas Revolution, fought in the battle of San Jacinto and received land grants around Refugio. He married a widow, Catherine Duggan, whose husband died of cholera on the voyage from Ireland.

Daniel O'Driscoll owned a tavern in Refugio and served as a county commissioner. The couple had two sons, Jeremiah born in 1838, and Robert born in 1841. O'Driscoll died in 1849 after he was hit on head with a cane wielded by Michael Whelan, a fellow commissioner. Catherine would follow Whelan around and point an accusing finger — "You killed my husband!"

When Catherine died in 1852 her sons Robert and Jeremiah (Jerry) became the wards of their half-sister, Mrs. Daniel Doughty. Jerry and Robert Driscoll (they dropped the O) fought in the Civil War and returned to Texas to expand the cattle operations their father left them. The brothers were in the cattle business with Dan Doughty and John Howland Wood of St. Mary's. The Driscoll brothers soon owned cattle and land in Refugio, Victoria and Bee counties.

Robert Driscoll married Julia Fox, a petite redhead, and they had two children, Robert Jr. born on Oct. 31, 1871 in Victoria and Clara born April 2, 1881, in St. Mary's. When Clara was a toddler and the family was living in a boarding house in

49

Rockport, the boarders taught her to chant in a sing-song voice, "I'm the black-eyed beauty, the belle of Rockport." She actually had brown eyes like her father and flaming red hair like her mother.

In 1884, D. C. Rachal purchased Martha Rabb's old ranch and after one bad winter he sold out to Robert Driscoll. Driscoll moved his family to the 83,000-acre Palo Alto Ranch, 22 miles west of Corpus Christi, near today's Driscoll.

Robert Driscoll added to his holdings, buying the 53,000-acre Sweeden ranch and La Gloria ranch in Duval County, the 20,000-acre Los Machos ranch in Jim Wells and the 8,000-acre ranch near Skidmore that he named the Clara Ranch after his daughter.

Clara grew up on the ranch where one of their favorite diversions was a South Texas version of fox-hunting. They kept greyhounds for chasing coyotes which, it was said, could run the pants off any fox. During roundup, Clara would join her father who would crack eggs in a shovel, fry them over a campfire and eat them out of the shovel. Clara's father disliked being cruel to livestock and prevented his ranch hands from using quirts or unduly frightening the cattle.

In the early 1890s Clara went away to school. She went first to Peebles and Thompson's in New York, a boot camp for young ladies, and on to a French convent near Paris called the Chateau Dieudonne, a far cry from chasing coyotes through the brush.

Robert Jr. went to Princeton, where he got into trouble and was reprimanded by one of his professors, Woodrow Wilson. He graduated in 1893 and went on to practice law for a time in New York City.

Julia Driscoll took Clara and Robert Jr. on a round-the-world trip. They spent a summer in India and visited most of the watering holes of Europe. Clara sent travel dispatches to the San Antonio and Corpus Christi papers under the pen name "A Texas Girl." Julia Fox Driscoll died in London on May 23, 1899. Clara and Robert brought her body back for burial in San Antonio.

Not long afterwards the 22-year-old Clara wrote letters to the Corpus Christi Caller and San Antonio Express describing the plight of the Alamo. Part of the Alamo property was up for sale

Clara Driscoll (shown in 1905) led a campaign to save the Alamo which was in danger of being demolished.

to private developers. Clara started a campaign to save the convent portion of the Alamo, where much of the fighting took place, which was in danger of being demolished to build a hotel.

When the Alamo campaign fell short of the needed funds, Clara put up $18,000 of her own money, along with $7,000 raised by the Daughters of the Republic of Texas, and with this $25,000 they made a down payment on the convent property. They needed $75,000 to buy the site. They didn't have the remaining $50,000 by the deadline so Clara signed five personal notes for $10,000 each. The state was shamed into refunding her money and taking the property off her hands. This second battle of the Alamo was one of those rare victories when everyone agreed the right side one.

Clara became the woman who saved the Alamo. It was a heady time. Her novel "Girl of La Gloria" and a collection of stories, "Shadow of the Alamo," were published and her play, "Mexicalli," was produced by the Schubert Theater. She married a former legislator from Uvalde, Henry "Hal" Sevier, whom she met while lobbying the Legislature for funds for the Alamo.

Clara Driscoll and Hal Sevier married on July 31, 1906 at the chapel of St. Patrick's Church in New York City. At the wedding, Robert Jr. whispered to a friend, "I thought she would never make it. Now I hope I won't have to be her valet anymore."

The New York Journal reported that, "When the demolition of the Alamo was threatened, Miss Driscoll displayed her patriotism by purchasing the property and presenting it to the state. Sevier, who was not acquainted with her at the time, of his own volition introduced a bill in the Legislature to reimburse her. Although the measure was hotly opposed he forced its passage. Mutual friends introduced them."

The newlyweds spent their honeymoon in Europe and returned to New York, where Sevier worked for the New York Sun and they lived next door to Theodore Roosevelt.

In the first decade of the 20th Century, Robert Driscoll Sr. made a deal to sell 78,000 acres of Driscoll ranchland to prospective farmers. The lands west of Corpus Christi were opened to agriculture. Settlers moved in and new towns flourished, including Robstown, named for Robert Driscoll Sr., and Driscoll, named for the family.

Robert Driscoll Sr. died in 1914. He was buried in the family plot at the Masonic Cemetery in San Antonio. People who knew him thought he was one of the best cattle ranchers in Texas. Clara said, "There never was a better cattleman anywhere."

—*March 30, 2016*

The Clara Driscoll story

"People who live in town forget how sweet the grass smells." —Clara Driscoll

After Robert Driscoll Sr. died in 1914 Clara and her husband "Hal" Sevier moved to Austin where he started the Austin American newspaper and she became active in Democratic Party politics. During World War I, Clara was a bandage-roller and canteen hostess for the Red Cross.

Her brother Robert, a confirmed bachelor, became the sole manager of the Driscoll ranches. In 1923, he was named president of the Corpus Christi National Bank and moved to Corpus Christi, where he was one of the leaders in the drive to establish the Port of Corpus Christi. He was the first chairman of the Nueces County Navigation District.

In Austin, Clara was elected national committeewoman at the Texas State Democratic Convention.

Corpus Christi entered a building boom after the port opened in 1926. Robert Driscoll started the Corpus Christi Trust Company in 1928, which became a full-fledged bank. After the Nixon Building was erected on the bluff, it was Robert Driscoll's brainchild to build a major hotel across the street. He created a company made up of Corpus Christi investors to build a hotel and San Antonio investors to run it.

The result was the city's largest hotel, the Plaza, which opened in May 1929. The 14-story hotel towered over the bluff at Leopard and Broadway. Both Robert and Clara had penthouse apartments in the Plaza. That summer Robert got a leg infection which resulted in two amputations. He died on July 7, 1929. He was buried in San Antonio alongside his mother and father.

Family lawyers advised Clara to sell the cattle and family land. "No," she said, "I'll keep the cattle and the land, every foot of it." As the only surviving member of her family, she felt her responsibility keenly. "We were a small family and very close," she said. "The work they started means everything to me." Clara managed the ranches in five counties, became president of the bank her brother established, the Corpus Christi Bank and Trust, and was a director of the Corpus Christi National Bank.

Her husband Hal Sevier was appointed ambassador to Chile by President Roosevelt. A banquet honoring the Seviers was held at the Plaza Hotel on Oct. 17, 1932.

The Plaza fell on hard times during the Depression and the Corpus Christi investors, who owned 67 percent of the hotel, sold out to Jack White, the main man behind the San Antonio interests. But Clara refused to sell. This led to a lawsuit which she lost. White gained control and changed the name to the White Plaza Hotel.

A story — perhaps apocryphal — said Clara threatened to build a hotel next door from where she could spit down on the White Plaza. (Careful writers, or editors, used "spit" but she probably said something else.) Another story said the falling out stemmed from a loud party in Clara's penthouse. When the hotel manager complained Clara called him a stuffy old owl. She was known as a sharp observer, with a sharp tongue, who could give as good as she got.

When the Seviers returned from Chile in 1937, Clara was granted a divorce, though she kept her husband's name until his death.

The land her father acquired was rich in oil and gas deposits and it made Clara immensely wealthy. She still had a taste for the ranch life. People who live in town, she said, forget how sweet the grass smells. "I like to go out there and get away from things. I can always find plenty to do. The ranch hands come in and keep me informed about what is going on." She went to a cattle auction at the Steiner Valley Ranch near Whitney, she said, "and got started bidding on the cattle and just couldn't stop."

Robert Driscoll Jr., shown in the 1920s, was one of the leaders behind the drive to build the Port of Corpus Christi. He died in 1929 after a leg infection required two amputations. Clara Driscoll (shown in a portrait) occupied a penthouse apartment in the Driscoll Hotel until her death, at age 64, on July 17, 1945.

She was instrumental — along with Roy Miller and Congressman Lyndon Johnson — in Corpus Christi gaining a new naval air station. She was also involved in national politics and was one of the leaders in the Garner-for-President campaign, before Roosevelt opted for a third term and sent Garner into retirement.

Clara built the Robert Driscoll Hotel on Upper Broadway in 1942, named after her brother. The Driscoll opened on May 25, 1942. With 18 floors, it towered over the 14-story White Plaza next door; it was far grander in every respect — a matter of bragging rights. Clara occupied a penthouse apartment, with 12 bathrooms, and if she had a loud party no one would complain.

She died at age 64 on July 17, 1945. They put her body in the chapel of the Alamo where thousands of Texans paid their last respects. She was buried in San Antonio with the rest of the Driscoll family.

Among her papers were found notes and drawings of her travels, with a large collection of souvenirs and picture-postcard views from around the world and the accumulated bric-á-brac of a lifetime. There was a list of flowers to be planted at her Long Island estate and recipes written for "Meta's cornbread, biscuits, and lemon pie" and a wardrobe inventory which included dresses for different occasions described as "old, fixed-over, and new." A rare violin from 1625 was found among her effects. There was also broken glass from a champagne bottle from when she christened the USS Corpus Christi, a World War II transport ship.

After Clara's death the big question was what would happen to the vast Driscoll fortune. The question was soon answered when her will was revealed. It said the money would be used to create a foundation to build and operate "a free clinic and hospital for crippled, maimed, and diseased children." The Driscoll Foundation Children's Hospital opened in February 1953.

The consensus was that the Driscoll wealth could not have gone to a better cause. The great fortune her family amassed from the land would be returned to fill a great need in South Texas.

The Robert Driscoll Hotel was closed in 1970, the building stripped to its frame and given a new facade of black granite. It still stands as an office and banking complex. The White Plaza was torn down in 1962 and the 600 Building erected on that site.

As for the Driscolls, their story is our history, and that is especially true of the woman who saved the Alamo. The story of Clara Driscoll has often been told. But not too often.

—April 6, 2016

The firemen's ball at Market Hall

"Two of the popular shows were titled Ten Nights in a
Barroom and The Yankee in Texas." —Andrew
Anderson

From the 1840s through the 1860s, butchers and fruit and
vegetable vendors occupied sheds and shanties on a patch of
ground between Peoples and Schatzel on Mesquite Street. It was
called Market Square. The butchers sometimes dumped rotten
meat around the square and every so often the city ordered a
general cleanup.

Two businessmen proposed building a structure, at no cost to
the taxpayers, to house city offices and with stalls that could be
rented out to the town's butchers and vendors. City officials liked
the idea. For years the mayor and councilmen held meetings in
various buildings around the city, including the Ohler, Hunsaker,
and Cahill buildings.

The businessmen were William "Billy" Rogers and Richard
Jordan. Rogers was a sheep rancher and had served a term as
sheriff. Members of his family were killed in a massacre on the
Arroyo Colorado on their way to the Rio Grande during the
Mexican War. Billy Rogers had his throat cut but survived.
Rumors later said he tracked down and killed the bandits
responsible.

Richard Jordan and his brother came to Corpus Christi in 1854
from Maine. They opened a lumber yard. During the Civil War,
Jordan denounced his brother as a Union supporter to
Confederate authorities. The brother had to flee for his life. One

account said Jordan was captured by Union soldiers and begged for his life.

In July 1871 the city accepted the offer by Rogers and Jordan to build a municipal structure for $10,000, which would cost the taxpayers not a nickel. To make sure that Rogers and Jordan didn't lose money on the venture the city made it illegal to sell meat or vegetables inside the city except at Market Hall. That gave them a monopoly. After 12 years, the building would become city property.

E. D. Sidbury, builder and lumber dealer, constructed a two-story-building that was 80 feet long, 32 feet wide, with a tin roof and brick floor. The ground floor was divided into stalls and the second floor included space for city offices, council chambers, and an auditorium.

When the building was nearly finished, a reporter for the Nueces Valley wrote that when completed it would give Corpus Christi "one of the finest meeting halls in Texas." It was called Market Hall.

When it opened, the meat market of H. L. Dreyer was on the Mesquite Street front. Dreyer was called the "boss butcher" because he was responsible for making sure the other butchers didn't dump their waste trimmings around the new building.

On the west end were quarters for the city's volunteer fire department, the Pioneer Fire Company No. 1. The firemen had a large cistern behind the building from which they could fill their water wagons. A wide stairway on the south side led to the second floor where there were city offices and a large hall for dances and public events. There was an elevated stage at one end of the hall.

The great fire bell, which weighed 787 pounds, hung from a cupola on the roof above the dance floor. The fire bell was rung to signal the beginning of the work day, school, lunch hour, quitting time, and when fires broke out. In 1874 the council stopped paying a full-time ringer and after a hurricane sent the bell crashing to the ground it was mounted on a concrete base at ground level behind Market Hall.

The first anniversary of the Pioneer Fire Company was celebrated on June 6, 1872 with a parade, followed by a supper

Corpus Christi's Market Hall, built in 1871, was located between Peoples and Schatzel facing Mesquite Street. The first floor was leased to commercial vendors and the upper floor contained city offices and a large auditorium used for dances and entertainments. Market Hall was torn down in 1911.

and fancy-dress ball at Market Hall, where they danced and partied for all they were worth. The Nueces Valley reported that "a more brilliant assemblage was never seen in Corpus Christi." The firemen's parade and ball became the big social event of the year, held on the last Tuesday of each November.

Coleman McCampbell wrote in "Saga of a Frontier Seaport" described one firemen's ball: "A parade by day, a ball by night. Hook and ladder truck and a fire engine, decorated with evergreens and oleanders. Hose carts for the wards and a spirited tug of war . . . The walls of Market Hall a cloud of green foliage and flowers . . . The firemen as hosts, the social elite as guests . . . Waltzes, polkas, schottisches and old-fashioned Spanish quadrilles . . . Supper arranged by kind and generous ladies . . . Turkeys, ham, a pig with ruffled collar and apple in his snout. Two deer, fashioned of butter, grazing on a lawn of parsley. Monstrous platters of salad, ornately garnished, stack cakes, five feet high, the top layer the size of a teacup topped by Goddess of Liberty in sugar icing . . . Full stomachs, aching feet, wilted finery, dawn."

The large auditorium was also used for traveling shows and entertainments.

In 1873 the Nueces Valley reported that the Royal Japanese Troupe of acrobats and jugglers played before a full house in Market Hall.

In 1902, George Landrum, an impersonator, put on a one-man show called "A Pair of Spectacles," in which he played eight characters, changing from one to another by voice, gesture and facial expression. Or so the paper said. Reserved seats cost 35 cents.

Andrew Anderson recalled some of the entertainments. "Two of the popular shows were titled Ten Nights in a Barroom and The Yankee in Texas. I remember especially how they would sell Hamlin's Wizard Oil from a wagon. Four fellows would sing beautifully and the whole street would be full of people listening to the singing. Finally, someone arranged for them to give an entertainment at the Market Hall. You paid 25 cents to hear them sing and they had a full house every night for a week or more. They sold lots of Wizard Oil."

At one ball, the town was outraged when a culprit sprinkled a quantity of cayenne pepper on the dance floor, causing fits of sneezing and coughing that disrupted the evening.

Market Hall in its 40th year was torn down in 1911. A new brick three-story City Hall was built on Market Square. There is a small park on that spot now, sandwiched between Schatzel and Peoples, where the old Market Hall was once at the very heart of the city, where they danced until dawn at the firemen's ball.

—March 13, 2016

Banks and bankers

The ups and downs of banks reflect the town's economic
history. The first banks were tied to the wool trade and
the first chartered bank came during the Ropes Boom.

Jacksonian Democrats like Sam Houston distrusted banking as
evil incarnate. Before the Revolution, there was only one bank
operating in Texas, in Galveston, which was chartered by the
Mexican government in 1835.

Ten years later, banks were still considered odious when the
Republic of Texas joined the Union. A new state constitution
prohibited the chartering of banks after the president of the
constitutional convention, Thomas Rusk, accused banks of
causing "ruin, want, misery and degradation." Texas merchants
had to keet their cash, make loans and provide basic banking
services.

After the Civil War, and after state government was
reorganized, nationally chartered banks were formed in several
Texas cities, but not in Corpus Christi. The first banks here were
private, evolving out of the wool trade.

In the decade after the Civil War, Corpus Christi was one of
the largest wool markets in the world. The town's wealthy wool
merchants handled millions of pounds of wool and hides at their
stores on Chaparral. The wool merchants kept a supply of cash
(mostly silver and gold) to buy wool and, by necessity, they
became part-time bankers.

Corpus Christi, founded in 1839, was three decades old before
it got a bank. The city's first banker was Perry Doddridge, a wool

merchant, who opened the town's first bank in 1871. His partners were Uriah Lott and A.M. Davis.

Norwick Gussett, one of Doddridge's chief competitors in the wool trade, opened his own bank in about 1883. Another contemporary was the Friend and Cahn Bank, started in the 1880s by Bertrand Cahn and a man named Friend. When the Friend & Cahn Bank closed the building was converted into the Bank Saloon.

Corpus Christi's first national bank was founded in 1890 by another wool merchant, David Hirsch. Corpus Christi National Bank was located in a small building on Chaparral. Hirsch's bank was said to be the smallest national bank in the country, with a measly $50,000 in capital. Within a year the bank moved into a new building on the corner of Schatzel and Chaparral.

In what was called the national money panic of 1893 a man tried to withdraw $5,000 in savings from Hirsch's bank. People were allowed to withdraw small sums but not large amounts. The customer, however, was adamant, demanding all his money. Thomas Hickey, the cashier, offered to give him the entire $5,000 if he would take it in silver. That would have been a heavy load to carry so the man left his money in the bank.

The Doddridge bank collapsed during this panic and collapse of the Ropes Boom. Perry Doddridge spent his own fortune repaying depositors 60 cents on the dollar, which left him bankrupt. It was said that the entire town, even the bank depositors who lost money, sympathized with Doddridge.

After the turn of the 20th Century, Clark Pease established a bank in 1904. It was reorganized and chartered in 1905 as the City National Bank. Pease built a four-story building at Chaparral and Peoples where DeRyee's drug store once stood. The City National Bank & Trust was the first bank in town to go under during the Great Depression.

Vincent Bluntzer opened the First State Bank in a rented room in 1907. A new structure was built at Mesquite and Schatzel the following year. First State later received a federal charter and changed its name to State National Bank.

In 1908 Burton Dunn, the son of Padre Island rancher Pat Dunn, went to work as a runner for Corpus Christi National

Corpus Christi National Bank (top) after the turn of the 20th Century. The bank was founded in 1890 by wool merchant David Hirsch. The City National Bank (below) in the late 1920s. The bank was established in 1904 by Clark Pease and in 1905 he built a four-story building at Chaparral and Peoples on the corner once occupied by DeRyee's drug store.

The First State Bank (top), founded in 1907 by Vincent Bluntzer, moved into a new building in 1908 at the corner of Mesquite and Schatzel. First State changed its name to State National Bank. Corpus Christi Bank & Trust (below), known as the Hill Bank, was established in 1928 by Robert Driscoll Jr. It was located on Leopard at Tancahua.

Bank as a "runner," his job literally was to run from place to place making collections. He didn't have far to run because the town was so small. Dunn later became president of the Corpus Christi National Bank.

J. E. Garrett opened the Texas State Bank & Trust in 1925. Garrett first came to Corpus Christi in December 1906 with his bride on a honeymoon trip to Mexico. He contracted typhoid fever and was hospitalized in Spohn Sanitarium on North Beach. The newlyweds never made it to Mexico. Garrett became a developer and land promoter.

Garrett's Texas State Bank lasted eight years before it went under during the Depression, along with the City National Bank. The bank failed because people couldn't repay their loans.

Rancher Robert Driscoll Jr. started the Corpus Christi Trust Company in 1928 and became its first president. It was first located in a rented building on Schatzel but moved into a new building on Leopard at Tancahua.

What became known as the Hill Bank was established to handle wills, trusts, and real estate but it was ready to open as a full-fledged bank when Robert Driscoll Jr. died in 1929. His sister Clara, famous as the savior of the Alamo, became the bank's president, a position she held until her own death in 1945.

In 1928 Citizens Industrial Bank was formed by a group of San Antonio businessmen, including bakery owner Henry Richter and Maury Maverick. The name was later changed to Citizens State Bank.

Corpus Christi National Bank and State National Bank merged in 1956. Ground was broken for a new building on Shoreline and the new institution was named the Corpus Christi State National Bank. This foreshadowed the frenzy of banking mergers that would come.

Beginning in the 1980s, local banks were absorbed by state and national corporate behemoths and their identities became blurred. Names were changed to MBank, First City, NationsBank, PlainsCapital and others. The historical identities of the banks were devalued and then lost. I thumbed through countless newspaper clippings of bank mergers, acquisitions and takeovers until I lost my way and could not persuade myself to continue.

The ups and downs of banks reflect the town's economic history. The first banks were tied to the wool trade and the first chartered bank came during the Ropes Boom. New banks opened in the first decade of the 20th Century as ranchlands were converted to agriculture. Other banks were launched in the 1920s after the port opened and they all prospered with the discovery of oil, the location of industries in the port area, and the building of the Naval Air Station.

The banking story of Corpus Christi is still evolving, but banks have come a long way since Thomas Rusk defined them as pernicious agents of ruin, want, misery and degradation.

—April 20, 2016

John Peoples joins the gold rush

"A large number of the men were unfit to go to
California by any route and will be unfit to stay there if
they ever arrive, unless they get a situation in the shade
next to a cologne lake." —John Peoples

Henry Kinney returned to Corpus Christi after a two-year
absence at the end of the Mexican War in 1848. The town he
founded was virtually deserted. It had languished after Zachary
Taylor's army marched away in 1846. He set about trying to
improve his town's prospects.

Kinney took advantage of sensational news. In January 1848,
the week before the treaty was signed that ended the Mexican
War, gold was discovered in California. A carpenter picked up a
nugget the size of a pea at Sutter's Mill near Sacramento and the
news spread like wildfire.

Newspapers reported that gold nuggets were there for the
bending over and picking up. In one story, a party of miners saw
the glitter of gold dust in a ravine. Each man threw himself down
and spread out arms and legs to claim the spot his body covered.

Gold fever spread across the land. Cornfields were left half
planted, houses half built, and some towns lost half their men as
thousands of gold-seekers made their way to California.

Songs of the miners were the hits of the time. One went: "Oh,
don't you remember sweet Betsey from Pike? / Who crossed the
big mountains with her lover Ike / With two yoke of cattle, a
large yellow dog, / A tall shanghai rooster and one spotted hog."
Another asked, "Oh, what was your name in the States? / Was it

Thompson or Johnson or Bates? / Did you murder your wife / And fly for your life? / Say, what was your name in the States?"

Like the rest of the country Corpus Christi was consumed with gold fever. The town's newspaper, the Star, was filled with news from California, news that described the gold fields, the techniques of mining and panning for gold, and the best way to get there.

Henry Kinney placed ads in newspapers in New York, Boston and Philadelphia asserting that Corpus Christi was the best route to take to get to the California gold fields.

In truth there was no easy way to get there. The main route was overland starting at Independence, Mo. Another was 18,000 miles by ship around the stormy Horn. Still another was by ship to Chagres, Panama then by foot or mule-train across the narrow Isthmus of Panama and board another ship on the Pacific side.

The route promoted by Kinney was by ship or packet boat to Corpus Christi then travel across South Texas and the Mexican states of Chihuahua and Sonora to California.

Goldseekers began to arrive in town in January 1849. They came mostly on the Neptune, a fast-sailing packet boat, or the Fanny, a packet steamship.

The town began to stir with the kind of economic activity it hadn't seen since Taylor's army left two years before. Wagons, horses and mules that were sold dirt cheap as army surplus after the Mexican War were sold at high prices. Gunsmiths, blacksmiths and coopers set up shop. The emigrants would need everything a town could supply.

Those bound for California were organized into companies, for mutual protection and assistance. They adopted bylaws, elected officers, and created their own judicial tribunals. Groups arriving in Corpus Christi included the Essex Mining Company of Boston, the Carson Association of New York, the Kinney Rangers (named in honor of Henry Kinney), the Holmes County (Miss.) Mining Company, and the Mazatlan Rangers.

Many Texans joined the exodus. Jack Hays, the famous Texas Ranger and Mexican War hero, left for California in 1849. Hays went on to become the first elected sheriff of San Francisco and helped found the town of Oakland.

Jack Hays, famous Texas Ranger captain and Mexican War hero, joined the gold rush to California in 1849. Hays became the first elected sheriff of San Francisco.

For months, the editor of the Corpus Christi Star, John Peoples, filled his paper with news about the gold rush. He came down with the fever and joined the Mazatlan Rangers, under the command of Col. E. W. Abbott. Peoples had been a war correspondent in Mexico and knew Abbott from the war. Abbott had led a regiment of Massachusetts volunteers.

Peoples departed with the Mazatlan Rangers in February 1849. They stepped off as chipper as larks, leaving their camp at Twelve-Mile Motts (near today's Calallen) and heading for the Rio Grande in the Laredo area.

They were not chipper for long. The trip across Texas took 33 days, longer than it should have. Pack mules carrying trade goods usually made the trip in 10 days. Peoples wrote a letter to the Star from the Rio Grande in which he blasted his fellow travelers as lazy layabouts who had no interest in anything involving work.

Peoples said some of them had paid their $150 fee to join the company and expected that nothing more was required of them. They deemed it below their dignity to do physical labor. He said their wagons were weighed down with useless personal possessions and were pulled by oxen and mules in poor condition.

On days when they should have been traveling, Peoples wrote, some refused to stir, forcing the entire company to waste time. "A large number of the men were unfit to go to California by any route," Peoples wrote, "and will be unfit to stay there if they ever arrive, unless they get a situation in the shade next to a cologne lake."

The Mazatlan Rangers broke up before they started across the arid region of northern Mexico. The main group, with Peoples, continued on across Mexico. It was a hard trip. They ran out of water and suffered dysentery. Crossing raging rivers was their most difficult undertaking. They had to caulk wagon beds and turn them into rafts. In crossing the Gulf of California Peoples was drowned.

Word spread that the journey from Corpus Christi across Chihuahua and Sonora was long, difficult and dangerous. An affidavit like that of the Mazatlan Rangers carried weight. The 49ers fell back on tried and true routes. They took ship to Chagres and rode mule-back across the isthmus or they went overland and over the mountains, like Sweet Betsy from Pike.

The gold rush, short though it was, represented an epic chapter in Corpus Christi history. We still have a reminder of that time in Peoples Street, named for John Peoples, editor of the Star who left for the gold mines of California and ended up at an unintended destination.

—April 27, 2016

The mystery of Henry Gilpin

Ruth Dodson said several women set their cap for Judge
Gilpin but got nowhere. He lived with a young man
named Graham and the two were "well suited to be
company to each other."

When Henry Addington Gilpin landed on the shore of Corpus
Christi Bay, where the city is today, no one was there to welcome
him. In 1829 there was no settlement. It was deserted, ten years
before Henry Kinney built his trading post that later grew into
the city.

Very little was known about Gilpin. He was a mystery man.
Some said he came from Canada, others from Rhode Island, but
people knew nothing of his family pedigree.

Though they didn't know it at the time, Gilpin came from a
well-regarded English family. His grandfather was the Rev.
William Gilpin, a celebrated author in England, and his father,
John Bernard Gilpin, was a British consul in Rhode Island.
Henry was born on May 13, 1808. His mother died when he was
six and his father retired and moved to Nova Scotia.

Henry Gilpin worked in a bank in New Jersey and by some
accounts "left suddenly." In 1829 he purchased trade goods and
arrived on a schooner from New Orleans. He landed at the site of
today's Corpus Christi and went on to Matamoros where he
became a trader and business partner of Frederick Belden.
Belden kept the store and Gilpin hauled merchandise into the
interior. On a trip in 1833 he carried $80,000 in goods to
Zacatecas (worth $2.3 million in today's dollars).

71

In the early 1840s Gilpin and Belden moved to Corpus Christi, which was a good spot to land goods destined for Chihuahua, away from the annoyance of Mexican customs officials.

Gilpin was elected chief justice of Nueces County in 1852. At a sheriff's sale, he bought 1,476 acres of land for $50, or 2.9 cents an acre, which became Gilpin's ranch at Penitas. It was 12 miles northwest of San Patricio, 50 miles from Corpus Christi, once part of Nueces County but now in Jim Wells.

Gilpin and Belden were partners in another ranch called Carmel. When Belden died in 1868 Gilpin administered the estate for his widow. In 1873, Gilpin was elected to the Texas House in a district that covered 22 counties from Corpus Christi to El Paso.

On Good Friday 1875, Gilpin was in a buggy heading to Corpus Christi when he was captured by bandits in the Nuecestown Raid. The bandits made their captives walk or run as they headed for Noakes store. A bandit who knew Gilpin shouted, "Andale! Don Enriquez! Andale!"

After Gilpin retired and moved to the ranch, he spent his time studying weather and making astronomical observations. Ruth Dodson, who lived nearby, wrote that his home had a wide porch where the judge liked to sit. He was an exotic neighbor, a courtly man with an English accent who would invite visitors to tea.

Several local women, Dodson wrote, set their cap for the judge but got nowhere. He lived with a young man named Graham. "They were well suited to be company to each other," Dodson wrote, "although Mr. Graham was much younger." Conventions of the time did not encourage speculation about domestic arrangements.

A daughter (which no one knew he had) came to visit the judge. She brought her husband and three children. The later story was that Gilpin was married and the father of two children before he fled to Texas.

Gilpin sold the livestock on his ranch and half the land but the fund evaporated. He was living in dire poverty when he died on Nov. 11, 1895. Judge Henry A. Gilpin was a man with a mysterious past. Whatever secrets he brought with him to Texas were buried with him.

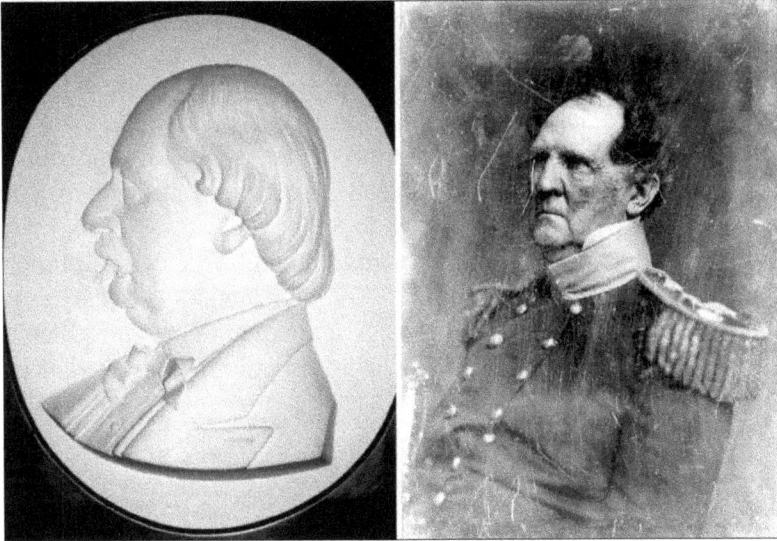

A bas relief shows Henry A. Gilpin (left), who landed trade goods for Mexico in 1829 at the site where Corpus Christi was later built. A Matthew Brady photo from the Library of Congress shows Gen. Winfield Scott (right) in 1849.

Old Fuss and Feathers

Ethan Allen Hitchcock was a senior officer with Zachary Taylor's command at Corpus Christi in 1845 before the war with Mexico. Later in Mexico he joined Gen. Winfield Scott as inspector general.

In "Fifty Years in Camp and Field," Hitchcock wrote an account of one of Scott's tirades over punctuation and misspellings in a letter copied by an aide. Scott was known as "Old Fuss and Feathers."

As Hitchcock tells it, "A funny scene occurred last evening that would require Dickens to describe. The General called for his letter-book to show me a letter from himself to Commodore Connor. It had been copied by Colonel Edmonson. An error was discovered and the General broke out: 'Colonel Edmonson! Colonel Edmonson!' 'Did you copy this?'

" 'Yes, sir.'

" 'My dear Colonel! That is not right; that interlineation should be there' (pointing with his finger) 'and not there. Don't you see? The sense requires it. I never wrote it so! It is not sense! You make me write nonsense! You will kill me! I'll commit suicide if you don't follow me. Follow me no matter where I go — follow me, if out of a third-story window. I'll commit suicide if you don't!'"

" 'Send that nonsense to the government? My dear Colonel! Don't you attempt to correct me! And here again — over here — there should be a period and not a semicolon. The capital letter shows it. How could you make it a semicolon? Correct that on your life.'

" 'And there, you've left a space at the beginning of the line! That shows a new sentence; but there was none — it was all one sentence in the original! Never leave a space at the beginning of a line except when beginning a new sentence. There! You've put a 'g' in Colonel Hardin's name. I'll bet a thousand — ten thousand dollars to a farthing — there was no 'g' in the original. I'll agree to be shot tomorrow morning if I put a 'g' in the original.

" 'Follow me — follow me. I'll kill myself if you don't! I'll kill six others and then kill myself! I'll die before I send such a copy to the government! What would be said of me? That I write nonsense and don't know how to spell Colonel Hardin's name! Hardin, d-i-n — there is no 'g' in it and never was! No matter how strange the spelling — follow me. Don't you attempt to correct my spelling!' "

Hitchcock said that was a fraction of the general's angry outburst. Besides being a great general, Old Fuss and Feathers was a man with a colossal ego and monstrous vanity. When it came to grammar and spelling, apparently he was a tyrannical nitpicker.

—May 4, 2016

Column 19

The vote-bribing trial of 1915

County Judge Walter Timon testified that he had never found it necessary "to buy a single vote to keep Nueces County in the Democratic column."

U.S. District Judge Walter Burns empanelled a federal grand jury in May 1915 to investigate alleged corruptions in the general election of 1914 and determine whether local officials conspired to corrupt the ballot in Nueces County.

A U.S. marshal took charge of ballot boxes and more than 200 witnesses were called. After months investigating, the grand jury returned indictments against 42 people on charges of committing "conspiracy to corrupt an election."

Prominent people were indicted, all Democrats. They included County Judge Walter Timon, District Judge W. B. Hopkins, Sheriff M. B. Wright, Tax Assessor Joe Bluntzer, County Clerk August Uehlinger, County Treasurer Ed Oliver, and Constable Lee Riggs. Others included Claud Fowler, city police chief, Russell Savage, city attorney, and Joe Acebo, owner of the St. Dennis Saloon. Congressman John Nance Garner, a political ally of Judge Timon, was in the courtroom when the indictments were read.

The trial began in September 1915. The courtroom was crowded with those eager for a spectacle and extra chairs were brought in. Top officials in county government were sitting in the dock, no doubt startled to be there. They were streetwise politicians who knew how to round up votes but they were unsure of themselves as defendants in a courtroom.

75

County Judge Walter Timon was indicted, along with other prominent Democratic office-holders in Nueces County, on charges of committing "a conspiracy to corrupt an election."

Others enjoyed the show. It was amazing, one wit said, just how much it lifted the town's spirits by putting a bunch of county officials on trial.

A witness for the prosecution, Fred Headley, testified that a meeting was held in Timon's office to discuss how much it would cost to bribe voters "on the Hill." Headley testified that Timon said it would take $2,500 to $3,000 to carry the Hill "as the other side will spend money like water."

Defense witnesses could not recall Timon saying that. Mayor Roy Miller testified and complained that prosecutors were impugning his integrity. The judge said Miller was perfectly able to defend himself. Timon testified that he had never found it necessary "to buy a single vote to keep Nueces County in the Democratic column."

Charges against 18 people were dismissed, 16 were acquitted, and five were convicted, including Tom Dunn, Henry Stevens,

Lee Riggs, Ed Castleberry, and August Uehlinger. The case against Timon was ruled a mistrial.

Federal prosecutors tried to revive the case but the issue of election fraud in Nueces County was dropped. They gave it up because the root of it was a fight over the control of political patronage in South Texas and in truth, as everyone knew, both parties openly spent money to "corrupt" the ballot.

In the euphemism of the time, "The Hill" meant Hispanic voters on the bluff. Campaign money paid for whisky, cigars and cash handouts to buy votes, a system of fraud that had been perfected over the years by both sides. The saying was, "As the money goes so goes the Hill, and as the Hill goes so goes the election." After the voter fraud scandal died down, county elections were soon operating as always, like an expensive well-oiled Swiss watch.

Knights of the Golden Circle

Large groups of strangers showed up in Corpus Christi in late 1860. They came by ship from New Orleans and they left town on foot, walking south and west. Who were they? Where were they going? No one seemed to know. The Ranchero, Corpus Christi's newspaper, solved the mystery. The men belonged to the Knights of the Golden Circle, a secret society.

The Knights of the Golden Circle, or KGC, was founded in Lexington, Ky., on July 4, 1856 by George Bickley. It spread across the South and into Texas. Local units were called castles and members were formed into three orders, a military corps, a financial contingent, and a leadership cadre.

The KGC advocated the creation of an empire of slavery that would extend to Central America, include Mexico and the West Indies, and the southern half of the United States, from Kansas to Maryland and from Texas to Florida. As the KGC envisioned it, this slave empire would control a monopoly on tobacco, cotton, sugar, rice, and coffee and become a world power to rival ancient Rome. The North would be free to go its abolitionist way.

The KGC had an influential following in Texas, including legislators and other state leaders. There were 30 so-called castles in the state, including one in Corpus Christi. In the fall of 1860, the mysterious movement of men toward the border was part of the KGC plan to conquer Mexico, which would be divided up and great tracts of land bestowed on loyal followers of the KGC. They had it worked out exactly how many acres each man would receive, with peons assigned as slaves to till the land.

In September 1860, the Knights began to arrive in Corpus Christi and left on foot, some heading for Brownsville and some for Laredo. The countryside filled with Knights and their campfires increased every night by new parties arriving during the day, a Galveston paper reported. One detachment of Knights passed through Corpus Christi and a week later another group arrived, the Ranchero reported on Sept. 15, 1860.

"Those who passed through last week are at Banquete," the Ranchero stated, "and it appears they are bound to suffer disappointment, as they expect to meet a large force subsequent to a march on Matamoros."

The KGC's plan to invade Mexico was badly organized and just fell apart. George Bickley, leader of the Knights, arrived in Texas and cited difficulties in raising money, buying weapons, and organizing such a large undertaking. He postponed the Mexican invasion to await the outcome of the U.S. presidential election coming in November. The dispirited Knights who had come to Texas to conquer Mexico turned tail and headed home.

Corpus Christi's own "castle" held a birthday party for the K.G.C. on July 4, 1861. Local Knights marched to Ziegler's Hall where there were speeches, toasts, and tables filled with good things to eat. It was their last hurrah.

Some Confederate militia units were formed from ranks of the Knights and several Confederate leaders were high in the order. But the Knights of the Golden Circle's dream of creating a pro-slavery empire to rival ancient Rome became one of the first casualties of the Civil War.

—May 11, 2016

Rip Ford at Palmito Ranch

"You can retreat and go to hell if you wish. These are
my men and I am going to fight." —Rip Ford to Gen.
James Slaughter

John Salmon Ford arrived in Texas a month too late for the
battle of San Jacinto but he didn't miss much else in the next 50
years of Texas history. His Confederate Cavalry of the West
fought the last land battle of the Civil War near Brownsville.

Ford was trained as a teacher and doctor and when he arrived
in Texas in 1836 he practiced medicine, did surveying, and was
elected to the Ninth Congress of the Republic. When war
threatened with Mexico he joined Texas volunteers under the
command of Jack Hays.

In Mexico, as Hays' adjutant, Ford send out death notices of
the Texans killed in battle and he would write RIP for "Rest in
Peace" at the bottom. He became known as "Old Rip."

After the war Ford was appointed captain of a Ranger company
and pursued Indians between the Nueces and Rio Grande. On
one occasion, Ford's Rangers were camped near Fort Merrill and
there was a skirmish with Comanches during the night. Ford
yelled to a Ranger, "Level, what's the matter?"

"Damn them, they shot my horse."

"Is that all?"

"No, damn them, they shot me, too."

After Texas joined the Confederacy Ford was put in charge of
conscription, which meant a desk job in Austin, for the first two
years of the war. Then, in December 1863, he was given

command of a regiment of cavalry made up of volunteers too young or too old for the regular army. Ford called his regiment the Cavalry of the West. He was promoted to brigadier general in 1864.

In March 1865 Union Gen. Lew Wallace, the man who later wrote "Ben Hur," traveled to Brazos Santiago. He sent a message to Confederate Gen. James Slaughter in command at Brownsville asking for a conference. Slaughter and Ford met Wallace at Point Isabel. The subject of this unusual meeting was the possibility of reaching an informal ceasefire in South Texas.

Gen. Wallace thought it would be useless to continue to fight on the Rio Grande, with the war all but over. But Slaughter and Ford emphasized that they could make no deals without specific instructions from their superiors, which they did not have.

Still, Ford left the meeting with the understanding that there would be a kind of peaceful co-existence along the border based on a simple handshake and gentleman's agreement reached between Wallace, Ford and Slaughter.

Not long afterwards, on April 9, Robert E. Lee surrendered at Appomattox. But it is a long way from Virginia to South Texas and news during the war traveled slowly. On May 11, the commander of the federal camp on Brazos Island sent a detachment of 300 men to take possession of Brownsville. The detachment of Union soldiers was under the command Lt. Col. David Branson.

Next day, Branson's soldiers attacked a Confederate outpost at Palmito Ranch near the old Palo Alto battlefield. Horses were captured and three Confederate soldiers were taken prisoner. The outpost was manned by Confederate cavalry under Capt. George Robinson. That afternoon, Robinson's troops tried to regain their position and the federals, assuming the Confederates got up reinforcements, fell back four miles.

When Ford got word that Union forces had attacked Capt. Robinson's regiment, he ordered Robinson to hold his ground. Over supper in Ford's quarters, Gen. Slaughter and Ford discussed their course of action. Slaughter wanted to retreat and Ford got angry. "You can retreat and go to hell if you wish," he told Slaughter. "These are my men and I am going to fight."

John Salmon "Rip" Ford in 1865. The skirmish at Palmito Ranch on the Rio Grande, between Rip Ford's "Cavalry of the West" and Union soldiers from Brazos Island, was the last land battle of the Civil War.

Next morning Ford, with 70 men and six artillery guns, marched to the scene of the battle from the day before. He deployed his forces to flank the federal position and told his troops, "We've whipped them before and we can whip them again."

Artillery fire was directed at the Union position and when Ford's men charged the Union troops began to run, retreating east to Brazos Island. Ford in a wry understatement said the Union soldiers left the battlefield "in a confused manner."

It was almost dark when Ford ordered a halt near Boca Chica Pass. Confederates and Yankees moved out in skirmish formation. A Union soldier, John J. Williams, a private in the 34th Indiana, was killed. His family later received a medal honoring him as the last soldier killed in the Civil War.

In the dying light, an artillery shell from Union guns struck near the Confederate position and a Confederate soldier in his teens — using "a very profane expletive for so small a boy" — fired a random shot toward the dunes of Boca Chica. It was believed to have been the last shot fired in the Civil War. (A local attorney, Michael P. O"Reilly, thinks Andrew Jackson Avant, his great great grandfather who was in the Cavalry of the West, could have fired that last shot.)

In the battle of Palmito Ranch or Palmito Hill, the federals lost 25 to 30 men killed and wounded and 113 prisoners were taken. Confederate losses were five wounded, though none seriously.

Later accounts said Ford learned of the surrender of Robert E. Lee and downfall of the Confederacy from the Union prisoners taken after the battle. The federals said they thought the Confederates knew the war was over, that they were sent to take possession of Brownsville and did not expect any resistance.

It has been pointed out that by continuing the fight time was gained to move a consignment of cotton across the river, into Mexico, to avoid confiscation by Union troops. Richard King and Mifflin Kenedy, friends of Ford's, had an interest in this cotton. But as Tom Lea wrote in "The King Ranch," Ford cared little about the cotton shipment but was angry that the agreed-upon truce made with Gen. Lew Wallace was violated by Union troops. In any event, the Palmito Ranch affair was the last land battle of the Civil War.

John Salmon "Rip" Ford, gray ghost of the border and great figure in Texas history, died in his bed after a stroke on Nov. 3, 1897. He was remembered for long years of fighting Comanches, Mexican soldiers, border bandits, and Yankee cavalry. His soldiers in the Cavalry of the West won the last land battle of the Civil War. They won a battle after the war was lost.

—May 18, 2016

Last sunset of the Karankawas

The Karankawa warrior was fascinated by the sight of the sun submerging itself into the sea, "gazing spellbound at the point on the horizon where the waters closed over and quenched this great ball of fire."
—Roy Bedichek

Roy Bedichek called the Texas Coast Karankaway Country. He wrote a book by that name in which he related the story of a Karankawa warrior mesmerized by watching the evening sun set.

The Karankawas roamed the coast from Galveston Island to Corpus Christi Bay, drifting in and out of their favorite places in following the food of the seasons. The men were over six feet tall and carried long bows of red cedar. The women wore deerskin skirts and smeared their bodies with alligator grease. The men's hair was braided with rattlesnake rattles, which made a rustling sound when they walked.

They poled dugout canoes on the lagoons and bays and ate great quantities of shellfish. Their old campsites left mountains of oyster shells that had been discarded over the centuries. Their guttural language consisted of whistles, sighs and grunts and in conversing they avoided eye contact. Some accounts say they were cannibals.

When Cabeza de Vaca was shipwrecked on a barrier island in 1528, a curious Karankawa reached out to touch his face. Cabeza took this as a gesture of shared human identity. Still, they kept him as a slave for years before he and three companions escaped and walked to Mexico. Two decades after Cabeza de Vaca's sojourn, 300 survivors of a shipwrecked Spanish fleet washed up on Padre Island. Karankawas attacked and killed the Spanish as they tried to flee down the island. All but two of 300 were slain.

In 1684 Sieur de la Salle and his French colonists built a settlement called Fort St. Louis on Garcitas Creek near Matagorda Bay. After being provoked, the Karankawas attacked the French settlement, killing all the colonists but five children, whom they took away. A Spanish expedition recovered four of the children. One said he went hungry rather than eat the flesh of a man the Karankawas had killed and prepared for a feast. He told how the Karankawas cried when the French youngsters were taken away.

In 1722 the Spanish established a mission and fort near the site of La Salle's old fort in an effort to civilize and convert the Karankawas.

A year later trouble erupted when a Karankawa living at the mission went into the hut of a soldier and asked for a piece of meat, his promised share of newly slaughtered beef. While waiting he shook his blanket and scattered dirt over the area where the soldier's wife was grinding corn. The angry woman ordered her husband to send the Indian away. The Indian refused to go until he had received his piece of meat. A fight erupted and spread until it took in the whole Indian population around the mission and fort. Soldiers and horses were killed and the Indians fled to the woods. Spanish soldiers captured some Karankawa women and imprisoned them in a small hut. Several were hanged. Others escaped.

After the uprising the mission and fort were moved west to the Guadalupe River and the missionaries were urged to do all they could to pacify the Indians. They were told to treat them with kindness, give them presents and supply their material and spiritual needs.

In 1749 the mission was moved again, this time to Goliad. The new mission Rosario was established on the banks of the San Antonio River. Within four or five years, about 500 Karankawas and Copanes lived around the mission. They helped put up buildings and work the fields, but the Indians did not understand the attempts to restrict their freedom and they often deserted to return to the coast. They were punished when they were caught.

A plain headstone with simple cross marks the grave of Mary (Amaroo) Pothoff, last known Karankawa Indian, buried in the Welder family plot in St. Joseph Cemetery in Beeville. Photo courtesy of E. Herndon Williams.

Fray Gaspar José de Solís inspected Texas missions in 1767 and wrote in his diary that the mission Rosario had 40 horses, 30 mules, 200 milk cows, 700 sheep and goats, and 5,000 head of cattle. Solís reported that the Indians would escape, preferring to live in their old savage ways rather than as civilized wards of the mission. The Spanish were never able to subdue the Karankawas.

In 1818 Jean Laffite's pirates on Galveston Island kidnapped a Karankawa girl and in retaliation, it was said, the Indians captured and ate two of Lafitte's men. In the battle that followed 30 Indians were killed and the rest of the tribe fled Galveston Island.

In the 1820s Stephen F. Austin's colonists signed a treaty with the Karankawas but killings on both sides continued. Austin wrote that the Karankawa Indians would have to be "exterminated" by civilization. Mexico's Manuel de Mier y Teran praised Austin's colonists for their reprisals against the Karankawas. "If the Indians kill a settler a large party of settlers hunt down and kill 10 of the tribe, of any age or sex."

They were soon killed off. By 1844 a few ragged Karankawa survivors were killed in a battle south of Corpus Christi. Several accounts say that the last Karankawas — reduced to a dozen families or more — were living in abject poverty in Tamaulipas, Mexico in the late 1840s and 1850s. From there they disappeared.

The last known Karankawas in this country were a sister and brother named Mary and Tom Amaroo. They were taken and cared for by the Welder-Power family. Tom Amaroo enlisted in the Confederate Army and was killed in the Civil War. Mary Amaroo married a man named Pothoff (sometimes spelled Pathoff) who was also killed in the war. She died in 1911 and was buried in the Welder plot in St. Joseph Cemetery in Beeville. The last known Karankawa was given a Christian burial, with a cross adorning her tombstone. The old Spanish friars won in the end.

Roy Bedichek provides us with a last appealing glimpse of the Karankawa. "Early explorers report a curious habit of the Karankawa warrior," Bedichek wrote. "At times he was fascinated by the sight of the sun submerging itself in the sea. The wonder of sunset over water was too much for the mind of this simple savage. He became still as a statue, oblivious to his surroundings, gazing spellbound at the point on the horizon where the waters closed over and quenched this great ball of fire. Finally, in the deepening dusk, he stirs. The fire has gone out. The sea is gray again. The rattles awaken as he moves away toward his camp behind the dunes."

—May 25, 2016

Town nicknames

"God's Most Livable Land and Most Lovable People."
—Robstown slogan

A photo taken by Doc McGregor in the 1930s shows a sign on old Highway 9 near Calallen. It identifies Corpus Christi as the Naples of the Gulf, one of the city's fanciful nicknames.

Before the turn of the 20th Century Corpus Christi was known as the Bluff City, the Texas Riviera, and more recent times as the Sparkling City by the Sea, though that is often employed with a heavy touch of irony. Such nicknames, or civic slogans, betray a town's ambitions.

In the 1890s, soon after its founding, Portland was called the Gem City of the Gulf. In 1914, when Aransas Pass was only a few years old, its slogan was "The City of Certainty, Where the Sails Meet the Rails." Aransas Pass hoped to be the next Houston with railroads connecting to a deepwater port on Harbor Island.

Ingleside called itself the Atlantic City of the Gulf, then changed that to Playground of the South. Taft's civic slogan sounds like a copybook maxim or admonishment: "Where Permanent Prosperity Rewards Honest Effort." Robstown's modest slogan was, "God's Most Livable Land and Most Lovable People." Alice billed itself — and still does — as the Hub City.

When Port Aransas was known as Tarpon, and famous for its sport fishing, the slogan was, "Where They Bite Every Day." And they did, too. Even President Roosevelt came there for the

The Port Aransas slogan — Where They Bite Every Day.

fishing. The slogan for Mathis was, "As Good as the Best and Better Than the Rest." The local Chambers of Commerce, I guess, once had a creative streak, though the idea of pairing Chamber of Commerce with creative gives one pause.

Street work

When going downtown I try to plot my course, like the captain of a ship at sea. I can't take Staples; it's all torn up by City Hall. I try to avoid the dog-leg around Spohn Hospital and Shoreline has become an obstacle course without the view. There's no easy way to get from my house to downtown.

This came to mind when reading a copy of the Corpus Christi Crony from 1902. It seems they had as much tolerance for the disruptions caused by street work as we do today.

The Crony described how streets were improved with a crew of 30 men with 16 wagons and mule teams. The 30 men, said the

Crony, get themselves with their wagons in the middle of the road where they can block traffic. When they have stood around for four or five hours, discussing various things, they move forward three or four feet and block traffic some more.

After three days they become exhausted and stop. At this point a foreman arrives with a spade and searches until he finds a place where the road is particularly smooth. There he digs a large hole and into this the men each drop a gravel. The 16 mule teams are driven over the hole and after a prolonged bout of pawing at the gravel the men all go draw their pay.

Sometimes, said the Crony, where the street is very good, they will improve it with a plow so that no one can pass that way again. But this is hard work and requires extra pay and two holidays.

Another writer noted that the streets would not be so bad if they were repaired in the middle and on both sides. The streets of Corpus Christi, he said, were all paved with good intentions. You wonder, if you could go back even further, if they had similar problems with their streets in Thebes and Babylon. Roadwork has certainly changed. We no longer use wagons and mule teams. Otherwise, our modern world is not so different. It wouldn't take much to please us: just good streets and roads, that never need maintenance, and paid for by someone else.

The first district attorney

D. for Daniel McNeill Turner came to Corpus Christi in the 1870s, got his law degree and bought a newspaper, the Gazette, then was elected to the City Council. In 1882 the office of district attorney was established and he ran for that position.

Turner's opponent was a man named McConnell, who listed his accomplishments in a campaign brochure. Before coming to Corpus Christi, he had had a large and successful law practice in Alabama. He had argued cases before the Alabama Supreme Court. He was running for district attorney, he said, for the honor of the thing and not for the money.

D. McNeill Turner took the opposite tack. He wrote that he had never had a large law practice, that he had never seen a supreme court, much less appeared before one, and that he was running for the money, hang the honor. He won easily.

Turner served 10 years as district attorney and then was elected representative to the Texas House. As district attorney he worked to convict evil-doers accused of committing the worst offenses of the time: horse stealing, cow stealing, sheep stealing, murder. Turner was paid $50 for every man convicted "and I sent them off by the carloads, either to be hung or cool their heels in prison."

Lynch law, he said, did him out of a lot of fees. "The law abiders (vigilantes) hung any thief they could get their hands on and if they figured a murderer had it coming they would hang him too."

Turner once recalled an incident in Judge J. C. Russell's (25th Criminal District) court being held in San Diego (in the old courthouse that later burned in 1914). Judge Russell had a bald head and nervous disposition. To keep flies off his shiny dome he wore a black skullcap. He hated the loud sound made by pistol matches, so-called because they sounded like a pistol being fired. The judge had a sign put up stating that it was punishable by a $10 fine to strike a pistol match in his court.

Two lawyers bought five boxes of pistol matches, cut the heads off, and scattered them in the courtroom. When the jury pool of 75 men came into court and their heels struck the match heads it sounded like the battle of Bull Run. Turner said Judge Russell went berserk, tore off his black skullcap, threw it down, and told the court he would give $100 to the man who brought in the culprit or culprits who caused the commotion, dead or alive.

—June 1, 2016

General Sherman's warm welcome

"I will not go down there. His march through Georgia
was a disgrace to the North." —Mayor John B. Murphy

William Tecumseh Sherman — Civil War general famous for
his quote "War Is Hell" — visited Corpus Christi in 1883.
Sherman was asked to travel to Corpus Christi to promote the
new railroad to Laredo, the Tex-Mex. The general was in Texas
inspecting military posts.

Eli Merriman, editor of the Caller, told the story. Merriman
was notified of the general's visit and responsibility fell to him to
get up a welcoming committee to meet the train from Laredo.
Merriman didn't think it would be a problem. The town's mayor
was John B. Murphy, a staunch Unionist. But Murphy refused to
attend any ceremony for Sherman. "I will not go down there,"
Murphy told Merriman. "His march through Georgia was a
disgrace to the North."

Merriman turned to Perry Doddridge, wealthy wool merchant
and banker. Doddridge was an Alabama native and former
Confederate, but he agreed to meet the general and drive him
around the city. When the train arrived, Merriman and
Doddridge, two ex-Confederates not thrilled with the assignment,
were at the depot to greet the famous Union general.

Before they could get him into a carriage, a black barber in
town named Will Leonard took center stage. He was dressed for
the occasion, wearing a fancy coat and plum-colored top hat. He
jumped on top of a baggage handcar and in a deep voice gave
three rousing cheers for Gen. Sherman, one of the Union

The visit of Civil War general William Tecumseh Sherman in 1883 caused some problems. When the town's mayor refused to roll out the welcome mat, the town's barber took his place.

generals, besides U.S. Grant, whose victories not only helped win the war but to end slavery.

Will Leonard's unscripted cheering no doubt was more heartfelt than any official welcome Gen. Sherman could have received.

Trial delayed by war

J. M. "Scotty" Jetton, a gatekeeper on King Ranch property on the Laguna Madre, was shot to death on Feb. 28, 1941. His drinking buddy, Phillip Trammell, a one-armed fence-rider, was indicted for the crime.

Sheriff's investigators found that in a gun fight Trammell was shot in the shoulder by Jetton's shotgun while Jetton was killed by two shots from Trammell's rifle. Trammell said, "He got me but I got him." What sparked the fight was never revealed.

The trial began the day after the attack on Pearl Harbor. Judge George Westervelt called a recess so jurors could hear President Roosevelt's day-of-infamy speech. Two walls of Jetton's cabin were reconstructed in the courtroom to show what happened. On

Dec. 13, 1941, jurors found Trammell guilty of murder. He was sentenced to 99 years. The conviction was overturned on appeal, but because many of those involved were in the military overseas it was not retried for six years.

In 1947, in the second trial, Rev. Lester Roloff arrived to protest Judge Cullen Briggs' decision to let jurors have a beer with their supper. Judge Briggs wouldn't back down, but he told the bailiff to allow each juror only one bottle of beer. At the end of this trial, Trammell was found not guilty.

Real money

John Howland Wood, one of the first cattle kings of South Texas, founded his ranch a decade before Richard King established the more famous King Ranch. Wood's Bonnie View Ranch stretched from Copano Bay to the present town of Woodville.

Wood was descended from a wealthy New York family. He went to New York in 1847 to collect part of his inheritance and returned to Texas with $60,000 in gold coins packed in wooden kegs.

Soon after the Civil War, crooked horse traders passed through the Corpus Christi region buying horses at remote Mexican-American ranches. They paid for them with worthless Confederate bills. After that, people refused to accept any form of paper currency. They wanted to be paid in gold or silver; there was no question about the value of that.

After the war, when he went on cattle-buying trips, Shanghai Pierce would be accompanied by his black cowhand, Neptune Holmes, leading a pack animal loaded with bags of gold and silver. When the cattle had been classed and counted, Shanghai would dump out the money on a blanket and pay the stockmen their due.

The late Ruth Dodson told a story of her uncle, free-range cattleman Martin Culver, who owned Rancho Perdido in Live Oak County and made a fortune trailing herds to Kansas. When her mother, Mary Susanna Burris, was young she visited the Culver ranch, in 1868. A cattleman friend of Culver's put down a sack of gold coins and told her that if she could pick it up she could have it. She couldn't lift it.

In 1873, William Brittain, rector of the Church of the Good Shepherd, submitted his resignation, angry over the church's delay in paying his salary. In a letter he reminded church elders what he was owed; he knew down to the penny. He asked for 44 dollars and 37 cents and he wanted to be paid, not in greenbacks, but in "coin dollars."

In Rockport in the 1870s Morgan Line captains bought hides from the packing houses with kegs filled with silver coins, fresh from the mint in New Orleans. The money was measured by weight, rather than counted, and barrels filled with silver coins were casually stacked on the docks of the Big Wharf. Barrels packed with silver were transported around town in freight wagons like so many kegs of nails.

E. H. Caldwell, a bank clerk in Corpus Christi in the late 1870s and early 1880s, recalled that silver coins in wooden kegs were hauled around the streets by the wagonload. When he was a bookkeeper at the Doddridge & Davis Bank, silver dollars served as the currency for all transactions unless otherwise specified. Gold was used to pay customs charges.

As freight collector for the Morgan Line steamers, Caldwell said he had to carry large sums of gold and silver. "These would accumulate and I would tire from lugging them around to the point that $1,000 in silver seemed to weigh a ton."

The value of paper dollars fluctuated based on the day's market. People didn't trust them. They preferred the satisfying weight of silver or gold coins, so bright and shiny, and often carried in soft leather sacks. That was the real thing while paper currency represented the concept of money. Gold and silver coins were what people sweated for, slaved for, and sometimes killed for. That was real money, the coin of the realm.

—June 8, 2016

94

Freighter wrecked at the Devil's Elbow

For decades, the remains of the old Nicaragua could be
seen off the sands of Padre Island.

The freighter Nicaragua wrecked on Padre Island in 1912. The
ship ran aground at the Devil's Elbow, 75 miles south of Port
Aransas. Rumors said the ship was carrying guns for Pancho
Villa, but the real story was simpler, if less romantic.

The steamer left Tampico for Port Arthur on Oct. 11, 1912. It
was loaded with cotton, lumber and other products. If it had been
carrying guns for Mexican revolutionaries, it was headed in the
wrong direction.

On Oct. 16, a late hurricane hit the Gulf and during the storm,
the Nicaragua was forced aground on Padre Island. The ship's
owners in Mexico reported the vessel missing, but no one knew
what happened for 10 days until members of the crew turned up
in a small boat at Port Aransas. Capt. Eschevarria and nine
crewmembers took one of the ship's boats and headed north.
They were spotted by the Coast Guard's Lifeboat Station and
rescued. The captain said the rudder chain was damaged in the
storm and the ship was thrown against the island breakers.

The revenue cutter Windom searched for the other 12 crew
members without success. They were presumed lost. But on Oct.
29, six of them arrived at Port Isabel after they had walked 54
miles down the island. They left behind two men on the ship who
were too sick to walk, who were later rescued.

Efforts to salvage the ship were unsuccessful. For decades, the
remains of the old Nicaragua could be seen off the island.

The boiler of the steamship Nicaragua (top) was a landmark at the Devil's Elbow of Padre Island in 1960. Below, the Nicaragua on the beach soon after it ran aground during a storm in the Gulf on Oct. 16, 1912. Top photo from the Central Library; bottom photo from Greg Smith.

Greg Smith, great grandson of Padre Island rancher Pat Dunn, said his grandfather, Burton Dunn, and a cousin, Dooley Dunn, got to the wreck shortly after its grounding. "Granddaddy got on deck with some effort and scrounged up some of the ship's cups and dishes," Smith said. "They had Nicaragua embossed on them. He proceeded to drop them over the side to Dooley who was on the beach. Dooley was all thumbs and couldn't catch the darn things, leaving not much more than broken pieces. The ones caught disappeared long ago, probably lost when the house at the head of the island was destroyed in the 1916 storm."

A reporter visited the wreck in 1922 and wrote that a rope ladder still dangled from Nicaragua's side and a galley door swung on rusty hinges as a gulf breeze swept through the cabins. By 1960, another reporter said only the giant boiler was still visible. There may be part of the old freighter resting on the Gulf floor off Padre Island. Otherwise, what remains of the old Nicaragua is its story.

Ranch named for laurel trees

Rancho de Los Laureles was the closest large ranch to Corpus Christi. It was named for the bay laurel trees near the Laguna Madre.

The great capitalist Charles Stillman bought the Laureles in 1844 and his brother Cornelius ran it. As the ranch grew, it took in the Flour Bluff area and much of what is now the Southside of Corpus Christi. After the Civil War, Mifflin Kenedy bought the Laureles and increased the size of the ranch to 300,000 acres. At the time it was larger than King Ranch.

In 1882 Kenedy bought La Parra Ranch and sold Laureles to investors in Scotland for $1.1 million. They called their holdings the Texas Land & Cattle Company and hired John Tod of Edinburgh to manage the Laureles.

Richard King tried several times to buy the Laureles before he died. Henrietta King finally acquired the ranch in 1907 and Kenedy's old Laurel Leaf brand was added to the King Ranch brands.

John Tod, the old Scotsman, returned to Edinburgh. An article in 1936 said he spent his last years at his club, sharing memories of his days managing the Laureles, one of the great cattle ranches of South Texas.

County seat

When Nueces County was created by the Legislature on April 18, 1846, it was bigger than some states, stretching from the Nueces to the Rio Grande. The first voting precincts were at Corpus Christi, Laredo, and Port Isabel. Corpus Christi was named the county seat and it has been the county seat ever since except for one brief period.

During the Civil War, after Corpus Christi was bombarded by Union warships in 1862, officials moved the county government to Santa Margarita, a ferry-crossing settlement on the west bank of the Nueces River near the present community of Bluntzer, which was considered to be safe from Union warships. Commissioners' minutes for the last two years of the war were noted "in vacation."

After the war, Nueces County was reorganized and the county seat was moved back to Corpus Christi. Corpus Christi has always been the county seat of Nueces County except for those two years when county officials were "in vacation" and hunkered down at Santa Margarita.

Low prices, low pay

In reviewing 1902 editions of the Corpus Christi Crony it's always shocking to see what things cost more than a hundred years ago. Compared to today's prices they seem mighty cheap, but they were not.

People could buy a Victor Monarch gramophone, with 12 records, for $25. At Lichtenstein's men could buy hand-sewn shirts for one dollar each. At R. G. Blossman's Grocery coffee sold for 15 cents a pound and a dozen cinnamon rolls cost 15 cents at Cooper's Clean Bakery.

At the Oriental Hotel Merriman a room cost $1 a day, without meals, or $2 a day with meals. At Uehlinger's Grocery a plug of Gravely's Blue Tag chewing tobacco or tin of Dog Fight smoking tobacco cost 10 cents. A full meal, with coffee or tea and dessert, cost 25 cents at J. R. Shaw's Restaurant. Three Havana cigars sold for 25 cents at Joshua Smith's Drug Store.

But to put in more perspective, the average worker was paid $400 a year in 1902. He would work 60 hours a week for that dollar and quarter a day. If that worker paid $1 to stay in the Oriental Hotel Merriman and spent 25 cents for a meal at Shaw's Restaurant, his hard-earned wages were gon*e and he would not have a dime left to buy a cigar or a can of Dog Fight tobacco. Those prices seem low today but they would not have at the time.

—June 15, 2016

<u>Column 25</u>

Tom Coleman's mansion

On their way home from the housewarming at the Fulton
Mansion, Mrs. Coleman told her husband, "If she can
have one (meaning Mrs. Fulton's new home) then I want
one twice as big."

Thomas Coleman and George Ware Fulton founded one of the
great ranches of South Texas, the Coleman Fulton Pasture
Company. Coleman and Fulton became rivals for control of the
company.

Fulton, who made his fortune from beef packing plants, built a
mansion he called Oakhurst. We know it today as the Fulton
Mansion. Among the guests at the housewarming party in 1877
were Thomas Coleman and his wife. On the way home Mrs.
Coleman complained to her husband, "If she can have one
(meaning Mrs. Fulton's home) then I want one twice as big."

Coleman lost no time in meeting his wife's demands.
Construction soon began on a new home on his ranch on the
south side of Chiltipin Creek (15 miles north of today's Taft).
When it was finished it looked like a much grander version of the
Fulton mansion. But it was out in the country, in the middle of
nowhere.

At the Colemans' housewarming party in 1880 guests left
Corpus Christi at sunrise to cross the reef road in buggies. They
carried a change of clothes for the two-day party. The gateway
was a mile from the house. Servants were posted along the route
to offer refreshments to the guests. Some 25 acres were
landscaped. There were stables and a race track.

Thomas Coleman's mansion, built on his ranch on Chiltipin Creek, north of Taft, was meant to out-lavish the Fulton mansion, the home of his rival, George W. Fulton.

Among the marvels of the new home was an acetylene lighting plant, indoor bathrooms with water supplied by cisterns, a billiard room, music room, and quarters for maids. There were beautiful hand-carved mantels and specially made furniture of ebony and walnut. Guests ate barbecue spiced with the little peppers that grew along Chiltipin Creek. That night they danced on the veranda surrounding the mansion.

The Coleman mansion cost $150,000, compared to $80,000 of the Fulton mansion. That $150,000 would amount to $3.5 million today.

The fierce rivalry between Coleman and Fulton reached a point where one of them had to go. Coleman sold out to David Sinton from Cincinnati whose son-in-law, Charles Taft, took over the ranch operations and the Coleman-Fulton Pasture Company became known as the Taft Ranch.

Coleman kept his great mansion on Chiltipin Creek. This was where the White children grew up after their parents died in the yellow fever epidemic in 1867. Thomas Coleman was the nephew of Edward White and brother Frank who settled at White Point across Nueces Bay from Corpus Christi.

When Edward White and wife died in the epidemic, their four children became wards of Thomas Coleman. There were two sons and two daughters, Thomas, Frank, Alice and Eddie. In time, Eddie White married Edwin Atlee McCampbell in Corpus Christi. Her son, Coleman McCampbell, wrote the well-known history of Corpus Christi, "Saga of a Frontier Seaport."

After Thomas Coleman died in 1896, the house was sold to John Welder and used briefly as a summer house then stood vacant until it was demolished in 1930. It was built as a result of wealth, envy and one-upmanship. After they were gone it was torn down.

What a deal

A British consul reported in 1837 that Corpus Christi Bay would never be of any consequence as a harbor because extensive sandbars hampered navigation. When Zachary Taylor's army arrived in 1845 transport ships had to be lightered and even shallow-draft lighters had to be dragged over the mudflats in the bay.

Corpus Christi founder Henry Kinney bought a steam-powered dredge in 1848 and hired a crew to deepen the channel at the entrance to the bay. After this effort languished John Moore headed an effort to dredge a channel. His dredge boat was burned to the water line by federal ships during the Civil War. What was left of the dredge, tied up at a wharf at Corpus Christi, gradually disappeared as people ripped it up for firewood.

In the early 1870s Augustus Morris and James Cummings dredged an eight-foot-deep channel across the bay. The Morris & Cummings Cut allowed the first ocean-going vessel, the Gussie, to dock at the Central Wharf on May 31, 1874, which was a big day for the city.

After the 1919 storm wrecked the new port on Harbor Island, Corpus Christi's struggle to get a deepwater port reached a critical time. After years of lobbying, Congress authorized the

Corps of Engineers to make a recommendation on where a new port should be located. The Corps at Galveston had to choose between Port Aransas, Aransas Pass, Rockport, and Corpus Christi. The recommendation would be made to Congress by the district supervisor of the Corps, Maj. L. M. Adams.

Corpus Christi advanced several arguments. The other coastal cities were more vulnerable to hurricanes than Corpus Christi, which was hard-hit in 1919 but mainly in the low-lying areas of the city. Much of Corpus Christi was built on high bluffs, the highest elevation on the Gulf Coast. Another point in Corpus Christi's favor was its size, compared to its rivals, and the fact it was served by three railroads while Port Aransas had no railroad link and Rockport and Aransas Pass had one.

Roy Miller, Corpus Christi's former mayor and most influential booster, took the Corps' Maj. Adams on a hunting trip to King Ranch on a hot day in December 1920. They drove around until Adams shot a buck.

That night at the King Ranch's Big House, Miller got a bottle of whisky and took it to Adams' room. After a few drinks and some conversation, Miller came out and whispered to Richard King, the banker and grandson of the ranch founder. Miller told him, "We got it."

Sure enough. Adams made his report to Congress and recommended Corpus Christi over the over coastal cities as the best place for a new port. Whether that was the basis of an impartial assessment or whether a deal was made will never be known for certain. In 1926, on the anniversary of the 1919 storm, Corpus Christi residents watched the first ships enter the turning basin of the new port. It was the culmination of 75 years of effort.

In 1930, when Maj. Adams retired as district supervisor of the Corps of Engineers, he was named director of the port of Corpus Christi. If eyebrows were raised, it went unreported. It sure looks like a deal was made over a bottle of bourbon at the King Ranch.

—June 22, 2016

Wrong-Way Corrigan was never lost

He had no parachute or radio. His monoplane named
Sunshine cost $325. He made the trip on $62 and 26
cents. That was for gas and oil. For himself, he had a
quart of water, two packs of fig bars and two bars of
chocolate.

"Isn't this Los Angeles?" the flier asked.

"Los Angeles! This is Dublin, Ireland!"

That was July 18, 1938. The flier was Douglas Corrigan, who
had filed a flight plan to take off from New Jersey and land in
California. When he landed in Ireland, he said he had flown the
wrong way. From that day on he was known as Wrong-Way
Corrigan, the man who flew from New Jersey to Ireland, across
the Atlantic, on his way to California.

Douglas Corrigan grew up in Aransas Pass. His father was an
engineer on the Aransas Pass ship channel. When Douglas was
15, his mother died and his father was killed in a train accident.
Corrigan took flying lessons and worked as an airplane
mechanic. He helped to build Charles Lindbergh's "Spirit of St.
Louis."

In July 1938 Corrigan asked permission to fly across the
Atlantic to Ireland. Authorities turned him down, saying that his
plane was not airworthy. He went ahead and traveled without
official permission. He had no parachute or radio. His Curtiss
Robin monoplane, named Sunshine, cost $325. He made the trip
on $62 and 26 cents. That was for gas and oil. For himself, he
had only a quart of water, two packs of fig bars and two bars of
chocolate.

Douglas Corrigan, the pilot who grew up in Aransas Pass, became famous for making a navigational error that landed him in Dublin, Ireland, instead of California. Friends said he knew exactly where he was going.

When he landed in Ireland and asked, "Isn't this Los Angeles?" it was all so much blarney. Corrigan knew exactly where he was. But he played the string out and stuck to his script. He kept the "Wrong Way" joke going.

Others who knew Corrigan knew better. He was not some lost clodhopper but an experienced pilot who always knew what he was doing. Barbara Erickson London, a pilot and friend, said he was too good a pilot to make that kind of mistake. "It's unfortunate that the buffoonery was played up instead of recognizing the fabulous feat that he accomplished." They made a movie of the spectacular flight in 1939 called "The Flying Irishman." Corrigan ended up in California after all, where he bought an orange grove. He died in 1995 and was buried in Santa Ana. To the end of his life, he stuck to his story — with, it was said, a twinkle in the eye and the trace of a smile. But those who knew him well insisted that he was never lost.

The wolf-bit man

Rabid coyotes, skunks, dogs and cats were always a danger on the remote ranches of South Texas. A mad coyote, it was said, would run among the pack biting and infecting every other animal.

The danger from rabid animals increased during a drought. Wild game came in close to the ranch houses in search of food and water and the coyotes followed them. It was a drought year in 1888 when Will Chamberlain, usually called Willie, was bitten by a mad coyote. Chamberlain was taking a nap on the porch of his ranch house near Brownsville when a mad coyote bit him on the cheek. At the time, this meant an almost certain and painful death.

But Chamberlain was lucky. Word was sent to his half-sister, Henrietta King, the matriarch of King Ranch, who sent the family physician, Corpus Christi's Dr. Arthur Spohn, in her buggy to treat her brother. Dr. Spohn had just read of a medical breakthrough in the treatment of rabies by a French doctor.

Dr. Spohn took his patient to Galveston and from there they sailed on a fast clipper ship across the Atlantic. Once in Paris, Willie Chamberlain, bitten by a rabid coyote on a ranch in South Texas, became the first to be saved from the horrors of a death by rabies by the vaccine developed by Louis Pasteur.

Pasteur himself administered the vaccine, one shot each day for 14 days. Chamberlain returned to Texas and died 47 years later. He had been bitten by a mad coyote, but he was always known as the wolf-bit man.

Henry Kinney's faulty title

A legal dispute over who owned the land on which Corpus Christi was built caused a lot of distress in the 1870s.

Henry Kinney established his trading post in 1839 in what would become Corpus Christi. He was a squatter, without rights to the land. Two years later, the owner, or so it was thought, showed up. He was a Mexican army officer, Capt. Enrique Villarreal, and he brought some 200 Mexican cavalry soldiers with him to reclaim his land. Kinney offered to buy the land, giving Villarreal $3,000 for one league of the 10-league Rincon del Oso. Kinney later bought nine more leagues from Villarreal's heirs for 21 cents an acre.

Levi Jones, a land speculator, did not believe Villarreal had clear title. He located two men, Jose Bargas and Miguel Bosquez, who held patents issued by the Republic of Texas to tracts of land on which the city was later built. Jones acquired these patents for a few dollars.

In 1849 Jones sold part of this land to J. Temple Doswell and the two men took the case to court. The case was shunted around for two decades. In 1873, long after Kinney's death, the case reached the Supreme Court, which sent it back to the U.S. Circuit Court in Galveston where the Doswell-Jones claim was upheld and the Kinney-Villarreal title ruled faulty.

This was shocking news for Corpus Christi. Most homeowners and businessmen purchased their land from Henry Kinney. After the court ruling, they no longer owned the land on which their homes and stores had been built. Jones and Doswell established a firm — the Corpus Christi City and Land Company — to resell property, lot by lot and tract by tract, to the erstwhile owners. A great deal of Corpus Christi money was transferred to Jones and Doswell. Some who could not buy back their land were evicted.

Anna Moore Schwien said her friend "Uncle Dempsey" owned two lots on Tancahua Street but as a result of the Jones-Doswell victory in court he had to repurchase both lots. "His friends counseled him not to pay, as he had already bought the lots once, but he thought he had better pay. He did and later events showed his wisdom, as many other people had to pay many times what he did to secure title to their property."

Probably the three most hated men in Corpus Christi in the 1870s were land speculators Levi Jones and J. Temple Doswell and Henry Kinney, the town's founder.

—June 29, 2016

108

Causeway opened up remote island

"Padre is to become one of the biggest watering places in
the nation. Two causeways will connect it with the
mainland to admit artesian streams of restless tourists."
—Bernard Brister

The Padre Island Causeway was opened to traffic on June 17,
1950. The first to pay the $1 toll was Frank Morris, a cotton
farmer from Portland. The long skinny island that was once the
haunt of Karankawas, Spanish explorers, pirates and cattlemen
would never again be as isolated and mysterious.

Before the Causeway, Padre Island had always been a remote
place. In 1847, a schooner carrying John V. Singer, his wife and
two children were caught in a storm and washed ashore on Padre
Ballí's island. They built a house of driftwood and became a
Crusoe-like family. The Singer homestead was on the site of
Padre Ballí's Rancho Santa Cruz, which the Singers called Las
Cruces Ranch. The Singers left during the Civil War and never
returned.

After the Singers there was the Curry Settlement, started by
preacher Carey Curry and extended family. Their place was 17
miles below Corpus Christi Pass. In the 1870s, a meat-packing
plant was built on Packery Channel, during the hide-and-tallow
era when packeries did a killing business along the coast.

Pat Dunn moved his cattle to the island in 1879. The cattle
grew fat from sedge grass and whatever they could find in the
surf. Their hides showed spots of tar from the blobs that wash up
on the beaches. Dunn sold the island in 1926 to Sam Robertson,

The beach on Padre Island was crowded on July 4, 1950, the first holiday after the Padre Island Causeway was opened to traffic two weeks before.

who planned to develop it into a tourist resort, until the Great Depression and a hurricane put an end to his dream.

The new causeway that opened in 1950 was built by Nueces County; the $1.2 million cost was repaid through a $1 per vehicle toll. After the bonds were paid off, the causeway was turned over to the state and it was later renamed the JFK Causeway.

Bernard Brister, a reporter in the 1930s, foresaw the future for the island when he wrote that, "Padre is to become one of the biggest watering places in the nation. Two causeways will connect it with the mainland to admit artesian streams of restless tourists. Back in the sand dunes, radios will send music floating out through the tall sea grass and the tourists, settling down in their trailer cars for the night, will quarrel shrilly."

That prediction started coming true when the Padre Island Causeway was opened to traffic on June 27, 1950.

Ferries on the Nueces

In 1847, the first act of the newly formed Nueces County Commissioners Court was to set ferry tolls on the Nueces River and Rio Grande, since Nueces County took in all the territory in between. Tolls were fixed at 25 cents for a pair of oxen, 25 cents for a horse, and 25 cents for every wheel on a wagon.

The main ferry on the lower Nueces was at the Santa Margarita crossing below San Patricio. The Paso de Santa Margarita, an ancient crossing, was a good place to ford, where the river was wide and shallow with a rocky bottom.

In the 1850s Samuel Reed Miller ran a ferry at Santa Margarita. During the Civil War, Miller's Ferry was a major stopping place on the Cotton Road. Unfortunately, wagons loaded with cotton were too heavy for the little ferry barge so when the river was high the drivers would camp and wait until it was fordable.

After the war, Sylvanus Gerard Miller ran a ferry at Lagarto. For a few years there were two Miller's Ferries on the Nueces. By the 1870s Samuel Reed Miller's grandson, Alonzo Quinn, took over and the ferry was known as Quinn's Ferry. Borden's Ferry was above Nuecestown, near where Calallen is today, a half-mile from Sharpsburg. Sidney Borden owned the ferry and a store. At Nuecestown was O.H. Hearn's Ferry. The road leading to the ferry was called Hearn's Ferry Road. Below that was Bitterman's Ferry at the mouth of the Nueces. Borden's Ferry was the last still in use, until 1913, after which bridges were built across the river.

Roping a wild turkey

Vaqueros taught the cowboys how to handle the half-wild longhorns, which is why the language of the cowboys is filled with mangled Spanish root words. Another skill the vaqueros taught the cowboys was how to make and handle rawhide lariats and bullwhips.

J. Frank Dobie described how these were made. He said no machine ever invented could cut the leather cords like a vaquero.

A large hide would be stretched on the ground. A small hole would be cut in the center and strips cut round and round until there were four strands of equal length. The strips were scraped of hair, soaked in ashes and water, greased, and plaited to make a bullwhip or a lariat.

It took great skill to know when to widen or narrow the strips, depending on the thickness of the hide, so that when they dried they would be the same width. For texture, flexibility, balance of weight, and beauty, wrote Dobie, rawhide bullwhips and lariats (la reata) could not be equaled.

There was also great skill in using them. A vaquero, it was said, could pick a fly off a fence post with a rawhide bullwhip. The pop these whips made sounded like a pistol shot. J. Williamson Moses, a mustanger of the 1850s, saw Cristobal Benavides, brother of the later famous Confederate general from Laredo, Santos Benavides, rope a wild turkey as it lifted to fly.

"We had seen a couple of fat gobblers between the Pintas and San Fernando creeks, and gave chase," Moses wrote. "Cristobal, spurring his pony, threw his cabestro over the turkey, just as he was four or five feet from the ground, with his wings spread. It caught him around the neck and under one wing. It was a beautiful throw of the lasso, neatly and gracefully done."

In the book "Rincon" by Maude Gilliland, a family traveling to the Valley by wagon came on a flock of wild geese. As the geese took wing, the vaqueros traveling with them spurred their horses to ride into the midst of the geese, popping their bullwhips in the air. They brought down several wild geese, plucked from the air by men on horseback with rawhide whips. The geese were cleaned and mixed with flour and water (to make gravy) and cooked in an iron pot covered with hot coals. It made them a fine supper.

—July 6, 2016

Billy Sunday's sermons

"Nightclubs are the vestibules of hell." . . . "The
Constitution was cradled in prayer." . . . "It is the
skunk's publicity that gets him killed." —Billy Sunday

William Ashley "Billy" Sunday opened a revival in Corpus
Christi on March 3, 1929. It brought in thousands of visitors
from throughout South Texas during its five-week run, which
concluded on April 7, 1929.

Billy Sunday gave up professional baseball to preach the
gospel. He played right field for the Chicago Colts, later renamed
the Cubs, and turned down a contract to play for the Phillies so
he could preach the gospel. He was the most famous preacher of
his time.

The revival meetings were held at the Port Compress plant on
19th Street, between Agnes and Comanche streets. More than
5,000 seats were built for this "tabernacle," with a nursery for
infants and youngsters built behind the compress. The city
repaired the streets leading to the site in anticipation of the
thousands who would attend the famous evangelist's meetings.
Most of the evening sessions drew from 5,000 to 6,000 people.
They came from all over South Texas.

The sermons of Billy Sunday, known as a brilliant speaker who
would quote Shakespeare as well as the Bible, were covered in
the Caller.

A few of Sunday's pungent quotes from his Corpus Christi
revival were: "Nightclubs are the vestibules of hell." "The
Constitution was cradled in prayer." "In an endeavor to serve

The Rev. Billy Sunday, a former baseball player, opened a five-week revival in Corpus Christi on March 3, 1929. Thousands came from all over South Texas for meetings held in a shed at the Port Compress.

God and mammon, the church is cross-eyed." "We came from the Garden of Eden, not from a zoological garden." "You know what you are by where you are." "It is the skunk's publicity that gets him killed."

Barrileros and street vendors

In times of drought when cisterns behind each house ran low, water carriers called barrileros traveled the streets, going from house to house, selling water. The water was hauled in barrels on two-wheeled carts pulled by a donkey. Around the turn of the 20th Century they sold water for 15 cents a barrel.

The city didn't get a municipal water system until 1893 and then it was limited. Many residents relied on cisterns and the barrileros who filled their barrels at a standpipe on the bluff.

There were other street vendors besides barrileros. Almost anything a family could need was delivered or sold door to door. The bread man would carry a large tray on his head loaded with loaves of "pan" and "pan dulce." An oyster man brought buckets of oysters. He would use a skimmer to scoop up the oysters, which were sold by the quart or gallon.

Before telephones were installed in the 1890s, a grocery clerk would visit regular customers in the mornings to take their orders, which would be filled and delivered in time to cook supper.

Wagons loaded with mesquite firewood and charcoal briquettes were a common sight. Housewives bought charcoal to heat their irons. After the city's first ice plant was built in 1878, mule-drawn ice wagons made daily deliveries, at least until the time when an epidemic killed the city's mules.

Three Mile Point

Legend held that Three Mile Point (now called Airheart Point) was used as a lookout for Lafitte's pirates. In the late 19th Century, boys went there to hunt rabbits, way out beyond the confines of the city. It was where the Alta Vista Hotel once stood. In the 1890s, during the Ropes Boom, a steam-dummy railway line ran from town to Three-Mile Point.

The Alta Vista had a grand opening on Aug. 14, 1891. The hotel closed after the financial panic of 1893. It was purchased by J.J. Copley in 1904, who added a bathhouse, pavilion and pier in the bay. As part of the project, the city, county and Copley each paid one-third of the cost of building a new shell-topped road to the hotel, called Ocean Drive. The hotel reopened on June 1, 1905.

After Copley went broke the Alta Vista was leased in 1911 for the Peacock Naval College, operated by the Peacock Military Academy of San Antonio. Classes were held in the hotel and the pier built by Copley was used to dock Navy cutters on loan to the school. The Peacock Naval College closed in 1912.

The old derelict stood vacant until June 9, 1927 when it burned in a spectacular fire. In 1930, V. M. Donigan bought the site and built a palatial home called Donigan's Castle, still standing today at Lafitte's old lookout at Three-Mile Point.

Other places have "point" in the name. Rocky Point gave Rockport its name. Cattle pens and chutes were built there in the 1870s to ship cattle by sea. The point was dynamited away in 1936 when the yacht basin was dredged.

During the Civil War, raiding parties from federal warships landed at Ingleside Point to burn homes and steal cattle. Ingleside Point was cut away when the La Quinta Channel was dredged.

White Point, across Nueces Bay, was named for Frank and Edward White, early cattle ranchers, who died during the 1867 yellow fever epidemic. It was originally called White's Point.

Indian Point on the Portland end of the causeway was supposedly named for an Indian campsite. It was where the Reef Road ended. The point jutting out to meet it from North Beach is Rincon Point, where the Reef Road began. Avery Point, where the port turning basin is today, was where Judge James Webb lived in the 1850s. The Avery who gave the place its name was said to be one of Lafitte's old pirates who first settled there.

Mustang Point, on the western end of Mustang Island, was where Union soldiers were buried during the Civil War. A quarantine station was located there in 1879, but was later moved to Harbor Island, which became known as Quarantine Shore. Point of Rocks on Baffin Bay supplied rocks to build the Aransas Pass jetties. The rocks were loaded onto flat-bottom barges which were pulled by tugs. The origin of Starvation Point, on Baffin Bay, is unknown.

There is also Live Oak Point, Blackjack Point, Black Point, Nine-Mile Point, Mud Island Point, Mosquito Point, Rattlesnake Point, Hannibal Point and Copano Point. Redfish Point is where, on June 2, 1836, Major Isaac Burton led his mounted rangers and by a ruse captured the Mexican ship "Watchman" which was loaded with supplies for the retreating Mexican Army. Burton's rangers became known as the Horse Marines.

—July 13, 2016

Column 29

House with the iron front

When Confederate Gen. Hamilton Bee threatened to
hang Conrad Meuly, the fierce Unionist said, "General,
issue your orders. I am here."

Conrad Meuly, from Switzerland, invested $16,000 in trade
goods — silk hose, scarves and alpaca — for the Santa Fe
Expedition in 1841.

The expedition was actually a secret venture to encourage New
Mexicans to revolt against Mexico. Members of the expedition
were captured and forced to walk 1,400 miles to Mexico City.
Those who survived were imprisoned until April 1842.

After his release, Meuly (pronounced "Miley") returned to
Texas and opened a bakery in Corpus Christi. When Zachary
Taylor's army landed in 1845, he sold coffee, pastry and bread to
the troops.

Meuly married Margaret Rahm and in 1852 he began building
a two-story structure on Chaparral. It was constructed of oyster
shell concrete (shellcrete), with Florida pine and Louisiana
cypress. The walls were two feet thick and the ceilings were 14
feet high. The house was decorated with ornate grillwork shipped
from New Orleans. It was completed in 1854, and people called
it the house with the iron front. The family lived upstairs and
Meuly ran a dry goods and grocery store on the first floor.

He bought the Rancho Puentecitas at Santa Petronila. During
the Civil War, Meuly, a Union supporter who was not shy about
voicing his opinion, was threatened by Confederates, who vowed
to hang him. He moved the family to the ranch near Banquete.

The front of the Conrad Meuly house at 210 Chaparral, photographed by Arthur Stewart in June 1936 for the Historic American Buildings Survey. The 100-year-old house was torn down in the early 1950s to clear the site for a Fedway department store. That site today is occupied by the Education Service Center.

In late 1863 Confederate Gen. Hamilton Bee stopped at the Meuly ranch. Bee was running from the Union Army at Brownsville but took time to threaten a known Union supporter. He called Meuly a traitor and threatened to hang him. Meuly told Bee, "General, issue your orders. I am here." Bee walked away and left the annoying Unionist alone.

At war's end Meuly took a herd of cattle to Brownsville, to sell to Union authorities and on the trip he caught yellow fever and died on July 9, 1865. He left a widow and 12 children.

A year later, on May 15, 1866, a lynch mob stopped at the Meuly home. The mob was dragging along a man named Jim Garner, who had killed a storekeeper for refusing to give him credit for a pair of boots. Someone threw a rope over the iron grillwork on the Meuly home. Margaret Meuly ran them off, brandishing a broom. They found a mesquite at the arroyo with a limb high enough to hang Garner.

118

Dr. Arthur Spohn, after he arrived in town in 1869, had his office in the house and boarded with the Meuly family.

After Margaret Meuly died in 1912, family members continued to live in the house. In 1938, it was listed in the Historic American Buildings Survey for the Library of Congress. The survey pointed out that the house had survived hurricanes in 1875, 1886 and 1919. The 1919 storm destroyed a five-room ell at the back and in the 1930s two car accidents knocked out the wrought-iron posts under the porch.

The home was torn down in the 1950s for a Fedway store; that site today is occupied by the Education Service Center. The razing of the Meuly house — the old house with the iron front — was a great loss to the city.

The year of Spanish flu

They called it the Spanish flu epidemic. It began in the summer of 1918 and at the height of the epidemic in this country, in late October, health officials recorded 40,000 deaths.

The flu spread rapidly across the country. The Caller in October 1918 printed rules of hygiene and warned people to avoid crowds, refrain from spitting in public, and practice "uncompromising cleanliness."

Mayor Roy Miller urged people to stay home and many activities were suspended. Schools and businesses closed. The city closed theaters and warned people not to congregate in hotel parlors. Poolrooms, domino parlors and soda fountains were shut down. Restaurants were permitted to stay open if they moved their tables at least five feet apart.

The Caller urged people to avoid streetcars and walk to work, to move away from those who coughed or sneezed. The paper said it might have to suspend publication because so many linotype operators were stricken. Camp Scurry, an Army training camp, was placed under quarantine. The Red Cross opened a soup kitchen at the high school on Leopard. The soup was prepared there and delivered to those at home who were sick.

On Oct. 26, 475 people were stricken with the flu in Corpus Christi and 21 died within two weeks. Bodies were brought in from outlying communities for burial and caskets were stacked at the train stations.

The worst of the epidemic was over by the time Germany surrendered on Nov. 11, 1918. Schools, churches and businesses were reopened. The quarantine at Camp Scurry was lifted and the soldiers held a dance to celebrate victory and the end of the epidemic.

Trolley line to Ward Island

During what we know as the Ropes Boom, in 1892, John Ward bought a triangle of land between the Oso and Corpus Christi Bay. He paid $1,448 for the 250 acres. Ward planned to build a resort. A year later, in an economic depression, Ward's plans fell through and he left for Beaumont, but his little triangle of land kept his name — Ward Island.

In 1914, investors planned to build an amusement park on Ward Island. They put up $40,000 in what was projected to be "the greatest amusement park of its character in the South." The plan called for constructing a trolley line from Corpus Christi to Ward Island, a distance of eight miles.

Construction of the line began on July 6, 1916 on Chamberlain Street (now Alameda) and by the end of July the tracks reached the city limits. A hurricane struck on Aug. 18, 1916 and workers building the Ward Island Interurban were diverted to clean up storm debris. Construction of the trolley line was suspended.

The newspaper said a shipment of rails and ties had been delayed, that work would resume when they arrived, then the newspaper ceased to mention anything about the Ward Island Interurban. Most likely, the storm and changing economic conditions led investors to pull out, but whatever killed it, it was no longer news and no trolley line ever reached that small peninsula that was John Ward's island.

—July 20, 2016

120

Landing at Copano ignites Revolution

"Couriers were flying, volunteers enrolling, and the
preparation for resistance resounding throughout the
land." —Noah Smithwick

The Texas Revolution began at Copano five miles east of the
present town of Bayside. The port at Copano, with 18 feet of
water, was the deepest harbor in the western Gulf. Ships could
anchor in the bay within easy distance of land and supplies to
support an army could be landed. Roads led to Refugio, Goliad,
Victoria and beyond to San Antonio de Bexar, Brazoria and
Texana.

The port and network of roads made Copano important.

On Sept. 20, 1835, Gen. Martin Perfecto de Cos landed at
Copano with 500 troops, heavy guns and supplies. This was an
event of considerable gravity. Before Cos landed the Texans
knew that war was likely, but now they knew it was certain. The
landing of Cos's forces and the response it provoked marked the
beginning of the Texas Revolution.

James Power, the Irish empresario, watched the arrival of the
Mexican ships and sent a warning to Texas leaders at San Felipe
de Austin. A call to arms went out and Texans began to prepare
for the coming fight.

Cos's landing sent a clear signal of the intentions of Mexico's
ruler, Antonio Lopez de Santa Anna Perez de Lebron, or Santa
Anna for short. Cos was Santa Anna's brother-in-law and he
arrived at Copano with orders to arrest Texas leaders (he had a
list) and to confiscate their weapons.

A few months earlier, in May 1835, federalists in the Mexican state of Zacatecas resisted Santa Anna's grab for power by refusing to disband their militia. Santa Anna unleashed his army on Zacatecas and hundreds of civilians, including women and children, were killed in an orgy of murder, rape and pillage.

Zacatecas bore witness that Santa Anna would use any means to impose his will and that he would show no mercy for the defeated. Cos had orders to disarm the Texans, root out the troublemakers, and expel American Anglos who had arrived since 1830 — essentially illegal immigrants — which included a majority of the population.

To send an army to arrest Texans, confiscate weapons and deport families was to incite a revolt if one was not already underway. Being deprived of weapons would leave the colonists at the mercy of marauding Indians. This was a match thrown into a tinderbox, intended to provoke a reaction by forcing Texans to fight or submit. If the colonists resisted, Cos could flush out the traitors and Santa Anna could arrive to finish them off. End of rebellion.

Noah Smithwick, a blacksmith, was at Victoria when a messenger rode in with the news that the government had ordered the disarming of the colonists and soldiers were on their way to enforce the order. "Couriers were flying, volunteers enrolling, and the preparation for resistance resounding throughout the land."

Cos spent several days at Copano, disembarking supplies and troops, then marched to Refugio. He reached Goliad on Oct. 2. There were 900 Mexican troops at Bexar (San Antonio) and Cos had 500 at Goliad, but these would soon be on the march to reinforce the San Antonio garrison. The line of supply and communication for Cos's campaign was Copano-Goliad-Bexar.

While Cos was at Goliad, the commander at Bexar, Col. Domingo Ugartechea, sent a detachment of soldiers to the Green DeWitt colony of Gonzales, 70 miles east, to demand the return of a brass six-pounder cannon that had been given to the settlement to protect it from Indians.

Ugartechea's demand for the cannon reinforced rumors that the colonists would be disarmed. The town's alcalde resisted the

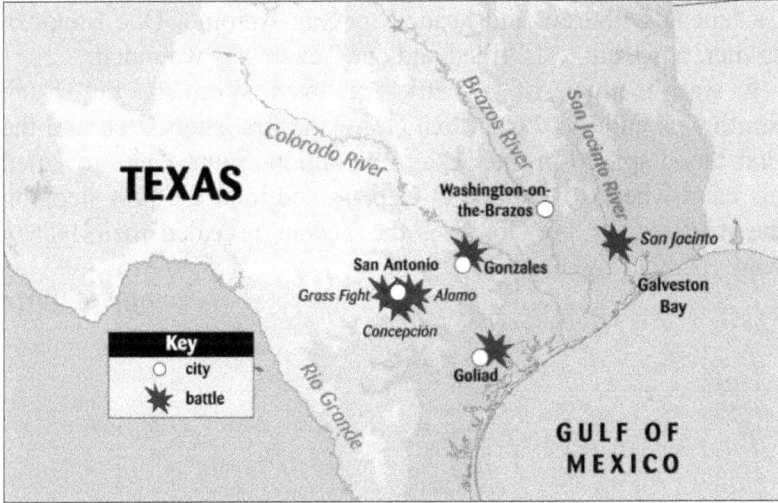

Map shows the battleground of the Texas Revolution was contained in South Texas, from the coast near Corpus Christi to San Antonio, until the epic encounter at San Jacinto.

order, to gain time, and sent word that trouble was brewing. Volunteers poured into Gonzales.

After the detachment failed to obtain the cannon, Ugartechea sent a larger force of 100 dragoons commanded by Capt. Francisco Castaneda. When he arrived on the west bank of the Guadalupe Castaneda conferred with Texas spokesmen. He insisted that the cannon had been loaned to Gonzales and in view of the political situation it was thought prudent to repossess it.

Talks were broken off. During the night 150 Texas volunteers crossed the river. It was a foggy morning on Friday, Oct. 2, when the Texans formed a line of battle on the west bank of the Guadalupe. In command was Col. John H. Moore of LaGrange.

In the center of the front line was the disputed brass six-pounder, mounted on cartwheels. Someone at Gonzales had a way of putting things, for over the cannon flew a banner fashioned from a bed sheet with the taunt, "Come And Take It."

As the two forces faced each other volleys were exchanged and the six-pounder, loaded with scrap metal, was fired. Before artilleryman James Neill could reload for a second shot,

Castaneda withdrew and headed for San Antonio. One Mexican soldier, a private, was killed and one Texan was wounded.

It wasn't much of a battle, or even skirmish, but Noah Smithwick called it "our Lexington," the first shots fired and the first blood spilled in the Texas Revolution. Santa Anna revealed his hand when Cos landed at Copano and took the first steps on the road to war. At Gonzales the Texans revealed theirs. They were ready to fight.

—July 27, 2016

Column 31

Texans capture fortress at Goliad

"Boys, the scoundrels shot off my powder horn!" —
Henry Karnes

After the clash at Gonzales Gen. Martin Perfecto de Cos left Goliad and by forced march reached San Antonio de Bexar, 95 miles away, where he took command of the garrison from Col. Domingo Ugartechea. In what would prove to be careless, Cos left behind a small skeleton force at Goliad.

Capt. George Collinsworth, a planter at Matagorda, recognized the military importance of Goliad, which guarded the route inland from Copano Bay, protected the road to San Antonio and linked San Antonio with the port of Copano. He organized a volunteer force to capture Goliad. He started with 52 men but others from Refugio, Victoria and surrounding country joined the expedition. Collinsworth's force reached the outskirts of Goliad after dark and scouts were sent to reconnoiter the town.

Ben Milam, who had escaped from a prison in Mexico and was on his way home, was hiding in the brush when he heard English being spoke. Milam identified himself and joined the descent on Goliad. The Texans reached the fort about 11 p.m. on Oct. 9, 1835.

The La Bahia presidio was the strongest fortress in Texas, with reinforced walls up to six feet thick and defensive parapets. But Cos left only 24 men under the command of Lt. Col. Francisco Sandoval to man the fort.

Before midnight Collinsworth's men assaulted the presidio. They knocked down a heavy door leading to Sandoval's quarters and forced him to surrender. Some of Sandoval's men continued firing from their barracks. They were called on to surrender and an interpreter warned that if they did not give up immediately the colonists would kill every one of them. A trembling voice pleaded, "Oh, for God's sake, keep them back. We will surrender."

In the fight which lasted half an hour three Mexican soldiers were killed and one Texan was wounded. The Texan was Samuel McCulloch Jr., a free black, who was hit in the shoulder by a musket ball.

The Texans found 300 muskets, several cannon, huge supplies of powder and lead, flour, sugar, coffee, whisky, rum, and $10,000 in silver specie. With the capture of the Goliad fortress the Texans cut Cos's supply and communication line between Copano and Bexar and had him cornered in San Antonio.

Collinsworth's report to the Council of War at Gonzales said, "I arrived here last night at 11 p.m. and marched into the fort by forcing the church doors and after a small fight they surrendered. (The Mexicans) have dispatched couriers for troops to several points and I expect I shall need your aid."

On Oct. 28, more than 300 Texans marched out of Gonzales heading toward San Antonio. The Texan volunteer force, called the Army of the People, was under the command of Col. Stephen F. Austin, who was ill and reluctant to take command.

On the march was the brass cannon and its flag with the provocative taunt "Come And Take It." Capt. Almeron Dickenson was in charge of the cannon. Halfway to San Antonio the cart broke down and the cannon was dumped into a creek.

The Texans camped on Salado Creek south of San Antonio. Austin wanted to move close to where Cos had concentrated his forces to put the town under siege. Austin sent Col. James Bowie with 92 men to explore the old mission at Concepcion

Mission Concepcion, two miles from San Antonio, was where Col. James Bowie with 92 men made camp on Oct. 27, 1835. Next morning, Bowie's detachment routed a 400-man Mexican assault force in the battle of Concepcion. Photo from the Library of Congress.

to see if it would serve as a base of operations. They rode through the trees along the San Antonio River to the old mission, two miles from town. They made camp in a wooded bend of the river, about 200 yards from the mission.

During the night of Oct. 27 Gen. Cos dispatched an assault force of 400 dragoons and infantry to attack the Texans. Next morning a heavy fog hung over the river bottoms. In the gray mist a Mexican soldier stumbled into a Texan sentry, Henry Karnes, whose warning shot alerted the Texans. Karnes yelled, "Boys, the scoundrels shot off my powder horn!"

As daylight showed in the ghostly mist Bowie's men saw Mexican troops deploying to attack. The Texans took a defensive position behind a high bank in the horseshoe-shaped bend, with the river behind them and on their flanks and an open field of fire in front of them. Bowie's men were divided into two companies commanded by Capt. James Fannin and

Capt. Robert Coleman. The Mexican assault forces were commanded by Col. Domingo Ugartechea.

About 8 a.m. Ugartechea's soldiers advanced across an open prairie behind two cannon. The Texans took cover in a pecan grove in a bend of the river. Noah Smithwick, the blacksmith, said Mexican grapeshot crashed through the pecan trees overhead and pecans rained down on them. "I saw men picking them up and eating them with as little concern as if they were shaken down by a norther."

As the sun burned off the fog the Mexican infantry made clear targets. The Mexican gunners at the cannons were all shot down. The Kentucky long rifles of the Texans were deadly at up to 300 yards while the British-made "Brown Bess" muskets carried by the Mexican soldiers were effective at only about 60 yards or less.

The Mexican troops were decimated by the accurate fire of the Texans. They charged three times before retreat was sounded and they retired, leaving one of their two cannons behind. Ugartechea lost 76 killed or wounded while one of Bowie's men was killed.

During the battle Smithwick saw Richard Andrews of Lavaca go down — "lying as he had fallen, great drops of sweat gathering on his white, drawn face, and the lifeblood gushing from a hole in his left side. I attempted to raise him. 'Dick,' I cried, 'are you hurt?' 'Yes, Smith,' he replied, 'I'm killed; lay me down.' I laid him down and put something under his head." He was the first Texan killed in the Revolution.

October was a momentous month for the Texans. It began with the clash at Gonzales on Oct. 2, the capture of Goliad on Oct. 10, and the battle of Concepcion on Oct. 28. Concepcion was the first real battle of the revolution, in which a large number of men were killed. There would be more — and far deadlier — battles to come.

—Aug. 3, 2016

Fort Lipantitlan falls to Westover

"We arrived in front of the fortress (Fort Lipantitlan) about dark." —John J. Linn

In October 1835, the month after Gen. Martin Perfecto de Cos began his campaign to disarm and chastise the Texans, three battles, or skirmishes, were fought — at Gonzales, Goliad, and Concepcion outside San Antonio.

The new commander of Texas forces at Goliad was Philip Dimmitt. He replaced George Collinsworth who captured the presidio. Dimmitt sent 40 men under Capt. Ira Westover to capture Fort Lipantitlan guarding a ford on the Nueces River. Another 14 men joined Westover, including John J. Linn, the alcalde of Victoria, and empresario James Power.

Fort Lipantitlan was built four years before to guard the Santa Margarita crossing on the Nueces River below the Irish settlement of San Patricio, 30 miles from today's Corpus Christi. The fort was built of dirt walls studded with huge wooden rails to hold the dirt in place. Linn described it as, at best, a second-rate hog pen.

Capt. Nicolas Rodriguez, commander at Fort Lipantitlan, heard from spies that the Texans were on their way so he took 80 men to ambush them on the Goliad Road. Westover, however, took a route to the south and they reached a ranch that was five miles downriver from Fort Lipantitlan.

Linn wrote that "A Mexican informed us that Capt. Rodriguez was on the Goliad road, at the head of his men, expecting to intercept us. We proceeded up the river and with the aid of a canoe crossed the river, which was swollen in volume. We arrived in front of the fortress about dark." The Texans planned to attack at daylight on Nov. 5, 1835.

That night two Irishmen from San Patricio came into the Texas camp. One of them, James O'Reilly, offered to convince the Mexican militia inside the fort to give up. They surrendered when they were assured they would not be harmed. There were 21 men inside, mostly militia, who were released after promising not to take up arms against Texas.

To their great surprise the Texans captured the fort without a shot being fired. Found inside were two four-pounder cannons, eight old Spanish cavalry guns called "escopets," and a supply of gunpowder, but no shells for the cannon.

The following day, Nov. 6, the Texans burned several buildings inside the fort, including an unfinished barracks, but the earthen walls studded with timber were not easily burned. They took the two cannon and prepared to cross the river to return to Goliad. A norther blew in and the sky turned dark. A cold rain started to fall.

Capt. Rodriguez and men were almost to Goliad when he heard Lipantitlan had been taken. They rushed back and reached the river as the Texans were trying to cross. Westover was caught with half his men on the east side of the river. Rodriguez attacked in a cold driving rain. The Mexican soldiers were cut down by the accurate rifle fire of the Texans before they could get within range of their muskets. They retreated and Westover's men crossed over to the other side. They had trouble with the two cannon and dumped them in the river.

One Texan, William Bracken, was wounded in the battle. A musket ball tore away three fingers of his right hand. Rodriguez lost 28 men, killed or wounded. Among them was Marcelino Garcia, his second in command, who was friendly with the Texans. He was wounded and taken to San Patricio. He was buried by the Texans, with full military honors, in the San Patricio Cemetery.

After the capture of Lipantitlan, plus the presidio at Goliad, Santa Anna's forces held one stronghold in Texas, San Antonio de Bexar, and Cos's forces there were isolated and under siege.

From his vantage point in the belfry of San Fernando Church, in the background of Military Plaza, Gen. Perfecto de Cos could see the Texans attack his pack train along Alazan Creek, a mile from town. He rushed 200 men and one cannon to rescue them. The battle came to be called the Grass Fight.

The Texans heard rumors that a relief column was on its way to San Antonio carrying a large amount of silver for the pay and subsistence of Cos's beleaguered troops. Patrols were increased and Texas soldiers debated over how they would split the loot.

On Nov. 26, 1835, Deaf Smith's scouts sighted a pack train escorted by 150 cavalry troops on the Laredo Road west of San Antonio. All the Texans were eager to join the fight so they might share in the plunder.

Col. Edward Burleson sent James Bowie with 40 men to capture the pack train. (When Stephen F. Austin was commissioned to travel to Washington to represent Texas interests, Burleson was appointed to replace him in command of the Gonzales army.)

The two sides clashed a mile from San Antonio near Alazan Creek. The Texans were outnumbered three or four to one but they attacked like furies. The Mexican soldiers fought their way to an old creek bed where they took a defensive position. Seeing the pack train in trouble from his vantage point in the town (probably the San Fernando Church), Cos rushed 200 men and one cannon to rescue them.

131

Burleson led a reserve force of 50 cavalry troops to reinforce Bowie. The Texans attacked the Mexican infantry in the creek bed and the cavalry charged head-on. The Mexicans fled in disorder until they were reformed. They made another charge, a frontal assault straight into the firing line of Bowie's men, before the rifle fire of the Texans sent them rushing back to San Antonio.

The Texans ripped open the sacks of the pack train and discovered they were filled not with gold or silver but grass. The six-week siege had exhausted the supply of fodder for Cos's cavalry horses and the pack train detail had been out cutting hay on the meadows west of the town.

Seventy of Cos's soldiers and five Texans were killed or wounded in the Grass Fight. It was the fifth encounter of the Revolution, after the clash at Gonzales, the capture of Goliad, the battle of Concepcion and the skirmish at Lipantitlan.

In the battles and skirmishes since the siege began six weeks before, Cos lost about 200 men but still had 800 in San Antonio. His forces were divided between fortified plazas in the center of town and the Alamo east of the river. Cos learned at Concepcion and in the Grass Fight that his troops caught in the open were no match for the sharpshooting Texans with their superior guns and skilled marksmanship.

—Aug. 10, 2016

Sniper kills Ben Milam

"We were surrounded by crude bumpkins, proud and overbearing." —Mexican officer at San Antonio

Gen. Martin Perfecto de Cos landed at Copano on Sept. 20, 1835 with 500 troops and orders to arrest Texas leaders and confiscate their guns. Three months later he was trapped in San Antonio de Bexar, under a state of siege, a virtual prisoner himself. His plan to subdue Texas had gone awry.

Cos sent his second in command, Col. Domingo Ugartechea, with 100 dragoons to Laredo to bring back reinforcements.

The Texans besieging San Antonio pushed past a cornfield into cannon-range of the Alamo, where many of Cos's men were quartered. The Texans would fire their cannon and the Mexicans would return fire. When the Texans ran short of ammunition they searched the cornfield for spent Mexican cannon balls which they collected and fired back.

After a seven-week siege the Texans were bored and clamoring for action. Col. Frank Johnson issued a challenge: "Who will go with old Ben Milam into San Antonio?" More than 400 men volunteered. They were divided into two columns, one commanded by Johnson and the other by Milam.

The night before the battle, on Dec. 4, 1835, a norther blew in bringing with it a heavy fog. Herman Ehrenberg, a young German in the New Orleans Greys, said at two o'clock in the morning guards went from tent to tent to wake the sleeping soldiers. They stood in line, wrapped in their blankets, waiting for the order to move.

As the Texans crept into position, everything was still. They were led into town by a San Antonio man, Jesus Cuellar, called Comanche because he was half-Indian. Dawn showed over the adobe rooftops as the Texans attacked in two columns: Johnson's along Soledad Street and Milam's on Acequia Street. A third contingent led by James Neill attacked the Alamo in a feint meant to draw Cos's forces away from the town.

The defense was stubborn. Mexican sharpshooters fired from the flat roofs and every adobe structure became a fort to be defended or stormed. Texans moved from building to building by using battering rams to punch holes through adjoining walls, avoiding Mexican artillery fire that swept the streets with murderous canister and grapeshot.

Ehrenberg said they became thirsty and would run down to the San Antonio River to fill a bucket, then it became too dangerous because of heavy enemy fire. A woman in the house they were occupying offered to get water. They told her not to try it, warning that the Mexican soldiers would shoot her.

"She insisted," Ehrenberg wrote, "and laughingly said that we knew very little of the Mexican attitude about women. Before we were aware of it she was on her way to the stream. She filled the buckets and was on the point of returning when she was hit by a hail of bullets and dropped lifeless to the ground. Several men rushed out to bring in the unfortunate woman. The enemies had discharged their muskets and the dead body was brought in without a single shot being fire." In the lull after her death several Texans ran to the river and filled their buckets and returned.'

The fighting raged all day with Cos's men still holding the Alamo and central plaza.

In the second day's fighting the Texans continued to advance from house to house, flanking the Mexican artillery positions. Mesquite trees and brush along the river caught fire and the Texans were able to move up their artillery to answer the Mexican guns. On the third day there was furious fighting near the central plaza, with Mexican snipers on the roofs and concealed in the bell tower of San Fernando Church picking off exposed Texans.

The courtyard of the Veramendi house on Soledad Street (shown in 1910) where Ben Milam was killed, picked off by a sniper.

At a meeting held at the Veramendi house a Mexican sniper shot Ben Milam in the head, killing him instantly. The Texans learned later that the sniper was named Felix Garza, reputed to be the best marksman in the Mexican Army. He was killed soon after he shot Milam.

It was cold, wet and rainy on the fourth day. Ugartechea arrived from Laredo with 500 reinforcements and the beleaguered Mexican garrison rejoiced by ringing church bells. The celebration was short-lived. The reinforcements were untrained conscripts who arrived exhausted, half-starved and not eager to fight. They did not help Cos, but actually made his situation worse. They were unwilling to take orders and consumed scarce provisions that were needed by those who were fighting.

As the Texans closed in on the central plaza, Cos withdrew his forces into the Alamo. Soon after daylight on Dec. 9 a white flag was raised and Cos sent his senior officers to ask for terms. His men were completely fought out.

The terms were liberal. Cos agreed to march back across the Rio Grande. He and his officers pledged not to take up arms against Texas again and Cos's retreating army was allowed to keep one cannon, in case they were attacked by Indians, and 150 muskets with 10 rounds of ammunition for each. They would be supplied with provisions, which they would have to pay for.

One Mexican officer, a colonel of engineers, who did not hold his opponents in high esteem, was disgusted with the surrender. "We were surrounded by crude bumpkins," he said, "proud and overbearing."

A curious sense of leisure came over these "crude bumpkins." They thought the war was over. They volunteered for the duration and now it had come to an end, they thought, with the last Mexican stronghold in Texas taken. They were in high spirits and content to rest on their laurels. The objective had been obtained: They had beaten Cos and sent him packing. With the Mexican troops now gone, the Texans moved into the Alamo and made themselves at home.

It wasn't the end of the conflict but the end of the first phase, which lasted from the time Cos landed at Copano on Sept. 20 until his surrender at San Antonio on Dec. 10. In between, Texas scored victories at Gonzales, Goliad, Concepcion, Lipantitlan, in the Grass Fight, and with the fall of San Antonio and the capture of the Alamo. The second phase would begin in February with a complete reversal of fortunes. The war for Texas independence was just beginning.

—Aug. 17, 2016

Santa Anna's march to San Antonio

"We put in the wagons some of the dying wretches we found on the road." —Soldier in Santa Anna's army

Texans thought they had won the war when they beat Gen. Perfecto de Cos, captured San Antonio and occupied the Alamo. But Santa Anna at San Luis Potosi was gathering a more powerful army to deal with the upstart Texans.

By the middle of February 1836 Santa Anna's expeditionary force totaled 6,000 men. While the quality of that force has been disputed, one historian called it "the flower of the Mexican army."

Santa Anna planned for the main army to cross the Rio Grande above Laredo at Guerrero (Presidio de Rio Grande) and make a quick forced march to San Antonio. But getting there would become an ordeal they were unlikely to forget. In the south, Gen. Jose Urrea would lead a smaller force from Matamoros and enter Texas by way of San Patricio, Refugio and Goliad.

A blizzard struck as Santa Anna began to move, with snow and a bitterly cold wind that cut like a razor. Then there was rain and more snow. It turned to a frozen slush and then mud. Marching through mud was more tiring than wading through snowdrifts.

Munition wagons and gun carriages carried those too weak to march. Many died along the way. Oxen, pulling overloaded carts through the mud, died in harness. Pack animals froze to death. The ground behind looked like a battlefield, strewn with broken wheels, discarded equipment, abandoned wagons and dead animals.

"We put in the wagons some of the dying wretches we found on the road," said one soldier. "I remember a poor wretch we found, art the point of death, unable to move, loaded down with gun and pack. We placed him in one of the wagons but he expired before the day's journey was over."

Santa Anna, insulated from the suffering of his men, rode ahead with the First Division and reached San Antonio on Feb. 23. With him was his brother-in-law, Perfecto de Cos, who had given his parole when he surrendered the Alamo in December. He violated that parole by returning to Texas.

The rest of the army reached San Antonio in 10 days. They arrived exhausted and half-starved from their ordeal. They came in sight of the Texans, who watched from the Alamo. They were a long time passing by.

In the south, Gen. Urrea's division consisted of 600 conscript militia from Yucatan and a cavalry regiment. They crossed the Rio Grande on Feb. 18 as a norther hit. Urrea's thinly-clad soldiers, accustomed to warmer weather, suffered through bitter cold, sleeping in the open, exposed to freezing wind and rain. Six men died before Urrea reached San Patricio on Feb. 27.

Urrea heard from a network of spies that Col. Francis W. Johnson was at San Patricio with a handful of men. Urrea planned to capture him.

Johnson was one of the Texas heroes at the battle of San Antonio in December. Johnson and Dr. James Grant favored invading Mexico, by way of Matamoros, and had been given freedom of action by Texas authorities, which all but removed them from the command structure of the army. The Matamoros Expedition was an ill-starred and foolish plan that was ultimately a failure.

Johnson and Grant had been off on forays to buy or steal horses. They rode to Santa Rosa Ranch (near today's Raymondville) and rounded up 100 horses. Johnson and half the men returned to San Patricio, which was largely deserted; the families had evacuated to Victoria. Grant was away looking for more horses. Johnson and 30 of his men settled down to wait out the bad weather. Because of the cold, rain and miserable conditions, Johnson posted no guards.

The original San Fernando Church (later remodeled) where, in February 1836, Gen. Santa Anna ordered a red flag to be flown, which meant there would be no quarter for Texans besieged in the Alamo.

Urrea's forces arrived before dawn, after a forced march of 20 miles through freezing rain and surrounded several houses in which the Texans were quartered. When the firing began, shortly after 3 a.m., Johnson and five of his men slipped out the back door of one of the houses and escaped.

Most of the Texans were holed up in the largest house in the town square. They shot several Mexican soldiers who tried to set fire to the house. The Mexicans eventually set the house on fire and the Texans surrendered. Ten Texans were killed and 18 captured. In his diary, Urrea noted that Texans at Fort Lipantitlan and in the town defended themselves resolutely. He inflated the numbers, saying that 16 men were killed and 24 taken prisoner.

Meanwhile, on March 2, Dr. Grant and his party, unaware of the battle at San Patricio or the presence of Cos's forces, were returning from their horse-hunting sortie. They were ambushed by a detachment of Urrea's men at Agua Dulce. Except for six who escaped, Grant and all his men were killed.

One who was captured, Reuben Brown, later described how Grant died. (Of the differing accounts of Grant's death, Brown's is considered the most likely.) When the party was ambushed,

Brown said, Grant, Placido Benavides and himself might have escaped. "We were well-mounted and some distance in advance, but our first impulse was to relieve our party . . ." Grant told Placido to ride for Goliad, to spread the alarm. Grant and Brown rode six or seven miles before they were chased down and surrounded. "I felt myself fast in a lasso thrown over me. After Grant fell, I saw ten or dozen officers run their sword through his body." Brown was taken prisoner.

Urrea wrote in his diary that Dr. Grant "was attacked and vanquished by the parties under my command and that of Col. Francisco Garay. Dr. Grant and 40 of the riflemen were left dead on the field, and we took six prisoners besides their arms, munitions and horses." Texans claimed 12 were killed, four captured, and six escaped.

In San Antonio, the siege began on Feb. 23, when Santa Anna arrived with his army of 6,000 men, and the Texans moved into the Alamo and worked to strengthen the walls of the fortification. The Texans ventured out at one point to burn down houses in a section of town called La Villita, which provided cover for Mexican troops. Santa Anna ordered a red flag to be flown from the San Fernando Church. The red flag meant no quarter.

—Aug. 24, 2016

Santa Anna's small affair at the Alamo

When the cemetery was full, the remaining bodies of the
1,544 slain Mexican soldiers were dumped into the river
until it became choked with corpses. The 188 Texan
dead in the Alamo were stacked in a pile and set afire.

The days passed from February to March with Santa Anna's
red flag flying from San Fernando Church. His army occupied
San Antonio while beleaguered Texans under the command of
William Travis watched from the Alamo. Travis sent appeals for
help, signed "Victory or Death!" while Mexican gunners
bombarded the bastion and Santa Anna planned his attack.

The Alamo celebrated when 32 men from Gonzales slipped
past Mexican lines to join the defenders. Davy Crockett played
his fiddle and another man played the bagpipes.

Travis sent a final appeal on March 3: "This will be the last
man we can send out." Next day, Santa Anna and his generals
held a strategy meeting and agreed to attack within 48 hours.
Santa Anna repeated orders that no prisoners were to be taken.
The Texans were pirates, unprotected by rules of warfare.

On Saturday, March 5, a warm clear morning, wounded men in
the Alamo were carried out into the courtyard. Every man, except
those on guard, heard Travis address the 188 men and, according
to legend, use his sword to draw a line in the sand. They were
outnumbered 20 to one, he said, and their only option was to die
fighting, to sell their lives dearly. If they had to die they would
die hard. Every man but one crossed the line to join Travis. Only
an old private named Louis Rose, a Frenchman who had fought

in Napoleon's Army, declined to stay. He slipped over the wall and disappeared.

Santa Anna's plan of attack was brutally simple. Ranks of infantry, *en masse*, would charge entrenched artillery protected by expert marksmen in strong defensive positions. It was a recipe for slaughter. Santa Anna would overwhelm the garrison by sheer numbers, whatever the cost in lives of his men.

In the early hours of Sunday, 4,000 assault troops in five battalions moved into position. Four columns, 40 men per rank, 20 lines deep, would attack the four walls. The fifth column would be held in reserve. Cavalry troops would cut off escape.

The men lay on the ground waiting for the signal. Snoozing Texas sentries were killed and bugles sounded the attack at dawn. The bands of the army, across the river, played the Deguello, the "cutthroat" tune meaning no prisoners. As they rushed forward the attackers yelled "Viva Santa Anna! Viva Mexico!"

The Mexican columns were so dense that only the first ranks could fire their weapons. Some carried ladders and ropes to scale the walls. The Texans hardly had to aim. If they missed one man they would hit another. The 21 guns of the Texas artillery decimated the close ranks of Mexican infantry with shrapnel made of nails, chopped-up horseshoes and door hinges. It was butchery.

The first charge broke up. No Mexican soldier got within 10 yards of the walls. The defenders cheered as Mexican officers reformed the lines for a second charge, which was also beaten back. Texans on the walls had a half dozen loaded rifles each. Many of the slain Mexican soldiers were shot in the head. Travis, one of the first Texans to die, was shot in the forehead and fell down an earthen ramp.

Santa Anna ordered his reserves to join the third assault. The northwest corner of the wall had been breached by cannon fire and Mexican forces concentrated there. The infantry charged from four directions but the west and east columns veered and joined the attack on that northwest corner. They overwhelmed the defenders and streamed into the Alamo, firing at Texans from the rear.

The front of the Alamo (Mission San Antonio de Valero) in 1936, 100 years after the improvised Texan stronghold was attacked and captured by Santa Anna's army. One hundred eighty-eight Texans and 1,555 Mexican soldiers died in the battle and aftermath on March 6, 1836. Photo from the Library of Congress.

The defenders fell back to prepared defensive perimeters, their backs to the wall. Literally. They gave ground stubbornly, using clubbed rifles and Bowie knives to parry bayonets. The plaza filled with Mexican troops. The defenders retreated to the long barracks, which had been made ready for a last stand, with sandbags and loaded shotguns inside. A cannon on top of the long barracks fired shrapnel into the Mexican ranks before the gunners were shot down. The doors were blasted open and each room taken by musket and bayonet. The Texans died hard.

The chapel was the last to fall. On top of the building was the main artillery emplacement with guns manned by Almeron Dickenson, James Bonham and others. The artillery position was ripped by musket fire and the gunners killed. The biggest gun the Texans had, an 18-pounder, was captured by Mexican troops and used to blast away the doors of the chapel.

By 8 a.m. it was over. Santa Anna and his aides ventured into the Alamo. The supreme leader was fuming when prisoners were brought forward. Didn't the men understand his orders? They were to die, every one of them.

Six wounded Texans were killed by bayonet. Jim Bowie, who had been too ill to fight, was killed in bed. Some revisionist accounts maintain that Davy Crockett and five or six of his men were captured and brought before Santa Anna, who ordered their immediate execution, and his aides fell on them with swords and hacked them to death. Other accounts say it didn't happen that way, that Crockett died fighting, with slain Mexican soldiers around him, that he never surrendered, that the word itself was no part of his character.

Santa Anna released three survivors, Susanna Dickenson, whose husband was killed firing the guns, her baby, and Travis's slave Joe. He wanted Susanna to spread the word, to sow panic among the Texans, but it only strengthened Texas resolve.

The alcalde of San Antonio was ordered to dispose of the bodies, which lay thick on the ground. When the cemetery was full, the remaining bodies of the 1,544 slain Mexican soldiers were dumped into the river until it became choked with corpses. The 188 Texan dead were stacked in a pile, layered with kindling, and set afire. The pile burned all day and throughout the night. The air was filled with the sickening stench of burning bone and flesh.

After the fighting was over, after the injured and the few who were captured were slain, with the huge funeral pyre burning in front of the Alamo, Santa Anna turned to an aide and said, "It was but a small affair."

—Aug. 31, 2016

The massacre after the battle

"I looked back at the place where my friends were bleeding to death. The enemy was still shooting and yelling." —Herman Ehrenberg at Goliad

Sam Houston, supreme commander of Texas forces, ordered James Fannin to destroy the Goliad fortress and join him at Gonzales. "We must not depend on forts," Houston wrote. "The roads and ravines suit us best." He would fight a war of movement, not try to hold fixed fortifications against superior Mexican forces. He would retreat and buy time until he was ready to fight.

Fannin, who held the strongest fortress and commanded the largest Texas army in the field, dithered. But if he dallied too long he could be trapped and destroyed like Travis at the Alamo. Gen. Jose Urrea was close.

While Fannin vacillated, Refugio settlers pleaded for protection as they prepared to evacuate their homes and join the exodus spooked by news of the Alamo and the approaching war.

Fannin sent a 29-man company, the Kentucky Mustangs, commanded by Capt. Amon King, to assist the families. King found them at the Refugio mission surrounded by 150 Texan-Mexican rancheros loyal to Santa Anna. He fought his way into the mission and sent a courier to Fannin asking for reinforcements.

Fannin dispatched the Georgia battalion of 120 men under Col. William Ward. At Refugio, Ward and King argued over who was in command; Ward was senior in rank but King said he was there first. King took his men to attack a Tejano ranch and before they could return they ran into Urrea's cavalry. They took cover among trees by the river a mile from town.

At the mission, Ward was surrounded by Urrea's army of about 1,000. A fierce battle raged on March 14 as Ward's men beat off four attacks. During the night the Texans slipped out of the mission to try to reach Victoria or Goliad, leaving behind their wounded with women, children and two caretakers. When Urrea's men entered the mission next morning they bayoneted the wounded and caretakers. One man, hidden under a mattress by the women, survived.

Amon King and 29 Kentucky Mustangs were captured and marched back to the mission. They were all shot. Their bodies were stripped of clothes and left for scavengers. The bones could be seen for a long time.

Fannin, tired of waiting for the return of Ward and King, on March 19 ordered 300 men at Goliad to load the wagons for the trip to Victoria. They left in a heavy fog, had trouble along the way, and made slow progress. They might have made it to the safety of woods near Coleto Creek but a wagon broke down and Fannin ordered a halt to let the oxen graze.

It was a terrible decision and they were caught in the open. When Urrea's cavalry was sighted, Fannin placed his men in a hollow square with artillery on the corners. There was furious fighting as Urrea's cavalry and infantry charged.

Herman Ehrenberg, one of the New Orleans Greys, said horses were running without riders while others were screaming and wallowing in blood . . . The men were enveloped in such dense gun smoke they had to advance slightly from the square to see their targets . . . The battlefield was covered with dead men, horses, guns, pieces of cloth, all kinds of objects.

During the night some wanted to make a dash for Victoria. This would have meant leaving 70 wounded behind, which most of them opposed. Fannin himself was among the wounded. They spent a miserable night without food and what little water there was had to be kept to cool down the cannons. A light drizzle in the night was not enough to ease their thirst. At daylight their position looked hopeless. Fannin surrendered.

The chapel of Presidio La Bahia at Goliad. On Palm Sunday, March 27, 1836, 342 captured Texans in James Fanning's command were marched away from the old Spanish fort and massacred. The photo is from 1936, Library of Congress.

They were marched back to Goliad and confined inside La Bahia. A week later, on March 27, Palm Sunday, nearly 400 Texas prisoners were told to get ready to march. They thought they were going to Copano, where they would board ships bound for U.S. ports.

Ehrenberg said the day was hot and close. They realized they were marching the wrong way, toward Victoria, not Copano, and it was strange that the soldiers escorting them were not carrying knapsacks for a long march.

A mile from the fortress they were stopped and told to kneel. The shooting began. After several volleys the Mexican soldiers fell on the wounded with bayonets and swords. At least 30 Texans played dead until they could make a mad dash for the San Antonio River.

Ehrenberg ran to the river, plunged in and swam to the other side. "I looked back at the place where my friends were bleeding to death. The enemy was still shooting and yelling."

At La Bahia 50 wounded prisoners were dragged outside and killed. James Fannin gave his watch to the Mexican officer in charge and asked to be shot in the chest, not the head, and be given a Christian burial. The officer took the watch, but had Fannin shot in the head and his body dumped with the others.

The cold-blooded murder of helpless wounded and unarmed prisoners was done by the express and explicit order of Santa Anna, the head of the government. What did it prove? Except to confirm just how right the Texans had been to revolt against such absolute power in which the lives of individuals counted for so very little.

The bodies of the Texas were burned, as they were at the Alamo, in huge piles with layers of wood. The official Texas figure is that 342 men, Texans and Anglo-American volunteers, were slaughtered on Palm Sunday in Goliad. Another 28 escaped.

Several were saved through the intercession of a common-law wife of one of Urrea's captains. Her name is given as Alvarez or Alavez, Francisca or Panchita. This kind-hearted woman intervened in behalf of Texas prisoners on several occasions. She saved the life of Reuben Brown, captured with Dr. James Grant, who was about to be shot. At Goliad, she pleaded with Col. Don Francisco Garay to save those he could and she hid several men in her quarters and later helped them escape. Her real name may be lost but she will always be known as the Angel of Goliad. But if an angel was there that day, so was the devil.

—*Sept. 7, 2016*

Caught napping at San Jacinto

Santa Anna told his soldiers to get some rest. Cos's men
were worn out after the forced march. Santa Anna also
took a nap in his brown-and-white striped tent.

Only mopping up operations were left, Santa Anna thought,
after his army reclaimed the Alamo and destroyed Texas forces
at Goliad. He split his 6,000-man force into four parts and
planned to make short work of Houston's ragtag army.

Sam Houston burned Gonzales and retreated, leaving a
scorched earth behind him, while settlers trying to get away from
the war fled in the Runaway Scrape.

Houston had 400 men, some without weapons, and most
without training. They marched to the Colorado River and
crossed at Burnham's Ferry. Houston burned the ferry after
crossing the river and they marched up the east bank to Beason's
Crossing. Gen. Ramirez y Sesma, leading one of Santa Anna's
armies, camped west of the rain-swollen river, which was too
high to cross. The armies watched each other across the stream.

A week later Houston's army pulled out at dusk, leaving
campfires burning, and marched to San Felipe then to Groce's
Plantation. The men wanted to stand and fight and were near the
point of mutiny, but Houston was not going to get trapped
between converging Mexican columns.

At Groce's Houston drilled the army and tried to instill
discipline among soldiers as likely to debate an order as carry it
out. Houston was getting it from all sides. David Burnet, interim

president, wrote a sharp reprimand: "You must retreat no further. The country expects you to fight."

Houston learned that Santa Anna was leading a detached regiment trying to capture Texas leaders, who had moved to Harrisburg. This was an opportunity to catch Santa Anna away from his main army.

Perhaps Houston intended to retreat to Nacogdoches, where the piney woods would provide ideal ground for Texas rifles and hamper Mexican cavalry. It would put him closer to support and succor from American friends. But when he came to a fork in the road he chose the one leading to Harrisburg. His men cheered, knowing they would run no more.

Santa Anna's 750-man special task force found Harrisburg deserted. Texas leaders fled to the coast and escaped across Galveston Bay in a small boat. Santa Anna turned back and made camp between Buffalo Bayou and San Jacinto River. It was a park-like area, with lush green grass, that lived up to its Spanish name, Jacinto, for hyacinth. Houston's army camped in woods 400 yards away.

Santa Anna ordered his men to build a makeshift breastwork and sent a courier urging Perfecto de Cos, who was 20 miles away with 500 men, to join him.

Cos arrived at 9 a.m. on April 21, 1836. Santa Anna had expected Houston to attack early that morning but when the Texans failed to show, he told his soldiers to get some rest. Cos's men were worn out after the forced march. Santa Anna also took a nap in his brown-and-white striped tent. (The tale that he had a private interlude in his tent with a young black woman named Emily has never been substantiated beyond one hearsay reference of doubtful veracity.)

About 3:30 that afternoon Houston ordered his men to form lines to attack. Houston rode in front on a charger named Saracen. The Texan artillery, the six-pounders called the Twin Sisters, anchored the middle. The Texans crept through tall grass and were within 200 yards of the Mexican camp before the alarm sounded. Santa Anna was caught napping.

The Twin Sisters ripped holes in the breastwork as a four-man Texas band played an old Irish folk tune, "Will You Come to the

Sam Houston rode in front of the charging Texas lines on a big stallion named Saracen at San Jacinto on April 21, 1836. Houston was hit in the ankle and had two horses shot from under him, including Saracen, during the battle. From a painting by S. Seymour Thomas.

Bower?" The Texans broke into a wild charge, yelling "Remember the Alamo!" "Remember Goliad!" as they streamed over the breastworks and into the encampment, attacking with ferocity.

Mexican soldiers, confused and fleeing in panic, were shot, stabbed, or clubbed to death as they ran or tried to surrender. Mexican officers tried vainly to rally their men to their own defense. The battle lasted 18 minutes but the slaughter continued until dark.

In a blind and furious rage, the Texans killed everything that moved. Without mercy. Houston tried to stop them. "Gentlemen," he berated his men, "I applaud your bravery but damn your manners." The frenzied killing was done in the heat of battle, unlike the cold-blooded murder at Goliad, but it left a stain on the day's victory.

Col. Pedro Delgado, on Santa Anna's staff, made it to Buffalo Bayou before he was captured, with other bewildered Mexican survivors. They were marched to the woods where they saw a huge bonfire. Delgado thought they were going to be burned alive in retaliation for those Texas bodies burned at the Alamo. "We were relieved when they placed us around the fire to warm ourselves and dry out our clothes."

Six hundred and eight Mexican soldiers were killed, 208 wounded, 730 captured. The Texans lost six killed and 26 wounded. It was one of the most lopsided battles ever fought.

Santa Anna was captured next morning, looking wretched in stolen clothes and still wearing red Moroccan slippers from his nap the afternoon before. How the mighty had fallen. So this was His Excellency, the generalissimo, the Napoleon of the West. He was brought before Houston, who was being treated for a gunshot wound in his ankle. Santa Anna asked for the opium from his tent and it was given to him.

The Texas soldiers would have liked nothing better than to have stood Santa Anna before a firing squad, but Houston shielded him, knowing he was more valuable alive than dead.

In the battle of San Jacinto, Houston defeated one part of the Mexican army, leaving powerful contingents in the field, under more capable generals than His Excellency. The lopsided victory would not have ended the war except for Santa Anna's capture. Houston and Santa Anna conferred. Santa Anna agreed to order a withdrawal of Mexican forces to below the Rio Grande. That agreement and retreat did end the war.

At San Jacinto, the bodies of the Mexican soldiers lay unburied on the field of battle, becoming at one with the landscape, for all flesh is like the grass and the past buries itself. As Santa Anna said after the fall of the Alamo, it was a small affair — but one that changed the course of history.

Note

(There are enough books to fill a large library on the Texas Revolution but as one who dabbles in Texas history I have never written much about it, though I have read widely on the subject. The Texas Revolution lasted 215 days, from beginning to end, but those 215 days, or seven months, represent the high peak of Texas history. It is an old old story, but it is the story of Texas and it is a story always worth telling.)

—Sept. 14, 2016

The story of Crockett's death

Crockett and several of his men were taken before Santa
Anna shortly after the battle was over and Santa Anna
ordered them killed on the spot.

The late Dan Kilgore, a Corpus Christi accountant and
historian, was president of the Texas State Historical Society
when he gave an address in 1975 about the circumstances of
Davy Crockett's death. It was published in a booklet titled "How
Did Davy Die?"

Kilgore relayed eyewitness accounts of seven Mexican soldiers
who said that Crockett and five or six of his men did not die in
the fighting, but were captured after the Alamo had fallen and
were executed.

One account came from Mexican officer José Enrique de la
Peña, published in Matamoros in 1836. In De la Peña's account,
Crockett and several of his men were taken before Antonio
Lopez de Santa Anna shortly after the battle was over and Santa
Anna ordered them killed on the spot.

The long-held legend was that Crockett, the former
congressman from Tennessee, was killed fighting to the end,
using his long rifle to bludgeon to death a score or more of
Mexican soldiers whose bodies piled up around him as he went
down swinging. Susanna Dickinson, a survivor of the Alamo,
passed by his body shortly after the battle ended.

Kilgore's account, for some, was heresy. As the late Bill
Walraven wrote, Kilgore received hate mail, personal insults and
threats of violence. One overheated critic called him "a mealy-

155

David Crockett, the former congressman from Tennessee, was killed in the Alamo, fighting to the end. That was the legend. Historian Dan Kilgore wrote that Crockett was executed after the battle on the express orders of Gen. Santa Anna.

mouthed intellectual who should have his mouth washed out with soap" and another said, "This gives me a rash."

Yet Kilgore's version was accepted by many historians. In Stephen Hardin's "Texian Iliad" Crockett and six of his men fought on until they were overwhelmed. They were marched before Santa Anna who ordered their immediate execution. "Nearby staff officers who had not taken part in the assault fell upon Crockett and the others with their swords and hacked them to pieces."

This does not serve the legend, which requires a heroic end. Other historians stood by the original version. Bob Boyd in "The Texas Revolution: A Day-by-Day Account" wrote that Crockett died fighting back-to-back with two comrades. "Before they had finished, a pile of dead enemies, estimated at between 14 and 24, lay around them. The evidence for this is undeniable. Susanna Dickinson passed by his body minutes after the battle ended and described the scene."

Which version is right? If some conscientious scholar unravels the true story does that invalidate the legend? Probably not, for there will always be questions of fact and interpretation. In John Ford's classic Western "The Man Who Shot Liberty Valance," congressman Ransom Stoddard (played by Jimmy Stewart) told a story of the old days and then asked a newspaper editor, "You're not going to use the story, Mr. Scott?" The editor replied, "No, sir, this is the West. When the legend becomes fact, print the legend." Dan Kilgore learned that the hard way.

Confederates in Mexico

After Robert E. Lee surrendered on April 9, 1865, Texas Gov. Pendleton Murrah and Gen. Alexander Watkins Terrell decided to escape to Mexico. They feared that the victorious north would punish high-ranking Confederates. Terrell had led the 34th Texas Cavalry, called Terrell's Texas Cavalry, in the Red River Campaign in Louisiana.

Murrah and Terrell left for Mexico and other leading Confederates joined them, including several Southern governors and many famous generals. Before Murrah died of consumption in Monterrey, he gave Terrell a letter to Maximilian, the French-imposed emperor of Mexico, in which Murrah asked Maximilian to help find a home for Southern exiles.

Maximilian granted former Confederates freedom of worship, exempted them from paying taxes for a year, offered each family 640 acres of land, and allowed them to keep their slaves as so-called apprentices. Nothing like having friends in high places.

The former Confederates tried to reinvent their lives. Henry Allen established the Mexican Times. Matthew Maury, the first naval officer of the Confederacy, was named commissioner of colonization. John Henry Brown, Texas newspaper editor, surveyed lands. Sterling Price planted coffee beans and Hamilton Bee planted cotton. They found that cotton did not thrive in the hot humid climate and the soil would not grow crops they understood.

A Confederate colony was established at Villa Carlota, named for Maximilian's wife, west of Veracruz. It was described as a poor village with Southern-style clapboard houses and pigs rooting around in bare yards. Another Confederate colony was at Tuxpan.

The Emperor Maximilian was under attack by Benito Juárez and Porfirio Diaz. He was captured and died on June 19, 1867 before a firing squad. His execution ended the French attempt to rule Mexico by proxy. The ex-Confederates, having backed the emperor, had to flee once again.

Alexander Watkins Terrell slipped across the Rio Grande wearing a sombrero and his old gray uniform. Back in Texas, he was elected to the Legislature and became known as the father of the University of Texas.

French and Belgian soldiers who fought for Maximilian escaped to Texas and settled in Corpus Christi. One of them, Auguste Dutailly, who was a bugler in the French army in Mexico, worked as a bartender in a saloon on Mesquite Street and served as lamplighter for city streets.

The Confederate sojourn in Mexico wasn't the first or the last time that people fleeing war, revolution and oppression looked for sanctuary on the other side of the river, "el otro lado del rio."

Skyrocket

A top attraction at the Bayside Amusement Park during North Beach's golden years, in the late 1920s and early 1930s, was the rollercoaster called Skyrocket. Its high looping shape was a dominant feature of the landscape.

On July 27, 1931, a 13-year-old girl — Tessie Mae Hunsucker — was killed when she was thrown from the coaster. The newspaper account said she stood up after the train left the spiral turn at the south end of the ride, lost her balance and fell through the framework to the ground. She was rushed to Spohn Hospital but died soon afterwards from a fractured skull.

Not long after that a woman was killed when a car jumped the track and the roller-coaster was closed down and dismantled. The famed Skyrocket on North Beach was one of those sights we will never see again.

—Sept. 21, 2016

Fire at St. Patrick's

The flames spread from the south belfry to the north belfry. The fire damaged both towers, the choir loft, and smoke blackened the interior.

St. Patrick's Cathedral on Carancahua was damaged when a fire broke out in the church's south tower on Nov. 28, 1938. St. Patrick's, the second Catholic Church of the same name in Corpus Christi, was built in 1882 at a cost of $18,000.

The building was designed by Charles Carroll, father of Mary Carroll, a longtime teacher who became superintendent of the Corpus Christi school system. A story in the Caller-Times said Carroll went to New Orleans to select the lumber for the new church. When the structure was completed, Carroll climbed the church tower to place a gold cross atop the steeple.

Leading contributors to the new church were Mifflin Kenedy, who donated money, murals and pews, and his wife Petra, who gave bells, pipe organ, and windows for the sanctuary. Mayor J. B. Murphy and wife donated the side altars and statues.

On Nov. 28, 1938, fire broke out in the south belfry and spread to the north belfry. The fire damaged both towers, the choir loft, and smoke blackened the interior.

A fund drive for a new cathedral was started and the John G. Kenedy family donated the lot on which his home was located on North Broadway for the site. Ground was broken for the new cathedral in March 1939 and the building finished the following year. The change of name from St. Patrick's to Corpus Christi Cathedral was not well-received, even though it came about from

St. Patrick's Cathedral was damaged when a fire broke out in the church's south tower on Nov. 28, 1938. A fund drive for a new cathedral was started the next day and ground was broken on the site of the new cathedral on March 1, 1939. St. Patrick's was dismantled in 1951.

a suggestion by Pope Pius XII. St. Patrick's, the splendid old church (no longer a cathedral), was pulled down in 1951. The material was salvaged and used as a framework for Our Lady Star of the Sea on North Beach.

Mayor John B. Murphy

John B. Murphy, mentioned as a main contributor when St. Patrick's was built, was elected mayor in 1880 and 1882. One of his problems was the condition of downtown streets, which were so damaged by heavy wagons and ox-carts that they turned into an almost impassable quagmire after every rain. Mayor Murphy, with little money in the treasury and citizens unwilling to pay more in taxes, put city prisoners to work improving the streets and digging drainage ditches to the bay.

Mary Sutherland in "The Story of Corpus Christi" said that Murphy was known for his honesty and practical methods. "He drained our streets by cutting ditches. He worked city prisoners on the streets and if the prisoner worked he was given three good meals a day; if not, he was idle on bread and water." When he died during his second term, Sutherland related, the city had "not one cent of debt and a cash balance of $12,000. Taxes were small and our streets were clean."

Cheap labor

John B. Murphy wasn't the only mayor to turn to creative manpower to repair streets. When Roy Miller was mayor, Camp Scurry was established south of the city, beginning in September 1916. Some 3,500 federalized National Guard troops were stationed at the camp. Miller asked John Hulen, commander of the camp, to divert soldiers from military training to repair UpRiver Road. He was told to go through channels.

Miller wrote Gen. Frederick Funston, commander of the Army's Southern Division. Miller had once taken Funston duck-hunting on King Ranch. Orders came through authorizing the project. Charles Duff, a soldier at Camp Scurry, remembered how they shoveled truckloads of shell on a long dusty road.

"We ran trucks to the beach between two rows of about 30 men. Each man threw two shovels of shell on the flatbed trucks. By the time the trucks reached the end of the row they were loaded. Other men scooped the shell out on to the roadway as far as Calallen." For a long time, UpRiver Road was known as Shell Road.

Tito P. Rivera, boy captive

Tito P. Rivera, a successful businessman in Corpus Christi in the 1880s and early 1890s, was the first Hispanic elected to the City Council. He had been captured and held by the Comanches as a young boy.

163

Rivera's story was told in the Record of Southwest Texas, published in 1894, and it was repeated by the late Frank Wagner, a Corpus Christi researcher who furnished material for the Handbook of Texas.

Based on that story, Rivera was born on the Pacific Coast of Mexico in 1843, the son of Julian and Josefa Rivera. His father was a wealthy owner of silver mines. When Rivera was nine, in 1852, his father sent him over the mountains with a party to procure food for the miners. The pack train was attacked by Comanches and the boy was taken captive. The Comanches returned to their home on the Brazos (near today's Mineral Wells), quite a long journey for the nine-year-old captive.

When the chief of the tribe learned Rivera could read and write, he had him write the Indian Agency at Camp Cooper. In one letter Rivera, who had not lost the sense of his own identity, explained that he had been captured. Robert S. Neighbors, superintendent of Indian Affairs, paid the Comanche tribe $125 to release the boy, who had been a captive for three years.

Once liberated, Rivera did not return to Mexico; his father had died and his mother remarried. He lived with Neighbors until Neighbors died in 1859. In 1861, he enlisted in the Confederate Army. After the war he worked as a clerk in Victoria, married Mollie Holloway, then moved to Corpus Christi to work as a cashier for the Doddridge & Davis Bank.

Rivera owned a book, stationery and office supply store and was elected to the City Council in the early 1880s. He was one of the original investors of the Corpus Christi Caller in 1883 and he built a large two-story home on Chaparral in 1885. Rivera, Dr. Alfred G. Heaney and John Stayton established the Corpus Christi Electric Light Company and the city's first telephone system. Rivera, his wife and children were all active in the Episcopal Church of the Good Shepherd.

The last journey of Tito Rivera was not a long one. He died at his home on Chaparral, on Dec. 13, 1894, and was buried a few blocks away in Old Bayview Cemetery.

—*Sept. 28, 2016*

Big S Curve on Ocean Drive

It was a hot issue when Mayor Farrell Smith ordered the
S Curve straightened after several major accidents.

Plans to straighten a dangerous curve on Ocean Drive around
the Donigan home site, where the old Alta Vista Hotel once
stood, became a hot issue in the 1950s and 1960s. Farrell Smith,
elected mayor in 1955, ordered the S Curve straightened after
several major accidents. The plan was to buy part of the Donigan
property on the bayside of the drive. On one hand Smith was
accused of trying to block the project; on another, he was
accused of standing to benefit from it since he was an Ocean
Drive property owner. It sounds crazy, but politics has its own
logic.

Smith and the City Council pushed ahead. The city went to
court to buy the land needed to straighten the curve. A
condemnation court awarded the owners of the Donigan property
— Mesog Donigan and Lucy Welch — $20,925.

Equipment was moved to the site and then the project became a
central issue in the city election campaign in 1959. It led to
Farrell Smith's defeat in 1960 by Ellroy King. After the election,
the King administration gave the land back to the Donigan family
and abandoned the project.

There were several fatal accidents in the 1960s, including one
in 1963. Three 16-year-old boys were killed when their car
crashed in the curve. Property owners along Ocean Drive urged
the city to put up flashing lights and railings. In 1969 the
roadway of Ocean Drive was widened into a four-way drive, that

An aerial photo of Ocean Drive, taken on June 17, 1937, shows the S curve around the Donigan estate, at 3276 Ocean Drive. The dangerous curve became a major political issue in the 1950s and 1960s.

smoothed out the sharp corners of the S Curve and ended most of the problems.

Picture palaces

The first motion pictures in Corpus Christi were one-reel films called flickers that were shown in storefront buildings. The city's first theater opened in 1905. The second was the Grand, next to Weil's Grocery on Mesquite. Coming attractions at the Grand were written on the sidewalk and ticket-stub drawings were used to hype interest. The big prize was $5 worth of groceries.

After the Grand came the Pavilion on Water Street, the Crystal and Palm Garden Theater on Chaparral, the Lyric on Starr, and Seaside Electric across from the Seaside Hotel on Water Street.

After 1910 the Rex on Chaparral opened and the Amusu was built on Mesquite in 1912. After the Queen opened in 1919, it became a favorite with kids because it showed Saturday serials.

Theodore Fuller, in his memoirs, wrote that he was terrified the first time a serial left off with a girl tied to the railroad tracks and a train thundering toward her. "The next week," Fuller wrote, "a switch appeared just before the distressed lady would have met her doom."

The Aldine opened in 1922 across from the Model Pharmacy. The Aldine and Amusu had a package deal. A ticket stub from one would get you in the other for 10 cents.

The Palace on Chaparral opened in 1926. The Leopard Street Theater opened in 1927 with a tile mosaic of a leopard in the lobby. It became the Melba. Across the street was the Grande where movies from Mexico where shown.

The Ritz on Chaparral opened on Christmas Day 1929. This was the city's most prestigious cinema, with an art-deco design of a Spanish courtyard and the ceiling painted to resemble a glittering night sky much like the Majestic Theater in San Antonio.

The Rio opened on Chaparral in 1933. The Tower at Six Points, built in 1937, was the city's first suburban theater. The Harlem on Staples and the North Beach Theater opened in 1942. The big new movie house built downtown was the Centre Theater, with a stage curtain of blue velour copied from the Roxy in New York.

The old picture palaces were done in by changing times. People moved to the suburbs and watched TV. They didn't go downtown to see a movie; downtown was no longer where the action was.

The Palace was gutted by a fire one night in 1953. It gave the guests at the nearby Nueces Hotel one last extravaganza as they watched the flames from their hotel windows. It was the kind of dramatic scene Hollywood might have invented. The Ritz closed in 1972 and efforts to restore the building have been underway. The Ritz and Centre Theater are standing reminders of the city's historical and cultural past, but there is something forlorn about vacant theaters and empty stages.

Murder at the P. O.

One of Corpus Christi's more shocking crimes of the decade of the 1930s occurred on May 19, 1939 when Postmaster Gilbert McGloin and Assistant Postmaster Albert Dittmer were found shot to death in McGloin's office on the second floor of the federal building on Starr Street. Both were shot in the head. A .45 was found near Dittmer's body. Two bullets had been fired.

Gilbert McGloin was first appointed postmaster by Calvin Coolidge in 1927 and re-appointed by FDR. He was popular and known as a man with a keen sense of humor.

On May 19, 1939, the bodies of McGloin and Dittmer were discovered by an attorney from Tyler. McGloin and Dittmer had been shot in the head. A .45 caliber handgun was found under Dittmer's body. Two bullets had been fired from the gun.

Investigators said McGloin was sitting behind his desk (he had taken off his glasses) when he was shot. Dittmer was shot behind the ear. No explanation was given, but it was considered an open-and-shut case: one murder, one suicide, one gun, two bullets fired. Investigators said there was an argument leading Dittmer to shoot McGloin and then put the barrel of the .45 behind his right ear. What was the quarrel? We will never know.

Gilbert McGloin's widow, Ameta, was appointed postmaster to succeed her late husband at the urging of Congressman Richard M. Kleberg. Mrs. McGloin was the fourth woman to serve the city as postmaster. Before her were Georgia Welch (1915), Hannah Taylor (1867) and Jane Marsh (1865).

The deaths of McGloin and Dittmer gave rise to reports that the second floor of the federal building was haunted. Not long after the slaying, post office operations were moved to a new building on Upper North Broadway and a new federal courthouse on Shoreline Boulevard was occupied in February 2001. Construction of the old federal building was completed in December 1916, so it is now 100 years old. The building today is occupied by the Thomas J. Henry law firm.

—Oct. 5, 2016

Column 41

When Company B left for Korea

"The civilian look still was fresh upon the features of the
Marines of Company B when they were swept away to
war." —John W. Johnson

On Saturday, June 24, 1950, North Korea struck across the
38th Parallel dividing North and South Korea. When President
Truman ordered American troops into Korea, the Caller-Times in
an editorial said, "It's war, all right, and there can be no backing
down."

On Aug. 6, the reality of the war was brought home when 80
members of the local Marine reserve — Company B of the 15th
Marine Infantry — departed the Missouri Pacific Depot for
Korea. A Caller-Times reporter and photographer recorded the
scene, in words and pictures.

Red Moores was a good photographer prepared for that split
second, that brief flash, in which an ordinary image becomes
transformed into something more lasting, something printed in
the memory. Moores captured one such image on the morning of
Aug. 6 when a young woman was lifted up to the train window
so she could kiss her boyfriend goodbye.

The reporter, John W. Johnson, conveyed a different picture,
one with flashes of telling detail:

"The civilian look still was fresh upon the features of the
Marines of Company B yesterday when they were swept away to
war. Many of the men, especially the younger ones, scarcely
more than boys, wore a look of incredulity as though they were
asking themselves: 'Can this really be me, going off to war?' A

A young woman (later identified as Sharlene Harper) kissed her Marine boyfriend (Robert Whitley) goodbye as members of a local Marine reserve company left for Korea on Aug. 6, 1950. The two were later married. Photo by Red Moores.

few days ago these boys were engrossed in dating their girlfriends, making plans for college . . . the older men had been immersed in raising their families . . . Their only contact with military life had been the one night a week during which they got together for drill as members of the Marine Corps Reserve.

"Yesterday everything changed. College plans were suddenly abandoned, civilian jobs deserted. Sweethearts, wives, and families were gathered on the platform to see these men on their way to war.

"Tears, despite the hot sun, did not dry too effectively in the humid air and there were few un-streaked faces. One tall erect man embraced his young uniformed son for uncounted minutes. A mother, swept by a torrent of emotion at seeing her son leave, had to be carried sobbing from the platform . . .

"As the train pulled out, faces pressed up hard against the windows, eyes searching out loved ones gathered on the platform. Then, as the train picked up speed, the faces became a blur that faded from sight. The watchers at trackside lingered a few moments, then drifted away. The platform stood deserted in the hot sun."

One of the Marines who left that morning was Pfc. Richard C. Garza, who was killed in action on Sept. 25 while serving with the First Marine Division. He was the first man from Corpus Christi to be killed in Korea.

The die-up and skinning war

Eighteen seventy-one and 1872 were drought years, when it was ferociously hot and dry in the summer followed by bitterly cold weather in the winter. With lack of grass and water, weak undernourished longhorns died by the many thousands. This was called a die-up.

The spring following the 1871 winter cowboys carried skinning knives to strip the hides of dead cattle. Because of a depressed market for beef the hides were worth more than the whole steer.

Every man with a horse and skinning knife went into the country looking for cattle that were dead or soon would be. For the honest skinners, brands identified the owner, who was to be paid the value of the skin less the amount owed the skinner for his work.

But many skinners were thieves or bandits. The resulting conflict between ranchers and outlaw skinners was called the Skinning War.

The skinners — or hide thieves — killed cattle and skinned them where they fell. Some used a long knife fixed to a pole to cut tendons of the cattle to immobilize them, then shot or stabbed them to death and skinned them. One notorious outlaw skinner was Alberto "Segundo" Garza. His band of 60 men killed and skinned cattle in Nueces and Duval counties.

The Nueces Valley reported the wholesale slaughter of cattle by Garza's band. "At one place there were 275 carcasses, at another 300, and at another 66. These robbers seem to be well-supplied with ammunition, rodeo the cattle, and shoot them in their tracks, until a sufficient number is killed for the day."

Garza sent a taunting message to the town of San Diego demanding that they bring enough money to buy the hides his men had collected or to send enough men to fight.

Jasper Clark, James F. Scott and other cattlemen took up Garza's challenge and led an attack on his camp. Garza and his hide thieves escaped in such a hurry they left saddles, bridles and bloody hides behind. Near the camp the posse found the carcasses of 80 cattle that had been killed and skinned.

This was a lawless time when rustlers, hide thieves, and robbers rode in heavily armed gangs — from 10 to 100 men. With brazen confidence, they could take on just about any force they ran up against. If truly threatened, they could find sanctuary across the Rio Grande. The Skinning War was a time of general slaughter and reciprocal violence, of wounds given and wounds received between the outlaw skinners and the hard-riding vigilantes.

Battle at Lake Trinidad

In 1854 a wagon train carrying army supplies was attacked by Lipan Apache warriors. Patrols were dispatched from every fort in the region, including Fort Merrill, 50 miles above Corpus Christi.

South of Ben Bolt, at Lake Trinidad, the Fort Merrill patrol ran into Indians who had just killed three mustangers. Lt. Blake Cosby ordered his men to charge. The Indians fled into mesquite timber and turned to fire on the soldiers. When the soldiers ran out of ammunition, the fight became hand-to-hand.

Three soldiers were killed and five wounded, including Lt. Cosby, who led his battered detachment back to Corpus Christi, which was army headquarters for the region. The wounded were treated at the army hospital in town.

We know the details of this fight because it was covered in a report by the Secretary of War to Congress. That report led Gen. Winfield Scott, in charge of the Army, to order soldiers at Texas forts to be armed with Colt six-shooters and Sharp's rifles.

—Oct. 12, 2016

Putting on city airs

"Went to town in the afternoon. A street railway is all
the talk there now. Notice they are putting up electric
light poles. Corpus Christi will be a city yet." —Joseph
W. Page

Joseph W. Page came to Corpus Christi from Houston at the
height of the E. H. Ropes' boom in 1890. This was a time of
prosperity when the sky was always blue and the sun was shining
like a twenty-dollar gold piece. Page took note of what was
happening around the town in his diary.

On Jan. 7, 1890 he wrote — "Went to Corpus Christi today.
The town is rather dull, though I understand they will have the
electric light wires up. Corpus Christi is putting on city airs."

On Feb. 15 he wrote — "Went to town in the afternoon. A
street railway is all the talk there now. Notice they are putting up
electric light poles. Corpus Christi will be a city yet."

On March 15 he wrote — "Everybody talking railroads,
electric lights, and street railway."

On April 12 — "They have the electric lights up at last.
Everybody is well pleased with them."

May 24 — "The town is booming. Land is selling like hot
cakes at $20 and $30 an acre. The town is full of prospectors."

May 31 — "Land excitement still booming. Col. Ropes is
dredging a channel through Mustang Island. There are great
hopes for deep water for Corpus Christi."

That's the end of Page's diary entries that I ran across. Within
two years, the Ropes' boom came to an end in the great financial
panic of 1893, a worldwide recession. Before that, during the

Sketch of Col. E. H. Ropes. He left town broke, with all his grand projects unfinished.

three-year period of the Ropes' boom, Corpus Christi got its first municipal water system, electric lights in the downtown area, its first streetcar operation (from downtown to the Alta Vista Hotel) and telephone service.

Then came the collapse, Ropes' grand projects were left unfinished, and the soaring land prices came crashing down. The town, stunned by the calamity, went into a long decline and for about a dozen years nothing changed but the seasons.

Suitcase sand

Texas oilmen, like the cowboys of an earlier generation, created their own colorful and specialized language rich in words taken from their original context and given new meaning.

In an oil field, a "dead man" was a buried anchor to which guy wires were attached to help hold the derrick in place. A "Christmas tree" was an assortment of valves that controlled the flow of oil from a producing well. The "stabbing board" was a platform above the derrick floor from which casing was "stabbed" into the well. An inexperienced oilfield hand was called a "boll weevil" and his station on a drilling rig was the boll weevil corner.

A "monkey board" was the platform on which the derrick-man worked. A "rat hole" was a small hole at the end of the regular well bore. "Soup" meant nitro and "shooting" referred to the use of explosives in a hole. A "shooter" exploded nitro in wells to shatter a producing sand and improve the yield.

The "doghouse" was a shed on a drilling site used as an office and in the doghouse the "knowledge box" contained the records and history of the drilling operation. A "suitcase sand" referred to a formation that would yield no trace of oil or gas, meaning it was time to pack up and move on, or look for another line of work.

Lighthouse on the bluff

In 1857 the U.S. government built a lighthouse on the bluff in Corpus Christi to guide ships across the bay. The lighthouse was in operation only a short time though the building stood for two decades.

No photos have survived but we know it was a rectangular building with a round tower above it. It was described as "concrete brick" but it was shell concrete, called shellcrete in local parlance. It was plastered and probably painted white. The light was a sixth-order Fresnel lens with a 12-sided lantern.

It was first illuminated on Jan. 1, 1859 then the lighthouse went dark in November of that year, by order of the Lighthouse Board. The Ranchero newspaper criticized the decision and noted that "never has the adage of 'penny wise and pound foolish' been more strikingly illustrated than with the decision to close the lighthouse."

But it remained dark.

During the Civil War, in August 1862, a cannonball from a Union warship smashed through one wall. The following year, when it looked as if Corpus Christi might fall into Union hands, Confederates lit a charge under the lighthouse which destroyed a corner of the building.

After the war the ground floor was used to store gunpowder. Some boys with time on their hands took some of the powder, put it in a butter churn, and lit a trail of powder leading to the churn. The explosion was tremendous. The boys ran and hid at the Salt Lake, expecting to be chased down by the constable and imprisoned for life.

There are conflicting stories about what happened to the lighthouse. Dee Woods, who wrote historical columns for the Caller in the 1930s, wrote that one night the town was awakened by a loud explosion. The lighthouse had been blown up. People suspected two prominent citizens blew it up because it was a dangerous place for kids to play.

In another version Peter Benson, a former sheriff, recalled that in 1878 or 1879 a city councilman named Dick Jurdan wrote to the Lighthouse Board advising that the building was hazardous and should be demolished. A government official replied that it was federal property and could not be condemned by city authorities. Soon afterwards, Benson said, men with ropes and mules pulled down the old lighthouse in the dead of night.

That wasn't the end of the story. There was a question about who owned the property where the lighthouse had stood: the federal government or Mrs. Caroline Morris. The government bought the property from Henry Kinney in 1857. But land purchased and resold by Kinney was later claimed by land speculator Dr. Levi Jones. After decades in court, the case was decided in favor of Jones. The government did not own the land on which the lighthouse was built. It took an act of Congress before a quit-claim was issued. The Morris home was built on the site and in 1953 the Southern Minerals Building (Somico) was built there. It was later the main headquarters for HEB before it decamped for San Antonio.

—*Oct. 19, 2016*

LBJ in 1959

The full photo captured the quintessential LBJ, with his
hair slicked back, his big ears, glittering dark eyes that
were somehow friendly and sinister at the same time,
the suggestion of forward motion of a man in a hurry.

I was looking through a file on Lyndon Johnson, with no
purpose in mind, and sorted through old newspaper clippings, a
few photos, not a thick folder considering the subject. There was
the 1948 Senate election, the helicopter campaign, Coke
Stevenson, George Parr, Box 13. As I spread this out on my desk,
one photo stood out.

It was taken on Nov. 5, 1959 when Johnson was leaving the
Driscoll Hotel and leaning out the car window to wave to the
photographer. He was on his way to Kingsville to speak to
students at Texas A&I.

The photo that ran in the paper was badly cropped, leaving
only Johnson waving. The rich context — the sign on the wall of
the garage, the men in the car with him, presumably aides — was
removed, which turned an interesting photo into one with no
interest.

The full photo captured the quintessential LBJ, with his hair
slicked back, his big ears, glittering dark eyes that were somehow
friendly and sinister at the same time, the suggestion of forward
motion of a man in a hurry. He is every bit the candidate on the
hustle. It is easy to read all this into the photo because we all
knew LBJ and he was always LBJ — larger than life, a caricature
of himself.

On Nov. 5, 1959, Lyndon Johnson waves as he leaves the Driscoll Hotel for Kingsville, where he addressed students at what was then Texas A&I. Johnson, the Senate majority leader, spent two days making speeches around the Coastal Bend. On the trip he denied having any interest in running for president.

The 1960 presidential campaign loomed, but Johnson was not a candidate, he averred, and everywhere he went on this trip — Kingsville, Robstown, Beeville, and Corpus Christi — he stressed that he was not running for president. Why should he? He had the best job in the world, as senator from Texas, and as majority leader of the Senate he wielded real power.

You can tell, though, as he leaned out the open window to wave, that Johnson was in an all-fired hurry to get somewhere. And it was not to Kingsville.

County's election history

The first time that Nueces County voted in a presidential election was in 1848, two years after Texas joined the United States. The election pitted Zachary Taylor, hero of the Mexican War, a Whig candidate, against Lewis Cass, a Democrat.

The few voters in Nueces County favored Taylor because he had commanded a large expeditionary army that trained at Corpus Christi in 1845 and early 1846.

County results tallied in that election showed 66 votes for Taylor and 56 for Cass, though Cass won the state. When Taylor was inaugurated as president the Corpus Christi Star noted that Taylor supporters "celebrated the occasion by the firing of cannons and other demonstrations of rejoicing."

In the next two presidential elections in the 1850s Democratic candidates were favored by county voters. They backed Franklin Pierce over Winfield Scott, the Whig, in 1852 and favored James Buchanan over John Fremont and Millard Fillmore in 1856.

Then came the election of 1860, on the eve of the Civil War. Corpus Christi's newspaper, the Ranchero, wrote on Nov. 10, 1860 — "Election day in Corpus passed off quietly and good feeling seemed to pervade those who attended the polls." Nueces County voted for John Breckinridge, the Southern Democrat running against John Bell, a Constitutional Unionist. The Republican candidate in that election was not even on the ballot. Local voters were never able to cast a single vote for Abraham Lincoln.

After the interregnum of the Civil War and Reconstruction, county voters chose Horace Greeley, the Democratic candidate, over U. S. Grant, the Republican candidate. While Grant had been a young lieutenant with Taylor's army in Corpus Christi, the bitterness of the Civil War took away any chance of his winning Nueces County.

The next presidential contest in 1876 was the closest American election in history, until the Bush-Gore contest in 2000. Samuel Tilden, called Whispering Sammy, won Nueces County over Republican Rutherford B. Hayes though Tilden lost nationally.

Nueces County voted Democratic for the rest of the 19th Century, a trend that continued in the 20th Century. In 1928 the county voted for the Democrat, Alfred E. Smith, over Herbert Hoover, who won the election.

Franklin D. Roosevelt in his four elections received heavy majorities in Nueces County, as did Harry Truman in 1948 when he surprised everyone, even himself, by beating Thomas Dewey.

In Nueces County, Adlai Stevenson edged out Dwight Eisenhower in 1952 but in 1956 Ike took the county by less than 100 votes. It was the first time that Nueces County voted

Republican. It did so again in 1972 when Nixon thrashed McGovern.

The county voted Republican again in 1984, favoring Reagan over Mondale, and it voted Democratic in the two elections won by Bill Clinton in 1992 and 1996. It voted Republican in favor of George W. Bush over Al Gore in 2000 and Bush over John Kerry in 2004. The county continued the Republican trend by voting for John McCain over Barack Obama in 2008 and for Mitt Romney over Obama in 2012.

There have been 40 presidential elections from 1848 to 2012 and in those 40 contests Nueces County voted once for a Whig (Taylor), seven times for a Republican, and 32 times for a Democrat. This record has no especial relevance for the upcoming election, since every presidential tussle has its own peculiarities. This one certainly does. It will be wonderful when it is over and with any luck we won't ever have another one like it. Knock on wood.

Dr. Spohn at work

The Corpus Christi Gazette reported on Jan. 30, 1876 the details of an operation performed by Dr. Arthur Spohn, which gives us a glimpse of the surgeon at work. "The Gazette learns that on Thursday Dr. A. E. Spohn, in the presence of Drs. Knott, Turpin, Lawrence and others, performed an operation on the body of the wife of Secario (perhaps Cesario) Falcon, which speaks volumes for his skill as a surgeon.

"The unfortunate woman had been for years with a tumor in her abdomen, threatening her life. She was put under the influence of chloroform and kept under it for an hour and a half. Her entrails were laid bare to the view and kept warm by the application of soft clothes dipped in warm water. The tumor that was extracted, Dr. Spohn stated, weighed 45 pounds. The incision was sewed up and the lady was reported improving and cheerful," as if a great weight had been lifted from her.

—Oct. 26, 2016

Column 44

Tarzan at the Palace

It was not the big sale at Penney's that turned out so
many en masse but the second day's showing of
"Tarzan, the Ape Man" with Johnny Weissmuller.

Doc McGregor stood on the roof above Draughon's Practical
Business College, as best as I can determine, and took a photo of
the east side of the 600 block of Chaparral Street. That was 84
years ago, on April 2, 1932, a Saturday.

In the photo a long line of people stretched for a block down
Chaparral. The occasion seemed to be a big sale at Penney's.
Must have been a hell of a sale, I thought. No department store
sale would ordinarily bring out that many people, and this was
1932, during the worst of the Great Depression. There probably
hadn't been such a crowd on Chaparral since the day in 1866
when they got together a quorum and lynched Jim Garner.

On closer look part of the line was facing away from Penney's.
A quick visit to the library's microfilm machine provided the
answer to this little mystery. It was not the big sale at Penney's
that turned out so many en masse but the second day's showing
at the Palace of "Tarzan, the Ape Man" with Johnny
Weissmuller. This smash hit accounted for the busy scene on
Chaparral.

This kind of scene was not all that unusual in the 1930s. The
downtown was a lively place and the 600 block of Chaparral was
at the heart of it.

At the Starr Street corner on the east side was Penney's. It had
been at that location seven years, in a building owned by Hugh

181

Sutherland. Before Penney's opened there in December 1925, the premises were occupied by Scogin Brothers Auto Accessories and Folsom Café. Long before, this corner of Starr-Chaparral was the site of John Woessner's bank and wool warehouse. It was said that dances held on the second floor of Woessner's wool warehouse were the best around, with a dance floor that was "springy and fine." In the middle of the 600 block on the east side was the Palace Theater and on the south corner was the Nueces Hotel.

Because of the camera angle you can't see the west side of the street in this photo, but there was the W. T. Grant store on the corner opposite Penney's, followed by Kress, Woolworth and McCrory. The City Bank Building stood on the south end across from the Nueces Hotel.

In the middle of the block, across from the Palace, was Ben Garza's Metropolitan Café where the special that Saturday was a fried chicken dinner for 35 cents. Nearby was Muttera's Federal Bakery which was selling sugar cookies, a dozen for nine cents, and cream puffs, two for five cents. The air around Muttera's, people who remember it have told me, was infused with a warm bakery smell, an open solicitation for those cream puffs.

The sign on Penney's said "Celebrating 30 Years Value Giving" in observation of the chain's 30th anniversary. The first Penney's — called the Golden Rule Store — opened in Kemmerer, Wyo., on April 14, 1902.

The 30th anniversary sale at Corpus Christi posted some bargains: Turkish towels, four for 49 cents; ladies' shoes, high-heels and low-heels, $3.98; leather handbags, 98 cents; women's house frocks, three for 98 cents; and silk hose, 45 cents a pair. (Perhaps these were not such great bargains in the context of the wages of the times: firemen in Corpus Christi in 1932 made on average $2 a day, laundry workers made 65 cents a day, and farm workers made 40 cents a day, if they were lucky enough to have a job.)

Doc McGregor's photo captured some of the vitality of the downtown during its heyday, or golden age if you will, which lasted roughly from the opening of the port in 1926 until the late 1950s. The city began to spread out to the south and west, 1950s.

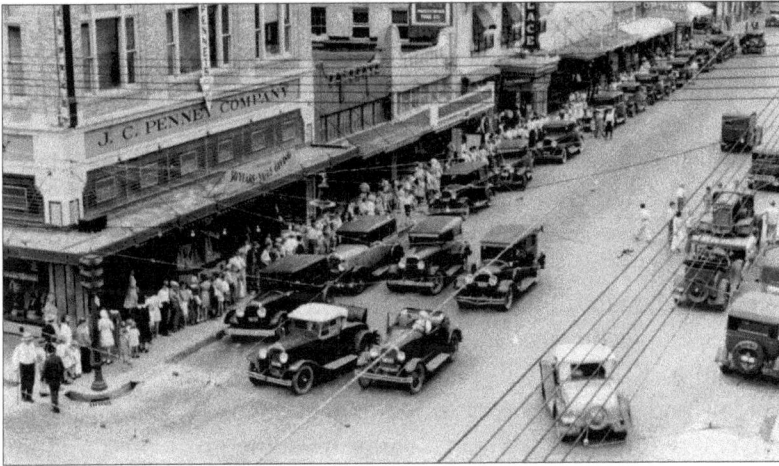

A large crowd lined the 600 block of Chaparral (looking south) on April 2, 1932. The major event was the showing at the Palace of "Tarzan, the Ape Man" with Johnny Weissmuller. Photo by Doc McGregor.

The city began to spread out to the south and west, swallowing farms and leaving the old uptown and downtown behind. The 600 block of Chaparral in 1932 was a street with a decided personality, but it has nothing in particular to recommend it today.

Penney's fought a losing battle to hang on. In 1949 it moved into a new five-story building at Chaparral and William but in 1978 it closed downtown, after 52 years, due to "declining sales and profits." Other businesses joined the general exodus.

Since I came here the subject of how to reverse the downtown decline has exercised many minds. There have been some successes but we will never come close to restoring the commercial liveliness, busyness and bustle of downtown's golden age, such as it was on that spring day in 1932 when Tarzan at the Palace was the best show in town.

Land rush

In the droughty 1880s and 1890s ranchers began to sell grazing land to recover cattle losses. This was the beginning of the land rush, which took off with the arrival of George H. Paul, a promoter from Iowa who came to Corpus Christi in 1907.

Paul made a deal with Robert Driscoll to sell ranchland north of what would become Robstown. He put together an organization and bought four Pullman cars to bring down prospective buyers (called home-seekers). The "George H. Paul Special" arrived every two weeks. The sale of 12,000 acres of Driscoll lands started in 1907. Paul started on another 60,000 acres and began selling Taft Ranch lands in San Patricio County.

Prospective buyers would arrive in Corpus Christi and make the trip to Robstown. Typically, they would reach Robstown on Friday and spend two days looking at land. Buggies carrying buyers would make a long caravan, sometimes 50 or more, traveling slowly and stopping often to view the land. Each agent carried a map showing plots for sale. Men on horseback rode back and forth with questions for the agents.

In 1907 Paul sold 56,000 acres of Driscoll land. In 1908 he sold 56,000 acres of Taft Ranch land. In 1910 he sold 70,000 acres of Welder ranchland. In two years, he sold 200,000 acres in Nueces and San Patricio.

Before the land rush was over, Paul brought in many thousands of settlers and sold half a million acres. He was called the father of Robstown and was instrumental in founding Driscoll, Taft, Sinton, Portland, Gregory, St. Paul and Sodville. George H. Paul made a fortune selling Texas ranchland but suffered reverses and died in Omaha in 1965 in extreme poverty.

—Nov. 2, 2016

A new kind of darkness

"That night, the atmosphere was tense and the
darkness so thick you were leery about going
outside." —Louis Anderson

Early in World War II, in the second month of the war after the
attack on Pearl Harbor, the Caller-Times carried instructions for
the first blackout drill. The newspaper warned people that it was
not an occasion for parties but a serious event requiring serious
cooperation. It was held on Jan. 19, 1942.

The piercing wail of six air-raid sirens positioned around the
city (Menger Elementary, City Hall, North Beach and three other
sites) warned that the drill had begun.

As darkness fell, photographer Doc McGregor stationed
himself on the roof of the White Plaza Hotel (the highest vantage
point in town, except for the Driscoll) and snapped a time-
exposure photo of a silver stream of lights from traffic just before
the test began. A shot taken after the drill began showed almost
total blackness except for two pinpricks of light on North Beach
where someone didn't follow the drill. Navy planes flew over the
city, the pilots looking for signs of light.

Most of the city was in absolute blackness, like being on the
inside of a cow, said one man, with an intermittent crescent
moon that was barely visible, and it was as quiet as the
proverbial grave. "That night," Louis Anderson, a Caller-Times
reporter, wrote, "the atmosphere was tense and the darkness so
thick you were leery about going outside."

Ten days later, on Jan. 29, 1942, the blackout was not a drill
but the real thing. It was prompted by a U-boat sighting in the

Gulf near Port Aransas, lying in wait off the ship channel. A smoke bomb, used as a danger signal from one U-boat to another, was seen four miles away, suggesting another U-boat was in the vicinity.

In the Jan. 29 blackout, merchant ships were ordered to remain in port. Navigation lights were doused. Airplanes were grounded. Trains were allowed to run but coach lights could not be turned on. To prevent ships from being silhouetted against the bright lights of the city skyline, a blackout from sunset to sunrise was ordered by military authorities Corpus Christi, and also for Port Aransas, Aransas Pass, Ingleside, and Portland.

The city's two radio stations, KEYS and KRIS, were ordered off the air. The Naval Air Station was blacked-out and air-raid wardens in uniform and carrying nightsticks patrolled the city, banging on doors and cautioning people inside if they saw a light. When police were warned that code signals were being flashed from the Driscoll Hotel they went to check and found a torn curtain flapping back and forth in front of an open window near a fluorescent light.

The blackout lasted 12 hours and 12 minutes, from dusk to dawn. People were off the streets and in their homes, with the black cloth used for blackout curtains drawn tight, in accordance with blackout regulations. The blackout this time was not so black because the moon (a gibbous moon just shy of the full) was not participating. As the old song says, the moon was the only light they could see.

The next day's paper reported that during the blackout all sound was hushed: "Standing on Mesquite Street it was possible to hear the chirrup of crickets on downtown streets. Occasionally a motor glided out of the shadows, creeping towards an intersection and then disappearing, traveling at a cautious crawl. The few persons on the streets moved in quiet groups, speaking in subdued tones. Travelers who reached the city too late to find a hotel dining room open went to bed without their supper."

"If you had credentials maybe you walked the streets that night," Louis Anderson wrote. "The moon was shining brightly and you didn't have to worry whether you would blunder into the side of the Driscoll. If you managed to work your way down-

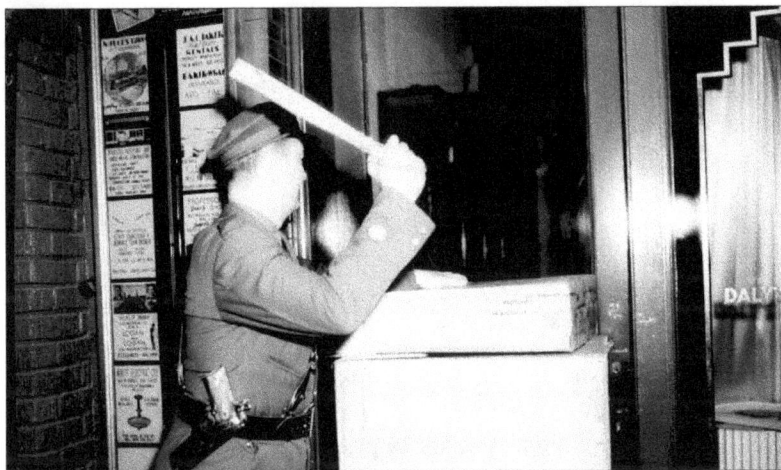

An air-raid warden made his rounds on Peoples Street, stopping to check for a light in the window of Daly's Camera Store during a citywide blackout on Jan. 29, 1942. The sighting of a U-boat near the Aransas Pass ship channel led to the city's second blackout. Ships became easy targets when silhouetted against city lights.

town you found the business houses all closed. If you happened to be in the know you could stop in for a few minutes and drink a cup of coffee, but the way those cafes were blacked out you'd never have found them by guessing."

There were other blackouts during the summer of 1942, when the U-boats were ascendant and sinking tankers and freighters all over the sea lanes of the Gulf. Military officials back then said the blackouts were merely a precaution, practice runs to be ready for the real thing. What they didn't say, because of strict wartime censorship, was that the blackouts in 1942, except for that first drill, always followed the sighting of U-boats just offshore. Most people didn't know how close the war had come. Details of the U-boat menace were revealed only after the war was over.

If people were not afraid during the blackouts, as most accounts suggest, they weren't bored either. Louis Anderson, the reporter, thought it might be indiscreet to talk about what went on during the blackouts, but said that people got into the spirit of the thing. "We might be able to tell about those nights to our children, when they get old enough to know not to question a few more details we can work up by then."

After 1942, when the U-boat threat diminished, things got rather quiet and dull.

Treasure legend

The legend of Casa Blanca, an old Spanish ranch near Orange Grove, was told by Mrs. S.G. Miller in "Sixty Years in the Nueces Valley."

The legend was that a wealthy rancher planned to return to Mexico with his two sons and daughter. He packed up his wealth, which include 10 kegs of gold and silver. The day before they were to leave an Indian war party was seen and the rancher submerged the kegs in a small lake near a lone mesquite.

When the Indians attacked the rancher and sons were killed. The daughter survived, moved to Mexico and many years later, when she was an old woman, returned to search for the treasure. There were no landmarks she could recognize. There was brush where the lake had been and a mott of trees where the mesquite once stood. She never found the buried kegs. Others searched for the lost treasure over years, presumably without success, so perhaps it is still there. If it ever existed.

—Nov. 9, 2016

Texas Brigade at Camp Scurry

"We were at the Amusu Theater when officers were summoned. The soldiers had come into town with their shirttails out, threatening to ride Mayor Miller out of town on a broom." —Mrs. Ray Starner

In August 1914, at the outbreak of World War I in Europe, Corpus Christi was focused on the revolutionary turmoil on the Texas-Mexican border. After Pancho Villa attacked Columbus, N.M., in March 1916, Gen. John Pershing was sent to the border with 10,000 troops. Pershing crossed into Mexico in pursuit of Villa. By August 1916, 100,000 state militia troops were stationed on the border. Of that number, 11,000 were Texans.

Five regiments of National Guard were ordered to move from Laredo to Corpus Christi but Laredo officials objected and promised to improve unhealthy living conditions in the camps. The orders were rescinded.

Corpus Christi Mayor Roy Miller lobbied Maj. Gen. Frederick Funston, commander of the Army's Southern Department, to move some state militia units to Corpus Christi. Miller promised that Corpus Christi would provide a model camp.

After the hurricane of 1916 flooded army camps in the valley, in August 1916, Gen. Funston considered moving the Second and Third Texas Infantry Regiments, which made up the Texas Brigade, from the Brownsville section to Corpus Christi. Brigade headquarters at Harlingen might join in the move.

On Aug. 27, Gen. John Hulen, commander of the Texas Brigade, came to Corpus Christi to inspect the proposed camp in a cow pasture south of town. Orders were confirmed four days later and Corpus Christi was designated as a station for two regiments of Texas militiamen stationed in the Brownsville section. Orders to move the Second and Third Infantry regiments, with 3,500 men, were issued by Funston.

The next day, on Sept. 1, Maj. A. C. Dalton, an army engineer from Fort Sam Houston, arrived to begin laying out the camp. This area was bordered by Buford, Santa Fe, Louisiana and Ocean Drive. It occupied the area where Spohn Hospital and the Del Mar neighborhood are today.

The city employed 300 workers to clear the 200-acre site of brush and prepare the camp. Thomas Born was given the contract to erect 24 screened 20-by-80 wooden mess halls. Huge piles of brush were burned, water lines were laid, drainage ditches were dug and the Corpus Christi Railway and Light Company strung wires to the site. The streetcar line was extended from Third and Elizabeth to the camp.

The site was ready in a week. The camp soon had shell-topped roads, wooden mess halls to serve 3,500 soldiers, and hundreds of tents, each one designed to house eight men. A trainload of rations (23 boxcars) and 33 new Packard trucks arrived. The Caller and Daily Herald reported that the militia units would soon be on their way and said, "Thirty-five hundred troops will mean a great deal to Corpus Christi."

The Third Infantry Regiment, under the command of Col. George Rains, came by train from Harlingen on Thursday, Sept. 7, 1916. The regiment marched through town with Company C from Corpus Christi leading the way. Company C, called the Musketeers, was under the command of Capt. John King. The Second Infantry Regiment, under the command of Col. Benjamin Delameter, arrived from Pharr the next day. Brig. Gen. John Hulen established his headquarters near Ocean Drive, with a good view of the bay.

Mrs. Georgia Welch, the city's postmaster, was authorized to establish a branch post office at the camp, tentatively called Alta Vista, but with a branch post office it had to have an official name. Hulen named it Camp Scurry after Gen. Thomas Scurry, a veteran of the Spanish-American War and commander of the Texas Brigade who died in 1911.

Soldiers in the Texas Brigade, state militia federalized during border troubles, at Camp Scurry in 1916. The camp was located in the area where Spohn Hospital and Del Mar neighborhood are today. Karl Swafford Photo from Jim Moloney.

On Tuesday, Sept. 12, the city held a welcoming reception for the soldiers. Five thousand colas and 600 cakes were ready at a big tent. The cakes (chocolate, banana, angel food) were baked in the kitchens of the mayor's wife and high society ladies of the town. Things began to look ugly at the festivities when competing bands of the Second and Third Infantry got into a brawl.

Gen. Frederick Funston, commander of the Southern Department, visited Corpus Christi on Oct. 2 and after lunch with Roy Miller, Funston and aides were taken for a swim off North Beach. A regiment of jellyfish, no respecters of rank, attacked. It was a tactical problem that forced Funston and his aides to retreat to the beach. That night, the general was the guest of honor at a dinner at the Nueces Hotel.

On Wednesday, Oct. 11, the entire Texas Brigade paraded down Chaparral Street in honor of the Order of the Eastern Star holding its convention in Corpus Christi.

Mrs. Ray Starner, wife of one of the officers, said in a later interview that soldiers went on a near-riot, angered by rumors that they were going to be put to work building a road at the request of Mayor Miller.

"We were at the Amusu Theater when officers were summoned," Mrs. Starner said. "The soldiers had come into town with their shirttails out, threatening to ride Mayor Miller out of town on a broom." The officers ordered the men to return to camp and obey orders, whatever they might be, and the disturbance was quelled.

The rumors were true. When Mayor Miller asked John Hulen, commander of the camp, to use soldiers to repair UpRiver Road he was told to go through channels. He wrote Gen. Funston, whom he had taken duck-hunting on King Ranch, and orders came through approving the project.

Charles Duff, a soldier at Scurry, said they shoveled truckloads of shell on a long dusty road. "We ran trucks to the beach between two rows of about 30 men. Each man threw two shovels of shell on the flatbed trucks. By the time the trucks reached the end of the row they were loaded. Other men scooped the shell on to the roadway as far as Calallen." For a long time after that UpRiver Road was known as Shell Road.

The Second and Third Regiments were composed of machine-gun companies. Mules were bought from King Ranch to use as pack animals, but when machine guns were strapped to their backs the mules turned into conscientious objectors. They stampeded, running into the mesquite beyond the camp. Soldiers spent days tramping through the brush, alive with rattlers, chasing runaway mules and retrieving machine guns which were strewn for miles.

—Nov. 16, 2016

Scurry fielded a great football team

The Second Texas team ran up 432 points while
allowing the opposition 6. It never came close to losing a
game and was called "the best team that ever played."

In late 1916, Camp Scurry at Corpus Christi was home to two regiments of the Texas Brigade. The soldiers spent the winter on practice marches and cheered themselves hoarse at football games of the Second Texas Regiment squad, which was called "the best team that ever played the game."

The camp guardhouse burned on Thursday, Nov. 9, the fire believed started by the inmates. The 66 prisoners who escaped into the night were rounded up and locked up in the city and county jails, where they were held until a new guardhouse could be built.

A four-day march and field exercise began early on Wednesday morning. The soldiers marched out of Scurry with full packs and in fine order. It was a sunny day and the men were in good spirits. A wagon train followed with rations. They camped in a large cornfield at 1 p.m. for lunch. Hot coffee and field rations were served and the march resumed at 2 p.m.

At Calallen they made camp in an open field across from the railroad depot. They pitched pup tents, campfires were soon blazing, and the regimental bands began playing patriotic airs. The men went wild when the Third Regimental band struck up 'Dixie.'

It looked like a pleasant place to spend the night and was so warm they hardly needed blankets. Before midnight, though, the camp was hit by heavy rain as a fierce norther blew in. Tents were blown down and orders passed on that it was every man for himself.

Some took shelter in the schoolhouse, others at the depot, some in churches and private homes. Though it was raining and freezing cold some tried to sleep in bedding rolls on the ground. Others found shelter in a lumberyard and built bonfires of "perfectly good lumber."

It was not a smart turnout next morning. The men were wet, cold, and caked with mud. Some weren't there. In the confusion of the storm a few deserted and it took weeks before they were rounded up, from as far away as San Antonio.

The planned four-day field maneuvers were halted after that miserable night in Calallen. In Corpus Christi, the Caller reported that the rumor mill said the four-day march was cut short because of a mutiny involving almost the entire brigade. The rumors were untrue, said the Caller, only one company was "involved in the alleged mutiny."

The true story, said the newspaper, was that an officer found several soldiers at the Calallen depot who said they had been given permission to take the train back to camp instead of marching back. The officer said that would not be permitted so the men returned to their units.

Back at Camp Scurry on Friday, officers said they were pleased with the march and though they did not complete the planned four-day exercise the men "demonstrated their fitness for a strenuous field campaign."

Another march was made to Sinton, from Nov. 16 through Nov. 20. The field maneuvers were cut short again, this time at the request of Mayor Roy Miller, who wanted the troops in town for the opening of Exposition Week. After four days in the field the brigade returned "in splendid condition."

The Third Regiment made another practice march on Nov. 28, this one for 17 miles. There was some amusement over the complaints of the regimental clerk, F. K. Smith, who was not taken on the march but left to perform his desk duties. After some ragging the clerk asked to be transferred to the ranks so he could show them that he could "soldier with the best of them."

The Second Texas Infantry stationed at Camp Scurry fielded what was called the greatest football team ever. In this photo the Second Texas team (striped jerseys) were taking on the New York Infantry in a contest on New Year's Day 1917. The Second Texas won 102-0. Photo from Corpus Christi Central Library.

He was made a mounted orderly, put on an unruly horse, and after being thrown a few times asked to be returned to his desk job where he could "clerk with the best of them."

The Second Texas Regiment fielded a football team made up of former college players, some from the University of Texas, Texas A&M and Baylor. They built a practice field at Santa Fe and Booty where the team trounced the country's best military teams, also composed of former college players. The Second Texas beat them by such lopsided scores that they were called "the best team that ever played the game."

On Nov. 22, in a game in Corpus Christi at the Exposition Grounds the Second Texas beat the Missouri Third Field Artillery 33 to 0. Three days later, the Second Texas played the First Wisconsin Infantry, which had not lost a game. Before a crowd of 2,500, the Second Texas beat the Wisconsin team 60-0, winning with ease, the newspaper reported, "outclassing them in all departments of the game."

On Dec. 6, a rematch against the Missouri Artillery was played at Laredo. The Second Texas won again but by a more modest 13-0. A week later Second Texas played the Virginia Artillery in San Antonio, winning 52-0. The Fourth Nebraska Infantry team came to Corpus Christi and lost 68-0, with many of the Second Texas team's best players on the bench.

In a game against the New York Infantry on New Year's Day, players on the New York team, made up of All-Americans from Princeton and Syracuse, were overheard saying they planned to go easy on the Texans. Second Texas whipped them 102-0. The only team that scored against Second Texas was the 12th Division All-Stars, which lost 34-6. Warren "Rip" Collins said, "The game was played in a blizzard and they scored against us when we put the fourth string in."

From November 1916 into early 1917 the Second Texas team ran up 432 points while allowing the opposition 6. It never came close to losing a game and was called "the best team that ever played." Best ever? How could we tell? It only played other military teams. The Second Texas was scheduled to play Texas A&M, which would have given us a reasonable measure of how good the team was, but the match was cancelled by A&M.

Best ever or not, the Second Texas was certainly one of the great teams in history. Knute Rockne, the legendary Notre Dame coach, was making some point at a football clinic when he said, "Not even the Second Texas could do that."

—Nov. 23, 2016

Column 48

World War I kept Scurry open

Camp Scurry was ordered closed. The Second and Third
Regiments were to be demobilized. That changed when
the United States entered the war in Europe.

With tensions on the border easing, Corpus Christi reconciled
itself to the closing of Camp Scurry. More than 3,500 Texas
National Guard troops at the camp, the Texas Brigade, were
awaiting orders to be sent home. Then everything changed. It
was to be war after all.

In February 1917, troops at Camp Scurry were agog with
excitement after hearing rumors that all Texas guardsmen were to
be returned to their home stations for demobilization. The rumors
were true. Orders arrived on Feb. 18 to a great roaring cheer.
They were going home.

This meant, the Caller reported, "that by March 7 all units of
the National Guard will be out of the federal service, leaving the
patrol of the border to the regulars." The news cast a deep gloom
over the city. "There is no denying that the stationing of the two
regiments and other units here for the past six months has been a
life-saver," the Caller said. "The boys arrived at a time when
business conditions were unusual, caused by the drought that has
prevailed for more than a year." Camp Scurry was ordered
closed. The Second and Third Regiments were to be
demobilized. Some 700 men would dismantle the camp.

That changed on April 6, 1917 when the United States entered
the war in Europe. The Second and Third Regiments were called
back into service and sent to Camp Travis.

But Camp Scurry would still be needed as the machine of war was set in motion. The government renewed its lease and the camp was selected as a training base. Two trains brought 539 officers and enlisted men of the Fifth Engineers, a regular army unit from El Paso, on June 26. They joined the remaining units of Third Texas Infantry, about 700 men, which brought the population of the camp to 1,200.

While the Engineers were in Corpus Christi they dug trenches to simulate trench warfare and practiced bayonet drills daily.

On June 13, 1918, the Fifth Engineers were sent to Camp Merritt, N. J., where they joined the 7th Division and sailed for France. After the Fifth Engineers departed Camp Scurry became the training base of the Fourth Field Artillery, which arrived on Sept. 7, 1918 from Camp Logan in Houston.

Dermot Meehan from New York was stationed at Scurry with Battery A of the Fourth Field Artillery in late 1918 and early 1919. Meehan said his group of six batteries went on short maneuvers in the area and sometimes fired their 295 mounted guns. He said the regiment had about 1,400 mules.

"I remember a bunch of us bought a boat and rented a net," he said in an interview. "We would drag it around the bay and catch shrimp, then have a shrimp feast. Everybody would donate a nickel for catsup and we'd eat shrimp till we were sick."

The camp was off limits during the height of the influenza epidemic. It began in the summer of 1918 and intensified that fall. Many normal activities of the city were suspended. Schools, theaters, poolrooms, domino parlors, closed. Restaurants stayed open but tables had to be five feet apart. Hotels also stayed open but people were not allowed to congregate in main lobbies.

During the worst of the epidemic Camp Scurry was placed under quarantine. Soldiers were not allowed to leave the base and civilians were not allowed to enter the camp. On Nov. 11, 1918, a young Corpus Christi girl, Anita Lovenskiold, wrote in her diary: "Oh, what a grand and glorious day is today! The war has ended. This morning whistles blew, bells rang, and music began to play. We heard a lot of yelling. It was a parade and we sure did some running to catch up. I lost my money and goodness knows how many hairpins."

Camp Scurry MPs gather around the Confederate Memorial Fountain on the bluff in 1917. The MPs occupied office space on the third floor of City Hall between Schatzel and Peoples. Photo from Corpus Christi Central Library.

A few days later the epidemic had run its course and the city's ban on public gatherings was lifted. Camp Scurry held a dance on Nov. 16 to celebrate the end of the quarantine and the end of the war.

It was miserably cold that November and because of icy conditions the men were not drilled. They lounged in tents which were made a little warmer with the arrival of new Sibley stoves. The men were awaiting orders. Many enlisted for the duration of the war and with the war over they expected to be discharged. They went to Eidson's, Lichtenstein's or Gugenheim-Cohn to buy civilian clothes. They hoped to be home for Christmas.

The expected discharges did not come before Christmas. The Fourth held a field day on New Year's Day, with the public invited. Most of the day's contests involved mules in one way or another. As an independent breed, mules could make things interesting because they were, well, mulish.

There was a slow mule race, in which the last mule to finish the course won, with a prize of an extra pail of oats. There was a mule chariot race, in the manner of Ben Hur, with four wild-eyed mules pulling any kind of two-wheel vehicle. The winning charioteer received a box of cigars. There was the mounted officers pie-eating contest. Contestants rode bareback to the pie stand, where they had to consume a pie (frosted chocolate) with their hands behind their backs, then remount their mules and race to the finish line. The winner received a towel, soap, and toothbrush.

On Jan. 4, 1919, the Fourth Field Artillery marched out of town for Camp Stanley near Leon Springs 175 miles away. The regimental band took the lead playing, "It's a Long, Long Trail."

The march took two weeks and much sweat, by man and mule, before they reached shade and cool water at Leon Springs. They were to spend two weeks at Camp Stanley and return to Camp Scurry in the middle of February. But new orders came through and many were discharged, as the Army began to slim down for peacetime. Only 12 men in the quartermaster's department were left at Camp Scurry to lock up and turn out the lights. They too were soon gone and Camp Scurry was closed for good.

—Nov. 30, 2016

A long day's journey into war

Movies playing that Sunday, Dec. 7, 1941, had titles that
seemed to be a premonition of coming events. "I Wake
Up Screaming" was showing at the Ritz and "Kiss the
Boys Goodbye" was at the Amusu.

In the first week of December 1941 Christmas lights were
switched on downtown. On Friday, Dec. 5, Santa Claus landed in
a Navy seaplane on Corpus Christi Bay, taxied to the Peoples
Street T-Head, then rode around town in a convertible escorted
by a firetruck. Columnist Bob McCracken recalled old-time
Christmas when Santa traveled by sleigh, not seaplanes and
convertibles.

On Saturday, Dec. 6, in Austin, the Longhorns, with Jackrabbit
Jack Crain, ran all over the Oregon Webfoots (later called the
Ducks) 71-6.

Sunday, Dec. 7, was cool. The bay was a little choppy for the
Corpus Christi Sailing Club's mid-winter regatta. Lichtenstein's
advertised Nelly Don dresses from $2.98 to $10.95 and there
were full-page grocery ads for Limerick's, Biel's and Piggly
Wiggly.

The paper reported that another historic building — Billy
Rogers' home on Chaparral, built in 1871 — was about to be
razed. Hilltop Terrace near Old Robstown Road, a development
by George and Annie Blake Farenthold, and Dahlia Terrace off
Ayers Street, were holding open house.

A news article advised young women to "Pack away the
overalls, girls" because there would be no defense jobs at the
Naval Air Station for a long time.

Movies playing that Sunday had titles that seemed to be a premonition of coming events. Betty Grable and Victor Mature starred in "I Wake Up Screaming" at the Ritz, Ann Sheridan and Jack Oakie were in "Navy Blues" at the Tower, and Don Ameche and Mary Martin were in "Kiss the Boys Goodbye" at the Amusu.

It was an ordinary Sunday until . . .

Marcus Norvell, an optometrist, played hooky from church. He was fiddling with his short-wave radio when he got a station in Honolulu playing music. He heard loud "booms" and an announcer explained that the Navy was conducting aerial target practice. A minute later a woman's voice came on yelling, "Clear the airways! This is an emergency! Pearl Harbor calling. A foreign power has attacked the United States." Then the station went dead. Norvell thought it was some Orson Welles-like hoax.

It was 12:25 in Corpus Christi when a radio bulletin reported that Japanese planes had attacked the U.S. navy base at Pearl Harbor. People learned of Ford Island . . . Battleship Row . . . Hickam and Wheeler Fields . . . Schofield Barracks . . . the USS Arizona, Utah, Oklahoma . . . Zeros . . . Rising Sun . . . Meatballs . . . And eventually Naguma, Yamamoto, Tojo, and Hirohito.

An ordinary Sunday was turned into a day they would never forget. Mrs. Guy Coffee, who lived on Santa Fe, recalled that "we had just come home from church when we heard it on the radio. We were stunned. We couldn't imagine anything that terrible happening."

"I was 11 years old when I heard the news on the radio," one man said. "I misunderstood and thought the Japanese had bombed the harbor in Corpus Christi. I ran to the post office and hid."

Another said, "I was 12 years old and listening to 'The Shadow' on radio ("The Curse of Baldring Heights" was airing) when I ran out and told my father. He told me not to get my radio shows mixed up with real news. He came to listen and heard it himself. Then we sat down and cried."

At the Naval Air Station all leaves were cancelled and extra guards were posted at the gates. Base commander Capt. Alva

A man reads a Caller-Times Extra on the Japanese attack on Pearl Harbor on the evening of Dec. 7, 1941 in front of the S&Q men's store in the Nueces Hotel building. Caller-Times Photo.

Bernhard said there was indignation among Navy men over "treacherous" nature of the attack. Young cadets took the news in stride. One said, "Damn, now we will have to wear uniforms and I just ordered a new suit."

At the Caller-Times, linotype operators, printers and reporters showed up in Sunday clothes to prepare a special edition, which came out later that evening and sold like hotcakes. The paper's phone was ringing constantly with people wanting news, any news, about what was happening in Hawaii. Many calls came from those with relatives at Pearl. During all the uproar one man called who wanted to know the time.

Telephone operator Virginia Adams said when the news was announced on radio the switchboard lit up. "The lights were all over the board. You couldn't take care of them there were so many."

To prevent sabotage guards were posted at the Mathis Dam, the port, Humble Refinery at Ingleside, the Westergard shipyard at Rockport, the main water line to the Naval Air Station, and the city's water line from Calallen.

On Monday at the Assembly & Repairs hangar at the Naval Air Station, hundreds of sailors and civilian workers gathered to hear President Roosevelt deliver his address to the nation. At the Courthouse (1914), Judge George Westervelt called a halt in the murder trial of Philip Trammell, accused of killing Scotty Jetton, so the jurors, witnesses and court personnel could listen to Roosevelt's speech.

Men in Corpus Christi were raring to fight. They flooded recruiting offices that Monday at the Federal Building on Starr Street. Most of them were turned down because of age, physical condition, or marital status. One man was rejected by the Army and then the Navy because of an old football injury, a trick knee. Another was 45 years old with one eye. He insisted he could be useful, that even an old one-eyed tomcat could still fight.

"If you sat here as I have and interviewed men like that," said a Navy recruiter, "you would never wonder again how our country became the great nation that it is."

Within days the city learned about its first casualties of the war. Warren Sherrill, who attended Corpus Christi High, was killed on the Arizona and "Billy Jack" Brownlee was killed in the bombing of Hickam Field. In his last letter to his parents, Brownlee wrote, "The island is perfectly protected from an enemy raid."

Seventy-five years ago, on Dec. 7, 1941, the world was turned topsy-turvy with the attack on Pearl Harbor, which launched America's entry into the second world war. People in Corpus Christi, as elsewhere, were uncertain about what was coming, about how their lives would be changed in the weeks and months and years ahead, but they all knew what they had to do.

—*Dec. 4, 2016*

School days at David Hirsch

Theodore Fuller said that his teacher, Miss Pearl
Bauerfeind, decided they needed a pencil sharpener in
the classroom and asked each student to bring a nickel to
defray the expense.

Theodore (Ted) Fuller, in his memoirs "When the Century and I Were Young," recalled an episode at the David Hirsch Elementary School in 1918. He was nine and in the third grade.

"Three grade schools in Corpus were the last word in modern school architecture," he wrote. "Our school, David Hirsch, was one of these." Fuller recalled that his teacher, Miss Pearl Bauerfeind, decided they needed a pencil sharpener in their clroom and asked each student to bring a nickel to defray the cost.

Fuller said a hand-powered sharpener would have cost $1 or $1.50 and with more than 30 students in the class a nickel from each would have been enough. Three days later Miss Bauerfeind wrote on the blackboard "collected" and "needed" and the totals underneath. Some didn't have a nickel to bring and they were short 25 cents.

A boy named Jack Giles (Elbert Jackson Giles; his father, Dr. H. R. Giles, would later be mayor) gave a quarter. Fuller was so impressed he never forgot Jack Giles' quarter. Had Fuller possessed such great wealth, there was no end of things he would buy, starting with candy and fishing lures. "It would never have entered my mind to have done as Jack did. My envy was boundless."

David Hirsch's school baseball team is shown in perhaps the late 1920s, though the date and identities are unknown. The photo is from Murphy Givens' collection.

David Hirsch was one of three new ward schools built in 1912, at a cost of $11,000 each, and opened in 1913. The other two were George Evans and Edward Furman.

David Hirsch was a brick structure built on North Water Street, a rock's throw from Hall's Bayou. It was on the site once occupied by Benny Anderson's mule yard (where the Museum of Science and History is today). The school was named for wool merchant and banker David Hirsch who served as the first president of the school board.

David Hirsch students came from Irishtown, that area north of the courthouse, and from North Beach, a ritzy residential area before the 1919 storm.

Mrs. Ameta McGloin, a teacher at David Hirsch, recalled that streetcars passed the school on their North Beach run. (She later became postmaster after her husband was shot to death in the post office in 1939.)

One who attended the school, besides Ted Fuller and Jack Giles, was Atlee McCampbell, who recalled that during recess the boys would shoot marbles on the playground or play baseball on a nearby field. When school let out they could go crabbing in Hall's Bayou.

Although David Hirsch was damaged in the 1919 storm, the principal, C. N. Coleman, said it could have been re-opened soon

David Hirsch Elementary, built in 1912, was located on North Water Street. The school was closed in 1962. The Museum of Science and History is on that site today. Photo from Central Library.

after the storm but the student population had been swept away. The school was surrounded by devastation and suddenly served an area with no population at all.

David Hirsch Elementary stood empty for six years before it was re-opened in 1925. Mary McBride was the principal until she was succeeded by Freeman Martin, who held the post from 1931 until 1948. The school was closed in January 1962.

One year later the school building was used as a backdrop to film an episode of the TV series "Route 66." The episode centered on the story of a boy who came to the school to get his younger sister to run away with him. A stalwart crew from Casa Linda (Norma Thomas's fourth-grade class) was brought in to help film the scene.

For a short time the old playground was alive again with girls jumping rope and boys playing basketball, as they performed for the camera. Martin Milner and George Maharis, co-stars of the show, were not there. Milner was visiting patients at Ada Wilson's Crippled Children's Hospital and Maharis was in New

207

York. They were fortunate to have missed it. It was freezing cold and 19 degrees outside when the scene was filmed.

David Hirsch Elementary was torn down in August 1966. You wonder if it was lamented. Who remembers with any pleasure or fondness his elementary school? I don't. David Hirsch was no doubt like all elementary schools, a place of confinement and torture for generations of oppressed schoolchildren, where they learned their letters, under duress, and endured the manifold miseries of education.

Dazzling lights

Kerosene lamp fixtures were on the street corners in Corpus Christi in the 1880s. A man would go around each evening and climb up, replenish the fuel, and relight the lamps and return in the mornings to put them out.

One of the city's lamplighters was Auguste Dutailly, a Belgian who had fought with Maximilian's forces in Mexico before he immigrated to Corpus Christi. (One of his four daughters, Annie, married Rafael Garcia, a longtime employee of Lichtenstein's.)

The city in 1889 began to consider installing the new Edison electric lights, invented 11 years before. The Caller on Oct. 26 reported that a contractor for the Edison light system, F. P. McMullen, proposed to substitute 70 coal-oil lamps with 16-candle-power Edison incandescent lamps. It would cost the city $2.50 per lamp per month.

A week later, the paper said the Corpus Christi Electric Company had perfected arrangements for lighting the city by electricity. The company was organized by Dr. Alfred Heaney, John Stayton, and T. P. Rivera.

The Caller was enthusiastic. "The City Council have wisely decided to light our streets with electricity instead of the ancient oil lamps now in use — which only serve to make the darkness visible — and to that end have closed a contract with the company for 70 lights.

"With our streets, business houses, and residences illuminated with electric lamps, our city will be a thing of beauty, Empress of the Gulf. Ere the winter visitor takes his departure electric lighting will be an accomplished fact. Corpus Christi is emerging from darkness and sloth and before another year passes will have taken her stand in the dazzling light of commercial push and energy."

The electric lights were up by April 1890. Wood was used for fuel at the power plant on Water Street. When usage was heavy more wood was added to keep the lights from dimming. Electricity was available only at night. It was not until almost two decades later, in 1908, that the city got 24-hour electric service when the new the Peoples Light Company was organized to compete with the original Corpus Christi Electric Company.

—Dec. 7, 2016

North Beach in 1939

The traveler's eye would have caught passing glimpses of shed-like shanties selling seashells, Mexican pottery and curios, followed by cheap tourist cottages and more shops selling curios.

I ran across a good photo by Russell Lee showing North Water Street in 1939. While most North Beach photos of that era focused on the crowded amusement park or people doing nothing on the beach and the usual scenes on the waterfront, this one shows how the main drag would have appeared to tourists as they drove in on highways 77 and 181.

The traveler's eye would have caught passing glimpses of shed-like shanties selling seashells, Mexican pottery and curios, followed by cheap tourist cottages and more Mexican curios. Nothing quaint or charming, but the North Beach-ness of the place is palpable.

The photograph was taken in the dead season of February, when profitable activity was slow and businesses had trouble paying the overhead, even in the good years, and this was the Great Depression. But come warm weather and North Beach would be overrun by an invading army of tourists and summer celebrants and the business climate would become much more solvent.

The photo led me to look up the type of businesses that lined the main drag on North Beach in 1939. Water Street stretched from the Bascule Bridge to the 3100 block. The side streets it crossed were Bessie, Bennett, Pearl, Market, Garner and Vine. Some of those names were changed — Bessie, Garner and Vine

A photo by Russell Lee, Farm Security Administration photographer during the Great Depression, shows North Water Street on North Beach in 1939. Photo from Library of Congress.

are no longer there — but I'm using those that were still there in 1939.

In the 2500 block, the first block after crossing the Bascule Bridge, there was North Beach Grocery and Fruit Market in a white stucco building on the west side of the street, which housed several businesses.

In the 2600 block, from Bessie to Bennett, were several tourist courts, including Shell Beach Cottages and Chandler Cottages. That block also included a fruit stand called Polly's Place and Theo Davis's Grocery Store.

The next block, the 2700 block, from Bennett to Pearl, featured the Aztec Curio Shop, Ollie and Ben Tunnell's Grocery Store, and the first Dragon Grill. Doc Mason's Dragon Grill moved out to Timon Boulevard in 1941, where it burned, and the third Dragon Grill was located in Corpus Christi proper in the old Elks Building.

In the 2800 block, from Pearl to Market, were J. D. Brown's Court (also cottages), Brown's Barbecue and Mexican Curios, and the Beacon Drug Store. The 2900 block, from Market to Garner, featured the Half Moon Confectionery, Rex Lodges, and the Owl Drug Store and Sandwich Shop. The 3000 block, from

212

Garner to Vine, included the North Beach Drug Store, Biel's Grocery No. 4, the Tip Top Café, and Beach Haven Court.

That gives us a commercial snapshot of North Water Street in 1939 when North Beach had the languid air of a seaside resort and tourism was the mainstay of whatever prosperity there was. As one oft-quoted North Beach businessman said, tourists were more profitable than growing cotton and much easier to pick.

We look back at North Beach of the 1930s and 1940s as a golden age, a sunny pleasure place before a slow attrition set in, Harbor Bridge was built, and the flow of traffic across the peninsula seemed headed in one direction — away. The tourists gradually disappeared and along with them went the tourist cabins and curio shops and North Beach came on hard times. Maybe that attrition had already begun by 1939. At least, Russell Lee's photo makes the place look awfully transient.

Corpus Christi's first doctor

Dr. David H. Lawrence, Corpus Christi's first doctor, came to the United States from England in the early part of the 19th Century. He lived at Dayton, Ohio, briefly before coming to Texas, shortly after the Revolution. He arrived in Corpus Christi in 1840, soon after Henry Kinney founded the town in 1839.

Dr. Lawrence had heard of the Gulf Coast weather ("like a dream of the French Riviera," someone said) and hoped that the mild climate would help his son recover. T. M. had been in poor health.

After the death of his wife, Dr. Lawrence married Ellen Pettigrew of Corpus Christi, considered a local beauty. On Feb. 16, 1846, she led the opening dance at the Annexation Ball with Gen. Zachary Taylor.

Dr. and Mrs. Lawrence had twins, a son named Marion, and a daughter named Mary. There was another daughter named Dora.

Dr. Lawrence's son married Ellen Pettigrew's niece, Sarah Quinn. T. M. Lawrence enlisted as a private in W. S. Shaw's company of light infantry in February 1860. He was serving in Shaw's company when the city was bombarded by Union warships in 1862.

Near the end of the Civil War Sheriff Mat Nolan, who was also a Confederate major, was shot on Dec. 2, 1865. He was carried to the nearby home of Dr. Lawrence, on Mesquite Street (where the Caller-Times parking lot is now). Lawrence told Nolan his wound was fatal.

During the yellow fever epidemic of 1867, Lillie Rankin said the doctor's treatment consisted of having the patient's feet soaked in a bucket of hot water mixed with ashes and mustard, then the patient was wrapped in blankets and sweated to discharge the fever. The doctor's son, T. M., died in the epidemic. He left a young son, T. M. Lawrence Jr., who was born in 1861 at the family home on Mesquite.

Dr. Lawrence had an office in the 300 block of Chaparral. He later moved to the St. James Hotel and kept an office there until he died on March 14, 1879. He was buried in Bayview Cemetery. Mary Sutherland in "The Story of Corpus Christi" said Lawrence was a much-beloved doctor of the old days.

The younger Lawrence, the doctor's grandson, married Cora Garrett of Alabama in 1880 and they had three children. He was one of the first to grow truck farms in Nueces County. He grew tomatoes and cabbages which were shipped out by rail in the 1890s. He was appointed county commissioner in 1902 to fill the unexpired term of another farmer, J. H. Roark. Lawrence, known as Buddy, was later elected and served as county commissioner until 1932. His home was on Shell Road.

We still have Lawrence Street in downtown Corpus Christi, which was named by Henry Kinney in 1852 for Dr. D. H. Lawrence, Corpus Christi's first physician. Buddy Lawrence Drive was named for his grandson, a longtime county commissioner of Precinct 1.

—Dec. 14, 2016

The Ironclad Oath House

When the war ended, Corpus Christi was occupied.
Union soldiers used this house as their provost marshal's
office. Citizens who wanted to affirm loyalty to the
Union went to this house to take the Ironclad Oath.

Looking at photographs of Chaparral in the 1930s I came across one interesting enough to warrant a closer look. The Doc McGregor photo taken on Dec. 16, 1935 shows a convoy of cars with signs advertising a movie preview. In the middle of the shot, between Vaky Apartments and the Railway Express Building, was a white framed house that looked out of place.

Most downtown homes were gone by 1935. They lost out to commercial encroachment. Bur this one had survived. A little research discovered that it was the Royall Givens' home, at 802 N. Chaparral, on the northeast corner past the intersection of Taylor Street, just east of the Caller-Times.

I was excited to find a photo of this building because it was called the Ironclad Oath House just after the Civil War. I had looked for a photo of this place without luck and here it was, hiding in a general street scene of 1935.

Long before it was Royall Givens' house it was the old Russell home. It was built between 1853 and 1855 by Charles Russell after he married Mary Eliza Dix, the daughter of Capt. John Dix. The house stood unoccupied after Mary Eliza died of yellow fever and Russell, a Confederate soldier, was stationed on the border.

When the war ended and Corpus Christi was occupied by Union soldiers, U.S. officers used this house for their quarters

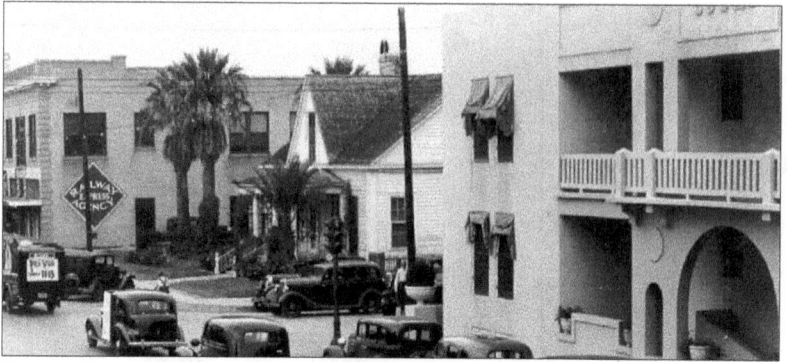

Royall Givens' house on North Chaparral, squeezed between Vaky Court apartments and Railway Express Agency office, was once known as the Ironclad Oath House after the Civil War. Photo by Doc McGregor.

and as the provost marshal's office. Citizens who wanted to affirm or reaffirm loyalty to the Union went to this house to take what was known the Ironclad Oath. The oath ended with, "I will faithfully support the Constitution and obey the laws of the United States and will, to the best of my ability, encourage others to do so. So help me God."

Some ex-Confederates argued about whether they should take the oath. Since the South had been whipped like a borrowed mule, as Thomas Noakes noted in his diary, "We came to the conclusion that we would have to conform to their measure sooner or later and we considered it the best policy to do so at once." He took the oath.

In the 1870s the Russell house was occupied by a succession of owners. Royall (also often spelled Royal) Givens bought it in 1888 and had it remodeled. The house had high ceilings, sliding doors, and a large cellar built of shellcrete.

Royall Givens (not related to my family) had a fish and oyster business with a packing plant and cannery on North Beach. He shipped seafood throughout the United States and Mexico, operated his own oyster beds, and was called the Drumfish King because he shipped out drum under the name of White Rock.

Anyone who visited the Givens packing operation on North Beach would be treated to a free oyster lunch. Judge George C. Westervelt, an article in the Caller said, always carried a bottle of

216

hot pepper sauce in his pocket in case he found himself in the vicinity of the packing house at lunch time.

Mrs. Leona (Gussett) Givens, the daughter of Norwick Gussett, was interviewed in her home on Chaparral in 1940. She recalled the fish fries that were held at the Givens' packing house complex on North Beach, near the reef on the north near Nueces Bay. "Fifty or sixty young people would gather for these occasions, spreading the supper on the long tables used to open the oyster shells."

She said her husband was in the insurance business for a long time but was best known as a wholesale fish shipper. "He was the first man ever to ship drum from Corpus Christi, but he called it White Rock. It was shipped in slabs and there was an enormous market for it. He patented the name Star Brand in Mexico, where a great quantity of his fish products was sold." He also supplied the turtles for turtle soup to restaurants in Boston and New York.

"Mr. Givens did a good business in shipping bones, too," she said. "They would be piled in great heaps as high as the house. Then they were loaded on ships, sometimes making up the entire cargo of a vessel. Bones were used in purifying sugar."

The Givens' packing house and seafood complex was destroyed in the 1919 storm. It was not rebuilt. He died in 1928 and his widow, Mrs. Leona Givens lived in the house until she died on Oct. 12, 1948. Not long afterwards the house was razed. There is nothing there now but a vacant lot. At least I have found an image of what the Ironclad Oath House looked like.

Buena Vista Hotel

Baffin Bay supposedly got its name as a joke. Before it was Baffin Bay it was the Salt Lagoon, as shown on old maps. During the Civil War salt was gathered from the banks of the Laguna Madre and Baffin Bay and traded inland for food. It was better tender than Confederate money, but almost anything was.

Some accounts say Mifflin Kenedy, who owned the Laureles Ranch, called it Baffin Bay as a joke, naming it after the one in the Arctic, one of the coldest places on Earth.

217

The Buena Vista Hotel on Riviera Beach was built by Theodore Koch, a banker from St. Paul, Minn., about 1912. The hotel was built to cater to prospective land-buyers in the land-boom era. The two-story hotel consisted of two buildings on Ebony Hill, with a fine view of Baffin Bay. The hotel had been closed for years when it burned in 1952.

In 1906, Theodore Koch, a banker from St. Paul, Minn., bought 20,000 acres from King Ranch and began two settlements, Riviera, and Riviera Beach, so named because Koch thought the coast resembled the French Riviera. He sold farm tracts and brought in trainloads of prospective buyers.

Koch built the Buena Vista Hotel, on Ebony Hill, with a captain's walk on the roof that provided a good view of Baffin Bay for the prospective land-buyers. He added a pleasure pier and bathhouse and spent $100,000 to build a railroad line, the Riviera Beach and Western Railroad (R.B.& W.), to run six miles between Riviera and Riviera Beach. It was one of the shortest and shortest-lived railroads in the world.

Riviera Beach, with its hotel, school, post office, and stores, flourished until it was wiped out by the 1916 storm. The storm destroyed almost every building at Riviera Beach and leveled several structures at Riviera. The hotel was left a derelict amid bare concrete foundations where homes and stores once stood. The railroad tracks were sold for scrap and the abandoned hotel burned in 1952.

—*Dec. 21, 2016*

Wooden causeway destroyed in 1933

Drivers were crossing over open water on wooden
planks and had to steer carefully to keep their cars from
jumping out of the u-shaped troughs and into the water.
Model-T's sometimes had to be fished from the Laguna
Madre.

The Don Patricio Causeway opened to traffic on July 4, 1927,
giving Corpus Christi access to Padre Island. The causeway was
the big thing of 1927 after the big thing of 1926, the port.

The island had long been the cattle ranch of Patrick F. Dunn,
known as Don Patricio, which gave the new causeway its name.
Until the causeway was built the island was hard to get to.
Fishermen had to get permission from one of Dunn's agents and
then they could cross the Laguna Madre by wagon or horseback,
following an oyster reef, or take a boat.

The island had long been used as a passageway to the border.
In 1845 Zachary Taylor's officers explored Padre, looking for a
route the army could take to the Rio Grande. The report by Lt.
George Meade said the island formed an excellent natural road
but that it was "not suitable for large groups of men camping
together." Taylor chose an inland route.

Texas Rangers would ride down the island to Brownsville. In
crossing the Laguna Madre, one wrote, it looked like they were
going to sea on horseback, with waves splashing against their
stirrups and saddles.

In 1879 Pat Dunn established a ranch on the island, called El
Rancho de Don Patricio. His men dug seep tanks in the sand and
made corrals of driftwood. Dunn sold the island in 1926 to Col.

Two women and children on the Don Patricio Causeway, which opened to traffic on July 4, 1927. Crossing the wooden troughs built on pilings cost motorists $3 for a round trip. The causeway was located a mile south of the present causeway. Photo by Doc McGregor.

Sam Robertson, who had big money behind him with the backing of wealthy oilmen from Kansas City (Albert Jones, Frank Jones, and J.M. Parker).

Col. Robertson was an army engineer. He helped build the St. Louis, Brownsville and Mexico Railroad, and served as a scout for Gen. Pershing during the border troubles with Pancho Villa. Robertson commanded artillery in France in World War I.

Robertson planned to develop the island as a pleasure resort, with a toll road called the Ocean Beach Driveway. On the lower end he built the Sportsmen's Hotel, the Twenty-Five-Mile Hotel and ran a ferry between Port Isabel and South Padre.

One of the Kansas City investors, J. M. Parker, told reporters, "The beaches on the island are better than can be found anywhere. Swimming and fishing can be enjoyed any time of the year. This place will have something to offer that no other section of the country can compete with."

On the north end the linchpin was the Don Patricio Causeway, built across the Laguna Madre at a ford called The Crossing. The pile-raised wooden causeway cost $95,000, about the same as $1.3 million in today's dollars, and was strictly functional, befitting the design of a military engineer.

It was a little more than three miles long and consisted of double wooden tracks built on 3,903 cedar pilings. It had a drawbridge in the middle to allow fishing boats to pass through.

The causeway opened at 9 a.m. on Monday, July 4, 1927. Col. Sam drove the first car across with civic leaders Edwin Flato and Lorine Jones Spoonts, president of the Chamber of Commerce. Behind them a long line of cars waited to cross. Toll collectors at a booth on the west end of the causeway were "as busy as a ticket-seller at a circus."

The toll was steep, $3 for a round trip, but people loved the new causeway. It was a complete success. The Corpus Christi Times said that July Fourth on the island was perfect. "The tide was low, the beach in a most inviting condition, and the occasion was a most pleasant one from every standpoint."

Drivers were crossing over open water on wooden planks and had to drive slow and steer carefully to keep their cars from jumping out of the u-shaped troughs — about 14 inches wide and the same depth — and into the water. Model-T's sometimes had to be fished from the Laguna Madre.

It was nearly impossible to keep wheels from rubbing against the planks which chewed up rubber tires. After having to replace a set of tires, the causeway may have lost some of its charm for some but it was still averaging 75 automobiles a day.

The Caller said this gave Corpus Christi a 70-mile scenic loop: across the Don Patricio Causeway, up Mustang Island to Port Aransas, across the ferry to Aransas Pass, and back to Corpus Christi over the state highway. That first month tolls were paid for 1,800 cars and for 2,500 the second month. Much of the traffic was by fishermen heading for Corpus Christi Pass.

Col. Sam's timing could not have been worse. Two years after the causeway opened came the Wall Street crash, which was followed by the Great Depression. He was forced to sell his island interests to one of the Kansas City oilmen, Albert Jones.

Then came a bad hurricane season in 1933. Storms destroyed the Twenty-Five-Mile Hotel and wrecked the Sportsmen's Hotel (it was rebuilt from salvage and renamed the Surf Side Inn). The last to drive over the causeway was an island squatter named Louis Rawalt, who inched his way across in his Model-A Ford,

The Don Patricio Causeway was a favorite place for fishermen, though anglers moved from one side to the other when a car approached. The causeway was destroyed by a hurricane on Sept. 5, 1933. Photo by Doc McGregor.

in pitch darkness, with hammering rain and screaming winds, as storm tides overflowed the causeway.

He made it to the mainland, a narrow escape for an hour later the causeway was demolished. Planks from the wrecked structure were found on King Ranch 20 miles away. The causeway was never rebuilt. Getting to the island was again reserved for the most determined, like Louis Rawalt, who put his Model-A on a homemade raft and poled his way across the laguna.

The connection between the mainland and the northern part of the island was broken and not re-established until the JFK Causeway was completed in 1950. Col. Sam died on Aug. 22, 1938. With a little luck, Col. Sam Robertson might have been to Padre Island what Henry Flagler was to Miami and Florida's Atlantic coast. The Great Depression and a storm in 1933 got in the colonel's way or, as Robert Burns once wrote, the best-laid plans of mice and men often go awry.

—Dec. 28, 2016

Chapter 54

Life and times of John McClane

The Pennsylvania sheepman was sheriff of Nueces
County in the troubled times after the war when cattle
rustlers and cross-border bandits cut a violent swath
across South Texas.

John McClane came to Corpus Christi in 1856 with a shipment
of merino sheep for Richard King from his father's farm in
western Pennsylvania. McClane stayed in Texas and soon had his
own flocks.

During the Civil War McClane was a blockade runner, carrying
cotton to Matamoros in an old sloop and bringing back military
supplies and tobacco for Confederate troops. His blockade-
running ended when he had to abandon ship and wade ashore to
escape capture.

When the war ended he became friendly with Union
occupation officers and in 1867 the military authorities appointed
him sheriff of Nueces County. McClane had stockpiled his wool
clips during the war and he made a deal with a Union Army
quartermaster named Daniel Haverty to sell 52,000 pounds of
wool in New Orleans. Haverty sold the wool and skipped out
with the money, which amounted to $21,000, the equivalent of
$321,000 today.

McClane found Haverty in Chicago and brought him back to
Corpus Christi. He locked him up in an iron cage kept in the
1854 courthouse. Despite his criminal record, Haverty had
influence with the ruling authorities. In June 1868 a military
board ordered his release and declared the office of sheriff
vacant.

John McClane at his home on Mesquite Street. He was a sheepman from Pennsylvania who brought a shipment of merino bucks for King Ranch in 1856. He stayed in South Texas and became sheriff of Nueces County during the violent times of Reconstruction. He died at his home on April 1, 1911.

McClane followed Haverty back to Chicago and filed a civil suit to reclaim his $21,000. There was little love in Chicago for ex-Confederates; McClane was held in jail for eight months until he agreed to drop the suit. McClane had exhausted all the options, except giving up. The wool money was gone. (This incident is told by Mary Sutherland in "The Story of Corpus Christi.")

In 1870 McClane was again appointed sheriff by Gov. E. J. Davis and he was later elected and served until 1876. He was sheriff in troubled times when cattle rustlers and bandits wearing crossed bandoliers cut a violent swath across South Texas.

On May 9, 1874 bandits killed four men at Morton's store at Peñascal on Baffin Bay. Two of the bandits were tried and sentenced to death. On Aug. 7, 1874 McClane gave them a drink of whisky and escorted them to a scaffold on the 1854 courthouse where they were promptly hanged.

The following year bandits terrorized Nuecestown and when the alarm spread to Corpus Christi McClane rode the streets, shouting, "Close your windows! Bar your doors! Arm yourselves! Protect the town!"

When McClane's term as sheriff ended in 1876 the books were audited and a shortfall of $13,000 was discovered. McClane sent word by Pat Whelan to Richard King, his lifelong friend, about the problem. King told Whelan, "Well, tell him I'll fix it." King hired an accountant who found that McClane's books balanced to the penny.

John McClane died at his home in the 1100 block of Mesquite on April 1, 1911. He was a sheepman, blockade runner in the Civil War, and sheriff of Nueces County during the bloody and violent times of Reconstruction.

Remember Muttera's Federal Bakery?

Sometime ago I was asked by one of my readers to write about Muttera's Federal Bakery, which monopolized the downtown baked goods trade for three decades or more. It was long gone by the time I got here, but several people told me about Muttera's and a little search through library files told me more.

The bakery was in the middle of the 600 block of Chaparral, facing east, across from the Palace Theater. It was established in 1919 and stayed in business into the 1950s. This was when Chaparral was a great thoroughfare, the street filled with cars and people. The 600 block was the heart of downtown and downtown was the heart of the city, which was more confined, compressed, and much smaller than it is today.

In 1919 Fred and Mae Muttera moved to Corpus Christi from Springfield, Ill. They rented an apartment across from Artesian Park and opened a bakery two blocks south on Chaparral.

A week later, on Sept. 14, the downtown and North Beach were devastated by the 1919 hurricane. Fred and Mae slept through the storm during the night and awoke next morning to find five feet of seawater below their second-floor apartment.

The bakery was gone, swept away like all the other homes and stores.

Fred Muttera bought a building a few doors down from the original site and opened Muttera's Federal Bakery. When he died in 1935 his widow Mae and his son William (Bill) ran the bakery.

In an interview in 1946 Bill Muttera said in the old days baking was all guesswork but it had turned into a scientific skill requiring precise measurements and attention to temperature, time, and the mixing of ingredients. The pastries, cakes and fancy bread at Muttera's, it was said, went down like a treat.

After Bill Muttera died in 1949 the bakery was run for several years by Wilbur Morse, who later worked as a bank teller and would tell people he decided to keep his hand in dough. The bakery was closed in 1958.

Two people have told me about their memories of Muttera's. Harriet Tillman said she grew up a block outside the city limits on the West Side and each Friday she and her mother would take the bus downtown, do some shopping at Perkins and go through the tunnel to downtown.

"On Chaparal there were three five-and-dime stores and Muttera's Bakery in one block," Harriet Tillman said. "We always stopped at the bakery and mother would buy a coffee cake and Wilbur would give us a cookie. If mother needed something from Penney's or K Wolens, we would cross the street and shop. My dad would pick us up on his way home from work. Friday was always a special day."

Tom Stewart knew the Mutteras well. He lived on Atlantic Street where the Muttera family had two homes. "Fred died the year I was born," Stewart said, "but I remember his widow as a generous person. Mae would give gingerbread cookies to children who came into the bakery with their parents." After the bakery was closed, Stewart said, "Mrs. Muttera stored the bakery recipes in their garage on Atlantic. They were lost when hurricane Celia hit. What I remember best were their butter biscuits, the angel food squares with white icing, and their salt-rising bread which made wonderful toast."

—*Jan. 4, 2017*

Strange fruit

Hanging had its own language. A man hanged kicked up
his heels in a Texas cakewalk, danced in the air, or
trimmed a tree. Mesquite, cottonwood, or post-oak, it
was said, produced human fruit.

Every community in South Texas in the 19th Century had its
hanging tree and the language was filled with veiled euphemisms
to hide the reality of what were often acts of coldblooded murder.
Some of those who were hanged were guilty of no crimes; they
simply were unlucky enough to be at the wrong place at the
wrong time.

Hanging had its own language. A man hanged was the guest at
a necktie party, dressed in hemp four-in-hand. He died with a
rope necklace, or of hemp fever, or he took a short ride under a
stout limb. He kicked up his heels in a Texas cakewalk, danced
in the air, or trimmed a tree. He was hung out to dry in a horse's
nightcap. Mesquite, cottonwood, or post-oak, it was said,
produced human fruit.

When five rustlers were caught in Matagorda County, a posse
strung them up on a dead tree. Shanghai Pierce, who led the
posse, said of the hangings, "You never can tell just how much
human fruit that dead tree might have borne had it only been
green."

Accounts of random hangings comprise a sad record of violent
times when South Texas was a lethal place.

On March 27, 1849, a vaquero who worked for Henry Kinney
was killed near Love's Ranch on the Nueces River. It was not a

hanging, but it started out as one. The Corpus Christi Star said two men tried to hang the vaquero but the limb broke. They tried a second time, but the limb broke again. They slashed his throat and left him with the noose around his neck. As it happened, a young boy came upon the scene and ran away. Two men were arrested for the crime but managed to escape.

At Port Lavaca in 1852 a man named Augustus Sharkey, a new arrival, bragged that he had killed three men in Mississippi. He got into a quarrel with a local man and attacked him with a slingshot. Sheriff James Fulkerson confiscated the slingshot and Sharkey returned with a rifle and shot the sheriff in the heart. He told bystanders, bragging again, he was the best shot in Texas. Sharkey was taken from the jail that night by a mob of irate citizens and next morning the best shot in Texas was found "trimming a tree."

Several men were hanged in Goliad during the Cart War of 1857. This was a fight between Anglo freighters, with four-wheeled wagons, and Hispanic freighters, who used old two-wheeled oxcarts. There was a big business hauling freight from the port at Indianola to San Antonio along the Cart Road.

Mexican-American cartmen, who lived simply and charged lower rates, claimed a greater share of the business. In retaliation, Anglo freighters destroyed oxcarts and killed Hispanic freighters. Some of the instigators behind the Cart War instigators were hanged from the hanging tree on the courthouse square in Goliad.

One account said as many as nine men were hanged from the old Goliad oak, which brought the Cart War to a close, but the Anglo freighters, as a result of the violent attacks on Hispanic and Mexican cart-men, came to dominate the Cart Road business.

In 1858, an old Mexican-American man was hanged in Live Oak County. A notice printed in Corpus Christi's newspaper, the Nueces Valley, said the vigilante committee of Live Oak County denounced the hanging and said it took no part in the incident. Members of the committee said the old man was innocent of the crime of being an accomplice of a band of Indians who had committed outrages in the area. The vigilante committee said the lynching was done by hard men from Atascosa County.

On Monday, Oct. 10, 1860, a man named Jesus Garcia was found hanging from a tree on the Agua Dulce Creek near Petronila. The Corpus Christi Ranchero said there was no trace of the killers and that, "Who done it, and what it was done for, is a mystery."

About 1860 a black man was charged with killing a man named Peter Dugat in Refugio and a mob took the black man from the jail and hung him from the courthouse windows.

The body of a man named R. J. Tevis was found suspended from a post-oak limb near Refugio on Feb. 21, 1861. The Ranchero said that Tevis was well known as "a professional dealer in other people's cattle" and had been advised to leave the county, and, failing to do so, had received his just desserts.

In 1862, the second year of the war, two Confederate deserters were hanged in Corpus Christi with signs pinned to their chests reading "Traitors Take Warning" and "Union Men Beware." The incident was noted by Thomas Noakes, a Confederate soldier from Nuecestown, who wrote in his diary for May 9, 1862 that his company marched into Corpus Christi "to a place above the town where a couple of deserters were hanging from a tree."

One of the most infamous hangings of the war occurred near Brownsville off the mouth of the Rio Grande. Corpus Christi Judge E. J. Davis, an outspoken supporter of the Union and fierce opponent of secession, went to Matamoros and organized the 1st Texas Cavalry, U.S.A., which was made up of Unionists like himself. Confederates were so eager to capture Davis they crossed into Mexico, in flagrant violation of Mexican sovereignty. They had learned that Davis and an aide, Capt. W. W. Montgomery, were staying at a hotel in Bagdad, Mexico waiting to board a ship.

The Confederate raiding party captured Davis and Montgomery and hustled them by rowboat across the river. The Confederates promptly hanged Montgomery and were in the process of putting a rope around the neck of E. J. Davis when Confederate Gen. Hamilton Bee arrived and stopped them.

Bee ordered Davis to be returned to the Mexican side with profuse apologies to Mexican authorities for violating their territory. Lt. Col. Arthur James Lyon Fremantle, a British military observer, saw the remains of Montgomery's body. He had been partly buried, with his head above ground and the frayed rope used to hang him still around his neck, said Fremantle.

Many believed that Montgomery, who was fond of taunting Confederates from his perceived sanctuary on Mexican soil, got what he deserved. As for E. J. Davis, he went on to become governor of Texas during Reconstruction. But at that time in March 1863, when Montgomery was hanged, he came within an eyelash of being the honored guest at his own necktie party.

—Jan. 11, 2017

The hanging of Chipita Rodriguez

Chipita sat on a wooden box of undressed planks for the
short ride to the river, a thousand yards from the
courthouse. She was wearing a white dress with blue
trim and a woman in town had fixed her hair.

The worst example of hanging times was that of Chipita
Rodriguez, the first woman legally executed in Texas. Some
believed then and later she was innocent and her hanging was a
legal lynching.

Events leading to Chipita's execution happened in 1863. John
Savage was on his way to Mexico with $600 in gold to buy
horses for the Confederacy. On Sunday night, Aug. 23, 1863, he
stopped at Chipita's cabin where the San Patricio Road reached
the Aransas River. A traveler could stop at Chipita's for a meal
and sleep on her porch. Chipita (her real name may have been
Josefa) came to Texas as a girl before the Revolution.

Savage stayed the night at Chipita's. Next morning a servant
from John Welder's ranch was washing clothes in the Aransas
River when she found a body in a burlap bag. It was Savage. His
head had been split open with an axe.

San Patricio Sheriff William Means found blood on Chipita's
porch. She said it was chicken blood. Her handyman, Juan
Silvera, of limited understanding, told the sheriff he helped
Chipita dump the body in the river. The sheriff did not find a
motive. It was not robbery. Savage's $600 in gold was in his
saddlebags. Sheriff Means arrested Chipita and Silvera and took
them to the courthouse, where they were chained to a wall.

The judge assigned to hear the case was Benjamin F. Neal, a lawyer and newspaperman who was the first mayor of Corpus Christi. At the start of the war Neal commanded a Confederate artillery company. When District Judge John McKinney died, Neal was elected to fill the vacancy on the 14th District Court. The court's fall docket included the trial of Juan Silvera and Chipita Rodriguez.

The trial was irregular. Sheriff Means served on the grand jury that indicted Chipita. Four members of the trial jury were under indictment for felonies, including murder. The foreman was a friend of the sheriff. Chipita would not assist in her defense.

The trial began on Friday morning, Oct. 9, 1863. The jury brought back a verdict at noon. Silvera was found guilty of second-degree murder and Chipita was found guilty of first-degree murder. The jury urged the court to show mercy for Chipita — "on account of her old age and the circumstantial evidence against her." Judge Neal sentenced Silvera to five years in prison and chose to ignore the plea for mercy. He sentenced Chipita to be hanged on Nov. 13, 1863.

When the day arrived, Judge Neal was gone and Sheriff Means was out of town. John Gilpin, the hangman, was entrusted with carrying out the execution, which normally was a responsibility of the sheriff.

Gilpin borrowed a farm cart and team of oxen. Chipita sat on a wooden box of undressed planks for the short ride to the river, a thousand yards from the courthouse. She was wearing a white dress with blue trim and a woman in town had fixed her hair. She was smoking a corn-shuck cigarette.

The wagon stopped at two mesquite trees by the river, one of which was used for the occasion. A rope was fixed around Chipita's neck and the sentence read. A lash of the whip moved the oxen forward but Chipita was so slight and the oxen moved so slow that the fall did not snap her neck. It took some time for her to strangle to death. An elderly man turned away and said, "It's a black day for San Patricio." She was buried in the plain wooden box under the hanging tree.

Corpus Christi had its own hanging three years later, a lynching, though there was no doubt of the victim's guilt. On

May 15, 1866, Jim Garner went into a store on Chaparral to buy boots. The storekeeper, named Emanuel Scheuer, knew Garner because both men had served in W.S. Shaw's Confederate militia company. Scheuer was a corporal and Garner a private.

That day at the store, Garner tried on a pair of boots and was about to leave without paying for them when Scheuer said he couldn't give him credit. Garner, without a moment's hesitation, shot Scheuer in the heart, killing him instantly.

Scheuer was laid out on his own store counter. He was a respected member of the community while Garner was a loafer who had killed a man in a saloon brawl when he was 16, in Helena. He had killed several others since.

Feelings were running high in the town. John Fogg, who owned saloon and livery, took charge of a mob that was forming. Fogg crossed Chaparral to Noessel's store (at the northwest corner of William) and grabbed a long rope. Garner was dragged to Noessel's where one end of the new rope was thrown over a sign that extended out from the store but Mrs. Noessel was adamant against using her store for a hanging and shooed the mob away.

They moved down Chaparral. Garner pleaded, "Give me a trial, boys! Give me a trial!" But the members of the mob showed a complete lack of sympathy. They stopped at the Meuly house, known as the house with an iron front because of its fancy wrought-iron balcony on the second floor. But before they could throw the rope over the balcony, Margaret Meuly ran them off, refusing to allow her home to be used for a lynching.

The mob dragged Garner down the block to the arroyo where there were a few stunted hackberry and mesquite trees. One tree had a limb just barely high enough for the job. The rope was attached to the limb.

Capt. John Anderson, who was there, said, "A lot of us boys caught hold of the rope down near the end. He kicked and kicked. The crowd was quiet. Everybody left pretty quick."

Helen Chapman wrote in her diary — "A terrible tragedy just enacted. An unoffending good citizen shot dead by a drunken loafing scoundrel who had killed several men before. About 50 citizens carried the murderer to the edge of town and hung him at once." W. S. Rankin said it was a terrible thing. "I didn't sleep for a week. I couldn't shut my eyes without seeing that tongue sticking out."

The day after the hanging Garner's father came with a wagon to take away the body and said, with no signs of sorrow, that he had gained a good long stake rope by the operation.

—Jan. 18, 2017

Busy time for the rope

"After satisfying ourselves that these were the only men
implicated in the murder and robbery, we took them to
Mean's village." —John Dunn

Texans have nostalgic feelings for frontier times. We admire
the spirit, hardiness and no-nonsense approach to life. But that
was also a time of casual lynching when scores were settled and
blood debts repaid with interest. It was a time when people took
direct action, without the sanction of law, to impose their sense
of order.

Law enforcement was mainly limited to the towns. Ranchers
and those who lived in the country protected themselves. They
banded together in vigilante groups and were not timid about
using a stiff rope and a short drop. The attitude was, who needs
lawyers, judges and legal precedent? "We got the guilty party,"
they would say. Sometimes it was true, but probably just as often
it was not.

The Nueces Valley reported — "The Mexican who shot
Sullivan, the butcher at Culver's Packery, was found hanging in a
thicket outside Nuecestown. The coroner's jury returned a
verdict of hanging by unknown parties."

Hobart Huson in his history of Refugio wrote, "Archey Reeves
at Ingleside found a Mexican hanging near the Corpus Christi
reef." . . . "James Hart was present at Corpus Christi when they
took a Mexican boy and brought him to the mott at Doyle's
Water Hole and five of Dan Doughty's vigilante company were
seen to go into the mott with the boy who was found hanging."

In January 1872, the Nueces Valley newspaper reported that a vaquero broke into the Elliff ranch house at Banquete while "Si" Elliff was away and Mrs. Elliff was visiting a neighbor. When Mrs. Elliff and her friend, Mrs. Hunter, came home they surprised the intruder. He threatened them with an ax. Mrs. Hunter, though 72, was able to wrest the ax away from him. The man was reportedly lynched by a mob at Banquete although some said he died from a loss of blood from a cut he received when he broke a window.

One of the worst crimes of the hanging era was committed on May 9, 1874 at Peñascal. This was a settlement with one store 50 miles south of Corpus Christi on Baffin Bay. John Morton, the store owner, his brother and two customers were brutally killed in a robbery.

Near sundown a cook was returning from the well with a bucket of water hid when he saw a band of 11 riders dismount. He heard shots and saw Herman Tilgner, a customer, run out. He was shot and killed. Michael Morton, brother of the store owner, was shot in the head and F. M. Coakley was tied up and executed. The store owner was shot in both arms, forced to carry out the thieves' plunder, then shot to death, his body riddled with bullets.

The alarm spread quickly. A posse led by "Red" John Dunn, which included several in his family, rode to Morton's store. There they found a trail of brown sugar that had leaked from one of the bags the bandits had stolen. The trail told them the killers were riding toward Corpus Christi, not the border as expected.

The posse scoured the country. A man told them he had seen sheepherders staying in an old jacal on the Nueces River. The posse reached the sheep pen at midnight where they found Hypolita Tapia and Andres Davila. "After satisfying ourselves that these were the only men implicated in the murder and robbery," Dunn wrote in "Perilous Trails," "we took them to Mean's village (Meansville)."

The two suspects were questioned but revealed nothing. Hypolita Tapia was taken out and a rope put around his neck as if they meant to hang him. Perhaps they did. But it helped to concentrate his mind and revise his attitude. He began to talk.

Tapia told them a Corpus Christi policeman overheard there would be a shipment of goods and money going to Peñascal by boat. He wanted to get 10 men to go get it. Tapia agreed to do it and got 10 men to go with him, including Davila and an American named Joe. At Peñascal, Tapia said, the boat carrying the shipment was sighted near shore and they assumed it had already landed, but it had not. When they hit the store the raiders found only $13 in the cash drawer.

Tapia and Davila were delivered to Sheriff John McClane for trial. Five other Mexican-Americans were arrested who were not implicated in the crime. Threats were made to burn Corpus Christi and free the prisoners. Armed citizens patrolled around the jail to prevent a surprise attack.

Tapia and Davila were found guilty and sentenced to be hanged on Friday, Aug. 7, 1874. Tapia asked to marry his common-law wife. The day before the hanging the two prisoners were shaved and dressed in white shirts and black pants. Tapia's friends and relatives attended the wedding at the jail.

Next day Tapia and Davila were still wearing white shirts and black pants from the wedding when they were escorted to the scaffold built from the second floor of the 1854 Courthouse by Sheriff McClane. Tapia's last words were — "My friends, I am here today to die by hanging. I have killed no person nor helped kill anyone. The people forced the party that was guilty to swear against me. But it is all right. Goodbye." Davila stared at the ground and said nothing.

A third suspect, the man who shot the storeowner, was taken out of the San Diego jail and "given a chance to look at the sky for the last time." A fourth suspect, the American named Joe, was identified as Joseph Delera, also known by the alias of Joseph Shane and "Jose el Americano." He was arrested in Matamoros by Brownsville police and "met some sort of accident" on the way to Corpus Christi. The policeman behind the attack was never brought to justice.

After the Peñascal slayings a Committee of Public Safety was formed in Corpus Christi. "Committee" did not mean what you might think it means. This "committee" wasn't started to hold meetings and keep minutes. It was a vigilante outfit. Similar committees were organized across South Texas. They were often called minutemen because they were supposed to be ready to ride at a moment's notice. They were the violent product of violent times.

—*Jan. 25, 2017*

Tragedy on Saus Creek

"What I saw at the Swift ranch changed me from a
simple-hearted country boy to a hard-nerved man boiling
for revenge." —John Young

On June 7, 1874, a Saturday, Thad Swift, a deaf sheep rancher who lived on the Saus Creek in Refugio County, took his wool clip to St. Mary's and sold it for $700, paid out in silver dollars. That night Swift was murdered, horribly cut to pieces, and his wife stabbed 25 times, her body left to be mangled by hogs. The Swifts' three small daughters woke to find the bodies of their parents. The oldest, who was eight, took her sisters to their uncle's house three miles away.

Word of the murders on Saus Creek traveled with lightning speed. The result was like kicking an anthill. Minutemen were riding in all directions, looking for suspects and longing for revenge. One of Swift's hands was named Juan Flores. He was with Swift when he sold the wool clip in St. Mary's and knew about the $700 in silver. He disappeared after the murders. A posse called Uncle Henry Scott's Minutemen followed the trail of Flores toward Laredo. Scott, a rancher who lived nearby, was considered to be a fair but harsh man.

Another posse was led by Edward Fennessey. It headed toward a ranch near Goliad, steered there by a cowhand named John Young. He became famous as the co-author, with J. Frank Dobie, of "A Vaquero of the Brush Country." Young in "Vaquero" said — "What I saw at the Swift ranch changed me from a simple-hearted country boy to a hard-nerved man boiling for revenge."

Young told the posse he knew of a "bad Mexican" named Moya who might have been involved in the killings. He offered no evidence beyond the fact that he was known to carry a sharp knife.

Based on this slim assumption the posse rode toward the Moya Ranch in Goliad County. They found the Moyas barricaded inside their house. They refused to come out. One yelled, "What do you want?" A member of the posse, Dan Holland, peered into a chink hole and yelled, "We want you." One of the Moyas fired and a bullet hit Holland in the head, killing him instantly. The posse laid siege to the ranch house, firing at random into the chink holes, trying to hit the shadowy Moyas inside.

While the Moya family was barricaded inside their home, the sheriff of Goliad County, Phil Fulcord, arrived and took charge. He urged the Moyas to come out, telling them they would be under the full protection of the law. They came out. There were two Moya brothers, Antonio and Marcelo, and their aging father. The sheriff convinced the Refugio minutemen to let him and his posse take the Moyas to Goliad.

After the sheriff and the prisoners left, the minutemen changed their minds. Young described what happened. "A lot of us did not propose to put off a punishment that we knew the Mexicans deserved. The guard and prisoners had only gone about three miles when we surrounded them. The guard offered practically no interference."

In the mêlée that followed the two Moya brothers and their father were killed — shot, beaten and stabbed to death. This wasn't just anger over the Swift murders. It was hatred. And there was no basis in truth that they had been involved in the Swift murders. Confusion about who the villains were seemed to be a recurring theme back then.

In Refugio County, Mexican-Americans suspected of complicity in the Swift murders were rounded up and taken to the courthouse at Refugio. Judge W. L. Rea, quoted in Hobart Huson's "Refugio" said, "I remember three were brought in and chained up in rooms of the old concrete courthouse. One night a mob took the three from the jail and hung them on the Saus Creek. I had seen them in the jail that morning."

The Weekly Gazette in Corpus Christi reported the incident with obvious approval. "Reliable information has reached us of the whereabouts of three of the Swift murderers. They were seen hanging on a tree near the house of Swift, two below and one above. Two of them were brothers, Silvestre and Refugio Flores, both well-known in Corpus Christi. The other had several aliases, including Pancho Luna. They were captured and lodged in jail, from whence they were violently taken and put on a limb. Three villains, long known as suspected horse thieves, were caught in their evil deeds and have gone to answer for their crimes." Their true connection to the main suspect or the crime was not established.

Henry Scott's Minutemen trailed Juan Flores who crossed into Mexico at Laredo. Scott sent a man across the river to make a deal with Mexican authorities. Some accounts say Scott paid $1,000 out of his own pocket to bribe officials to return Flores. The suspect was brought back to Refugio, tried and convicted. Before his sentence was carried out the condemned man, stoic to the end, admitted his guilt and expressed remorse from the scaffold.

Judge Rea in "Refugio" said Flores was hanged on the outskirts of town. "It was the first legal hanging in Refugio County and a large crowd turned out. I was present with the rest. Flores approached his end bravely and made a speech from the scaffold. He admitted his guilt and admonished the spectators not to act as he did, so that they would not come to the same terrible end."

One of the most horrific lynching incidents of the 1870s occurred when a posse led by Shanghai Pierce caught a gang of rustlers near Carancahua Creek in Matagorda County. There were three Lunn brothers, a stranger, and John Smith, who was called "All-Jaw" because of the shape of his face.

They had been killing and skinning cattle that didn't belong to them. They were caught with the bloody hides in their wagon, surrounded by a posse of 80 men led by Pierce. They were executed on the spot, all left hanging from the limbs of a dead tree. It presents an image in the mind, a tableau as it were, with a dead tree and dead weights gently turning in the wind. Pierce, the

Cattleman Shanghai Pierce led a large posse that caught and lynched five suspected cattle rustlers in Matagorda County.

great cattleman, a loud and profane man with foghorn voice, said, "You never can tell just how much human fruit that old dead tree might have borne had it only been green."

—Feb. 1, 2017

Lynchings after the Nuecestown Raid

Sidney Borden stood by as the pro-hanging crowd took
the two men off into the brush. They returned without
the prisoners. One of the hanged men was a Laredo
merchant, the other his servant.

The Nueces Valley newspaper in Corpus Christi urged
vigilante action in response to lawless conditions of the 1870s.
The newspaper editorial said, "Let the mesquite branches show
the fruits of their labor." This was akin to promoting murder as a
civic exercise. In that context, in the wake of the Peñascal
slayings and Swift murders, came the notorious Nuecestown
Raid.

In the last week of March 1875, a bunch of 33 bandits crossed
the river into Texas from below Rio Grande City and rode
towards Corpus Christi. They arrived on Thursday, March 25 and
camped on the Oso. After sunrise on Good Friday the bandits
ransacked two ranch houses and rode on to the Juan Saenz
community. At George Frank's store they swapped their boots
for new ones, took $80 from the cash drawer, and killed an old
Hispanic man who worked for Frank.

The roads were filled with people heading to Corpus Christi for
church services. The bandits took those they encountered
hostage. Rancher George Reynolds, his two daughters, their
governess Adele DeBerry, and ranch hand Fred Franks were
captured. When the bandits told Reynolds to take off his clothes,
he refused. The bandits didn't insist but made Fred Franks take
off his boots and trousers. Then they captured Henry Gilpin,

Laura Allen, Sidney Borden, Mrs. E. D. Sidbury and her daughter.

The bandits forced their captives to run as they headed for Nuecestown. One who knew Henry Gilpin shouted, "Andale! Don Enriquez! Andale!" One captive, Joe Howell, complained about having to run in his bare feet so they made him put on Laura Allen's slippers. He ran for a bit then sat down and refused to move. The bandits jumped their horses over him but left him behind unharmed.

As they herded the hostages along UpRiver Road four men from the numerous Dunn family trailed behind, keeping their eye on the bandits ahead of them. The bandits had Sidney Borden on foot and were forcing him up the road at a trot while one was riding Borden's prized race horse. Near Frank's store the Dunns and the bandits watched each other but kept a wary distance. There were too many for the Dunns to handle and the bandits were not disposed to initiate a fight.

Word reached Corpus Christi before noon. The alarm was sounded by James Hunter, who had escaped capture when Sidney Borden was taken. Sheriff John McClane lathered his horse riding the streets, urging people to stay inside and bar their doors. Women and children boarded the steamship Aransas and a lumber schooner and they moved out into the bay for safety.

At a meeting at Market Square several men agreed to form a posse to ride to Nuecestown to take on the bandits. Sheriff McClane tried to stop them. He warned that every man was needed to protect the town. Those joining the posse were George Swank, a roofer, Pat Whelan, brickmaker, Pat McManigle, bartender, Jesus Seguira, "Wash" Mussett, and Clem Vetters.

At Thomas Noakes' store at Nuecestown a man called "Lying" John came in to buy flour. As Noakes was getting it he saw the bandits ride up and as one raised his pistol to shoot "Lying" John, Noakes grabbed his Winchester and fired, hitting the bandit in the chest.

Noakes' wife ran from the store with their children. Noakes and "Lying" John scuttled through a trap door and hid under the floor. The raiders plundered the store then started a fire. After seeing her children to safety, Mrs. Noakes returned and poured

Sydney Borden led a posse that lynched two men near the Borjas Ranch in Duval County in the aftermath of the Nuecestown Raid.

water on the fire to put it out. Several times a bandit restarted the fire only to have her put it out before the flames took hold.

With the store on fire, "Lying" John left his hiding place and ran for it. He was shot and shot again as he lay on the ground. Noakes had his Winchester and was ready to shoot it out when Mrs. Noakes yelled that the bandits were gone. Mrs. Noakes ran into the burning store to save a prized feather bed.

The bandits took their plunder and captives and camped in the brush. When the posse rode up one shot was fired, killing George Swank, then the posse and bandits exchanged fire. The bandits escaped, leaving the captives behind.

The posse found a wounded raider, the man Noakes shot, who was placed in a cart to take to Corpus Christi. "Lying" John had been shot four times but survived. He said he was shot eight times.

On Saturday morning, Sidney Borden, who had been captured by the bandits the day before, arrived with a posse he raised at Sharpsburg. As they rode west past Borjas Ranch they captured two men. Most of the posse wanted to hang them. Borden argued that there was nothing to link them to the raiders.

Borden stood by as the stone-faced pro-hanging crowd took the two men off into the brush with two ropes. They returned without the prisoners. One of the hanged men was a Laredo merchant, the other his servant. The men were guilty only of being close at hand when the posse rode by. They had no connection to the raiders, as the Moya family had no connection to the Swift murders.

Borden's posse rode on to the Rio Grande and gave up. "Boys, I've brought you on a wild-goose chase," Borden said. "We'd better head for home." They turned back, having wasted time hanging two innocent men while the real bandits escaped into Mexico.

The cart with the wounded bandit rumbled into town. A crowd gathered behind it. Dr. Arthur Spohn was fetched to tend the bandit's wound before he was hanged. They drove down Leopard Street, looking for a place to hang him. They looped a rope around the steeple of the original St. Patrick's Church but cattleman Martin Culver ordered them not to desecrate a house of worship.

They found a gate with a convenient cross pole. A noose was put around the wounded bandit's neck. They drove the cart under the cross pole, a rope was thrown over it, the bandit was lifted into the air, and the cart drove on. Next morning priests from St. Patrick's came to take the body down. It was Easter Sunday.

—*Feb. 8, 2017*

Hanging times

"You ain't got no kick coming. You did lots worse
things and we're not going to hang you but once." —
Col. Crump to Pete Baldes

W. G. Sutherland, a teacher known as the Sage of Bluntzer,
told the story of a bad hombre named Pete Baldes who was
captured by a posse led by a Col. Crump.

Baldes, in Sutherland's account, was riding the horse of a man
who had been murdered near Collins. (This settlement was 40
miles west of Corpus Christi in what was then Nueces County,
near today's Alice. It became a ghost town.) As Crump's posse
put a rope around the bad man's neck Baldes asserted his
innocence. Crump told him his guilt or innocence didn't matter.
"You ain't got no kick coming," Crump told him. "You did lots
worse things and we're not going to hang you but once."

One notorious legal hanging happened in Beeville. The story
(told in "A Vaquero of the Brush Country") began when Ed
Singleton and John Dwyer rode out of Beeville for Rockport to
buy a wagonload of whisky. Dwyer planned to open a saloon at
Tilden.

When Dwyer's body was discovered a search began for
Singleton. He was caught boarding a ship at Indianola with
Dwyer's money warm in his pocket. Singleton was tried and
sentenced to be hanged. Since his friends vowed to free him the
sheriff let it be known he was going to move him to Galveston.
Instead of putting him on a train the sheriff took him to a thicket
and chained him to a tree where he kept him for two weeks.

He was brought to Beeville for the hanging. As the time drew near he wrote a will and asked that his body be skinned and the skin stretched over a drumhead and every year on the anniversary of his hanging the drum be beaten to the tune of "Old Mollie Hare." He was hanged on April 27, 1877. His last wishes were ignored.

In 1897, three members of a family, a couple and their daughter, were killed with an axe near Floresville. Farm worker Maximo Martinez was convicted and sentenced to be hanged. On hanging day they gave Martinez whisky in a tin cup and kept refilling the cup while he made speeches and sang songs from inside his jail cell.

W. L. Wright, a deputy sheriff (he later became a Texas Ranger) said a scaffold had been built out from a window of the jail. Wright put a black hood over the man's head and fixed the rope. Wright forgot to move away from the trapdoor, barely managing to jump aside at the last second. He said it would have been like the two Rangers who hanged a man in Brownsville and forgot to get off the trap door. "When the trap was sprung, they went through it, too, and fell six feet to the ground."

It was a gala day in Floresville on July 30, 1897 when the axe killer was hanged. "Everybody turned out," Wright said. "There must have been 4,000 people in town."

One of the worst crimes in Corpus Christi history occurred on April 21, 1902. The body of a young housewife, Eunice Hatch, who lived on a farm west of town, was found with her head split open by a hatchet. An infant daughter was crying in her crib near the woman's body.

A worker at the nearby McCampbell Ranch, Andres Olivares, was arrested. Blood was on his clothes and his shoes matched prints at the murder scene. Some urged Sheriff John Bluntzer to let them have Olivares but Jim Hatch, the husband, stopped any talk of lynching.

Olivares confessed. "I did it, but I do not know what was in me at that moment. I killed that woman, Jim Hatch's wife." Though he pleaded guilty, Judge Stanley Welch ordered a not-guilty plea to be entered. The trial lasted one morning and the jury found him guilty that afternoon. The judge ordered Olivares to be

Eunice Hatch and her husband Jim, believed to be their wedding photo.
She was killed in a brutal hatchet attack by a farmhand, Andres Olivares,
who was hanged in Corpus Christi in 1902.

hanged on June 3, 1902. On hanging day the condemned man was taken to a scaffold at the county jail, the noose fixed around his neck, and Sheriff Bluntzer opened the trap door.

Two years later a man named Apolinario Hernandez was hanged in Corpus Christi, on Dec. 23, 1904, after he had been convicted of murdering his wife in February 1903. The newspaper account said Hernandez was calm as he bid goodbye to those around him. A reporter talked to him before the execution. He confessed to killing his wife and asked to be forgiven if he had offended anyone.

A few days before Christmas in 1914 Harry Hinton, the jailer at the Oakville Jail, took the evening meal to two Mexican-American prisoners. He had been teaching them English, according to a history of Live Oak County, and they would write down a Spanish word and he would translate it into English for them. As the jailer squatted making translations one of the prisoners hit him on the back of the head with an iron bar. It had been slipped into the jail by an accomplice. The deputy was killed by the blow.

The prisoners escaped. One stole a horse and rode west. He was caught in Tilden. The other hid in the brush and was found by Sheriff Tullis. Both men were lynched, without a trial, one inside the jail and the other from a tree in front of the jail.

We have no idea how many people died because of legal and extralegal hangings during the last half of the 19th Century and the early years of the 20th Century. The worst of the hanging era came in the 1870s. The Peñascal robbery led to the deaths of eight men, by noose or bullet, the Swift atrocity also led to eight killings, and the Nuecestown Raid led to five. That is directly, but indirectly, who can say?

Bodies were found hanging from mesquite and live-oak limbs all over. Some were guilty but some were not. This was accepted as people argued that there was more than one way to pursue the end of justice. Remembering those rough perilous times helps us understand what people lived through back in the days when hangings were frequent and violent vigilantes rode the land.

—Feb. 15, 2017

Water Street is awash in history

Piers and wharves off Water Street reflected the city's maritime ambitions. The first pier was built by Hiram Riggs in 1844.

For a century, before the seawall was built, Water Street was the first street along the shore. It was from Water Street that early residents of Corpus Christi lived in close communion with the bay and Gulf beyond.

The story of Water Street begins with Henry Kinney. In 1839, he landed at the mouth of an arroyo, a natural watercourse that in time was named Blucher's Creek. Kinney moved to Texas from Illinois, where his venture to build a canal from the Mississippi to Lake Michigan collapsed, leaving him bankrupt. He came to Texas and opened a store at Aransas City, near where Rockport is today. He bought wool and hides and sold tobacco, cloth and manufactured goods. This was known in local idiom as the Mexican trade.

When Kinney landed at Blucher's Creek he was preparing to move his store from Aransas City to a site on Corpus Christi Bay. The attractions of the site included a high bluff and plateau overlooking a large bay. The beach was a place where goods had been unloaded for shipment to Mexico, called the Old Indian Trading Grounds. While details of Kinney's arrival are few, it was probably in September or October 1839.

The arroyo where Kinney landed emptied into the bay about where Cooper's Alley intersects with Water Street today. The bay at this point had the deepest water along the shore and for

251

that reason the first piers were built in the vicinity. Another natural watercourse was to the north, later called Hall's Bayou, where the port entrance is today. As the city grew Water Street stretched between these two tidal inlets along the shore.

Piers and wharves off Water Street reflected the city's maritime ambitions, despite being hampered by a shallow bay clogged with mudflats. The first pier was built by Hiram Riggs in 1844, located past the end of Lawrence Street. The base of the pier consisted of mattresses of mesquite limbs and brush filled in with shell to weight it down and topped with rough planks. The pier washed away in the early 1850s.

To the south was William Mann's wharf, built in 1848 near where Cooper's Alley joins Water Street today. Mann's wharf was 170-feet long and had a track for handcars leading to a warehouse and complex of buildings. Mann, like Kinney, dealt in the Mexican trade.

Ohler's Wharf was built for Edward Ohler in 1849, from the end of Peoples Street. The Government Wharf was built by John Willet in 1853; it later became the Central Wharf, which stretched into the bay from between Laguna and William streets. The Staples and Sidbury wharves were built in the 1870s to unload shipments of lumber from the pine forests of the South. The Staples Wharf was located off Lawrence Street where the old Riggs' wharf had been. It was washed away by a storm in 1875.

South of the arroyo where Kinney landed became the 100 block of South Water. The arroyo was the dividing line between street's north and south addresses. Here, on the water side, was William Mann's red house, which got the name from the color of the shellcrete bricks. Anna Moore Schwien said her mother, a slave named Malvina, said there were deep pits in the south bluff where the builders dug out red clay to make the bricks for Mann's place.

During an Indian raid in 1848 people forted up behind Mann's walls. The buildings were built around a central courtyard in the Spanish style. The main structure was three stories high, the largest building in town at the time, which included a store, rooms, and the Mann family residence. Traders arriving from

Cornelius Cahill's two-story building, constructed in 1848, in front of the Central Wharf in the 1890s. After Cahill moved to a new structure on Chaparral in 1859 his building on Water Street housed a store and the City Hotel. It was torn down after the 1919 storm.

Mexico to do business with Mann would stay in rooms at the Mann house. Mann's pier was in front of the buildings.

Anna Moore Schwein said after the Civil War the Mann place was used as a hotel, called the Virginia House. It was on the site of the later Guth Park, which is now an empty lot just north of U&I Restaurant.

Annie (Schallert) Bagnall said her parents lived in a house in the first block north of the arroyo, where she was born in 1862. "Mr. and Mrs. Prokop Hoffman lived across the street from us." In the next block, the 200 block, was the old Mullen home, at 203 North Water, which was said to have been one of the first five homes built in Corpus Christi.

Conrad Meuly's bakery was in the 200 block past the intersection of Laguna (now Sartain). Meuly, an immigrant from Switzerland, came to Corpus Christi at the time of Zachary Taylor's encampment in 1845. He built his home on Chaparral behind the bakery. During the Civil War Meuly's bread-and-biscuit bakery was demolished by Union troops, who ripped off the doorways and window frames for firewood.

Down the block from Meuly's bakery was Cornelius Cahill's store and home, which stood facing Central Wharf. Cahill came to Corpus Christi from Peru, Ill., where he knew Henry Kinney, the founder of Corpus Christi, before Kinney came to Texas. Cahill's two-story building, built in 1848 of shellcrete bricks, faced the long wharf that stretched out into the bay. It housed a store and family dwelling on the second floor. City aldermen held their meetings at Cahill's in the 1850s, dances were held there, and mass said at Cahill's before the first St. Patrick's Church was built.

Cahill built a three-story building on Chaparral in 1858, north of Conrad Meuly's home. Cahill's place on Water Street housed a store on the first floor, operated by J. Scott, and the City Hotel on the second. A grand ball was held on March 14, 1860 to celebrate the opening of the City Hotel.

Cahill's on Water Street stood a long time. The weather-beaten building was torn down with great difficulty after it was damaged in the 1919 storm. Dynamite blasts left only small breaks in the thick shellcrete walls, hardly larger than the space made for the dynamite sticks, so workers were forced to undermine the foundations. They used tractors to pull down the walls before they could bring the old building down.

—Feb. 22, 2017

Mail boats docked at Central Wharf

"The coming of the mail boat was announced by the
captain by blowing a cow-horn within a mile of the
town. The mail was brought up from the wharf on a dray
by a man named Webber." —Eli Merriman

Three mail boats made a tri-weekly run from Indianola to
Corpus Christi. They docked at Central Wharf, across from
Cahill's on Water Street. The mail boats were the Emily, the
Agnes and the Henrietta. This was after the Civil War. Before the
war, the mail boats docked at Ohler's Wharf.

"The coming of the mail boat was announced by the captain by
blowing a cow-horn within a mile of the town," longtime
newsman Eli Merriman said. The mail boat arrived on Sunday,
Wednesday, and Friday. "The mail was brought up from the
wharf on a dray by a man named Webber who delivered it to
postmaster Horace Taylor." The mail boat runs ended with the
coming of the railroad.

A cattle chute on Central Wharf was used to load cattle on the
steamships. Cattle shipped by sea were called coasters. "We
could hear the cattle bellowing way up at our house (blocks
away)," said Lillie Anderson Rankin. One resident recalled cattle
jumping into the bay, with men rushing in on horseback to herd
them to shore.

Central Wharf was a busy place during the wool era. The
Corpus Christi Gazette, on May 1, 1875, reported that the
steamer Mary left Central Wharf on April 27, 1875 with 178
bags of wool, 31 bales of hides and skins, five casks of tallow,
266 beeves, 74 calves, 115 mutton and other freight." Next day

the schooner Anna M. Dickenson left with 398 bags of wool, 4,128 dry hides, 294 wet salted hides, 30 bales of skins, and 5,000 horns.

Across from Central Wharf, three doors down from Cahill's, John Graham ran a café that featured, said the Nueces Valley, "fresh fish, oysters, and hot coffee." During the Civil War Graham served as captain of a Confederate militia company, the Mounted Coast Guards.

In the 300 block of Water, between William and Lawrence, was an ice plant built in 1878 and owned by Richard King and John Greer. Before it was built, blocks of lake ice packed in sawdust came in on schooners from Maine. After King's death in 1885 and Greer's soon afterwards, the ice plant was sold to George Blucher. Kate Smith Anderson lived next to Blucher's ice factory for 40 years. "I would gather the bark that fell from the wood at the factory for my own use. I have seen many a cord of wood unloaded at his place for boilers for the factory."

Near the ice plant, on the water side, was John Superach's fish and oyster business. When the Caller printed its first edition, on Jan. 21, 1883, they sent down to Superach's for a bucket of oysters for the pressmen. It was so cold the oysters froze to a block of ice in the bucket. Andrew Anderson said Superach built a pen in the water where he kept turtles to sell.

The Magnolia Saloon, in 1860, was located in the 300 block of Water. The Ranchero, on May 18, 1861 reported that the Magnolia "has been fitted up and opened. A marble-topped billiard table, the finest in western Texas, is at the services of the knights of the cue."

Down the street was James Hunter's Livery. Hunter, a Confederate cavalry officer in Terry's Texas Rangers, opened his livery in 1871. When bandits took hostages and burned Noakes' store in the Easter raid of 1875, Hunter was almost captured but escaped on a fast horse and rode to Corpus Christi to sound the alarm. He was the Paul Revere of the Nuecestown Raid. His livery was where the Water Street Seafood restaurant is today.

In the 400 block, past the Lawrence intersection, were two wool warehouses owned by Perry Doddridge and Uriah Lott. Elizabeth Hart's store, built in 1848, was in this block. Mrs. Hart

What may be the oldest known photograph of Corpus Christi shows Edward Ohler's building at the corner of Peoples and Water, in the early 1850s, not long after it was built in 1849. In the early years, the Ohlers lived upstairs and operated a store below.

from Ireland opened a store in Zachary Taylor's old commissary building at Taylor and Chaparral in 1848 then built her own shellcrete structure on Water Street. Her daughter, Rosalie Hart Priour, wrote an autobiography about the hard times during the Civil War.

In an upstairs room in a building on the corner of Lawrence Henry and William Maltby ran their pro-Confederate, pro-Secessionist newspaper, the Ranchero.

The Byington house, used by Zachary Taylor as his headquarters in 1845, was in the 500 block of Water, between Schatzel and Peoples. Myrtle Calloway, a visitor, was staying in this house in March 1902 when she came down with smallpox. The house was quarantined, a yellow flag flying from the roof, until she recovered and the quarantine was lifted. In 1910 part of the house was demolished and the rest used as a warehouse.

Eli Merriman built a home at 505 N. Water Street, on the corner where the old Swift home once stood, built in 1849 by J.T. Swift. Merriman's daughter Marion (Clemmer) said the older Merriman house was torn down and a new one built in 1900. She said people would stop by and, with remarks, help "supervise" the project. The Merriman home was wrecked in the 1919 storm.

At the Peoples Street intersection with Water were two identical buildings, the Hunsaker on the south side of Peoples and the Ohler building on the north side. Much of the activity of the 1852 Lone Star Fair occurred in front of Ohler's. Both buildings were constructed for Edward Ohler by Henry Berry from shellcrete bricks made in his kiln at the foot of south bluff.

Judge E. J. Davis had a law office in the Hunsaker building after the Civil War, before he was elected governor. The building was sold to Will Grant and became known as the Grant Building. The Sherman-Jones-Nueces Building was built on this site.

Across Peoples Street was the Ohler building. Eli Merriman said the two buildings, Ohler and Hunsaker, looked like twins. A photograph of the Ohler building, taken in the early 1850s, is perhaps the oldest known photo of Corpus Christi. The back of the photo identifies it as a landmark structure built on the waterfront in 1849. Based on a comparison of Rudolph Hollub's 1874 sketch of the waterfront, it is almost certainly the Ohler building. The Nueces Hotel was built on this site in 1913.

—March 1, 2017

Town shocked by Ohler scandal

Maria von Blucher described Matilda Ohler as pretty,
vain, and lazy, who was always attended by several
slaves. "At the table stands a black woman with a mighty
fan of peacock feathers, shooing off the flies."

Edward Ohler was in Veracruz during the Mexican War. He
was an army sutler and made a fortune selling goods to the U.S.
Army. Soon after the war ended in 1848 he moved to Corpus
Christi.

The Corpus Christi Star on Oct. 17, 1848 noted the arrival of
the Ohler family on the schooner Uncle Bill out of Indianola. It
docked at the Mann wharf. Ohler brought his wife, two young
sons, and a supply of merchandise "with the view to settling
permanently in Corpus Christi."

Maria von Blucher in a letter to her parents mentioned the
arrival of the Ohlers. Her husband Felix knew them from
Veracruz. She described Ohler's wife Matilda as pretty, vain, and
lazy, who was attended by several slaves. "At the table," Maria
wrote, "stands a black woman with a mighty fan of peacock
feathers, shooing off the flies." Ohler opened a grocery and dry
goods store on Water Street in a new building constructed by
Henry W. Berry.

Corpus Christi was a small town. Soon everybody knew about
a scandalous affair between Henry Kinney, who was fond of
other men's wives, and Matilda Ohler. Maria Blucher wrote that
"Mrs. Ohlers (sic) is the paramour of Col. Kinney. Felix
(Blucher) is not shocked at Mrs. Ohlers' affair and often goes
there in the evening. The most ignominious aspect of this is that

Mr. Ohlers, because of his pecuniary relation with Kinney, tolerates the affair and even favors it."

Young Andrew Anderson, who lived next door, said Mrs. Ohler would sit on the porch upstairs and ring a silver bell to summon a slave. One of her slaves called Old Rachel was accused of stealing some silver and was sentence to receive 25 lashes at the whipping post. Anderson watched as the constable whipped her with a leather strap.

Anderson recalled that Mr. and Mrs. Ohler would dress up and take a drive to North Beach; Ohler bought much of the property there. They rode in a carriage pulled by four black horses and were accompanied by two slaves, a driver and footman, wearing top hats. They must have cut quite a figure in the little frontier town of Corpus Christi.

Lt. John Kittredge landed at Ohler's wharf under a flag of truce in August 1862. Kittredge was the commander of the federal blockading fleet in the Gulf and the scourge of the coast. People called him "that pirate Kittredge" and used his name to frighten children. He demanded the surrender of Corpus Christi, and after those demands were rejected, Kittredge's warships bombarded the town. This came to be called the battle of Corpus Christi.

Ohler was put in jail as a suspected Northern spy. With the city under blockade and food scarce, Mrs. Ohler was accused of jacking up prices on foodstuffs. The town's low opinion of her dropped even lower. After the war, Mrs. Ohler, with the rest of the family, moved to Indianola, to the satisfaction of those who remembered her wartime profiteering.

Ohler's building was torn down in the 1870s. George F. Evans built a wool warehouse on the site. Evans owned a store on Chaparral and a ranch near Banquete. The Evans warehouse was later sold to Randolph Robertson to become the American Bottling Works.

Next to the Ohler building was Capt. John Anderson's place and next to Ohler's wharf was Anderson's wharf. Anderson's schooners "Flour Bluff" and "Two Brothers" docked there. Capt. Anderson came to Corpus Christi in 1845 carrying supplies for Zachary Taylor's army. He returned after the war with Mexico and built a home in the 600 block of Water Street in 1852.

John Anderson's windmill and home in the 600 block of Water Street north of the Peoples street intersection. Cords of wood were stacked in front of the windmill. To the left was the George F. Evans Warehouse. The Nueces Hotel was later built on this site.

When Kittredge's warships threatened Corpus Christi, Anderson took his family to the country. They could hear shells exploding and afterwards returned home to find a hole in their roof and their old gray cat missing an ear. The Andersons moved into a salt warehouse at Anderson Point at Flour Bluff to sit out the war.

In the 1870s Anderson built a windmill to grind salt and to power a saw to cut firewood. The salt came from the Laguna Madre and the wood from the Nueces River bottoms. Anderson acquired four old cannonball relics of Kittredge's bombardment and used them as ball bearings on his windmill. They allowed him to shift the blades into the wind.

Anderson's home and windmill were torn down in 1900. In 1913, the Nueces Hotel was built on the site of the Evans warehouse and Anderson's windmill. Scogin Brothers Garage was built next to the Nueces on the site of the Anderson cottage. At the north end of the 600 block, at Water and Starr, was the old Arlington home used as a boarding house.

Between Starr and Taylor, in the 700 block, a building on the southwest corner was owned by Edward Grant and used for storage. His home was next door. In later years, the Elks Club was on this site, then the Dragon Grill, and finally the Town Club.

At the other end of the block, near Taylor, was architect Charles Carroll's office. Carroll designed St. Patrick's Cathedral in 1881. Mary Carroll, one of his four daughters, became school superintendent; Carroll High School was named for her. In this block, in the 20th Century, was the Elks Building which later was converted into Doc Mason's famous Dragon Grill.

In the next block at the end of Taylor Street facing south was the home of John Dix, a retired ship captain who had served on a privateer in the War of 1812 and journeyed to the South Pacific. He moved to Corpus Christi in 1849 and built a large home at the bay end of Taylor and planted salt cedars by the water's edge.

During the Civil War Dix was an ardent and outspoken Unionist, not afraid to voice his opinion. With most of the town fiercely secessionist and Confederate, it took a brave man to stand up for the Union cause. Confederates believed that he was somehow communicating with Union blockade officers by using a lantern at his house to send pre-arranged signals. Even though his son John J. was a Confederate officer, that didn't prevent local Confederates from threatening to hang him.

—March 8, 2017

The dirt walls of old Fort Marcy

Near John Moore's home were the remains of the old
earth walls of Fort Marcy built by Zachary Taylor's
soldiers in 1845. These were dirt embankments. There
really was no fort except on paper.

Capt. John Dix, a retired sea captain, built a large home at the
end of Taylor Street which gave him a good view of ships
coming and going across the bay. During the Civil War Dix, a
confirmed Unionist, was suspected of using a lantern in his
window to signal Union ships in the bay. True or not, he was a
Unionist and that was enough. Local Confederates locked him up
and threatened him with consequence involving a rope.

After the war, with what must have been great satisfaction, Dix
was appointed chief justice of the newly reorganized Nueces
County government. The town's former Confederates, including
those who had threatened to hang him, were disqualified for the
post.

A school for former slave girls was conducted by Dix's wife
and the home rented rooms as the Dix House or Dix Hotel. Eliza
Ann Sullivan, who ran a boarding house in San Patricio, moved
to Corpus Christi to keep the Dix House.

Dix was chief justice of Nueces County when he died in 1870.
The homestead was eventually sold to Jack Ennis, who converted
it into the Seaside Hotel. William Jennings Bryan stayed at the
Seaside Hotel after he lost the 1908 presidential election to
William Howard Taft. The Seaside Hotel and Seaside Pavilion
were destroyed in the 1919 storm.

On the beach side of Water in the 1000 block the Confederate sloop Hannah was burned in 1862 to prevent her capture by Union warships. Wool dealer Ed Buckley, of Byrne & Buckley, built a fine home nearby, at Mann and Water, where the Princess Louise Hotel was later built. Mr. and Mrs. J. B. Murphy lived on the north end of this block.

In 1891 Robert Ritter built the Ritter Hotel and Bath House on a pier over the water between Resaca and Fitzgerald streets. The Caller on Jan. 8, 1893 reported that a ball held at Ritter's Pavilion was in honor of Adelaide Lovenskiold and Belle Skinner who were leaving for a tour of the North. The paper said the Ritter pavilion was decorated with evergreens, flowers and bunting. When the grand march was struck by the Favella orchestra, 50 couples fell in line, and the program of dances was taken up. The ball broke up as the sun rose. Ritter's Pavilion was destroyed by a storm in the 1890s.

At the intersection of Water and Fitzgerald, in the 1500 block, was the home of Col. John M. Moore. Before he moved to Corpus Christi, Moore was a wealthy plantation owner in Alabama and owner of the Alabama Coal & Mining Company. He sold his land holdings in Alabama and Mississippi and moved to Corpus Christi in 1858, bringing some of his slaves with him.

Moore became involved in efforts to dredge a channel across the bay in the late 1850s. Andrew Anderson recalled that he would take his father's dinner to him as he built a dredge boat for Moore. When it was finished, Moore used his slaves to work the dredge digging a channel across the bay. The work was stopped before the start of the Civil War when funds ran short; New York capitalists pulled their money out of the South and invested in Europe instead.

J. C. Riddle, captain of the dredge boat, wrote to Moore complaining about "not having a cent" to pay his workers. One of them, Thomas Noakes, tried for years to get his back wages.

During the Civil War Moore was involved in blockade-running and served as a purchasing agent in Mexico for Confederate authorities. During the occupation, two Union regiments of black soldiers camped at that end of town and the Moore home was

Robert Ritter's Hotel and Bath House was built on a pier over the water between Resaca and Fitzgerald streets in 1891. It was a popular place for dances and entertainments.

taken over by Gen. Charles Russell for his headquarters. Thomas Noakes visited Russell at the Moore home to lend him his painting of the battle of Corpus Christi.

Moore later bought the Corpus Christi Ship Channel Company and sold it to the city. His dredge boat, abandoned at the beginning of the war, disappeared as people pulled it apart for firewood. It was beached where Ritter built his pavilion.

Moore was one of the first members of the school board, with William Rogers and Nelson Plato, in 1873 and he was elected to a three-year term as mayor in 1877. He dabbled in mining and oil exploration; he drilled for oil around Spindletop long before the great discovery. He died in 1892. Moore's home at 1505 Water Street was a handsome two-story structure surrounded by an iron fence. It was sold to J. H. C. White, who owned the town's mule-drawn trolley system in the 1880s. At the rear of the Moore home was an adobe house where Moore's daughter taught school.

Near Moore's home were the remains of the old earth walls of Fort Marcy built by Zachary Taylor's soldiers in 1845. These were dirt embankments, or redoubts, but there really was no "fort" except on paper. The embankments were used to protect a Confederate battery during the battle of Corpus Christi in 1862. The walls could be seen after the turn of the century; Alex Weil

265

Sr. recalled playing on the old redoubts as a youngster. Over time they were leveled and built over.

The Stanley Welch home on the north end of Water was followed by a small bridge over the slough where the bascule bridge was built and where the ship channel is today. Hall's Bayou was a natural watercourse that drained into the bay. In the 1870s when North Beach was called Brooklyn there was a small wooden bridge across the bayou. Naturally it was called Brooklyn bridge.

Great changes came in 1919 when the storm destroyed much of waterfront, and then again in 1939-41 when the seawall pushed back the bay two blocks. Water Street was left high and dry and gone was the sharp tang of salt air smelling of the sea. Though Water Street was no longer on the water, it never lost its historic importance. From Blucher's Creek, where Kinney first landed, to the Central Wharf, from Cahill's building to Anderson's windmill, from Ritter's pavilion to the old earth fortifications left by Zachary Taylor, much of the city's history is connected to Water Street.

—March 15, 2017

The pride of Front Street

A lynch mob stopped at the Meuly home and tried to
throw a rope over the iron railing to hang a killer named
Jim Garner.

Eli Merriman, longtime editor and principal founder of the
Caller-Times, wrote that Corpus Christi had three main streets:
Water, Chaparral and Mesquite and of the three Chaparral was
the main commercial street, called Front Street; Mesquite was
Back Street.

At the south end of Chaparral, past Cooper's Alley, was a
thicket that may have given it its name. Guth Park was here later
and a parking lot is there today. The arroyo between Cooper's
Alley and Laguna (Sartain) was the dividing line between North
and South Chaparral addresses. The line was later moved south
to Cooper's Alley.

South of Cooper's Alley, on the east side, was a lumberyard
owned by W. N. Staples. He sold it to E. D. Sidbury. North of
Cooper's Alley, in the first block, on the west side, was William
"Billy" Rogers' home. Rogers survived a wagon-train massacre
at the beginning of the Mexican War and legend held that he
tracked down the killers who murdered his father and a brother
and one by one slit their throats.

Rogers' home at 101 Chaparral burned on Oct. 1, 1871. After
the fire, he organized the city's first fire volunteer department.
His replacement home was torn down in 1941. A parking lot is
on that site today. Across from Rogers' home, in the 20th
Century, was the San Antonio Machine Shop building.

Rear view of the Conrad Meuly house, in 1936, shows the round above-ground cistern used to store runoff rainwater from the roof. Library of Congress.

Across Laguna, on the east side, was Conrad Meuly's home built in 1851-1854. Meuly's two-story house had 14-foot ceilings and walls as thick as an ancient fortress. It was built of local materials — clay, oyster shell and lime — and the front of the house was decorated with iron grillwork. On May 15, 1866, a lynch mob stopped at the Meuly home and tried to throw a rope over the iron railing on the upper veranda to hang a killer named Jim Garner. Margaret Meuly ran them off. The man was hanged, without formality, from a mesquite tree at the end of the street.

Dr. Arthur Spohn had his office in the Meuly house and boarded with the family. The old home was torn down in the 1950s. Some cities preserve important historic buildings, for a grateful posterity . . . well, some cities. A Fedway department store was built on the site, which was later remodeled and enlarged to house the Education Service Center.

Past Meuly's was Cornelius Cahill's three-story building on Chaparral; he had an older building on Water Street, facing Central Wharf. Cahill held a party in 1859 to celebrate the opening of his new store. The Ranchero said the party was a pleasant affair and the "beauty of Corpus Christi never appeared to better advantage." The building was in ruins by the 1880s.

At the north end of the block was the Gravis boarding house shaded by a screen of oleanders along William Street. The Gravis place was built in 1846 by J.A. F. Gravis, a former Texas Ranger. It was called the California House in 1849 to attract the custom of prospective miners as they passed through on their way to the goldfields.

Gravis died of yellow fever in 1854 and though he and Henry W. Berry had built many of the early homes and stores in Corpus Christi, his estate was very small, valued at $27. Gravis's widow Irenah married Berry, her husband's partner in the building trade.

Irenah Gravis Berry continued to run the renamed Berry boarding house, which for a time was called the Sierra Madre Hotel. She would send one of her sons out with a bell fixed to a long wooden pole to summon the boarders at meal times. This site was later occupied by a two-story building leased by E. H. Caldwell for his hardware store, his third location, which still later became the auto dealership of J. C. Blacknall, who sold Plymouths and Dodges. The corner where the Berry boarding house once stood was still being used for a hotel well into the 20th Century; the Colonial Hotel was above Blacknall's.

Past Laguna on the west side of the street was Frederick Belden's warehouse, set back on the west side of the street, an adobe-like building that was used to store supplies for Zachary Taylor's army in 1845. Behind the warehouse, on Mesquite, were Belden's store and home.

In the middle of the block in the 20th Century, across from the Meuly residence, was a two-story boarding house run by J. L. Sowell called "The Chaparral."

Down the block in the 1860s, on the lot second from the corner, was the La Retama Saloon, located in a substantial shellcrete building. Saloons were usually two stories, with a bar below and rooms above. When a man had too much, he could stay the night and sleep it off upstairs. The Ranchero in its March 31, 1860 edition reported that the La Retama "is the name of the new saloon, opened opposite the Sierra Madre Hotel, Chaparral street." A fracas at the La Retama on Aug. 4, 1860 led to the fatal shooting of Deputy Sheriff Tom Nolan, brother of Sheriff Mat Nolan. This building was later used as a store.

The west side of the 200 block was burned in a spectacular fire on July 14, 1892. The fire consumed the Molander home, the Lay home, J. B. Mitchell warehouse, Biggio residence, Daimwood home, and Royall Givens' grocery store in the old La Retama building.

Ida Daimwood (Magnenat) once recalled the night of the fire. "It was mother who smell smoke first. My father had just come in and he ran down the street yelling 'fire!' The bell in the old Market Hall began to ring, which was the signal for volunteer firemen to drop everything and come running."

The Caller described the conflagration as the most destructive fire in city history. It led to building a pipeline to the Nueces River and establishing the city's first municipal water system. A 1900 Sanborn fire insurance map shows the south end of the block empty except for water cisterns behind the burned homes. The Royall Givens grocery store, in a shellcrete building with a tin roof, survived, for a time. J. C. Penney moved into a new five-story building on this site in 1949.

—March 23, 2017

The sign of the Indian chief

George Noessel's store featured a sign of an Indian chief
and displayed a Comanche buffalo hide shield
ornamented with red flannel, feathers, little bells, and a
brass plate.

One of the oldest buildings in town was the old Kinney House, built in 1845 on the northwest corner of Chaparral and William Street. It was diagonally across the intersection from the Sierra Madre Hotel.

The Kinney House was operated as a hotel when Zachary Taylor's army was camped in Corpus Christi in 1845 and early 1846. It was sold in 1848 to George Noessel, who had owned hotels in Matagorda and Bastrop before he came to Corpus Christi. Noessel renamed the Kinney House the Corpus Christi Hotel.

Army officers, including future Civil War general Phil Sheridan, stayed at Noessel's. Lt. Sheridan was on his way to his new post at Fort Duncan. When army moved the Eighth District headquarters from Corpus Christi to San Antonio in 1855, Noessel converted the hotel into a grocery and dry goods store.

Noessel's featured a sign of an Indian chief and displayed a Comanche buffalo hide shield. The Ranchero, on Feb. 23, 1861, said the shield was made of "bull hide ornamented with red flannel, feathers, little bells, a brass plate, doubtless taken from the lock of some unlucky traveler's carpetbag. It is a curiosity worth seeing."

Noessel had two sons, Otto and Felix. Felix was a longtime captain of the Pioneer Fire Company No. 1. In 1882 the old

Noessel building was rented become the first home of the Corpus Christi Caller. The first edition of Caller was printed on Jan. 21, 1883, a night so cold that a bucket of oysters brought from John Superach's for the pressmen froze solid.

Past the Caller's office, after 1883, came the Noakes Brothers' Machine Shop. An ad just after the turn of the 20th Century said Noakes Brothers' machine and blacksmith shop contained the latest machines and could fix anything from a clock to a steam engine. An ad in 1906 said Noakes was selling Cadillacs, that there were already four in town, and the shop would keep the machine in repair for six months, barring accidents or punctured tires.

Beyond Noakes was F. Lachman's tailor shop then Joseph Groome, a bootmaker, followed by Prokop (also spelled Prokoff) Hoffman's dry goods and grocery store near the end of the block. When he arrived in the early 1850s Hoffman cut hay outside town and sold it to the army. By 1859 he owned a "shaving and hair-cutting saloon" and a dry goods store. On the corner, I believe, was a restaurant and saloon run by Jacob Ziegler, who also ran a hotel-cum-boarding house on Mesquite. Later, on Ziegler's site, was Nueces Hardware.

On the east side of the 300 block, on the northeast corner, was the wool commission firm of Byrne & Buckley. In 1871 the Nueces Valley said that Byrne & Buckley "received this week by the steamer Austin a complete assortment of fancy groceries and other goods. Their store and warehouse is now crowded with merchandise." John F. Morton, who was later killed in the Peñascal raid, was a buyer of wool and hides for the firm.

Next door was a grocery and dry goods store owned by Wayman N. Staples. In the October 1859 Ranchero Staples advertised the arrival of a shipment of hoopskirts, family groceries, whisky, and said he would accept wool, hides, stock, lead, gold or silver in exchange. He also owned a lumberyard which he later sold to Edward Sidbury.

Mary Sutherland told a story about one of Staples' customers, as related by Joseph Fitzsimmons who was a bookkeeper for Staples. A nearby rancher came in twice yearly to settle up, Fitzsimmons said. "One day he came in for his account. I called

In the 300 block of Chaparral was the old Kinney House, left, built in 1845. It was sold to George Noessel and for many years housed Noessel's grocery store. To the right was Noakes Bros. Machine Shop, which advertised that its machinists could repair anything from a clock to a steam engine.

the amount, he hesitated before taking the bill. 'No, sir, that's not right,' he said, laying it on the desk and reaching in his pocket he brought out a stick covered with notches. 'You have charged me twenty cents too much.' Running his finger down the stick he said, 'This is ten dollars; this is five; one-seventy; two forty-five; tobacco, twenty-five; ax for John, seventy-five; one wash pot for the old woman, two-thirty; one dollar, what the devil? Oh, yes, two gallons of whisky for Old Jerry's wake,' and so on to the end of the stick. The clerks added wildly, the overcharge of twenty cents was actually found, and the old man settled up and cut a new stick."

Staples moved out to Last Street (which was changed to Alameda in 1942). The Staples building housed David Hirsch's store, beginning in 1869. In the early years, the family lived upstairs and on the ground floor Hirsch operated a grocery, general merchandise and men's clothing store. He became a major wool dealer, bought Martha Rabb's Magnolia Mansion on the bluff, founded the Corpus Christi National Bank and served as the first president of the school board. Hirsch moved his wool store to the west side of the 400 block of Chaparral.

After Hirsch moved out the Staples building housed the dry goods store of brothers Richard and Sam Jordan. Richard, in partnership with William Rogers, built Market Hall and leased it to the city. The Jordan brothers' father, S. W. Jordan, once tried to kill Sam Houston with an ax for criticizing Mirabeau Lamar's Indian policy.

The Crescent Hotel followed. An ad in the Caller in 1883 said the hotel was under the new management of Nick Constantine and had reduced its prices to $1.50 and $2 a day. It was soon afterwards bought by Capt. Fred Steen, a seafaring man who had once seen Napoleon Bonaparte in exile on the island of St. Helena. Steen lost a leg in a collision of ships at Brazos Santiago. Capt. Steen and his wife Nevada and renamed the Crescent as the Steen Hotel.

Next door was George Roberts' Favorite Saloon, which had been John Fogg's Saloon before that. The Favorite Saloon advertised "choice liquors, fine cigars, and polite bartenders." The Favorite had had a ten-pin alley and rooms above.

Past the Favorite Saloon, on the corner, was Frank & Weil, where E. Frank and Charles Weil sold dry goods and ranch supplies and, like many of the other merchants in town, bought wool and hides. Later at this site was McNabb Motors with the Model Rooms above.

—March 29, 2017

Historic landmark on Chaparral

The St. James Hotel was named after one in Kansas
City, but it was also the last name of the man who built
it, J. T. James, a cattleman on Mustang Island.

The commercial center of Corpus Christi in the 19th Century
was the 400, 500 and 600 blocks of Chaparral, where the most
successful businesses were located. The most dominant structure
in the 400 block was the St. James Hotel.

When Zachary Taylor's army was camped at Corpus Christi in
1845 Charles Bryant, an architect from Maine, built the Union
Theater at the corner of Lawrence and Chaparral. It hosted plays
and entertainments for the troops. Bryant was killed in 1850 by
Indians on Chocolate Bayou near the Wood Ranch.

A new hotel was built on the site of Bryant's Union Theater. It
was probably named after the St. James Hotel in Kansas City, but
it was also the last name of the man who had it built, J. T. James,
a cattle rancher on Mustang Island. Before the hotel was finished
James sold it to William Rogers, who sold his Palo Alto Ranch to
get the money. He paid $13,000 for the hotel and spent $5,000 to
get it ready to open. When Rogers died in 1877 William Biggio
became the manager of the St. James. Biggio was the pilot of the
Confederate ram Webb which was captured at the mouth of the
Mississippi and Biggio taken prisoner.

Under Biggio's management the St. James became known as
the headquarters of cattle ranchers, cowboys, politicians,
gamblers and gunmen. The hotel saloon, the Gem run by P. H.
McManigle, was one of the most popular places in town.

At the southwest corner of the 400 block of Chaparral was the St. James Hotel, built in 1869 (shown here in 1933). It stood on the site of the old Union Theater, built in 1845 to hold entertainments for Zachary Taylor's troops. Lichtenstein's was built on this site in 1941.

In 1896 a man named Foster and his wife opened a snake-collecting business next to the St. James. They bought rattlesnakes and shipped them away. One rattler escaped and had guests in the St. James on full alert. Complaints forced the snake couple to move on.

The St. James was torn down in 1937 and three years later Lichtenstein's new department store, its last location, was built on the site.

Past the St. James was a variety store, similar to a five-and-dime, owned by J. Levy, who moved to Corpus Christi from Banquete. The Bluntzer building was later constructed on the site of Levy's store. The Caller and Daily Herald moved from the Noessel building to the Bluntzer building early in the 20th Century. Cage Hardware was later in this building.

Past Levy's was a wool warehouse where, in the 1870s, David Hirsch was located, after he moved from the 300 block of Chaparral. Several merchants — Staples, Gussett, Lichtenstein, and Hirsch — occupied buildings at different locations. They moved around.

Down the street was Herman Meuly's News Depot — "Sign of the Big Book" — which sold newspapers, stationery, and

276

McGuffey's third, fourth and fifth readers. Meuly's father built the "house with an iron front" in the 200 block of Chaparral.

Past Meuly's was a vacant lot used to park wagons. Gugenheim-Cohn Department Store was built on this site in the 20th Century. After it was moved north a block, the building housed Eidson's Department Store, which moved from the 400 block of Mesquite.

Across from the St. James, on the northeast side, was the wool firm of Edey & Kirsten in the 1850s and 1860s. Uriah Lott, Perry Doddridge and Allen M. Davis bought out Edey & Kirsten. The Nueces Valley on Dec. 21, 1872 said the firm purchased more than one million pounds of wool the previous year. When Mary Sutherland arrived in 1876 she found a seeming tangle of carts and wagons, horses, mules and oxen crowding around the great wool emporiums on Chaparral. She described it as a perfect uproar of stamping hooves, cracking whips, and cursing in Spanish.

Perry Doddridge, an orphan who raised himself, became a wool merchant and opened the first bank in town in 1871. The Doddridge Bank was built on the old Edey & Kirsten site. Doddridge was elected mayor in 1873.

Above the Doddridge Bank, on the second floor, the Myrtle Club had its rooms, beginning in about 1885. Most of the town's prominent men were members. There was a reading room, a billiards room, and tables for card games like whist. They would sometimes hold ladies' night.

North of the Doddridge building was Wheeler's store. Lt. E. H. (Elijah Harvey) Wheeler arrived with Union occupation forces after the war and married a Confederate girl, Sarah McCampbell, and opened a shoe store. Wheeler's promised to refasten buttons on ladies' shoes for free.

Next door was Julius Henry's store with living quarters on the second floor. Henry arrived in Corpus Christi in 1858, penniless, and chopped cotton for John Dunn for $4 a month and board. Then he got a job with August Holthaus as a baker. When Henry Kinney, the town's founder, was shot to death in Matamoros in 1862, Julius Henry and Martin Hinojosa were with him. Henry lifted Kinney up as he was dying. Henry returned to Corpus

Christi after the war and opened a general store on Water Street then built a new building on Chaparral.

Past Henry's was Gradwhol's dry goods, which later became Friend & Cahn's Bank, and finally, after the bank failed, the Bank Saloon run by Jap Clark. Charles Parker's barber shop was next door.

In the middle of the 400 block on the east side of the street, W. E. "Uncle Elmer" Pope built the 10-story Pope building in 1929, later called the Medical Professional Building. That structure today is the Sea Gulf Villa Apartments.

Near the end of the block was Blumenthal & Jordt furniture, in a wooden building with three gables, making it look as if three houses had been squeezed into one. This firm later became Jordt-Allen and then Allen Furniture. It moved into a new building in 1912.

Next door, on the corner, was a long low barn-like structure that looked painfully functional like our prefab buildings today. It was shipped in component parts from New York by William R. Grace, mayor of New York City, who was a business partner of Matthew and William Headen, buyers of wool and hides. The Grace building was erected on the corner of Chaparral and Schatzel.

William Headen, the son, married John M. Moore's daughter and was elected mayor for a term, 1876-77. The Headen/Grace building was later occupied by J. W. Westervelt, a ship chandler.

— April 5, 2017

Mulberry tree and cabbage roses

Anna Moore Schwein said that Dr. Thomas
Kearney's pale pink cabbage roses were prized by
young men for their sweethearts.

One appealing feature of the 500 block of Chaparral was a
large mulberry tree behind a paling fence in the front yard of the
aptly named Bob Berry. The cognoscenti of the town's young
miscreants knew they could steal the blackberry-like fruit by
climbing Bob Berry's mulberry tree.

Next door to the south was Max and Otto Dreyer's candy store,
where youngsters could find firecrackers, toys, and soft drinks.
On the corner was a dry goods store owned by D. Schwartz, who
lived in New York and hired a local manager. The Nueces Valley
said Schwartz "has a large stock of dry goods, boots and shoes.
This house is connected with New York. They do a heavy
business." Corpus Christi National Bank was built in 1890 on the
Schwartz-Dreyer-Berry site.

Next to Bob Berry's to the north was George Mew's ship
chandlery, followed by F. Brose, cobbler. On the corner was the
Uehlinger building which housed Lichtenstein's store, its second
location, and then Gugenheim-Cohn after it moved from the 400
block. The Uehlinger building was later torn down to build
Montgomery Ward.

On the northeast corner was Keller's Saddlery, the building
decorated with the painting of a white horse. Fred Gold, another
saddle-maker, later moved into Keller's old building. Past
Keller's was E. Morris's dry goods. Morris operated in a store

half a block south in 1870 but moved into the new building in 1872.

Morris was shocked one day in August 1874 when a cow and a calf trotted into his store. The cow was being driven home, the newspaper reported, and took a shortcut through the store. Past E. Morris was the Pat McDonough building, with a stationery business on the ground floor and club rooms upstairs.

The Shaw building at Chaparral and Peoples was remodeled to become Norwick Gussett's store and bank. Gussett, who had been a sergeant in the Mexican War, became the city's richest merchant. He bought wool and hides and shipped them to New York on his three schooners named for his three daughters.

Gussett sold tobacco, cloth and manufactured products to be transported back to Mexico. This was how the money was made; this was the city's great enterprise in the 19th Century. Corpus Christi was founded for, and sustained by, this trade. Gussett was one of a dozen or more major wool dealers in town. Traders from Mexico called his store, identified by a rooster weathervane, "la tienda del gallo."

At Peoples and Chaparral, on the northwest corner, was the DeRyee Drug Store in a shellcrete building. Dr. William DeRyee collected driftwood on the island to frame the doors and windows. DeRyee's front window always displayed some curiosity, like a duck with its bill clamped in an oyster shell. Dr. DeRyee, a chemist, came to Corpus Christi in 1857 with John Moore. He made candles which were in great demand during the Civil War. DeRyee's drug store was torn down in 1908 to build the City National Bank Building, which still stands.

Down the block was Johnny Hall's tin shop, decorated with a stove sitting on a pole. Hall's was followed by Eli Merriman's mother's boarding house. After Eli's father, Dr. Merriman, died in the yellow fever outbreak in 1867, his widow sold their Banquete ranch to open the boarding house. Eli, a boy at the time, met the buyer in Banquete and was paid in twenty-dollar gold pieces. He feared robbery and put the money in a sack and rode to Corpus Christi holding his six-gun "with a vigorous grip." Mrs. Merriman combined two adjacent houses to establish the Oriental Hotel Merriman.

J. B. Mitchell's store dominated the 600 block of North Chaparral in 1880. To the left of Mitchell's was Evans & Hickey Groceries and to the right was the first location of Morris Lichtenstein's Department Store.

This end of this block was later dominated by McCrory, Woolworth, Kress, and Grant. Ben Garza's Metropolitan Café were also located in that block. Joe Mancias, a newsboy, said when he sold his papers at the Metropolitan Café Ben Garza never failed to urge him to stay in school.

On the east side of Chaparral, past Peoples, was a wooden building with a slanting porch that served as an awning. This building housed Morris Lichtenstein's first store. Lichtenstein was a Confederate veteran who fought with Sibley's Brigade in New Mexico. After the war, he opened a store in Indianola, then moved to Corpus Christi in 1874, the year before a great hurricane virtually destroyed Indianola. In 1889 Lichtenstein moved into the Uehlinger building, which was torn down to build the new Montgomery Ward building. Lichtenstein's moved three times, always on Chaparral.

Next door to Lichtenstein's was James McKenzie's paint store. "Little Mac" McKenzie was killed when he was run over by Elihu Ropes' steam-dummy streetcar.

McKenzie's was followed by J. B. Mitchell's hardware and furniture store, which had been Mitchell & Evans for many years. Louis Trevino, the purchasing agent for the firm, traveled all over South Texas and Northern Mexico to buy wool and hides for the firm. Mitchell's two-story building was later occupied by E. H. Caldwell's hardware store. In 1913, the Nueces Hotel was built on the site of the Lichtenstein's first store and Mitchell's hardware.

Past Mitchell's was Evans & Hickey Groceries. The Palace Theater was built on this site in 1925.

The Kearney cottage followed Evans & Hickey. Dr. Thomas Kearney was brought to Corpus Christi from Cuba during the yellow fever epidemic of 1867. Anna Moore Schwein said he sent back to Havana for four rose bushes, which he planted in the front yard. Kearney's pale pink cabbage roses were prized by young men for their sweethearts. The old Kearney cottage later housed the Customs Office.

At the end of the block at the intersection with Starr Street was John Woessner's place. It included a store and a wool warehouse and residence behind the store, on Starr, all built around 1871. John was the son of William Woessner, a blacksmith.

As Prokop (Prokoff) Hoffman got his start by cutting hay for army horses, John Woessner got his by selling water from a "roly" barrel, as Red John Dunn recalled. Woessner went on to become a wealthy wool dealer. Dances were held in the second-floor hall of the wool warehouse; Walter Timon once recalled that Woessner's had the best dance floor in town, which was "springy and fine." In the 1920s Hugh Sutherland built a two-story brick building on the Woessner site, which, beginning in 1925, housed J. C. Penney's.

—April 12, 2017

282

The James Ranahan block

In 1862, during the bombardment of Corpus Christi, the Ranahan home was hit by a shell, which left a hole in the wall.

You could call the 700 block of North Chaparral the Ranahan block. James Ranahan died building a structure on the northeast corner of the block, at Starr, while the home he built stood at the southwest corner at Taylor.

Ranahan, a brickmaker and builder from Belfast, Ireland, came to Corpus Christi in 1849. His brick kiln was on the slope of the bluff near the top of Taylor Street, about where the Caller-Times is today. In late 1866 he was building a two-story shellcrete structure at Chaparral and Starr when he died.

The building was finished and housed the Holthaus grocery and bakery, run by a German man, August Holthaus, and his French wife. Robert Adams worked for the Holthaus couple as a 15-year-old in 1862 and said that Mrs. Holthaus was a demanding boss who was very hard to please. August Holthaus died during the yellow fever year of 1867. Mrs. Holthaus sold the business to George French in 1873. French operated a retail and wholesale grocery business at the site. The Holthaus/French building was later occupied by Cooper's Clean Bakery. I believe the Mayflower Café was in this old building. K Wolens department store was later built on the site.

In the middle of the 700 block on the eastern side was the Horne Apartment building, built in 1899. The Horne building was badly damaged in the 1919 hurricane, but was rebuilt and survived. Past Horne Apartments to the north was Vaky Apartments, built in 1922.

On the northwest corner, past Starr, was the John Grant building, constructed in 1908 on the site of a Chinese laundry, which later became John Selvidge's Corpus Christi Steam Laundry. He moved to a new building on Mesquite.

The Grant building housed the City Drug Store, later Davis Drugs, with Draughon's Business College above. After 1912, a streetcar line ran from the City Drug Store corner to the Breakers Hotel on North Beach.

At the north end of the block was James Ranahan's home, a shellcrete structure built in 1852. Shellcrete buildings were constructed of adobe-like bricks made of crushed shells which were covered with plaster. In 1862, during the bombardment of Corpus Christi, the Ranahan home was hit by a shell, which left a hole in the wall.

The Ranahan home (also known as the Fitzsimmons home) later housed Jack Brown's carpentry shop which stood next to the Ritz Theater. When the building was torn down in 1938 house-mover Ed Brennan was killed when a wall fell on him. Ed was known as the strongest man in town; it was said he could lift a 500-pound bale of cotton as easily as if it were a 50-pound sack of sugar. He was 54 when he was killed.

Diagonally across the street was the home of Royall Givens, a fish and oyster dealer. It was the old Russell home before Givens bought it. After the Civil War Union occupation officers used this house as their headquarters. Citizens went here to take the "Ironclad Oath" of loyalty. It became known as the Ironclad Oath house. The old Russell/Givens house was torn down after the death of Mrs. Leona Givens in 1948.

The Givens Apartment Building followed and in later years there was a Piggly Wiggly and the Plaza Apartments. On the west side was Peterson's Food Store (later Guy's) on the corner. It was followed by the parsonage for the Church of the Good Shepherd. Next to the parsonage was the Otto Dreyer home, built in 1881. Dreyer and his brother Max owned a candy store in the 500 block of Chaparral. The Dreyer home was moved and the site cleared in 1957. Artesian Park was north of the home.

A rooftop view of the 700 block of Chaparral shows Cooper's Clean Bakery on the corner with Starr. The Mayflower Café was here and K Wolens department store was later built on the site. Across the street was the Grant building which housed Davis Drug Store.

Down the block on the east side was a two-story shellcrete store and home of William Baker Wrather. At the beginning of the Civil War Wrather commanded the first militia company of Confederate soldiers. In a ceremony on the courthouse steps, Capt. Wrather accepted a Confederate flag from Mary Woessner. After the ceremony, the captain and Miss Woessner were married. The old Wrather house was demolished after it was wrecked by Hurricane Celia.

Next to the Wrather place was Dan Reid's home, on the corner. This two-story house was built about 1850. Reid, an architect and builder, designed and built many of the downtown structures, including the First State Bank on Mesquite. He was elected mayor in 1908. The Reid place was sold in 1950 and torn down soon afterwards.

Across the street from the Reid home was the Deposit Guaranty building, constructed in 1926. The building was restored in the 1980s.

On the west side of the 1000 block of Chaparral, at 1001, was the Tito Rivera house. Rivera was captured by Comanches as a boy but he was purchased, for $125, by Robert Neighbors, superintendent of Indian Affairs. In the 1870s Rivera moved to

Corpus Christi and worked as cashier in the Doddridge Bank. He owned a stationery and book store and was elected to the City Council in the 1880s. The Rivera house, built in 1885, was sold to Walter Timon in 1902. It was torn down in 1962.

Past the Rivera/Timon house, later, was Doc McGregor's Studio. McGregor bought a home on that site, built in 1928, which he enlarged over the years. He had been trained as carpenter by his father. In the next block, the 1100 block, in the 20th century, were the Henderson and Giles hotels.

The Herman Cohn home was in the 1300 block. Cohn was the co-founder of Guggenheim-Cohn department store. In 1914, he built a mansion on South Broadway, considered the city's finest home. Near the old Cohn home on Chaparral was the Hoover Hotel which opened in 1926. In the 1400 block was the August Ricklefsen home.

Chaparral, or Front Street, was Corpus Christi's main shopping thoroughfare. It stretched from south of Cooper's Alley, past the arroyo, to Hall's Bayou. Chaparral, covering 17 city blocks, was home to Conrad Meuly's house with the iron front, to the old Kinney House in the 300 block, from the St. James Hotel to Bob Berry's mulberry tree, from J. B. Mitchell's Hardware store to the Mrs. Merriman's Oriental Hotel, from the Holthaus Bakery to Tito Rivera's home. We reach the end of Chaparral Street. There is no need to walk back.

—April 19, 2017

The south end of Back Street

"There were bales of cotton and boats floating around the house. We were wiped out." —Matt Pellegrino

Mesquite was spelled Mezquit but it was often called Back Street, which was easier to spell. It was established, from early times, as the city's third most important street, after Chaparral, the main commercial thoroughfare, and Water Street, but Mesquite was of equal importance in the city's history.

In the 100 block of Mesquite, on the east side, was the Pellegrino home on the corner. Matt Pellegrino, who would become a city detective, lived here, in the home of his father, Frank Pellegrino.

Before the 1919 storm struck, Matt Pellegrino was planning to go to Matamoros with friends to see a bullfight. It was raining so hard they decided not to go. When the storm hit, Pellegrino led his family and others through the raging waters to safety on the bluff. After the storm was over on Monday morning he went down to see what was left of their home. "There were bales of cotton and boats floating around the house. We were wiped out. Didn't have anything left. The house was there but everything was ruined."

Down from Pellegrino's home was the Corpus Christi Mattress Factory, which later moved to Laredo Street, followed by the Corpus Christi Steam Laundry, owned by John Selvidge. His first location was at Chaparral and Starr, in the 700 block before he moved to Mesquite.

Because of the encroachment of the bluff, there was almost nothing on the west side of Mesquite until William Street, except for one business. On the corner on the west side of the 100 block was the first grocery store of Vincente Lozano, in 1906.

Lozano, from Bagdad, Mexico, came to Corpus Christi in 1891. He worked in the fishing business then worked as a clerk in Peter Baldeschwiler's grocery store selling charcoal for five cents a bucket and cleaning the oil lamps. When he was 20, in 1899, he married Elvira McCarthy and in 1902 opened his own store in a rented building on the east side of Mesquite.

Lozano had $20 in capital and some borrowed stock. The store rent was $8 a month. When it was raised to $12, in 1906, Lozano moved across the street and built a small store at Mesquite and Broadway. He built a new building on Staples Street and moved out there in 1913.

In the 200 block of North Mesquite, on the east side, was the store of Frederick Belden, an early merchant who was engaged in the Mexican trade. He settled in Corpus Christi in the 1840s. He had been at Matamoros then moved to Lamar and from there to Corpus Christi. He married Mauricia Arocha in Matamoros and was considered a spokesman for the Hispanic community, where he was known as "El Juez." He was a friend of Zachary Taylor when the army was concentrated at Corpus Christi in 1845 and early 1846.

Capt. W. S. Henry, who dined with Belden and Mauricia soon after his arrival in Corpus Christi, said they gave him a dish called "themales." "It is made of corn meal, chopped meat, and cayenne pepper wrapped in a corn husk, and boiled. I know of nothing more palatable."

Before the army left Corpus Christi to march to the border, in early March 1846, Mauricia held a dinner party for Gen. Taylor and some of his officers. At the dinner Mauricia asked the general about the prospects for war. Taylor said if war broke out, he intended to march on and capture Mexico City. Mrs. Belden bet him he would never get there. While Taylor didn't capture Mexico City — Winfield Scott did — he sent Mrs. Belden a silk dress from Mexico. As an aside, Mauricia's sister married a rancher on the Nueces, Robert Love. Belden died in 1867 and Mauricia in 1896. The old Belden home was later a boarding house run by an Irish woman named Annie Dugan.

Workers gather in front of the Corpus Christi Steam Laundry at 112 N. Mesquite one day in 1907. The laundry was established in 1904 at Chaparral and Starr by John Selvidge. The new location was near Cooper's Alley.

In the 20th Century, past the Belden home, was the Russell-Knight Whippet auto dealership, at 204 Mesquite. The building became a popular restaurant in the 1930s, the Rendezvous Grill. Near the end of the block, east side, was a blacksmith and wagon wheel shop.

On the corner was the home of photographer Louis de Planque, whose photo studio was behind the home, fronting on William street. He came to Corpus Christi in 1868 after stints in Mexico and Indianola. People would stroll by his studio to see the photos in the windows. De Planque was one of the finest photographers of that era. It's unfortunate that so few of his photographs have survived. Later on, Roy Murray Motors was located on this northeast corner and, more recently, La Bahia Restaurant.

On the west side of Mesquite in the 200 block was the sloping ground of the bluff. In the middle of the block, in the 1850s, was a small adobe building where Fr. Bernard O'Reilly taught young children. After the school closed, the Corpus Christi Female Academy occupied the building, about 1860, until the academy was moved north on Mesquite, in the 700 block. The O'Reilly building housed the Post Office for a time in the 1870s and after it was torn down the site was used as a parking lot for teams and wagons. This was directly across Mesquite from the old Belden home.

In 1909, a speaker's platform, or pergola, was built on the side of the bluff where Spohn Park is today for President William Howard Taft to make his speech. Taft was in the area to visit his half-brother Charles at the Taft Ranch. The president spoke about the importance of harbor improvements and the need for a deepwater port, subjects dear to Corpus Christi.

After Taft's departure, Eli Merriman, editor of the Caller, ran into Annie Dugan, who ran the boarding house in the old Belden home across from where the president spoke. She said, "Mr. Merriman, why didn't you put in the Caller that the President of the United States made a speech in front of my gate? I would have liked to have sent a copy to Ireland."

The 200 block of Mesquite, around Spohn Park, was visited in 1909 by President Taft and in 1846 by Zachary Taylor, who became president in 1848, so two presidents were connected to this block of Mesquite.

—April 26, 2017

Livery stable dominated 300 block

"The public are informed that John Fogg still holds forth at his old stand on Mezquit Street." —Newspaper ad

The creak of leather, the jingle-jangle of chains and harnesses, the neighing of horses and braying of mules — must have been the sounds coming from Fogg's Livery in the middle of the 300 block of Mesquite. This was an important institution in town, in the age of the horse.

Fogg's included the main livery building, wagon sheds, and hay storage building. An ad for Fogg's from the 1870s said, "The public are informed that John Fogg still holds forth at his old stand on Mezquit Street." Fogg also operated a saloon and a San Antonio-Brownsville stagecoach line. When a drunk shot a storekeeper in 1866, Fogg led the mob that hanged the culprit at the end of Chaparral.

Fogg distrusted banks, it was said, and kept his money hidden on his property. A man who had done some job of work for Fogg went to his home to get paid. Fogg went out back around his chicken house and returned with a handful of gold coins. After Fogg died on Oct. 30, 1896, his backyard looked like Swiss cheese with holes dug by people searching for his buried gold.

Fogg's Livery later became Pitts Livery, which sold and serviced the town's first automobiles. Coleman Furniture was later built on this site in the mid-1930s. North of Fogg's, near the corner, was Zip Battery owned by Cipriano "Zip" Gonzalez.

On the north corner was the Russell boarding house run by Kate Fletcher and Myrtle Russell. It later moved into the old

Pitts Livery, shown in 1907, stabled horses, rented buggies, conducted funerals, and serviced the town's first automobiles. It was located on the site of John Fogg's livery, which dated back to the 1860s. Coleman Furniture was built on this site in the 1930s.

Timon house in the 600 block, past the Amusu Theater. On the corner to the south of the 300 block was the variety store of John Peterson. Later it was Thayer's Yankee Notions store, which sold guns, cigars, guitar strings, perfume, Montgolfier balloons, and eight-day clocks.

On the west side of the 300 block, on the corner with William, was the Baldeschwiler home. The Baldeschwilers were among the earliest to settle in Corpus Christi. Blaize Mathias Baldeschwiler and his wife, Swiss immigrants, came to Corpus Christi in 1844. She ran a boarding house and Blaize did carpentry work. Their son Andrew followed in the carpentry trade and married Margaret Murphy of San Patricio. After the turn of the century, Peter Baldeschwiler lived in the family home, rented rooms, and ran a grocery store.

In 1928, a new building was constructed on the Baldeschwiler corner that housed Tribble's Meat Market. Down the block was Stanley's Trading Post, a used furniture store owned by Stanley Tomlinson. He later moved to Agnes Street. In the 1930s, at the end of the 300 block on the west side, was the Crescent Bakery.

In the 400 block of Mesquite, on the east side, was the Constantine Hotel, on the corner with Lawrence. When the Constantine was remodeled and renamed the Bidwell, one of its 25 bedrooms was turned into a bathroom, a novel idea at the time. The Caller said, "Surely there is such a thing as being too nice, this craze about washing all over." The Bidwell was turned into a furniture showroom in 1940 and torn down in 1999.

Past the Bidwell was saloon row before Nueces County went dry. The Richelieu Bar was followed by a pool hall and then the Magnolia Bar, which was later changed to the Alamo Bar. After that came the Buckhorn Saloon, with rooms above, and across the street was the Palace Bar. After county voters approved prohibition in 1916, the Richelieu Bar became Allison's Domino Parlor and the Alamo Bar became the Alamo Café.

Near the end of the block was Farrell Smith's Grocery on the lower floor and the Miramar Lodge of the Knights of Pythias on the upper floor. The knights called it a "castle." On the corner was Boyd's Hardware in an old two-story former residence. This was later Heath & Son's Emporium and still later on that site was Citizens Industrial Bank.

On the west side of the 400 block, on the corner opposite the Bidwell, was Robert Ritter's Bazaar, which opened in the 1880s. It was called a racket store because it sold children's toys that made a loud racket. The Ritter building later housed Weil Brothers Grocery, opened in 1903 by Alex and Moise Weil, who ran the store until 1945. Past Weil's was a building occupied by the Caller-Times before it moved to Lower Broadway. Above the newspaper was the Cadillac rooming house.

In the middle of the block was the Uehlinger bakery. This building was moved and, in 1903, Joe Mireur's saddlery shop was built on that site. Eidson's Department Store was near the end of the block before it was moved to Chaparral.

At the end of the block, I believe, was the old Ziegler place. It's hard to be sure since no ad or newspaper reference gives a specific location for Ziegler's. It was variously referred to as Ziegler's Hall, Ziegler's House, and Ziegler's Hotel. More properly, it was probably a rooming house. There is also mention of Ziegler's Restaurant and Saloon.

The Ranchero on March 9, 1861 refers to Ziegler's restaurant on Chaparral. I think this was at the north end of the 300 block, where Nueces Hardware was located later. Others refer to Ziegler's on Mesquite. For a time in the 1870s, Ziegler leased and ran the St. James Hotel. He must have owned and operated several businesses at more than one location.

Ziegler, who came from Germany, arrived in Corpus Christi in the 1850s and opened a rooming house, or hotel, and a restaurant and bar. An ad in 1869 said the well-known house of Ziegler's "has been fitted up and renovated in a style unsurpassed in Western Texas. The table will be well supplied with the best meats the market affords." The Weekly Advertiser on April 8, 1870 said, "Louis de Planque, the photographer, has fitted up rooms at the Ziegler building, on Mezquit street, and will be ready to receive visitors."

Jacob Ziegler died on Nov. 4, 1883. Based on a few clues I surmise that Ziegler's original establishment was on the southwest corner of Mesquite at William. That's an informed guess, at best. Sometimes we have to recognize what we don't know as well as what we do know.

—May 3, 2017

The demise of Market Hall

In 1911, a new brick city hall was built on the site of
Market Hall on Market Square, between Schatzel and
Peoples.

A triangle of blocks between Schatzel and Peoples is fan-
shaped, with the small end under the bluff and the large end on
the bayfront. The Schatzel-Peoples triangle contains the 500
blocks of Water, Chaparral, and Mesquite. At the top of the fan
between Schatzel and Peoples, in the 500 block of Mesquite, was
Market Hall in Market Square. This was the civic heart of old
Corpus Christi.

In the 1880s, Robert Simpson's grocery and liquor store stood
on the corner of the east side of the 500 block. Simpson, from
Delaware, was a single man who lived in a boarding house. The
State National Bank, a red-brick building with a round tower,
was built on this site in 1908 (originally called the First State
Bank).

Next door was Conrad Uehlinger's saloon in a shellcrete
building with an Alamo-shaped roofline. It had a hitching rail in
front. It was said that late at night when Uehlinger's closed there
was the loud clip-clop of horses' hooves as cowboys rode back to
the ranch. The Alcove Chili Parlor was on this site later.

The McCampbell Building on the corner had law offices
upstairs and William Rankin's grocery store below. The brick
Seeligson building was later constructed on the McCampbell site.

The west side of the block was dominated by Market Hall.
From the earliest times, this block was called Market Square,

Market Hal in 1907. On the west end of Market Hall was the belfry housing the fire bell. Fire ladders are propped against the building. Market Hall was torn down in 1911 and a new City Hall built on the site.

with a collection of sheds occupied by butchers and vegetable vendors. In 1871 William Rogers and Richard Jordan built a two-story building on the site. They rented stalls on the first floor to butchers and vendors and provided free space on the second floor for the mayor and aldermen. A large hall was reserved for dances and social events.

One of the biggest events of the year was the Firemen's Parade and Ball, observed on the last Tuesday of November. There was a parade during the day, featuring fire engines and hose carts covered with flowers, and competitive events between fire units. A supper and dance followed at Market Hall.

North of Market Hall was a small building of the same design, intended to house city offices, but it was leased to bring in extra revenue. Market Hall and its auxiliary building were torn down in 1911. A new brick city hall (with an irregular shape, like the other modern buildings on Schatzel) was built on the site. Lumber from Market Hall were salvaged and used to build a home on the bluff. The demise of Market Hall marked the end of one era and the beginning of another.

R. G. Blossman's Grocery was in the 600 block on the northeast corner. In the 1930s and 1940s Thomas Boucher's

Pharmacy was on Blossman's old site in a corner of the Furman building. North of Blossman's was a small home occupied for a time by Dr. Arthur Spohn after he married Sarah Josephine Kenedy. They later moved to the Kenedy mansion on the bluff. The Amusu Theater was built here in 1912.

Gale Gibson, with whom I worked, once told me that in the 1940s he would take the bus from hihome in the Hillcrest area to go to the Amusu on Saturday mornings. "I would get on the bus and half the kids in the neighborhood would be there," Gibson said, "We'd go to the Amusu because it always had a double-feature Western, a serial and a couple of cartoons. You could ride the bus for a nickel, and a token would get you back, and for a quarter you could get into the movie and buy popcorn and a drink."

Past the theater was the home of John Timon, father of the later county judge Walter Timon. Six years after the house was built, on a February day in 1891, Mrs. Timon and her daughter returned from Beeville to find a wrecked house and the body of John Timon. There were signs of a struggle but no clear indication of how he had died. If it was a case of murder, it went unsolved. The old Timon home became the Russell House, which moved from the 300 block. The house was torn down in 1955.

Mrs. E. D. Sidbury built a new home on the southeast corner with Starr, which was later sold to R. H. Bingham. His drug store was at the other end of the block. Bingham's home was later the site of Barry Hendrix drug store, then the Taylor Brothers Jewelry store expanded to take in this location.

On the west side of the 600 block, on the corner, the Hatch & Robertson building was constructed in 1891. The structure had many tenants over the years, including Bingham's Drug Store. After the 1919 storm found valuables were displayed in Bingham's windows, a sad display of watches, rings and necklaces of people who lost their lives in the storm. That old building is still there.

Past Bingham's was the B. R. Harris Grocery store. Findlay's Café followed, in the 1920s, and later this building housed the A&G Army Store. Next door was the post office before it moved into the new federal building. Afterwards, it housed Oscar Nau's hardware store. The upper floors of several buildings in this block were partitioned for rented rooms.

Near the end of the block was Norwick Gussett's lumberyard, which was wrecked in the 1874 hurricane. At the end of the block was an old blacksmith shop that was rented by the First Baptist Church in 1883, before it moved to a new brick building a block north.

In the early 1930s the Citizens Industrial Bank was on this southwest corner, then Dr. Fred Stamm and his wife opened a jewelry store and optometrist's clinic in the building. This was followed by Stever's Jewelry, before it moved to Chaparral next to the Center Theater.

Jim Stever said his father did not do well at this location, with stiff competition from Taylor Brothers across the street, but he did well next to the Center Theater, where many of his customers were from the Naval Air Station. "Whenever Tyrone Power came into the store," Stever said, "the sales girls scrambled to see who would get to wait on the famous movie star."

—May 10, 2017

Union soldiers raided Mat Nolan's home

The Union commander on Mustang Island, Major
William Thompson, led a raiding party to reclaim
Nolan's souvenirs taken from the battle of Galveston.

The Mesquite story covers 15 blocks of what people called the Beach Section of the city. Most stores and commercial activity could be found in the first eight blocks of Mesquite, from the southern limits at Cooper's Alley. The north end of the street was mostly homes, including the area once known as Irishtown.

Sam Shoemaker's blacksmith shop, in the 700 block, was on the east side of the street. Shoemaker was one of the town's first volunteer firemen in 1871. Past Shoemaker's was Alexander Kinghorn's wheelwright shop.

One of the three homes on the east side was that of Sheriff Matthew Nolan, a Confederate colonel, and his wife Margaret McMahon. Nolan fought in the battle of Galveston and brought back two captured American flags and a sword. The Union commander on Mustang Island, Major William Thompson, led a raiding party to reclaim Nolan's souvenirs. Thompson's men landed on Jan. 21, 1864 and surrounded the Nolan home where they found Mrs. Nolan, her mother and sister. Thompson took away the sword and flags. They ended up in Iowa.

Later that year, across from the Nolan home, Mat Nolan was shot with a double-barreled shotgun by the Gravis brothers. He died soon afterwards and was buried in Old Bayview.

At the end of the block was later the Magnolia Service Station, which was one of the city's first service stations, built in 1917.

On the west side of the block, past Starr Street, was the Corpus Christi Female Academy run by Professor J. D. Meredith from 1880 to 1896. The State Hotel was built on this site. An Armenian immigrant named Vartan Manasseh Donigan — V. M. Donigan — built the State Hotel in 1907, considered Corpus Christi's first modern hotel. Donigan managed the hotel with his sons, Mesog and Parnot. The family lived in the hotel until Donigan built a show place on Ocean Drive called Donigan's Castle.

At the end of the 700 block on the west side was George Hobbs' wheelwright and blacksmith shop, on a small part of where the Caller-Times parking lot is now.

In the 800 block on the east side corner was the home of Cheston L. Heath. Heath and his father owned a hardware store. The younger Heath became president of the school board; after he died in 1918 the Cheston L. Heath Elementary School was named for him.

Down the block was the grassy, shaded Artesian Park, which got its name from a well drilled there in 1845 by Zachary Taylor's soldiers. The soldiers wouldn't drink the water because, said one critic, one taste made you want to pull out your hair and run. But the mineral water was considered a cure-all and prized by many. Artesian Park was the scene of political rallies, band concerts, horseshoe and domino games. On the west side of the street, on the corner, was the Baptist Church, which moved to this new brick building from an old converted blacksmith shop a block south. A new church was built on Ocean Drive in 1950.

Beyond the church, at the end of the block, was the residence of E. B. Cole, a real estate developer, gave the city land along the bay for Cole Park. The story was that it was the result of a mistake. City workers were plowing up a small city park which adjoined Cole's bayfront property. They plowed up Cole's six acres by mistake so Cole gave his six acres to the city. The Austin J. Wright Park became the larger Cole Park. The Caller-Times was built on the old Cole home site.

On the east side of the 900 block, at 912 Mesquite, was the home of Priscilla Hawley, a heroine in the Civil War. When Union forces threatened a Confederate post on Mustang Island,

The 700 block of Mesquite in the 1930s shows the front of the State Hotel (left) followed by Texas Motor Sales and across the street the Mesquite Street entrance of the Ritz Theater. The distinctive dome of the First Methodist Church can be seen in the distance.

the soldiers there prepared to retreat but the only men who knew the twisting channel around Harbor Island were gone. A 14-year-old girl said she knew the channel and she piloted the boatload of Confederates to safety. Mary Sutherland identified her as "Grace Darling" because she didn't want her name told; she thought her actions "unladylike." She was Priscilla Stephenson who married Henry Hawley.

In the 1000 block, between Mann and Aubrey, was the First Methodist Church, built in 1912 to replace an older church built in 1872. The 1912 Methodist church was a landmark until the new church was built on Shoreline in 1955.

On the east side of the 1000 block, second from the corner, was the Martin Kelly home, built around 1857. During the Civil War when Corpus Christi was bombarded by Union ships cannonballs smashed through the roof and kitchen wall.

Next door was the home of John McClane, who came to Corpus Christi as a sheepman in the 1850s. McClane was a blockade runner during the Civil War and became sheriff of

Nueces County in the 1870s during reconstruction. McClane died at his home on April 1, 1911.

Across the street was the Nueces County Courthouse. The first one was built in 1854 and the second was built in 1875, designed by Rudolph Hollub and called the Hollub Courthouse. Hollub was a mapmaker during the Civil War, making sketches from balloons. He worked as an engineer building the Tex-Mex Railroad, and he was an architect and artist. In 1913 the county's third courthouse was built south of the older structures, which were torn down. The 1914 courthouse still stands.

Mesquite north of the courthouse was mostly homes in an area known as Irishtown. Lillie Anderson Rankin said Irishtown was so-called because so many families were of Irish descent, although there were many of German descent as well, including the Vetters, Shaws, and Fitzsimmons.

Mesquite has a rich history. In the 200 block, at Frederick Belden's home, we see Zachary Taylor discussing over dinner his plans for war with Mexico. In 300 block we see John Fogg leading a lynch mob in the hanging of Jim Garner. In the 700 block we see Union soldiers ransacking Mat Nolan's home to carry away trophies captured in the battle of Galveston. Each of the city's three principal downtown streets — Water, Chaparral and Mesquite — opens a window into the city's past.

—May 17, 2017

Roosevelt loses a big fish

"I told Mr. Roosevelt, 'I am going to lose your first tarpon.' Sure enough, the fish jumped and shook the hook out." —Barney Farley

Eighty years ago this month, in May 1937, President Franklin D. Roosevelt traveled to Port Aransas to go fishing for tarpon off the Texas coast near Port Aransas.

Roosevelt and aides left Washington by train on April 28 and at New Orleans they boarded a Navy destroyer which carried them to the Aransas Pass channel. There they met the presidential yacht, Potomac, which anchored off the lighthouse.

On Sunday Roosevelt went fishing with Port Aransas guide Barney Farley. Nine tarpon were caught, but none were caught by the president though he said he felt four good tugs.

On Monday, Roosevelt went fishing again with Farley. He hooked a tarpon and worked it to the boat. When Farley saw the fish, he realized that the hook had torn a large hole in the tarpon's mouth. "I knew that when I took hold of the leader, the tarpon would jump and the hook would fall out or tear out. I told Mr. Roosevelt, 'I am going to lose your first tarpon.' Sure enough, the fish jumped and shook the hook out. The only thing he said was, 'You called that right.' "

Roosevelt later landed a four-footer and Corpus Christi photographer "Doc" McGregor, in a boat nearby, snapped a shot of Farley and Elliott holding up the tarpon.

Roosevelt received news on Friday morning that the German airship Hindenburg had exploded at Lakehurst, N. J. He sent a

President Franklin D. Roosevelt caught a four-foot tarpon off Port Aransas on May 3, 1937. His son Elliott and fishing guide Barney Farley hold up the fish. Photo by Doc McGregor.

telegram to Adolf Hitler with condolences. On Saturday, the president's last day of fishing, he went out again with Farley. That afternoon he landed a five-foot tarpon as a newsreel camera crew recorded it. The president was so excited, Farley said, he would rub his hands on the tarpon and then on his khaki pants.

The Potomac left on Sunday for Galveston where Roosevelt met, for the first time, Lyndon Johnson, newly elected to Congress.

Back in Washington, Roosevelt's court-packing plan, which would give him control of the Supreme Court, went down to defeat. Cartoonists remembered the fishing trip to Port Aransas and the big tarpon with a hole in its mouth. Roosevelt's plan to reconstruct the court was shown as the big fish that got away.

Alternative facts

History is littered with what some might call Alternative Facts, as we find in the Brundrett story. George Brundrett moved his large family from Detroit to Corpus Christi in 1845. He was a blacksmith and probably worked for Zachary Taylor's army in

304

Corpus Christi. In 1847, when Nueces County was formed, Brundrett was elected one of three county commissioners. In September of 1848 he came to an untimely end and we come to the Alternative Facts.

Historian Hobart Huson wrote in "Coastal Bend Trilogy" that George Brundrett was the captain of a boat operating between Corpus Christi and Port Isabel, that he drowned when thrown overboard at Aransas Pass. Another version comes from the book "Aransas." In this account Brundrett bought a schooner and the boom of the mainmast knocked him overboard. The book said his body was never found, that foul play was suspected because the money he had on him was missing. So which version do we believe?

Well, there's another. It comes from the Sept. 9, 1848 edition of the Corpus Christi Star. In this account, Brundrett had been working at Port Isabel as a blacksmith and was returning home on the Black Bird schooner commanded by Captain Smith. A shift in the wind caused Brundrett to fall overboard and being unable to swim he drowned. Capt. Smith spent five days searching for the body, which was recovered on Sunday after he had drowned on Tuesday. His body was taken to St. Joseph's for burial.

Brundrett was a passenger, not a captain, and his body was recovered and buried on St. Joseph's. Surely that is the accurate story, published a week after the accident. As Shakespeare's hermit of Prague said — that that is, is.

Brundrett's widow Hannah remarried twice and lived to an old age. Two sons, George Jr. and John, served with Confederate forces on Mustang Island. Sara Ann, a daughter, married William Roberts, the first keeper of the lighthouse on Harbor Island.

Subtracting sheep and counting goats

W. G. Sutherland was known as the Sage of Bluntzer and besides running a store he was a longtime schoolteacher, so he may have gotten this story first-hand. By his account, a teacher was explaining the mysteries of subtraction to a pupil named Jimmy.

The teacher asked: "If 12 sheep were on the left side of a wall and four jumped to the right side, how many would be left?"

"None," said Jimmy.

"Oh, Jimmy, think. If 12 sheep were on the left side of the wall and four jumped to the right side, wouldn't there be eight left?"

"No," said Jimmy. "That may be the way with figures, but not with sheep. If four jumped across the wall then all the sheep would follow." Jimmy knew the exact equation: 12 sheep minus four equals zero.

If subtracting sheep is problematical, so is adding goats, as Ranger Captain Rip Ford learned. Ford, also a lawyer, was asked by a goat rancher named Champini to represent him before a congressional committee meeting in Brownsville. The committee was considering claims for reparations due to bandit raids. This story is told in "Rip Ford's Texas."

Champini claimed bandits had stolen his goats over five years and Ford presented a claim for 150 goats plus whatever their natural increase would have been. The committee, puzzled, wanted to know how many goats they were talking about.

Ford figured. A goat has three kids in March, two in September, and the March goats have their own kids when they are 18 months old, and these have their own kids . . . Ford put down his pencil. Champini's 150 goats, if left unmolested, would have increased to two million, five hundred and twenty-one thousand, and eighteen goats.

Ford became concerned about the goat crisis. "Lord help us," said Ford, "if this goat business isn't stopped, in 10 years the state of Texas won't be able to hold all the goats."

The committee decided Champini should be paid for the actual goats but nothing for the hypothetical goats. If Rip Ford gained a new nickname from this experience — such, let us say, as Count de Goats — I am unaware of it.

—May 24, 2017

Hy Vogel's caricatures in 1939

A famous caricature artist from Detroit captured the
likenesses of Eli Merriman, John B. Harney, A. C.
McCaughan, and Doc McGregor.

Hy Vogel, a nationally known artist from Detroit, came to
Corpus Christi in July 1939 to sketch the town's prominent
personalities as a promotion of the Caller-Times.
   Vogel completed caricature sketches of a number of civic and
business leaders, such as Willard Brown, insurance agent, John
Wright, bank president, George Clark, banker, David Peel,
funeral director, L. M. Thomas, pharmacist, Lon Hill, CPL
president — men of influence and repute. No women were on the
list, it being 1939.
   I chose four sketches for this article: newsman Eli Merriman,
Sheriff John B. Harney, Mayor A. C. McCaughan, and
photographer "Doc" McGregor, all heavy hitters on the local
scene. Though Vogel's sketches were gentle exaggerations, as
caricatures go, they do seem to tell quite a lot with a few pen
strokes. At least that's how I see them.

Eli Merriman

   Vogel's Merriman is of venerable age, with the gray of old
silver. He was 86 that summer and would die two years later.
You see nothing of the young boy who was in school when the
Civil War ended. His father pulled him out of class at the
Hidalgo Seminary to tell him the news.

Merriman was born in Hidalgo in 1852, the son of Dr. and Mrs. E. T. Merriman. The family moved to Banquete in 1857 where Dr. Merriman bought a ranch. Eli recalled being sent out to the creek to cut hackberry twigs which the women used as snuff brushes at quilting parties. He recalled Sally Skull coming to visit and bringing a packed jar of butter — large yellow balls.

Merriman started his newspaper career working for the Nueces Valley. In 1883 he and two partners established the Caller. After his partners left, he operated the newspaper until 1911 when he sold it to Henrietta King. He turned to real estate and insurance but continued to write for the paper, his first love. He died on Jan. 25, 1941. A former newsboy said Merriman "was always heart and soul behind every movement" that led to progress for the city of Corpus Christi.

John Harney

In the sketch of Sheriff John B. Harney, perhaps it is the impatient set of the hat that suggests he was anxious to be off, that he had other things to do than sit down and stare back at Vogel. Harney, with a shock of black hair, heavy-duty eyebrows and calculating eyes, looked something like Orson Welles in "A Touch of Evil."

Harney was elected sheriff in 1938 and took office in 1939. Before that, he served as the county inspector of cattle brands. He came from an old family that settled at Nuecestown in 1852.

Harney was a big man who wore a Stetson, hand-tooled Western boots, carried a six-gun, and flashed a badge rimmed with diamonds. In 1942 he was tried for murder involving the death of a man who was taken out of jail and shot, "attempting to escape." Harney was cleared by jury and when the state pressed charges of official misconduct he was acquitted. Harney's political power began to ebb and in 1952 he was defeated for re-election. He died on Sept. 23, 1959.

A. C. McCaughan

When Hy Vogel sketched A. C. McCaughan, he had been mayor for two years, after defeating Dr. Giles in one of the most

Nationally known caricaturist Hy Vogel came down from Detroit in July 1939 to sketch well-known people in Corpus Christi. Four of his subjects were Eli Merriman (upper left), John B. Harney (upper right), A. C. McCaughan (lower left) and "Doc" McGregor.

fiercely fought political contests in city history. Vogel's McCaughan looks like a buttoned-up bookkeeper, which was not far off the mark for he was known as a very precise and detail-oriented man. Allan Charles McCaughan's father was appointed U.S. consul in Durango, Mexico, and McCaughan served as vice-consul. In 1914, with Mexico in turmoil, McCaughan moved his family to Corpus Christi, entered the real estate business and was elected mayor in 1937.

McCaughan's tenure from 1937 to 1945 marked a time of great progress for Corpus Christi. With building the Naval Air Station and consequent growth of the city, new water and sewer lines were extended, new streets were constructed and old ones paved. Under McCaughan's guidance, the city added the seawall, T-heads and yacht basin to the bayfront. McCaughan died on Feb. 10, 1964.

Doc McGregor

It must have been a new experience for John Frederick "Doc" McGregor, having his picture made without a camera, but the result appears to nail him. Vogel depicts him with wavy dark hair, the suggestion of quick brown eyes, a long nose reaching toward communion with the chin, and a small half-smile as if he were trying to look serious and not quite making it.

"Doc" McGregor reached Corpus Christi by a fluke. He was from Pennsylvania, educated as a chiropractor, and was moving his family to California. They were driving to Harlingen to visit friends and stopped in Corpus Christi on Halloween 1929. They stayed. "I never intended to locate in Corpus Christi," he said later. "It was just fate."

He rented an office but it was the Depression and his patients couldn't pay. He was an amateur photographer and began to sell photos in his office. He became the unofficial photographer of the Caller-Times, working without pay but for a credit line. He built a studio, chiropractor's office and family home at 1015 Chaparral. His hobby became his mainstay and he developed a large portrait and photofinishing business. But he was always out with his camera, taking photos of anything going on, leaving the inside work to hired help.

Two of his most famous photos were his favorites. One was a shot of the USS Constitution entering the port in 1933. The other was a shot of President Roosevelt after he caught a tarpon on a fishing trip to Port Aransas in 1937.

McGregor died on May 17, 1986. By chance, or fate he would say, he became the city's photographic historian of record and left a rich legacy, especially of the 1930s and 1940s when he was most active as a photographer. That legacy is an estimated 250,000 negatives at the Museum of Science and History, a fine collection.

The artist Hy Vogel, by the way, became well-known for his caricatures of celebrities that decorated the walls of the London Chop House in Detroit. He died in 2001 at the age of 101.

—*May 31, 2017*

The day the Alta Vista burned

A dark smudge of smoke hung over the city as hundreds
of people drove out to see the spectacular fire.

Ninety years ago, on June 8, 1927, the Alta Vista burned in a
spectacular fire. The old hotel was a well-known landmark,
visible from far out in the bay and the last symbol of the Ropes
Boom.

Elihu Ropes built the Alta Vista in 1890, patterned after a
luxury hotel in Santa Monica, Calif. The Alta Vista was at Three-
Mile Point south of town. The three-story hotel had 106
bedrooms, billiard parlor and bar on the first floor, dining and
dancing facilities on the third floor.

Ropes came to Corpus Christi in 1888. With borrowed money,
he dredged a channel — Ropes Pass — across Mustang Island
and planned to build a railroad to Brownsville; grading started at
the end of Staples, which was called Dump Road because
railroad ties were dumped there.

Ropes bought 20 blocks of land for a development called "The
Cliffs" and planned Ocean Park that would extend five miles on
the bayfront along a street to be called Ocean Drive. He built a
steam-dummy streetcar line to the hotel and held a grand opening
on Aug. 14, 1891. A curved staircase arching over the lobby was
constructed of polished mahogany from logs salvaged on Padre
Island by J. E. Curry, one of Preacher Curry's sons at the Curry
Settlement.

At the height of the Ropes' boom, land that once sold for $8 an
acre soared to $1,000 an acre. Two elderly men fought over who

Elihu Ropes' Alta Vista Hotel, a luxury resort patterned after one in Santa Monica, Calif., was built at Three-Mile Point in 1890. The old derelict burned in a spectacular fire in 1927.

would get to buy a lot near the Alta Vista that was selling for $900. The same lot had recently sold for $10.

But it was a bad time for such unbridled ambition. The crash came during a recession in 1893. Ropes could not pay his taxes or bills. At the Curry settlement, the family joked about all the thngs they would buy "when Colonel Ropes pays us for the logs." Matt Dunn, an old Texas Ranger who lost money in the crash, attacked Ropes with a cane. He left town and sought sanctuary in New Jersey. Before he left Ropes filed a $20,000 suit against Dunn. It was dismissed. Ropes never returned. He died of a stroke, at age 53, on Staten Island in 1897.

The Alta Vista story didn't end with Ropes. In 1904 J. J. Copley bought it and added a pavilion and pier. Copley reopened the hotel in June 1905, but it was closed soon afterwards. David and Clarence Torrey of San Antonio leased the Alta Vista and opened it in the summer of 1906. Then it was closed again.

In 1911 the Alta Vista was leased by the Peacock Naval College in Corpus Christi. Navy cutters on loan to the school docked at the old Copley pier. The Naval College soon closed. Then it stood vacant again. Theodore Fuller looked inside the hotel in 1921. "The dust of decades, quarter of an inch deep, formed a habitat for an infinity of fleas," he wrote. "Heaven knows what they lived on."

The Caller on June 9, 1927, reported that the Alta Vista fire was believed started by vagrants. H. W. Palmer saw the smoke and ran to the hotel. He realized it was a goner and ran back to his own residence and organized a bucket brigade to try to save it but wind-blown sparks set it afire and it burned. The nearby Sumerlin home was saved by covering the roof with wet sacks. City firemen did not go to the scene because there were no water connections that far out of town.

A dark smudge of smoke hung over the city as hundreds of people drove out to see the spectacular fire. Automobiles lined the road from the hotel to the southern limits of Del Mar and hundreds of people gathered to watch the fire, no doubt hoping it would spread and provide an even greater spectacle.

Not long before the fire, the Caller noted, a man committed suicide in the Alta Vista and people talked of it being haunted. "But if there was a rattle of ghostly chains yesterday," the paper said, "it was drowned in the roar of the ravenous fire."

Loyd's Pleasure Pier

On Saturday night 103 years ago Loyd's Pavilion and Pleasure Pier opened. It was June 6, 1914. After selling 17,186 ten-cent admissions on opening day, the cashier said she wore out her fingers tearing off tickets. The Caller was enthusiastic, describing Loyd's as the "peer of piers and the Coney Island of Corpus Christi Bay."

J. E. Loyd's Pavilion and Pleasure Pier was built past the end of Mann Street on a pier extending 900 feet into the bay. It had a bathing pavilion, with 250 private bathing rooms, an amusement section with a dance hall, skating rink, merry-go-round and Ferris wheel. It had a soda fountain, café, and open-air picture show described as "absolutely flickerless."

There were 16 concession stands and a 21-piece band of "master musicians" that played each afternoon and evening. It was a dazzling place at night, with more than 1,500 lights reflecting off the waters of the bay. After opening day the Caller said the new

Bathers pose for the camera of Karl Swafford. In the background is Loyd's Pleasure Pier before it was heavily damaged in the 1916 hurricane. Karl Swafford Photo from Jim Moloney.

slogan was "Meet Me at Loyd's." People came from San Antonio and beyond on special railroad excursion rates to visit Loyd's.

Two years later, on Aug. 18, 1916, a hurricane severely damaged or destroyed every pier on the waterfront, including Loyd's. Only a portion of the pier was left.

Six years later, after another destructive storm in 1919, the city built its own Pleasure Pier off Peoples Street. The 1,000-foot pier had landing places for boats on the T-Head part of the pier. Downtown workers liked to stroll on the pier at noon and guests at the Nueces Hotel would take an evening promenade for a breath of Gulf air and view of the bay. An old fisherman's shack at the foot of the pier was remodeled to become the Pier Café, operated by John Govatos. Most of the town's 22,000 people got around to eating at the Pier Café, certainly one of the most popular restaurants in town.

Loyd's Pavilion and Pleasure Pier lasted little more than two years before it was wrecked. The city's Pleasure Pier survived the 1933 storms and lasted almost two decades. It was dismantled when the seawall was built in 1939-1941.

—June 7, 2017

316

What happened to Sodville?

A generation born to the farm moved to town and
Sodville, and places like it, withered away.

In the times before the 1920s, a woman named Christi Field, a
farmer's wife, looked forward to taking her daughters, Judy and
Addie Christine, on her trips to Corpus Christi, which was a big
city since it had paved streets.

When the day arrived, they would take the family buggy to
Taft. Since the road there was muddy or dusty — there was no
in-between — the girls would travel in their petticoats until they
reached Taft where they would change into their city dresses and
board the train for Corpus Christi.

They would go shopping, have a hamburger, and return on the
afternoon train. The horse was tied to a tree with a tub of water
and the buggy nearby. The girls would take off their city dresses
and ride home in their petticoats to Sodville. That story is told in
Keith Guthrie's San Patricio County History.

Sodville was one of the farm communities that grew out of the
homeseeker era after the turn of the 20th century. George H.
Paul, from Iowa, made such a success selling Driscoll Ranch
lands in Nueces County that he was contracted to sell 50,000
acres of the Taft Ranch in San Patricio County.

This was the great transition. Cheap, fertile land opportunities
brought down people from the Midwest looking for a place to
settle. They bought their acreage or farmed on shares and land
that had long been grazing pastures gained new patterns of
plowed fields and long rows of growing crops, mostly cotton.

317

New towns sprang up named Sinton, Taft, St. Paul and Sodville. The latter was seven miles south of Sinton and four miles west of Taft.

How Sodville came to be called that has been lost, but the name describes what it was and hoped to be. If some thought it a derogatory term, it was not for the people who lived there. It was a proud name evocative of the rich black sod that gave the place its name: Sodville.

By 1908 the Sodville school was built, a store opened in 1910, two gins were ginning cotton by 1912, and a Baptist church was established in 1914. One man closely identified with the history of Sodville was W. A. Dunn.

A Caller-Times reporter talked to Dunn in 1956. He moved to Sodville in 1913, bought a burned-out gin and general store, built another gin, then sold both gins and concentrated on the store.

Dunn told the reporter that running a country store in the days before paved roads required him to keep a large inventory on hand. People remembered that it rained harder then, unlike today, and for days on end. Maybe so. After a heavy rain Sodville became Mudville and on the dirt roads "the bottom dropped out."

Dunn said he kept a stock of $25,000 in staple groceries and foods, as well as a complete line of dry goods, hardware and harnesses for mules and horses. Where his store stood was known as the Dunn Corner. Dunn died in April 1961.

The specifics vary but in general what happened to Sodville happened all over the country, beginning in the Great Depression, when hard times became a way of life. Big farms got bigger and small family farmers and tenant share-croppers went broke. "If I was to start to hell with a load of ice," one said, "there would be a freeze before I got there." A generation born to the farm moved to town and became office clerks, service-station workers and short-order cooks. Sodville, and places like it, withered away.

You can find where Sodville used to be, at the intersection of Farm roads 1074 and 1944, and if you drive around there you will see scattered houses surrounded by plowed fields. A historical marker tells the story, concluding with — "As people left farms and rural areas for cities in the second half of the 20th

The Sodville 4-H Club took part in the Texas Centennial Parade in Sinton in 1936, with their farm wagon pulled by mules. Sodville was once a thriving farm community with a store at Dunn's Corner, a Baptist church, a large school and two cotton gins

Century, the population of Sodville declined. The school district was consolidated with Sinton in 1947. Dunn's store closed in the 1950s. The Sodville Baptist Church disbanded in 1961. A few homes were all that remained of Sodville at the end of the 20th Century."

That sums it up. The sod is there but the ville is long gone.

Jane Cazneau and manifest destiny

An ad in the Corpus Christi Star in 1848 read — "The undersigned is in expectation of receiving a complete assignment of dry goods, selected for the Mexican trade." The ad was William Cazneau's.

Cazneau, from Boston, opened a store in the town of Matagorda. He fought in the Revolution and was in charge of the squad that buried the Texan dead at San Jacinto. He moved to Corpus Christi and became a business partner of Henry Kinney. In March 1849 he led a trade expedition to Chihuahua called "The Great Chihuahua Train." That year he married Jane McManus Storm.

Cazneau was interesting, but his wife was on another level. She studied law with her father, a member of Congress from Troy, N.Y., and married Allen Storm and had a son. After she was separated she reportedly became a great friend (not platonically) of former vice president Aaron Burr when she was in her 20s and he was in his 70s. Mrs. Burr filed for divorce and named Jane Storm as the cause, for the usual reason.

Jane Storm moved to South Texas, bought land at Matagorda and encouraged German immigration to Texas, in partnership with Aaron Burr. She went to a ball in Matagorda City but was turned away because reports of the Burr scandal had followed her to Texas.

She wrote for the New York Weekly Sun and other papers under the pen name of Cora Montgomery and coined the term "Manifest Destiny" though it was attributed to a man. Her influential columns in the New York Sun helped shift public opinion in favor of the United States' annexation of Texas.

During the Mexican War, she accompanied Winfield Scott's assault on Veracruz and wrote dispatches from the front. Some called her the first woman war correspondent. A book on Jane Cazneau by Linda Hudson — "Mistress of Manifest Destiny" — published in 2001 was very interesting though the connection with Corpus Christi is marginal. Jane McManus Storm Cazneau was an unusual woman well ahead of her time. She died in a shipwreck in 1878.

—June 14, 2017

When the Green Flag flew

The Green Flag was symbolic of the city achieving some great success. When the Green Flag went up, business practically stopped while citizens congratulated each other.

In 1934, during the Great Depression, Corpus Christi got its first big industry, Southern Alkali. A delegation led by Maston Nixon persuaded the company to locate in Corpus Christi. When the deal was finalized, the Green Flag was flown over Leopard Street between the Nixon Building and Plaza Hotel. The Green Flag was symbolic of the city achieving some great success.

When the Green Flag went up business practically stopped while citizens congratulated each other. They knew that the Green Flag meant the city had landed Southern Alkali, like a fisherman who pulled in a very big fish on a small line. In 1934, with the city desperate for jobs, this was a big deal.

The Green Flag was flown again in November 1939 when Navy officials chose Corpus Christi for a new navy base at Flour Bluff. But what happened to the Green Flag, the city's symbol of civic success? Come to think of it, what happened to the Doddridge Bank Clock?

Perry Doddridge, a wool dealer, opened Corpus Christi's first bank on Chaparral in 1871. The Doddridge Bank collapsed during what was called a money panic in 1893. Doddridge spent his personal fortune repaying depositors 60 cents on the dollar, leaving him bankrupt.

On the day in 1893 when the Ropes Boom ended and the Doddridge Bank went under, its big clock in the lobby stopped,

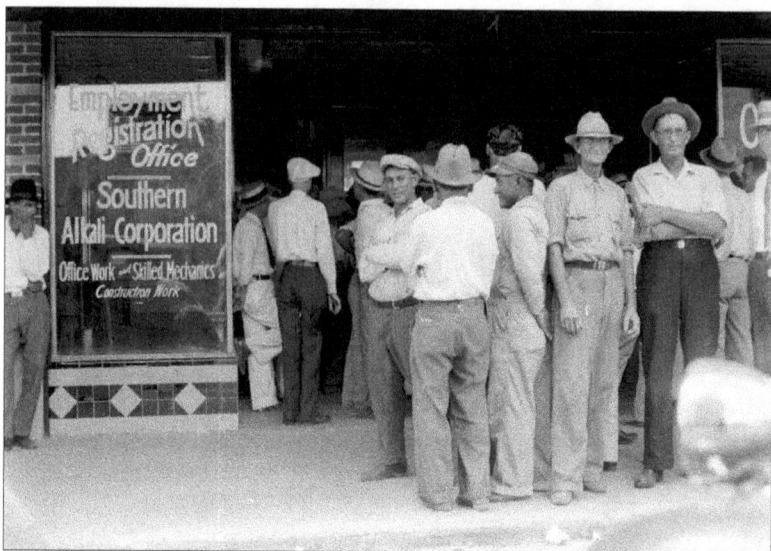

In the depths of the Great Depression in 1934, men wait outside an office on Leopard Street to apply for work building a new plant, Southern Alkali. It was the first major industrial concern to locate in Corpus Christi.

and as the clock stopped, so did Corpus Christi's economy. Lean years followed.

In 1906, as Corpus Christi was becoming accustomed to prosperity again, the Board of Trade was formed and the Doddridge Bank clock was repaired and set to running again. It decorated the office of the Board of Trade in the Garrett Building.

The Board of Trade lasted only a year. It was followed by the Commercial Club, which survived until 1920 when the Chamber of Commerce began operations. But, in the meantime, what happened to the old Doddridge Bank clock? Gone, I guess, to the same place as the Green Flag.

Starting for Kansas

The Nueces Valley newspaper reported on April 18, 1872: "Quite a number of our young men are about to start for Kansas again with cattle." In another edition, it reported that James

Bryden, trail boss at King Ranch, "starts off with the first drove of cattle for the Kansas market, his herd consisting of 4,120 head from Nueces County." The Corpus Christi area figures prominently in the epic history of the trail drives.

This was a tremendous undertaking. In 1871 more than 700,000 head of Texas cattle went north. The drovers gathered herds in the spring when grass was coming up. The drive would take about four months. For every 1,000 head there would be four to six trail hands, or waddies. They were paid about $30 to $40 a month. There was a trail boss, wrangler, and cook, also known as "Coozie. Trail-driving stories are in "Trail Drivers of Texas."

James Gibson of Alice recalled one drive when a young rooster went along as mascot. He crowed every morning, rode in the chuck wagon, and was a source of amusement for all. He made the trip to Dodge City and returned to South Texas with the cook.

Walter Billingsley, who drove herds to Kansas for King Ranch, said he was well-educated for the job. He graduated from the fourth grade with a diploma in herding goats.

Amanda Burks went north with a herd with her husband, John Burks of Banquete. She slept in a tent, like Lorena in "Lonesome Dove." She said she returned to Banquete in December "in much better health than when I left nine months before." Her story is told in Trail Drivers.

Cowboys would arrive in South Texas in the fall, dressed in store clothes they bought in Dodge City or Abilene and, said one, looking as though they were somebody sure enough. One said he would never forget the feel of the saddle, the heavy pull of a six-shooter on his belt, or what a blessing on a wet night was that old yellow rainslicker they called "fish".

Decrow's Point to Murdock's Landing

On the north side of Pass Cavallo is Decrow's Point, at the end of Matagorda Peninsula. A bar pilot named Thomas Decrow built a home and wharf there in the 1840s. In the 1875 storm, the wharf and buildings at Decrow's Point were destroyed. Nothing was left but concrete cisterns. Decrow's Point is an example of how coastal history can be traced by place names of early settlers.

Vinson's Slough, with Cedar Bayou, separates Matagorda from St. Joseph's. When the stage ran from Saluria to the village of Aransas on St. Joseph's, it made a rest stop at Vinson's Slough. But who was Vinson? All we can glean is that a long-bearded and cantankerous old man named Vinson lived there. He would, on some pretext, try to prevent the mail rider from crossing the slough where he lived

Jerry Stedman had a place on an island in Redfish Bay, off Aransas Pass, before he moved to Beaumont. The name Stedman's Island remained, along with Bludworth Island, Tally Island, and Dunham Island — all named for early settlers. Clark's Island was named for William Clark, a sea captain from Maine who also founded the town of Clarksville on the border.

Lydia Ann Channel, between Harbor Island and St. Joseph's, was named for Lydia Ann Wells, wife of James Babbitt Wells who commanded the Texas Navy yards at Galveston before moving to St. Joseph's. Their son, Jim Wells, was the political boss in Brownsville.

In 1892, John Ward bought Island A, between the Oso and Corpus Christi Bay. He planned to build a resort. When the Ropes Boom collapsed, Ward left town but his name remained with Ward Island, where Texas A&M-Corpus Christi is today.

Down Padre Island was Murdock's Landing, on the laguna side, named for William Murdock, described as a Yankee renegade and island scavenger who made buckskin for sale. There was a channel across the island called Murdock's Landing Pass. It was closed by the 1919 hurricane. Yarborough Pass was dredged there in the 1940s.

Of course, the family name with the longest tenure is that of Padre Balli, who began a cattle ranch on the lower end of the island in 1804. Ever since, it has been Padre Ballí's island.

—June 21, 2017

Walter Foster's Princess Louise Hotel

"You don't miss home so much, in a place like this."
—J. C. Robertson

One of Corpus Christi's finest resort hotels after the turn of the 20th Century was the Seaside Hotel, with its shady grove of salt cedars, and its annex and the nearby Seaside Pavilion on a pier in the bay. The Seaside, Pavilion and salt cedars were destroyed in the 1919 storm.

Corpus Christi sorely missed the Seaside Hotel, as a draw for tourists, so the Chamber of Commerce offered a bonus of $10,000 to anyone who would build a resort hotel in what was called the beach section of the city.

The Chamber's offer was taken up by Walter Foster, a railroad conductor and engineer, his wife and her brother, John Saunders. They bought a property at Mann and Water and built a 110-room hotel in 1927. The hotel's stucco walls were painted pink offering a colorful contrast with the red-tile roof. The stylish interior was designed to resemble a Spanish villa. It was named the Princess Louise, after Walter Foster's wife Louise.

It was a complete success and the owners were paid the $10,000 bonus. The hotel opened on Saturday night, Jan. 7, 1928. The first guests to register were Mr. and Mrs. J. C. Robertson from St. Petersburg, Fla. "You don't miss home so much," said the man, "in a place like this."

The hotel was managed by Walter and Louise Foster until She died in 1936. Walter turned over the management to Leslie Greer, though he kept an active hand in the hotel's operation. He

The Princess Louise as seen from its pier in the bay on March 26, 1936. The pink stucco hotel with a red-tile roof opened in January 1928 and became a downtown landmark. The building was converted into La Posada Apartments in 1965. Photo by Doc McGregor.

opposed building the seawall at first but later withdrew his objection. When the seawall was completed, Foster's hotel was two blocks inland. It was never the same away from the water.

Foster resumed management duties when many of his employees enlisted in the armed services during World War II. He was known as a philanthropist and "soft touch" who told a reporter he would rather be cheated by a scoundrel than fail to help a deserving person.

Walter Foster died on Nov. 15, 1948. He left the hotel to his secretary, Mary Ethel Noble, and in 1965 she had the hotel remodeled and converted into the La Posada Apartments. But it was nothing like what it once was, when the Princess Louise was a rose-pink, gaily colored, palm-fringed landmark by the wide blue bay. Like the Seaside Hotel before it, the Princess Louise Hotel was deeply missed.

Robert Love's Rancho Grande

Of Robert Love's Ranch — known as Rancho Grande — our first introduction comes from William McClintock, a soldier from Bourbon County, Ky. He was traveling through Texas to join the Second Kentucky Regiment, which was a week's march ahead of him, on the way to the Mexican War. McClintock rode through San Patricio on his way to Love's Ranch in October 1846.

In a letter home, McClintock wrote that it had been recommended that when he reached San Patricio to go down to Love's Ranch, three miles below the town, a stone's throw from the river. He reached the ranch about dark on Oct. 25, 1846.

"I was hospitably received," McClintock wrote. "The proprietor was sick. He had perhaps passed the meridian of life. Had spent several years in Mexico. A man of strong sense and correct judgement." He said Love had purchased and settled his ranch the previous spring. The tract Love acquired from the heirs of Toribio Molina "contains 18 square miles of unsurpassed richness and beauty."

McClintock left the ranch after two days and on departure gave some books to Love, in lieu of a payment that Love, a courteous host, would not accept. But he was an avid reader and kept the books. Robert Love was called a judge, although in those days anyone who had ever seen a law book was called a judge. He had been in Matamoros for several years where he married Maria de Jesusa Arocha, younger sister of Mauricia Arocha who married Frederick Belden. Belden became a Corpus Christi merchant, also called a judge. The Arocha sisters and their families remained close over the years.

J. Williamson Moses, who led a band of mustangers (later he was a real judge), visited Love's Ranch in the 1850s. "I saw two of Judge Love's little boys — Pendleton and Marcos, one about five and the other seven — with a lot of small children on the place," Moses wrote.

"They would go around and after gathering together all the chickens they could find, two or three of them would act as drivers and the others would take stands behind bushes and, with tough cords for lassos, they would rope the chickens as they were running by them.

"Pendleton or Marcos scarcely ever failed to secure a captive, while the old judge would laugh heartily when a successful lasso was thrown . . . The judge would encourage the youngsters in their sport. Some of the careful housewives, however, did not take quite so kindly to the 'carrera de los pollos' (race after chickens). Though the judge never failed to pay for a crippled or decapitated pollo, they denounced it as a barbarous pastime."

After the death of Judge Love, sometime in 1862, Marcos and Pendleton Love figured in two tragic incidents at Rancho Grande.

In one, on March 15, 1868, Pendleton Love and Margarito Martinez were killed by the same bullet. Pendleton Love was standing in the door of a house when he was shot by a man named Olgin. The bullet passed through Pendleton's body and killed Martinez who was behind him. Love died two days later. What the fight was about was unknown. The incident was reported in the Daily Ranchero in Brownsville.

The second event was also a terrible bit of bad luck. It happened the same year at a fandango at the ranch. A drunk cowboy named George Malloy, just back from a trail drive to Kansas, fired a shot at a lantern hanging from a tree. The shot was wild and killed a baby. Marcos Love shot Malloy on the spot. He was laid down on the front porch of the Love ranch house and died soon afterwards. It was the night of July 23, 1868.

Not long after the shooting, Marcos Love moved to a village in Coahuila, Mexico where he married and assumed, in the Spanish custom, his mother's surname. He was known as Marcos Love Arocha.

—June 28, 2017

Stylish homes lined South Broadway

In 1909, Ella Scott held a reception in her home for
William Jennings Bryan, after he lost the presidential
race to William Howard Taft.

South Broadway was a residential street where homes of the
well-to-do were built in the 19th and early 20th Century before
Ocean Drive became the showplace of fine homes.

The stately structures on South Broadway featured columned
porticos, wide balconies, spacious lawns, and carriage steps by
the street. These homes had a splendid view. The waterfront was
closer then and the residents could walk out on their columned
porches and watch sailboats tacking across the bay.

The dividing line on Broadway between north and south
addresses was the arroyo, which ran from where Blucher's Park
is today to the bay. Broadway, north and south, with a few
exceptions represented the city's most stylish residential street.

One exception was the wholesale fruit and vegetable
distributor, Desel-Boettcher, at 100 South Broadway. Another
was Corpus Christi Hardware across the street. Corpus Christi
Hardware later bought the Desel-Boettcher building to expand.

At 223 South Broadway was the home of George R. and Ella
Scott. It was called the Scott Mansion when it was built in the
1880s. In 1909, Ella Scott held a reception in her home for
William Jennings Bryan, who was in Corpus Christi licking his
wounds after he lost the presidential race to William Howard
Taft.

Mrs. Scott's daughter Lucille married a young lawyer in the
Scott law firm, Walter E. Pope, who was elected city attorney,

The residence of Mr. and Mrs. G. R. Scott at 223 South Broadway, a two-story house with a round turret, was built in the 1880s. It later became the home Mrs. W. E. (Lucille) Pope, the Scotts' daughter. The house was torn down in 1958.

state legislator and ran for governor. After G. R. Scott's death, Mrs. Scott and her married daughter Lucille, who became estranged from her husband, lived in the Scott Mansion. It was called the Pope-Scott home before it was torn down in 1958.

William Rankin's home was at 313 South Broadway. Rankin, born in 1856 to parents who immigrated from Scotland, established a thriving grocery business on Mesquite Street. After his marriage in 1885, Rankin lived in a cottage where the Amusu Theater was built. He built a new home on South Broadway in 1894.

Dan Reid, who built the Rankin home, looked at his plan and complained, "There's enough lumber in it for two houses," but Rankin insisted the specifications be followed. It was copied from a house he admired in New Orleans.

Most of the buildings on South Broadway were on the west side of the street facing east. But there were several homes and a church in the 200 and 300 blocks built on the east side of the street facing west. Most prominent of these was the home of Edwin and Winnifred Flato, at 316 South Broadway. The house

The Pat Dunn residence at 317 South Broadway was an 11-room home built in 1907. The Dunn family spent the summers on their island ranch and winters in town. The house was torn in 1955.

was two stories in front and four stories in the back. I have not seen a photo of that home, except when it was already half destroyed when it was being razed.

Edwin Flato was president of Corpus Christi Hardware, located two blocks north of his home. Flato was born in Flatonia, the town named for his grandfather. He moved to Kingsville in 1904, when he was 20, and worked for a lumber firm; he slept in the lumberyard and ate his meals in a tent. Two years later, he went to work as a bookkeeper for Corpus Christi Hardware and within a year was named president of the company. After the 1919 storm the business was separated, with the retail operation on Chaparral renamed Nueces Hardware while the wholesale operation moved to South Broadway.

The Flato home during World War II was often filled with officers from the Naval Air Station. The Flatos entertained with a dance every Saturday night. Flato's terraced gardens were famous for their flowers and shrubs, including a variety of hibiscus registered as the Edwin Flato Hibiscus. Flato's wife died in 1958 and he remarried. After his death in 1971 the house was torn down, along with the garden where the hibiscus grew.

The Pat Dunn home, at 317, was across from the Flato home. Pat Dunn owned a cattle ranch on Padre Island for more than 50 years. He built the home in 1907 for $10,000. Dunn's family spent the summers on the island and lived in town in the winters so the children could attend school. After Dunn's death, the house was sold in 1946 to Walter Foster, owner of the Princess Louise Hotel, and used to house his art and antique collection. The house was demolished in 1955.

Past the Dunn home was one of the city's oldest structures, one of the first built on South Bluff. It was the home of W. W. Chapman, an Army quartermaster stationed at Corpus Christi after the Mexican War. Chapman was a business partner of Richard King, Mifflin Kenedy and Charles Stillman. He imported some of the first Merino sheep to Nueces County.

Chapman purchased a four-acre lot from Henry Kinney for $900 and the Chapman home was built about 1855 with lumber shipped from New York. Chapman died at Fort Sumter in 1859 but his son William and his widow Helen returned to Corpus Christi after the Civil War.

Andrew Anderson recalled a school operated in the Chapman house about 1869. "Mr. and Mrs. [J. B.] Carpenter ran a school for boys and girls, having at times as many as a hundred scholars," Anderson said. "This was on the bluff in the Chapman house. The rules of conduct were framed and hanging up inside the door. Mr. Carpenter did not whip or slap anybody; if a pupil would not obey the rules he had to go home."

The students sat at tables, with two boys and two girls at each table, Anderson recalled, and once a month the school presented a program for the parents. The students would recite and sing songs such as "Johnny Schmoker" and "Go Tell Aunt Rhody" the old gray goose is dead.

In 1930 the Chapman house was moved to the back of the lot facing South Carancahua. There was major disruption in this area when the state in 1965-'67 built what was called the Midtown Traffic Exchange, which extended Agnes and Laredo into the downtown. It cut across Tancahua, Carancahua and South Broadway. The Chapman house was sold for $825 and moved to the Westside. Others were either moved or knocked down.

—July 12, 2017

Library occupied the W. W. Jones mansion

"My friend and I rode bicycles from Six Points to the
library and I can still remember the smell of wood floors
and books." — Joyce Lanphier

South Broadway was a fashionable residential street with
stately homes, columned porches, spacious lawns, with a clear
view of the bay from the high bluff. Upper Broadway was a
showplace of fine homes, homes loaded with historical
significance and character.

One was the home of Joseph and Sadie Hirsch, built in 1910 at
411 South Broadway. The house was moved to Carancahua in
1946 to make way for a YMCA expansion. It was demolished in
1956.

South of the Joe Hirsch home was Herman Cohn's residence at
425 South Broadway. What was described as a Greek-Revival
mansion was built in 1914 for Cohn, a partner in the Gugenheim
& Cohn department store. The Cohn house was noted for unusual
features.

One was a series of vents that relied on natural drafts to keep
the high-ceilinged rooms cool. The house had one of the first hot
water systems in the city and it had a vacuum-cleaning system in
the basement with air tubes in the walls connecting to the rooms.
The Cohn house was destroyed by a fire set by an arsonist on
June 8, 1976.

The Perry Doddridge home was at 435, although the numbers
on the street were changed later and the address became 501.
When it was built for Peter Schatzell in 1849 it was called
Mansion House. Schatzell, a bachelor, was a merchant in

Matamoros who became friendly with Henry Kinney, founder of Corpus Christi and chose to retire here. When Kinney hosted the 1852 Lone Star Fair, Schatzell loaned him $45,000 for expenses.

When Schatzell died in 1854, Samuel Fullerton, executor of the estate, pressed Kinney to repay the $45,000 loan. Kinney had to sell some of his ranch holdings to pay the debt. In the process, Fullerton acquired Mansion House, where he and wife Mary and daughter Rachel lived.

A young wool merchant named Perry Doddridge married Rachel Fullerton in Mansion House on June 12, 1862. Doddridge was a self-made man. His parents died when he was seven. When he was 14 he worked as a clerk in Brownsville for the riverboat line owned by Richard King and Mifflin Kenedy. After he married Rachel Fullerton he opened a wool business in Corpus Christi. The four-year-old son of Perry and Rachel Doddridge died in the yellow fever epidemic in 1867. He was buried behind their home.

In 1871 Doddridge opened the first bank in Corpus Christi, on Chaparral, and he was elected mayor in 1873. During those years the Doddridge home was one of the town's social centers. Every Thursday evening was open house where "old and young amuse themselves brilliantly and feast on the best fare," wrote Maria von Blucher. E. H. Caldwell noted in his memoirs that the Doddridge home "was a frequent gathering place for many of us young people. We attended dances, played games, conversed, and generally passed happy times."

The Doddridge bank went under in 1893 during a national depression and Doddridge spent his personal fortune repaying depositors 60 cents on the dollar, which left him bankrupt. Mary Sutherland in "The Story of Corpus Christi" said the entire city sympathized with Doddridge — "a good, honest man, whose greatest sin was his trust in his fellow man. He never recovered from the shock of the destruction of his life work." He died on June 11, 1902. Rachel Doddridge died the following year. Both were buried under hackberry trees in the yard where their young son was interred in 1867.

Rachel Doddridge left the property to the First Presbyterian Church. The old Schatzell-Fullerton-Doddridge home, Mansion

The W. W. Jones home, described as modified or Southern Colonial, was built in 1907. The Jones home was sold to the city in 1937 and used as the La Retama Library until 1955. It was torn down in 1957.

House, was a landmark on South Bluff for 80 years before it was dismantled to make way for a new First Presbyterian Church. It was built on the site in 1929. The remains of Perry, Rachel and their son were moved to New Bayview Cemetery.

E. E. Roscher, whose family home stood at Lipan and Carancahua, once recalled herding milk cows that his father owned from an empty lot next to the old Doddridge home, where the church was built later.

At 511 South Broadway was the home of W. W. Jones, built in 1907 by Dan Reid. While it was being built, the Jones family rented the Doddridge-Fullerton home nearby.

William Whitby Jones was one of the richest cattlemen in South Texas. He was also a banker, real-estate broker and later owned the Nueces Hotel. W. W. Jones was born in Goliad in 1858. His father, A. C. Jones, was a prominent merchant who later moved to Beeville. As a young man, W. W. Jones worked as a trail hand driving cattle to Kansas. He bought a ranch near Beeville and married Louella Marsden. About 1890 Jones bought much of the land that became Jim Hogg County. In 1905 he moved to Corpus Christi and later invested in building the Nueces Hotel, which opened in 1913. He bought out the other investors.

In 1937 the Jones' mansion was sold to the City of Corpus Christi for use as a public library. The city paid $26,000 for the property, although it was valued at $35,000. The library opened in its new quarters on Oct. 11, 1937.

Several people over the years have written me with memories of the library in the Jones mansion. Janis Wood said there was a magnolia tree in the front yard and librarians would pick the large white blossoms to keep in a vase at the front desk. "Patrons were greeted with a heavenly scent. These memories are probably responsible, in part, for the career I chose as a librarian."

Another who remembered the library from those years, Joyce Lanphier, wrote that, "I have fond memories of La Retama Library when it was in the old Jones house. My friend and I rode bicycles from Six Points to the library and I can still remember the smell of wood floors and books."

La Retama occupied the Jones mansion until 1955 when it was moved to the old City Hall building on Mesquite. The Jones home was torn down in 1957 to make way for a parking lot for the First Presbyterian Church.

—July 19, 2017

Clark Pease home built in 1905

"The home was built with a carriage house which was
converted into a garage for Pease's Maxwell." —Marie
(Pease) Crook

Stately houses filled with old furniture and family memories
once lined South Broadway. One of these was the Clark Pease
home. The Pease home was built at 521 South Broadway in
1905, the year after Pease came to Corpus Christi from
Wisconsin. He established the Clark Pease bank which became
the City National Bank, at the corner of Peoples and Chaparral.
He was elected mayor and served from 1909 to 1913.

The home was built with a carriage house which was converted
into a garage for Pease's Maxwell, said his daughter, Marie
(Pease) Crook. Pease died in 1929 and his wife in 1940. The
house was torn down in 1962.

On the next lot south, at 601, was the home of Charles and
Sarah Weil, who built a new home after the turn of the century
and moved from the family homestead on North Broadway, north
of Henrietta King's home.

The area around Broadway, Carancahua and Park streets
became the Weil neighborhood. The adult children of Charles
and Sarah built or bought homes within rock-throwing distance.
They included Mrs. Jeannette Kaffie (a married daughter),
Joseph Weil, Sylvan Weil, Jonas Weil, Alex Weil, and Carrie
(Weil) Lichtenstein.

The E. L. Barnard home at 611 South Broadway was purchased
and cleared by Richard King Sr., a banker, rancher, and grandson
of the great cattleman who founded King Ranch.

The Clark Pease home on South Broadway, built in 1905, included eight huge rooms, a large entrance hall, verandas, and back porch. Exterior and interior windows provided lighting in the time before electricity was available.

After King's home on North Beach was destroyed in the 1919 storm he moved his family into the King-Kleberg home on North Broadway before building a new home on South Broadway.

The two-story red-brick home built in 1926 became the home of King and his wife, Minerva Pierpont Heaney King, daughter of Dr. A. G. Heaney. In 1964, a new high school was named for Richard King. The Kings lived in their stately home on South Broadway until Mrs. King died in 1966 and he died in 1974. The King home was renovated and converted to law offices in 1990.

Next door to Richard King's mansion was the one-story home of Julius Lichtenstein and his wife Carrie (Weil) Lichtenstein, at 615 South Broadway.

Julius Lichtenstein was three years old when his father moved his department store from Indianola to Corpus Christi, in 1874. Julius married Carrie Weil in 1902 and in 1904, with the death of his father, he became the head of Lichtenstein's & Sons. In 1905 he built a house at 715 North Chaparral and in 1913 he built a larger house at 615 South Broadway.

Julius Lichtenstein died in 1923 and his widow Carrie in 1958. The house was sold to attorney Howell Ward and Hortense

The Julius and Carrie (Weil) Lichtenstein home at 615 South Broadway, which still stands today. The home, built in 1913, was later owned by Howell and Hortense Warner Ward.

Warner Ward, a local historian. After Mrs. Ward died in 1978 the house was sold and today serves as offices for Durrill Properties.

On the corner with Park Avenue is the Giles-Farenthold home. It was built by Dr. Clyde Watson, but it has long been known as the Giles-Farenthold house. It is mostly identified with Dr. H. R. Giles who served as mayor, owned the Giles Hotel on Chaparral, and practiced medicine for 50 years.

In 1935, Dr. Giles and A. C. McCaughan ran for mayor in one of the fiercest political races in city history. Passions were so heated that Texas Rangers were sent to keep the peace on election day. Giles won by a slender margin. In 1937, Giles ran for re-election and faced McCaughan in another heated contest. McCaughan won. Two years later Giles ran for mayor again but McCaughan won and Dr. Giles, in disgust, gave up politics.

Dr. Giles died in 1948 and the Giles place was sold and became the home of George and Frances "Sissy" Farenthold, state legislator and candidate for governor. It became known as the Farenthold home and gained the hyphenated name of Giles-Farenthold. Perhaps it should be called the Watson-Giles-Farenthold home, though you can take hyphenation only so far. It was purchased in 1990 by David Massie, who said it is a wonderful home that is now fully restored on its original site.

South of Park Avenue, one lot past the corner, was the home of Roy Miller and his wife Maud (Heaney) Miller. Their first home on North Chaparral was destroyed in the 1919 storm. Miller took the family to the Nueces Hotel on the morning of the storm and they remained there afterwards. He purchased the house at 703 South Broadway.

Roy Miller's second home was south of a vacant lot at the intersection of Park. The Church of the Good Shepherd was moved from Chaparral to this lot in 1926.

Miller's son Dale recalled that, "When I was young there was always a gathering on the lawn in the summertime. The bay was only about 75 yards away. People would drop in and play games." He said his mother "loved young people and would always be the ringleader in the fun, dancing and gaiety."

Roy Miller was born in Blue Rapids, Kansas in 1884. His family moved to Houston and Miller, after college, worked as a reporter for the Houston Post. He moved to Corpus Christi for a job as a railroad publicity agent. He married Maud Heaney, daughter of Dr. A. G. Heaney. He was named editor of the Caller and elected mayor in 1913. Miller's tenure was credited with paving downtown streets and completing the bluff beautification project. After three terms in office, Miller lost in the 1919 election to Gordon Boone.

Roy Miller was very much the political mover and shaker. And very good at it. He led the campaign for a deepwater port and was lobbying in Washington when President Harding signed legislation authorizing the construction of the port of Corpus Christi on May 22, 1922. Miller sent a short telegram to the Caller saying, "We win!" In 1929, Miller sold his interest in the Caller and went to Washington to represent the port and the city. In the 1930s he worked to promote the Intracoastal Canal. He died on April 28, 1946. He was 62. His widow, Maud Heaney Miller, died in 1965.

—July 26, 2017

Church moved to South Broadway

During the war the Civic Center became a popular
center for servicemen, where canteens were open and
dances were held three times a week.

South of Park Avenue, on the corner lot, was the Church of the
Good Shepherd. It had been moved from its old location at
Taylor and Chaparral in 1926. On its new site on South
Broadway the old church building was enlarged and remodeled,
given a new roof and brick front while the original nave and
chancery were preserved. A new church was built in 1950.

Across from the church, on the east side of South Broadway,
was a large building constructed by the church in 1938. It was
the Corpus Christi Civic Center. It was privately operated,
though the owned it.

The Civic Center was an all-purpose community building
where a variety of civic functions were held. Dances were held
every Saturday night. During the war years the Civic Center
became a popular center for servicemen, where canteens were
open and dances were held three times a week. The Civic Center
was remodeled and renamed Munds Hall in 1956.

Next to the church to the south was the Roy Miller home,
which I wrote about last week. Following that were the homes of
the Caldwell brothers, who were the first to build south of the
Doddridge place. The Caldwells, William Herbert and Edward
Harvey, were sons of the pastor of the First Presbyterian Church.
The brothers bought a sheep ranch in Duval County then entered
the hardware business in Corpus Christi.

A Doc McGregor photo of the Church of the Good Shepherd on South Broadway in 1936. The original church building at Chaparral and Taylor was moved to the south bluff in 1926. It was enlarged, a new roof constructed and a brick veneer added. A new church was built on the site in 1950.

In 1884, W. H. Caldwell built a home at 711 South Broadway. Originally it had five rooms but he added a second story in 1906. He planted palm trees below the bluff on Water Street, surrounded the house with flowers and opened the city's first floral shop from a stable adjoining the house. All the flowers sold by Caldwell were grown in his yard.

After Caldwell died his daughter Julia operated the floral shop into the 1950s. When she was growing up, Julia Caldwell once said, "the bay extended to the hill and was right in front of our house." She and her sisters would go bathing in the bay early each morning, screaming and playing until their mother came out waving a white towel to fetch them to breakfast. "Huge pumps were later used to drain the water out and then fill it in. We loved watching the seagulls grab the fish as the water was drawn up, and we found it interesting to watch the big machines."

A year after Julia Caldwell died in 1970 the old Caldwell home was dismantled for scrap lumber. The next house to the south, at 715, was the home of E. H. Caldwell. He was 21 when he came

E. H. Caldwell's old home on South Broadway in a dilapidated state before it was torn to build the Cliff House in 1964.

to Corpus Christi from Tennessee in 1872 to join his family. Caldwell worked for the Doddridge bank until 1875 when he and his brother William leased the Borjas Ranch west of San Diego and bought a flock of sheep.

In 1880, Caldwell married Ada Lasater and got out of the sheep business. He and his brother bought Mitchell's hardware store. E. H. Caldwell bought part of the Rayne tract on South Bluff, which was broken into lots and put up for sale in the 1870s. This area was known then as the South Side. Caldwell's lots extended from the water's edge up to Staples Street. He said in his memoirs he thought it was a perfect place to build a home.

Caldwell said the family stayed in Mrs. Merriman's boarding house on Mesquite while their house was being built. They moved in in March 1884. In 1910, Caldwell moved this house to the back of the property and built a larger two-story house on the site. They moved in on Jan. 1, 1911.

Edward Harvey Caldwell died at his home on South Broadway on March 14, 1940. Sarah Caldwell, his daughter, operated a tea room and antique shop in the old home before it was torn down to build the Cliff House in 1964. Sarah Caldwell moved next door into the Born house, which had been converted into four apartments.

The E. A. Born house, on the corner of Coleman at 723 South Broadway, was built in the mid-1890s. It was said to have been the first house in town equipped for electric lights. Born was

343

secretary of the school board in 1910-1911 when the new brick high school was built on Carancahua. The house was converted into apartments in 1941 then razed in 1965 to make way for a parking lot for Cliff House apartments.

One of the oldest houses in the city, built in 1851, was at 801 South Broadway. This was the Walter Merriman house. Merriman was Henry Kinney's lawyer who was also married to Kinney's sister. Anna Moore Schwien in her reminiscences said Walter and his wife lost their children in a yellow fever epidemic in 1854. The children were buried in the yard. Afterwards the Merriman couple moved to Indianola.

The three-gabled clapboard house was purchased by Banquete cattleman John Rabb in 1859 as a town home for his family. It was used as a hospital during the Civil War by Dr. E. T. Merriman (not related to Walter Merriman). After the war, the Walter Merriman home was occupied by Martha Rabb's daughter Lulu who married Wade Hampton. It was called the Hampton place. In the 1930s, the house was purchased by a retired physician, Dr. Ernest Bobys, and it became known as the Merriman-Bobys house. Perhaps it should have been called the Merriman-Rabb house. It was moved to Heritage Park in 1983.

Of all the old homes on South Broadway only four have survived. Richard King's mansion, Carrie Lichtenstein's home, and Dr. Giles' home still stand on their original sites. Walter Merriman's home is in Heritage Park. We're lucky they survived since our standard practice has been, "If it's worth preserving, tear it down immediately."

Most of the old homes on South Broadway were dismantled or demolished, laid to rest by bulldozers, pickaxes and crowbars. If homes like the ones of W. W. Jones and Clark Pease had survived, they would be considered historic treasures. But if they had survived would we treat them any better today? Probably not. Most likely we would bring on the bulldozers.

—Aug. 2, 2017

Tunnel linked downtown with uptown

"For kids, the concrete cave with its echoes was a playland. For adults, it was a cool walk protected from sun and rain." —Bill Walraven

A large crowd milled around City Hall between Schatzel and Peoples on the day the bluff tunnel was opened. That was in February 1929. The tunnel was planned during the bluff improvement project undertaken in 1914. The original plan called for a pedestrian tunnel to link downtown and uptown, but it wasn't built until more than a decade after the bluff project was completed.

Before the tunnel was finished, the Caller reported that Mary FitzSimmons asked permission to be the first to walk through the tunnel, although construction of the pedestrian underpass was still going on.

"Miss FitzSimmons encountered some difficulty in climbing out of the upper end of the tunnel at the new Plaza Hotel," the Caller reported. "She made easy progress until she reached the Plaza Hotel end. There she encountered what she called a chicken ladder, but she made it through safely, a path that will be trod by thousands moving to and from one portion of the business district to another."

The tunnel was opened a week later. It was never given an official name. It was just the bluff tunnel. It catered to uptown workers who wanted to shop at the stores below and to downtown workers who wanted to eat at the popular restaurants on the bluff above. The main tunnel entrance (or exit, depending on which way the pedestrian was heading) was behind City Hall between Schatzel and Peoples. The tunnel ended at the basement of the Plaza Hotel.

The tunnel cost $22,000 to build. It angled upwards 302 feet, under the fountain, under the balustrade, to the top of the bluff. It was (and is) seven feet wide, eight feet high, with concrete walls eight inches thick. Its deepest point is 20 feet below the surface.

In early years the tunnel exited below the Plaza Hotel where a barber shop and beauty shop operated for the benefit of tunnel travelers. The tunnel was later expanded south, under Leopard Street, to the basement of the Nixon Building. When the Driscoll Hotel opened in 1942 the tunnel was extended north to that hotel.

The late Eleanor Mortensen of the Caller-Times wrote on July 8, 1977 that the tunnel "even housed some shops — a barber shop, for one, complete with an old-fashioned lighted barber pole." What was called the Arcade was in the basement of the White Plaza Hotel off the tunnel exit. At the Driscoll exit was a bar with a spiral staircase that led from the lobby to the club. It was called the Deep Six Club.

Another columnist, the late Bill Walraven, wrote that the tunnel was a real convenience, providing a sheltered walk out of the sun and rain. The tunnel was as cool in the summer as a deep cellar. "The Nixon Café, the Morocco Room (at the Driscoll) were attractions on the bluff," wrote Walraven. "I remember the tunnel as a kid as a place of high adventure. My aunt's brother, Olin Patillo, was a barber in the White Plaza Barber Shop, which fronted on the tunnel from the hotel basement. For kids, the concrete cave with its echoes was a playland. For adults, it was a cool walk protected from sun and rain."

The city planned to dig another tunnel under the northbound lanes of Shoreline Drive from Memorial Coliseum to McGee Beach in 1952, but the idea was shelved.

Things began going downhill for the bluff tunnel in the 1950s. The decrease in pedestrian traffic no doubt matched the decrease in shopping venues, as stores moved away from the central business district to new shopping centers on the southside.

Fewer people used the tunnel. Newspaper accounts in the 1960s said the tunnel became a nocturnal hangout of drunks and

A large crowd turned out in February 1929 (left) when the city's bluff tunnel was opened. The tunnel in 1975 (right) when the city debated whether to keep it open or close it. The city closed it in 1977. Opening day photo by Sammy Gold; 1975 photo inside the tunnel by George Gongora.

"hippies." The walls were defaced with graffiti, broken bottles littered the floor, light bulbs were smashed, and there were often reminders of overnight bathroom use. What in the past had been light housekeeping for city workers became messy and costly chores.

There was a plan in 1962 to use the tunnel as a fallout shelter during a nuclear attack. Jim Sticktor, who pushed the idea, said, "It's deep enough for protection against fallout." The idea was dropped. In 1966 Mayor McIver Furman said the tunnel was more of a problem than an asset and that it should be closed. "I wouldn't take my wife and daughter through it."

A developer named Bill Sweetland got a lease on the tunnel from the city with a scheme to use it for a saltwater aquarium. There must have been something wrong with the idea, though I can't fathom what it might have been. The scheme was also dropped.

The City Council decided on Feb. 23, 1977 to close the tunnel. Iron bars were installed to seal off the main entrance between Schatzel and Peoples and the three exits on the bluff at the 600 Building (where the White Plaza stood), the Wilson Building (formerly the Nixon Building), and Corpus Christi Bank & Trust (formerly the Driscoll Hotel). The tunnel entrance and exits were shut, barred, and cut off from drunks, hippies and the outside world.

The tunnel has remained closed and the subject rarely comes above ground. But every so often there is talk of reopening the tunnel.

It would not be practical to reopen it as a pedestrian walkway since not many people make that trip on foot today. Some think it could be a tourist attraction. Maybe. They go to Vienna to walk through the sewers. Many travel through London's foot tunnels under the Thames. The bluff tunnel would not appeal to an old claustrophobe like me who prefers light, air, and plenty of elbow-room.

How much would it cost to renovate the tunnel — to paint and patch the walls, install new lighting and ventilation, provide handicap access? One estimate a few years ago was $200,000, far in excess of the $22,000 it cost to build. But what use has a pedestrian tunnel without pedestrians? Maybe the city could put it on the market for some private enterprise — a wine bar? mercado? Run an ad in the paper: Used tunnel for sale. Needs work. No reasonable offer refused.

Someday we may find a use for this historic hole in the ground, but until then we can't tear it down.

—Aug. 9, 2017

Old building hidden by 1940s façade

The Doddridge Bank Building was erected in 1883 on
the corner of Chaparral and Lawrence, across from the
St. James Hotel.

I always thought that the Doddridge Bank Building on
Chaparral was pulled down and one of those modern box-like
structures — sans architectural embellishment — was built in its
place. Now I wonder.

I suspect some old downtown buildings have survived with a
new façade, their underlying identity covered over and
unrecognizable, past and present mingled together. Old buildings
are interesting for their unique features, their individual styles,
which modernizing exteriors were intended to destroy. The
question is whether the Doddridge Building is one of those old
survivors hidden by a modern front. I suspect that it is.

The Doddridge Bank Building was erected in 1883. The bank
was established by Perry Doddridge, a wool dealer, in 1871 in
the old Edey & Kirsten Building on corner of Chaparral and
Lawrence, across from the St. James Hotel. And that site is
where the Doddridge Building was constructed.

The building has a unique history. In 1885 part of the second
floor was used for the Myrtle Club, a private men's club, with a
saloon, billiards, reading room, and tables for card games. Most
of the prominent men in town belonged to the Myrtle Club.

The Doddridge Bank collapsed during the national depression
in 1893, which also ended the Ropes boom in the city. Perry
Doddridge spent his own fortune repaying depositors 60 cents on

the dollar, which left him bankrupt. It was said the entire town sympathized with Doddridge.

On Jan. 26, 1903, a meeting was held in the Doddridge Building with John Nance Garner, the newly elected congressman for the district. Garner stayed at the St. James Hotel the night before and walked across Chaparral for the meeting with his constituents. At the meeting, he was told that Corpus Christi wanted, above all else, a channel dredged across the bay to give the city access to deep water. Garner's work toward this end put in motion the chain of events that eventually led to the Port of Corpus Christi.

In 1908, the Dixie Theater, Dixie Café and Dixie Rooms occupied the Doddridge Building and that area of Chaparral was known as the Dixie corner. In February 1919, the Corpus Christi Caller moved from the Noessel building in the 300 block of Chaparral into the Doddridge Building in the 400 block. Later that year, during the 1919 hurricane, the newspaper office was submerged in the storm surge. The press on the first floor was swamped, though the editorial offices and composing room on the upper floor escaped damage. The Caller was printed in Kingsville until the press was repaired.

In the mid-1920s, the Caller moved to Mesquite Street and the Doddridge Building was remodeled to house J. E. Garrett's Texas State Bank & Trust. The Doddridge Building became known as the Garrett Building. The Doddridge/Garrett building housed several tenants in the late 1930s. Across the street, the St. James Hotel was pulled down and a new Lichtenstein store was built. It opened in December 1941.

It was about this time that the Doddridge Building was torn down or renovated to house Buttrey's Ladies Wear, which opened in 1941. I think it was renovated and can see how that would happen, in the 1940s, when the downtown merchants all wanted their storefronts to look new and modern.

The building later housed Joos Shoes before it was closed. It stands vacant today, across from the new Cosmopolitan. The back of the structure is an old brick wall that would be consistent with the Doddridge Building. With more casual conjecture than solid evidence, I suspect the 134-year-old building survived with

The old Doddridge bank building on Chaparral was known as the Garrett Building in 1939.

The Doddridge bank building was renovated to house Buttrey's Women's Shop, shown in the 1940s.

a modern exterior that disguised its original façade. Despite change, the past is still there, sometimes literally.

End of the line

Daniel Hewitt from Tyler began the Corpus Christi and Interurban Railway in 1910. He had tracks laid on wooden blocks on unpaved streets with copper wires strung above. The line had four cars and Hewitt bought electric power to operate them from the Peoples Light Company. The inaugural run was made on March 28, 1910.

A year later, Hewitt sold out to the Heinley brothers of Denver. Vinton Sweet Heinley ran the operation while his brother Earl was a co-owner. The Heinleys added three cars and built a power plant that ran on oil from Mexico. They sold out in 1914 to a syndicate from Philadelphia.

The new owners added eight new cars, modified the older cars, extended the lines, and changed the name to the Corpus Christi Railway and Light Company. The car barn was north of the 1914 Courthouse. One line ran from the City Drug Store at Chaparral and Starr to North Beach. Another line was the South Bluff run, which terminated at Third and Booty. One line ran to the Segrest area and another was the Paul Court run, at Lipan and 13th. A fifth line ran to the Nueces Bay Heights.

When an Army training post named Camp Scurry opened in 1916 south of town, the trolley business took off. Between 1916 and 1917, the number of riders exceeded one million. This was the golden age of streetcar transit in Corpus Christi.

The trolleys had another two good years before the 1919 storm struck. After the storm, the streetcar system was virtually destroyed, with damaged cars and the power plant knocked out. It was put back into operation on Nov. 19, 1919. But old times were gone forever. The streetcar line soon went into receivership and sporadic attempts to revive it failed. On Jan. 31, 1931, the last trolley car reached the end of the line in Corpus Christi. The clang of the warning bell, the whine of the electric motor, and clackety-clack of the wheels as they hit the rail junctures were heard no more.

—Aug. 16, 2017

Grace building stood on Schatzel corner

"I thought I would be a millionaire if I could own that
building." —*William S. (Bill) Rankin*

The southeast corner of Schatzel and Chaparral, was a prime
business location going back to the 1850s. The history of a
commercial location, which puts us in touch with the past, can be
surprising. The first building on that Schatzel Street corner, that I
can trace, was a two-story wooden building connected to William
R. Grace, who was later mayor of New York City and the
founder of the W. R. Grace Company.

Longtime newsman Eli Merriman once wrote that the Grace
building was used in New York, dismantled, shipped to Corpus
Christi on a schooner, and erected on the corner of Schatzel and
Chaparral. It served as the business headquarters of William
Headen, a wool and hide dealer who was a business partner of
William Grace. Merriman put the date the building was shipped
here at about 1859.

In the 1890s, what had been the Grace-Headen building was
occupied by J. W. Westervelt, a ship chandler. Sometime after
the turn of the 20th Century it was sold to William S. (Bill)
Rankin, who owned and operated several grocery stores in the
downtown area. Rankin said that when he was growing up in the
1860s his ambition was to own the old Grace-Headen building.
"I thought I would be a millionaire if I could own that building."
Rankin later sold the building to Hugh Sutherland, who owned
several downtown properties (including the J. C. Penney
building). There was a grocery store on the ground floor operated

William Headen's wool business under his father's name of M. Headen was located in a frame building at Schatzel and Chaparral which had been shipped from New York by W. R. Grace, Headen's business partner. Photo by Louis de Planque from Central Library.

The old Grace building at Schatzel and Chaparral was renovated with a new front and called the Rankin Building. It was demolished in the 1930s to make way for a new Sun Pharmacy building.

by the Scogin brothers and on the second floor, around the 1920s, were law offices of Hugh Sutherland's son, H. R. Sutherland Jr. The Oil City Café took over what had been the Liberty Café in a corner of the building in about 1930.

The Grace-Headen-Rankin-Sutherland building was torn down in the mid-1930s and a new structure was built on the site just north of the Medical-Professional Building and Allen's Furniture. The new building housed the Modern Pharmacy and Hall's Credit Clothiers. By the early 1940s, Modern Pharmacy became the Sun Pharmacy. After the Sun Pharmacy closed, the building was occupied by Lester's Jewelry for many years and later a Maverick Market store. Urbana Market & Deli occupies that downtown location today.

Army headquarters

After the U.S. and Mexico signed the treaty of Guadalupe Hidalgo on Feb. 2, 1848, ending the Mexican War, the U.S. acquired a vast territory from Texas to California open to settlement and expansion. Forts would have to be built and supplied, a task for the Army.

The War Department created the Eighth Military District, known as the Department of Texas, which would be responsible for manning and supplying a string of new forts on the Rio Grande and the Texas frontier. Supplies came in by sea, through the port of Indianola, and were loaded on wagons and transported to military depots in San Antonio and Austin. From there they were sent on to army forts on the frontier.

The Army ordered Lt. Nathaniel Michler of the Topographical Engineers to accompany a trade expedition from Corpus Christi to Chihuahua, Mexico. He was to determine if a road could be opened between Corpus Christi and Fort Inge on the Leona River. Lt. Michler made his report on July 31, 1849. He reported that the region offered "every facility for opening a good road."

Two years later, Gen. Persifor Smith, commander of the Eighth Military District, made his own tour of inspection. He was accompanied by Capt. George B. McClellan, of the Corps of Engineers. They traveled from Corpus Christi to San Antonio and then on to frontier forts on the San Saba and Llano rivers.

In 1852, Gen. Smith ordered headquarters of the Eighth Military District moved from San Antonio to Corpus Christi. He dispatched Maj. William Chapman, the quartermaster at Fort Brown, to prepare the way for the move.

Chapman arrived in August 1852. He rented houses for officers, including Gen. Smith, Col. Joseph E. Johnston, Capt. McClellan, and others. He rented Matilda Ohler's large house on the bluff for $100 a month and rented facilities for the army supply depot. In a letter to his mother, Chapman wrote, "The village is built on a flat plain. Directly behind it, facing the bay, is quite a bold green bluff on which the best residences are built. There is far more beauty of scenery here than on the Rio Grande."

Chapman rented the old William Mann complex on Water Street, known as "Mann's red house." The store and house, built around a central courtyard with a wharf in the bay, were used as quartermaster and commissary storerooms, a saddler's and wheelwright's shop, and quarters for 14 men.

The supplies coming in by ship to Corpus Christi were mostly clothing and medical stores. Food and forage supplies were still being shipped through Indianola. Though Corpus Christi had the headquarters of the Eighth Military District, the main supply depot was still in San Antonio. Corpus Christi lobbied to have the depot moved to join the headquarters, but a report by Lt. Col. W. G. Freeman threw cold water on the proposal. He recommended the main supply depot remain at San Antonio because of a lack of freshwater at Corpus Christi and the shallowness of the ship channels across Corpus Christi and Aransas bays.

But Corpus Christi in 1854 kept the headquarters and officers and soldiers on their way to frontier forts arrived by mail boat from Indianola. Lt. Phil Sheridan, on his way to Fort Duncan, stayed at a hotel on Chaparral, the old Kinney House which had become the Noessel House.

Corpus Christi suffered a major blow in 1856 when the Army decided to move the Eighth District Headquarters back to San Antonio. The army's shops, forges and stables were closed. Wagon drivers, many of them immigrants, were out of work. The move was completed in the spring of 1857.

William Headen, a successful wool merchant who would later become mayor, once said that many of the town's residents had depended on the army paychecks of $15 a month. When the army left, they were driven to the country. "Some became farmers, others became stockmen, and not a few turned their attention to raising sheep."

—Aug. 30, 2017

Woolworth's built on Flato's corner

When the new Woolworth's opened on Saturday, Sept.
2, 1954, Dwight Eisenhower was president and theaters
were showing "Rear Window."

Across from the St. James Hotel, south of Lawrence Street,
stood the Nueces Hardware store. This was on the Flato corner, a
property long associated with the Flato family. Woolworth's
Department Store was later located on this busy corner.

The Flato corner started with Edwin F. Flato, who moved to
Corpus Christi in 1906 and became the bookkeeper and one-third
owner of the Corpus Christi Hardware Store. It was then located
across the street on the east corner, at 324 Chaparral. By 1914
Flato was president of the firm and the store was moved across
the street to 323 Chaparral.

When the hardware store was all but destroyed in the 1919
storm, Flato decided it was an opportune time to separate the
business, with one firm specializing in wholesale and farm
equipment and the other in retail and household goods. He
moved the wholesale operation to South Broadway, which
retained the name of Corpus Christi Hardware, and left the retail
operation on Chaparral, which was renamed Nueces Hardware,
located in a new building. His son Franklin Flato joined the
Chaparral store in the 1930s and became its president while
Edwin Flato was serving as mayor, from 1932 to 1934.

In 1949, Edwin and Franklin Flato made a deal to build a new
structure on the Flato corner to house the F. W. Woolworth store,
which at the time was located next to the Perkins Brothers store

Edwin F. Flato's Nueces Hardware store, across the street from the St. James Hotel on Chaparral, in 1935. Photo by "Doc" McGregor.

Flato's Nueces Hardware store was given a new façade in 1938. A new building constructed on the site housed F. W. Woolworth's downtown store from 1954 to 1989.

on Leopard. Woolworth originally was located in the 600 block of Chaparral Street, between McCrory's and Muttera's Bakery. Woolworth's moved to Leopard in 1939.

The new building on Chaparral was built for Woolworth's. The Flato family owned the property but Woolworth's signed a 30-year lease of the building.

When the new Woolworth's opened on Saturday, Sept. 2, 1954, Dwight Eisenhower was president, theaters were showing Alfred Hitchcock's "Rear Window," and top songs on juke boxes were "Sh-Boom" by the Crew-Cuts and "Shake, Rattle and Roll" by Bill Haley and the Comets.

Woolworth's stood on a busy intersection, on the corner of Chaparral and Lawrence. Tom Stewart, a longtime resident, said Woolworth's corner was usually a hub of activity. "Lichtenstein's was on the other corner of Chaparral and Lawrence and one of the city's busiest bus transfer stops was at the Woolworth side. When I worked in the downtown area I'd buy a bag of cashews at noon and the lunch counter was always busy." Two of the regular customers at the counter were Mayor Farrell Smith and County Judge Noah Kennedy.

Woolworth's downtown store was closed in 1989. That building, across from the new Cosmopolitan, stands empty today. It was once one of the busiest spots in downtown Corpus Christi, on the old Flato hardware corner.

Martin Culver

Martin Smythe Culver was born in Louisiana in 1838, the son of a steamboat captain on the Mississippi River. When his father was killed in a boiler explosion his mother remarried and moved to San Antonio. Culver in his teens went to work for his uncle, J. T. "Tom" James, a cattle rancher in Live Oak County who owned the St. James Hotel in Corpus Christi.

At the end of the Civil War, Culver came out of the Confederate Army and bought a small herd of cattle and the 600-acre Rancho Perdido, the Lost Ranch. He paid $1 an acre for 600 acres and hired Milton Dodson of Dinero to work for him. The ranch, with a crude ranch house at Penitas, was three miles southwest of Casa Blanca, 50 miles north of Corpus Christi. After buying Rancho Perdido, Culver married Kate Pugh of Gussettville and they moved into the ranch house.

South Texas after the war was overrun with unbranded cattle and Culver burned his brand on every longhorn he could find. His main brand was KL, which stood for his wife Kate and daughter Lizzie. Culver began sending herds of 1,000 head up the trail to Kansas. Within a few years Culver became a wealthy cattleman.

In 1868, Culver's half-sister, Mary Susanna Burris, visited and a year later she married Culver's foreman Milton Dodson. In 1870, Culver built a new ranch house for Rancho Perdido on Penitas Creek. A former sailor designed the house and did the carpentry. It included nine rooms, a wide front porch that extended along the front and one side and it was painted London purple with white trim.

In 1871, so many head of cattle were sent up the trail that beef prices fell to almost nothing. The value of a longhorn dropped to the value of the hide, tallow, horns and bones. Beef slaughter houses, or packing houses, began operating on the coast. Culver built a packing house at Nuecestown.

During the Nuecestown Raid in 1875, a wounded bandit was brought to Corpus Christi on an ox-cart. When vigilantes climbed to the roof of the Catholic Church to fix a rope to hang the bandit, Culver stepped in and ordered them to desist and not to desecrate a house of worship. The bandit was hanged from a gate with a cross pole off Leopard Street.

With the spread of barbed wire, free-range grazing was coming to an end. Culver sold Rancho Perdido for $5,000 to Milton Dodson, his brother-in-law. Culver moved to Dodge City where he became Trail Commissioner, responsible for inspecting herds up from Texas. In 1885, the Kansas Legislature passed a law preventing Texas cattle from entering Kansas, to stop the spread of tick fever.

Culver secured a lease for a three-mile strip of territory along the Kansas-Colorado line where herds from Texas could be taken up this new trail, skirting Kansas, and then on to Ogallala. Culver established a new town in Colorado called Trail City, which attracted all the gamblers and saloon girls from Dodge City. Trail City was short-lived. The coming of railroads ended cattle drives. Martin S. Culver was a successful cattleman on the open range who was there at the beginning and end of the great trail drives out of South Texas. He died on Oct. 5, 1887.

—Sept. 6, 2017

Chat 'N' Chew and Purple Cow

"I paid a man $75 for the place. When we started out, it
was just me, my wife, and the dishwasher." —O. V.
Jackson of the Chat 'N' Chew

French novelist Marcel Proust ate a tea-cake cookie called a
madeleine which brought a flood of memories that he turned into
three books, "Remembrance of Things Past." Another writer, A.
J. Liebling, said the Proust formula was TMB: Taste equals
memory equals Book. If certain foods produce recollections, I
wonder what lasting memories were evoked at the Chat 'N'
Chew, Bunk's Café, the Purple Cow Drive-In, or the Squeeze In
Diner? All were famous in their day.

O. V. Jackson and his wife Maudie were traveling in California
and they ate at a small diner in Alhambra called the Chat 'N'
Chew. When they returned to Corpus Christi they opened their
own 10-stool diner in Corpus Christi. It was across from Cudd's
Grocery Store and Sears, in the 1300 block of Leopard between
Alameda and Sam Rankin. They copied the name from the
Alhambra restaurant and called it the Chat 'N' Chew. That was
in 1935.

"I paid a man $75 for the place," O. V. Jackson said in 1984.
"When we started out it was just me, my wife, and the
dishwasher. I did the cooking, Maudie washed and cooked. We
did whatever needed to be done. We catered to oilfield workers
and their families. A T-bone steak was listed on the menu for 35
cents, a hamburger was 15 cents, a bowl of chili was 10 cents.

The Chat 'N' Chew Cafe, on Leopard across from Sears (where City Hall is today), shown in 1938. Photo by "Doc" McGregor, Museum of Science and History.

Bunk's Café, next to the Chat 'N' Chew on Leopard, shown in 1942. Photo by "Doc" McGregor, Museum of Science and History.

The Purple Cow Drive-In on Water Street, where the U&I is today, shown in 1939. Photo by "Doc" McGregor, Museum of Science and History.

We paid the dishwasher $7 a week." The Chat 'N' Chew was popular for five decades. It closed in 1989.

Another popular café was B. J. (Bunk) Spence's place next door to the Chat 'N' Chew. When he opened his café in 1937, he called it the Quality Sandwich Shop but it quickly became known Bunk's Café. A man from Chapel Hill, N. C., once wrote asking me about Bunk's Café. "My mother fondly remembers a restaurant named Bunk's Cafe or Bunk's Diner," Adam Ronan wrote. "My grandfather would take the whole clan out to Bunk's on payday. The place had the best chicken-fried steak anywhere." Bunk's was closed, I think, sometime in the 1960s.

A downtown drive-in that was short-lived but created lasting memories was the Purple Cow at 309 S. Water, decorated with its namesake on the roof. The Purple Cow was opened in the late 1930s by Cody Wyatt. A letter-writer named Mary Emmert recalled that when she moved to Corpus Christi in 1940, "We would tell our friends in the Valley to come visit Corpus Christi, the only town with a pink hotel (the Princess Louise) and a purple cow."

The name no doubt was inspired by that old Gelett Burgess poem, "I never saw a purple cow . . . I never hope to see one . . . but I can tell you, anyhow . . . I'd rather see than be one."

The Purple Cow was sold to George Zackie, who owned Zackie's Playhouse Drive-In. He took down the namesake from the roof and renamed the place Zackie's Restaurant No. 2. The U&I Restaurant is on that Water Street site today and the spot is still a favorite dining location.

On Mesquite Street, across from the State Hotel, was a tiny diner called the Fig Leaf Hamburger Stand. It became better known in the 1950s as the Squeeze In Café. Defitting its name, the Squeeze In was a six-seat diner. It was operated by Mrs. Jessie Dye and then later, in the 1960s, by Eunice and Clyde Linton. It was popular with downtown workers. On Dec. 18, 1969, Mr. and Mrs. Sam Susser hosted a full-dress party at their house, which started with cocktails, and then moved to the Squeeze In Diner for the house specialties — hamburgers, Mexican food, and scrambled eggs. Must have been a small, if convivial, party for such a confined space. I don't know when the Squeeze In was squeezed out and torn down. There's a vacant lot there today.

Fort Merrill

In February 1850 two companies of the 1st U.S. Infantry under the command of Capt. Samuel Plummer moved up the Nueces River, 60 miles north of Corpus Christi, and picked a site to build a new fort. It was on high ground with a view of the stage road and a bend of the Nueces River.

The purpose of the new fort was to provide protection for settlers and travelers on the stage road between Corpus Christi and San Antonio. The fort would also serve as a way station for wagon trains hauling army supplies to other new forts on the Texas frontier. Corpus Christi had replaced San Antonio as headquarters of the Eighth Army District.

Capt. Samuel Plummer's soldiers were quartered in tents as they built the new fort to the west of Corpus Christi near the Nueces River. Lumber and pine logs were transported by wagon from Corpus Christi to the site. The soldiers built officers' quarters, kitchens, a sutler's store, guardhouse, stable, and quarters for two companies. They named it Fort Merrill.

After it was built Texas Rangers under the command of Rip Ford camped below the fort. One night a Comanche raiding party tried to steal their horses. There was a skirmish and one of Ford's men, Mat Nolan (later the sheriff of Nueces County) rushed barefoot through prickly pear to shoot at the Indians.

After the fight Ford sent word to Capt. Plummer to tell him what happened. Plummer was surprised. He had no idea Indians were operating so close to his fort. But that was the trouble with forts like Merrill. They were built to protect the surrounding countryside but couldn't protect their own environs. Fort Merrill's foot soldiers, mounted on mules, were no match for Comanche warriors on their lean ponies, the greatest fighters on horseback since Genghis Khan's Mongol warriors.

Fort Merrill's infantrymen were moved to Fort Ewell in 1853, leaving a few men as caretakers. The fort was closed in December 1855. The fort's beginning and ending coincided with the time when Corpus Christi was headquarters for the Eighth Military District.

The state erected a monument on the site in 1936, which attributes the fort's name to "Captain Hamilton W. Merrill, Gallant Officer in the Mexican War." The name was wrong. Hamilton W. Merrill was a young officer stationed at Fort Mason at the time Fort Merrill was built. The fort was named for Maj. Moses E. Merrill who was killed in the battle of Molina del Rey in the Mexican War.

—Sept. 13, 2017

Column 89

The St. James was a famous hotel

The St. James was known throughout Texas. It was the
headquarters of ranchers, politicians, gamblers and
gunmen. John Wesley Hardin, Ben Thompson, and
Leander McNelly stayed there.

Charles Bryant, an architect from Maine, arrived in Corpus
Christi in 1845 and built the Union Theater at the corner of
Lawrence and Chaparral. It was built to cater to the troops of
Zachary Taylor that were concentrated in Corpus Christi in
preparation for the war with Mexico. Five years after he built the
Union Theater, Bryant was killed and scalped by hostile Indians
near Chocolate Bayou.

In 1869, a hotel was built on the site of Bryant's Union
Theater. It was built by J. T. (Tom) James, a stockman on
Mustang Island. He called the hotel the St. James, after a famous
establishment in Kansas City. The hotel was built by Edward
Sidbury, who owned a lumberyard. One of the carpenters on the
project was Dan Reid, who was later elected mayor of Corpus
Christi. It had a wide porch gallery on the east and south sides,
facing Chaparral and Lawrence. Before construction was
finished, James sold the hotel to William Long (Billy) Rogers.
Rogers sold 1,300 horses and 2,800 head of cattle from his Palo
Alto Ranch for $13,000 to buy the place and spent $5,000 to
furnish it.

The hotel became one of the city's most famous landmarks.
"Billy" Rogers died Dec. 17, 1877 and William Biggio became
the manager of the hotel. Biggio was a former Confederate sailor
who was captured and became a prisoner of war.

It was a gray Sunday on July 2, 1933 when "Doc" McGregor snapped his shutter on Lawrence Street. It looks to be early morning, the street empty except for a parked car and delivery truck by the St. James Hotel.

The St. James under Biggio's management was known throughout Texas. It was the headquarters of ranchers, politicians, gamblers and gunmen. John Wesley Hardin, who once backed down Wild Bill Hickok in Abilene, stayed there and so did Ben Thompson. When Leander McNelly arrived in April 1875, his Rangers camped outside town while McNelly put up at the St. James. Congressman John Garner stayed at the St. James and so did Gov. Jim Hogg.

The hotel saloon, the Gem, run for a time by P. H. McManigle, was one of the most popular places in town. The Falvella trio played at the hotel for balls and dances; one of their most-requested songs was "Listen to the Mockingbird." In the evenings, prominent citizens would lounge on the porch of the St. James and talk about the events of the day.

It was said that Biggio would never turn a man away hungry, whether he could pay for a meal or not. When he retired in 1905, the Caller said the patrons of the hotel, as well as many others, "will miss his friendly greeting, and the hotel under another manager will hardly seem the same." Biggio died soon after his retirement.

368

The St. James in the 1930s was operated as a rooming house. When it was torn down in 1937, one of the most famous landmarks in South Texas was gone. Three years later, Lichtenstein's fourth and last department store was built there. The Cosmopolitan Apartments building was recently opened on that site today.

News Briefs

Old newspapers provide us with a glimpse of what has been called the first draft of history. From the Corpus Christi Star, the Ranchero, Nueces Valley, Advertiser, and Caller, a few assorted "news" items from the pages of the past can illustrate the big news of the past —

1848, Star: The editor visited Agua Dulce country this week. Halfway there we camped at a water hole for the night and, having killed a buck, had a good supper. The mustangs came around us during the evening but did not frighten our horses. Next morning we came to a prairie covered with mustangs, deer, and antelope. So gentle were the deer we were frequently in range of whole droves. They would stare and frisk around us as though unaccustomed to the sight of man.

1848, Star: Complaints have been made of the insecurity of the reef road after many of the stakes were thrown down or displaced. The danger has been obviated by Gilpin and Parker, who crossed the reef in a wagon and drove in stakes where they were most needed.

1849, Star: The steamer Fanny arrived Thursday bringing another detachment of California emigrants. They number 32, stout, intelligent-looking men and appear to be well-calculated to brave the dangers of the overland trip to California.

1859, Ranchero: A big business is being done at Corpus Christi. There are now 17 stores in this city, and no small Mexican trade, besides the merchants of Live Oak, San Patricio, Webb and Zapata do their business through this place.

1861, Ranchero: The Lone Star Flag was hoisted on Cahill's flagstaff and one gun for each Southern state was fired. Considerable excitement exists concerning the election and a spirit is manifested by many citizens in favor of secession. The vote on secession in Nueces County: For, 164; against, 42.

1862, Ranchero: Food is getting short. Corpus Christi at the present juncture is provision-less, subsistence-less, less of everything to nourish the inner man.

1871, Advertiser: The Rio Grande City Stage arrived here at 6 o'clock on Friday evening. The mail boat did not start until next morning. This gave the passengers a night to rest.

1871, Nueces Valley: One train of Mexican carts brought in today 43,000 pounds of imported wool and 231 Texas hides.

1871, Nueces Valley: Laureles Ranch, the property of Captain Mifflin Kenedy, in this county, comprising 94,150 acres, has been assessed at $231,675. The fence is 37 miles long and cost $1,000 per mile to build.

1872, Nueces Valley: A number of our young men are starting for Kansas with cattle.

1885, Caller: Morris Lichtenstein left on the steamship Aransas for New York to buy his fall stock of goods.

1889, Caller: Dr. Spohn's team ran away Thursday morning, the horses coming to a halt in front of their favorite saloon, after having pitched the driver out and turned the buggy over in the street. The driver was stunned and bruised and had to be assisted off the ground.

1894, Caller: Mayor O. C. Lovenskiold issued an order to City Marshal Busch to arrest all persons found committing depredations on Artesian square and to stop the gathering of tough characters in the habit of meeting on the square every evening and filling the air with vulgar language. The mayor says the square was made for a resort for the public generally and not for tough characters who have no respect for the presence of ladies.

—Sept. 20, 2017

Column 90

Two buildings on Schatzel Street

On Schatzel, between Mesquite and Chaparral, is a large
empty lot where two old buildings once stood: the four-
story Gugenheim-Cohn Building and the Corpus Christi
National Bank.

Sometimes I drive around to look at empty spaces and try to
visualize the buildings that were once there and let the mind's
eye recognize the erasures in the downtown landscape. But it is
getting more difficult to visualize the old buildings as the empty
lots become more fixed on the mind. And there are lots of empty
lots.

On Schatzel Street, between Mesquite and Chaparral on the
north side of the street, is a large empty lot where two old
buildings once stood. One was the four-story Gugenheim-Cohn
Building and the one east of it was the Corpus Christi National
Bank. The oldest of the two was the bank.

The bank building was on the northwestern corner of Schatzel
and Chaparral, at 502 North Chaparral. It was built in 1891 by
William Rankin and leased to the bank, which had been founded
the year before and was located in a frame building where the
first Lichtenstein's had been. In its early years, the building
housed the telephone company on the second floor.

After the 1919 storm, the bank building stood in six feet of
water and the bank was closed for weeks after the storm. People
were encouraged to check the contents of their safe deposit boxes
which had been submerged by the storm tide. The building was
renovated three times over the years, in 1909, 1924, and again in
1936. After the bank merged with the State National Bank, it

Top, the Gugenheim-Cohn Building on June 20, 1961. It was demolished in 1981. Bottom,Corpus Christi National Bank, on the corner of Schatzel and Chaparral, undergoing renovation in 1936. "Doc" McGregor photos.

moved into a new building on Shoreline in 1960. The old building was demolished in 1961.

In the middle of Schatzel, just west of the Corpus Christi National Bank building, was the Gugenheim-Cohn Building, at 416 Schatzel. Simon Gugenheim and Herman Cohn, who owned the Gugenheim & Cohn Department Store on Chaparral, bought the lot in 1906 and built a three-story structure on the site the following year for $16,210.

A fourth floor was added in 1912 and leased for use as the federal court while the federal building on Starr was being constructed. One of the tenants in the building was Dr. P. G. Lovenskiold, the town's first dentist who served as mayor for 10 years, from 1921 to 1931. Another was First Savings, which later purchased the building, and the Nueces County Navigation District which occupied the entire fourth floor. The Gugenheim-Cohn Building was torn down in 1981 in favor of — what else? — another empty lot.

The Eyes of Memory

In the misty old times of Spanish Texas, a fortified ranch house on Ramireña Creek in today's Live Oak County was known as Rancho Ramírez and later as Fort Ramírez. This more than 200 years ago.

Fort Ramírez was built between 1790 and 1802 about the time Casa Blanca was founded by Juan José de la Garza Montemayor between Penitas Creek and the Nueces River. Historical records tell us that Fort Ramírez was built by Don José Antonio Ramírez and his son Don José Victoriano Ramírez, who came up from Camargo. They built the fortified ranch house of white caliche quarried from a hill not far away.

The Ramírez family filed for title to eight leagues of land (35,000 acres) on Ramireña Creek and said in the claim they had cleared fields, built corrals and ranch houses, and owned herds of cattle and horses in the river valley. It was a dangerous place. The people at Rancho Ramírez had to be on guard always for hostile Indians. They could not stray far from the stone walls and probably slept with their boots on.

In an attack in 1812 many were killed at Rancho Ramírez. The ranch was abandoned soon afterwards. It was said that livestock and even household goods were left behind. The Ramírez family survivors fled to Mexico, probably back to Camargo from where they came. Similar attacks occurred at Casa Blanca and other Spanish ranchos in the Nueces River Valley. There is only a faint outline of history here, like a distant hill you can barely see. The specifics, the details, were not recorded or have faded over time.

The Ramírez heirs did not abandon their claim to eight leagues between the Nueces and Ramireña Creek. In 1828, Leandro Ramírez petitioned the state of Tamaulipas to confirm the grant. It was approved in 1834. The Republic of Texas did not confirm the Ramírezes' title but the state finally did so in 1858. The heirs gradually sold off the land for pocket change.

In one sale in 1866 a section of land that included Fort Ramírez sold at auction for the amount owed in back taxes. The buyer, Peyton McNeill, paid $6 for the 640 acres. In that way, all the land thereabout passed into other hands. The outcome does no justice, but then, what does?

The old stone walls of Fort Ramírez still stood then, a reminder that others had been there before. But the walls were torn down by treasure hunters. I haven't walked over the ground but I understand that only faint traces remain today.

The chronicler of Fort Ramírez was the prolific storyteller J. Frank Dobie who grew up nearby on his father's ranch. In one article, he recalled that the Dobie house stood in a mott of live oaks overlooking Long Hollow Valley. He recalled how the house had a paling fence around it and a dirt yard kept bare to show snake trails, about how wild buffalo clover reached the stirrups of his saddle, how the horses would stamp on the caliche to knock off the red ants on their hooves, how the stillness of the afternoon was broken by the lazy sound of windmill lifting rods, how his horse Buck would point his ears when he walked into the pen to rope a mount — "seeming to ask if I were going to ride him or Brownie."

Dobie wrote in "Coronado's Children" that — "All I regret now is that the stones of Fort Ramírez have been carried away. I should like to stand on them once more in April and gaze across the winding Ramireña upon the oak-fringed hills beyond. Yet the hills could hardly be so lush with buffalo clover — as we used to call the bluebonnet — and red bunch grass, so soft and lovely, as they are in the eyes of memory."

—Sept. 27, 2017

Scene on Starr Street in 1939

A 1939 photo shows W. T. Grant's variety store on the corner, J. C. Penney's across Chaparral and, across from Penney's, the Mayflower Café.

A photo of Starr Street taken by "Doc" McGregor shows several buildings with an interesting history — the W. T. Grant building, J. C. Penney's, the Mayflower Café, and the Elks Lodge down the block. The date of the photograph, on Aug. 1, 1939, was one month from the beginning of World War II when Germany invaded Poland. We are as distant from that date as people then were from the stagecoach days of the frontier.

William Radeker in his memoirs said that for many years the corner of Chaparral and Starr, and extending back to Peoples and Schatzel, "was the center of Corpus Christi's downtown area. Every Saturday night the street was teeming with people because stores remained open until 9 p.m. to cater to shoppers who worked six days a week."

In the 1939 photo of Starr Street, looking east, W. T. Grant's variety store was on the corner of Chaparral. W. T. Grant opened its store at 623 North Chaparral in July 1933 in a building that had been occupied by the Simon-Cohn department store. Grant's eventually moved into a large new store south of the new Penney's in June 1954. Grant's closed in 1975, a victim of changing times.

Across Chaparral from Grant's, on the east side, was J. C. Penney's. The two-story brick building was constructed in the early 1920s by Hugh Sutherland and leased to Penney's, which

A Doc McGregor photo taken on Aug. 1, 1939 shows Starr Street looking east. On the right was W. T. Grant's with J.C. Penney's across Chaparral. On the left was the Mayflower Café, which was soon torn down for a new building that housed K. Wolens.

opened in December 1925. In 1949 Penney's moved into a new five-story building at Chaparral and William. It was closed in 1978.

Across Starr Street from Penney's, on the northeast corner, was the Mayflower Café in an old shellcrete structure built in 1866. It originally housed the Holthaus Bakery then, after the turn of the century, Cooper's Clean Bakery. Not long after McGregor took this photo the Mayflower was closed and the building pulled down. A new structure was built on the site and leased to K. Wolens Department Store, which opened on June 19, 1941.

Harriet Tillman said she would go shopping at K. Wolens with her mother. "They had little tubes the salesman put your money in. You could watch the canister go through the tube to the balcony where they would record the sale and send your receipt and change down to you. It was fun to watch. K. Wolens and Penney's had about the same quality goods."

East of the Mayflower Café, on the corner with Water Street, was the Elks Lodge building constructed in the early 1920s. At the time of the photo, the building was occupied by the Paradise Night Club where men could pick a dance partner for ten cents a dance. Then it became the Playboy Club. After "Doc" Mason's Dragon Grill on North Beach burned on Jan. 15, 1944, he leased and renovated the Elks Lodge building.

The Dragon Grill at Starr and Water opened on March 26, 1946. It quickly became known for its entertainment, its fine cuisine, and its illegal gambling operations on the third floor. Guests entered through hand-hammered copper doors. The main dining room, the Zodiac Room, featured floor-to-ceiling murals between panels in coral and silver. The second floor included living quarters for the Chinese cooks and private rooms for guests and gamblers. On the third floor was the Jalna Room, a supper club. Access to the gaming tables beyond was controlled with a system of warning lights and buzzers. Cards, dice, roulette wheels could be concealed behind moveable walls.

In August 1953, an enterprising policeman gained access to the gambling tables and Doc Mason was charged with keeping a gambling house. Not long afterwards he closed the Dragon Grill. Yes, the end of an era which many regretted ever after.

On Aug. 1, 1939, Doc McGregor was pointing his lens east on Starr. It was a two-way street then. Where Penney's was located is an empty lot, the old bus station building stands where the Mayflower Café once stood, W. T. Grant's building is vacant and long-closed. Only the Elks/Dragon Grill/Town Club building is in business as the Vietnam Restaurant and V Boutique Hotel.

Dr. Giles and Mr. McCaughan

The hottest election campaigns in Corpus Christi history came in three elections in the 1930s with hard-fought struggles between Dr. H. R. Giles and A. C. McCaughan for mayor. Giles won in 1935 and McCaughan came back to win in 1937 and 1939.

McCaughan moved from Durango, Mexico to Corpus Christi in 1914. He entered the real estate business and was elected to the City Council in 1933. In a three-way contest for mayor in 1935, McCaughan ran against Dr. Giles and G. O. Garrett.

It was a fierce contest. Texas Rangers were dispatched to keep order after telegrams were sent warning that the election might lead to violence. There was no bloodshed but it was a close contest. Giles received 2,914 votes, McCaughan 2,659, and Garrett 775.

In 1937, Giles ran for re-election and was faced with McCaughan again. It was widely anticipated that Giles would be re-elected. People liked him and were pleased with the achievements of his administration, which included the annexation of North Beach and closing some of the more troublesome joints. On election day, there were fist fights at polling places between Giles and McCaughan supporters. Much to the town's surprise, McCaughan received 3,506 votes to Giles' 2,317.

In 1939, it was another fierce contest. Dr. Giles and McCaughan charged each other with intimidating voters and promising city jobs for votes. McCaughan won by a two-to-one margin. Dr. Giles never ran again.

McCaughan's four terms as mayor marked great progress for the city. The bayfront project, with the seawall and the yacht basin, was started and completed during his administration. McCaughan oversaw the tremendous growth that came after the Naval Air Station was built.

McCaughan answered the chorus of complaints by pointing out that the city was going through intense growing pains, that the inconveniences were unavoidable as a small city was trying to serve the needs of a much larger population. A. C. McCaughan was not a candidate in 1945, after the city approved switching to the city-manager form of government. He died in 1964 when he was 94 years old. His longtime political nemesis, Dr. H. R. Giles, died in 1948.

—Oct. 4, 2017

A growing city in 1942

Corpus Christi was much smaller in 1942 but the downtown was in its glory days. Two of the three tall buildings on Peoples Street in this photo are still there: the Jones-Sherman Building on the left and the Driscoll Hotel building on the bluff.

A 1942 photo shows Peoples Street looking west from the Water Street intersection to the new Robert Driscoll Hotel on the bluff. On the left was George Plomarity's Manhattan Café followed by the Jones (formerly Sherman) Building and the Nueces Hotel was across the street.

The photo by "Doc" McGregor was taken at a time of great growth. A Chamber of Commerce report in 1942 pointed out that Corpus Christi had a population of 10,522 in 1920. After the Port of Corpus Christi opened in 1926, it climbed to 27,789, an increase of 264 percent. By 1940, it increased to 57,301, a gain of 106 percent. The city was gaining 10,000 a year and claimed to be the fastest-growing city in Texas, surpassing Houston.

At the time, the city's largest building, the 20-story Robert Driscoll Hotel, soared above the White Plaza Hotel next door. Lichtenstein's new store was open at Chaparral and Lawrence. Buccaneer Stadium was being built. The city limits were being pushed out to consume cotton fields to the south and west of Six Points. The newly built seawall, T-heads, yacht basin and Shoreline Boulevard were completed.

Two of the three tall buildings shown in this photo are still there: the recently renovated Jones-Sherman Building on the left, now the Nueces Lofts, and the Driscoll Hotel building on the

381

A 1942 "Doc" McGregor photo shows the Jones (Sherman) building on the left, the Nueces Hotel on the right, and the Robert Driscoll Hotel straight ahead on the bluff. This tall-building view of Peoples Street shows the downtown in its glory days, when the city seemed larger than it was.

bluff, now the Wells Fargo Building. It was white in 1942 and black today.

Nineteen forty-two was a time of great bustle and energy in Corpus Christi. The McGregor photo of Peoples Street, at the urban center of the downtown, captured the view of a city on the way up. Corpus Christi was much smaller in 1942 than it is today but the downtown was in its glory days then, with its concentration of stores, offices and tall buildings. It must have seemed more imposing and grander than today.

Craig v. Harney

On Friday afternoon, May 27, 1945, a minor landlord-tenant dispute case was heard in Nueces County Judge Joe Browning's court. The case would eventually reach the U. S. Supreme Court and become one of the landmark cases involving freedom of the press and constitutional law.

In the original case, Bush Jackson was the agent for the Flato family and Harry Heaney who owned the old Elks Club building at Starr and Water. Jackson leased the building to "Doc" Mason, who owned the Dragon Grill on North Beach which had recently been destroyed by fire. But there was a lease already held by Joe Mayes, who operated the Playboy Club in the building. "Doc" Mason wanted to establish a new Dragon Grill in that location.

When the case came up for trial on May 27, 1945, Mayes had been drafted and was stationed at Fort Hood. His wife was operating the Playboy Club in his absence. When the case went to a six-man jury on Saturday evening, Judge Browning told the jury to bring in a verdict in favor of Bush Jackson, breaking the lease held by Mayes.

The jurors balked. Twice they ignored the judge's instructions and returned verdicts in favor of Joe Mayes. Twice the judge sent them back with orders to reach a verdict for Jackson. At 10 p.m. on Saturday night, the jurors were confined in the courthouse jury room. On Sunday morning the judge told the jurors to bring back a directed verdict for Bush Jackson or he would lock them up another night. After 15 hours, the reluctant jury brought back a verdict in favor of Jackson, but with the verdict the jury issued a statement that said, "This verdict is rendered and recorded on the order of this court against the conscience of the jury."

A Caller-Times' editorial said, "A jury with a conscience last night refused to bring in a directed verdict that it did not agree with." Two days later, Bob McCracken, the paper's managing editor and page one columnist, wrote that Judge Browning's action demonstrated the need for judges to be trained in the law. Browning had been a rancher, without legal training. "Browning's behavior and attitude has brought down the wrath of public opinion on his head, and properly so."

Judge Browning was outraged. He issued a contempt citation for the publisher, Conway Craig, the managing editor, Bob McCracken, and reporter Tom Mulvaney. At a hearing, Browning found all three guilty of contempt, turned them over to Sheriff John Harney and ordered them held in jail.

They were booked, finger-printed, and mugshots taken. McCracken carried his portable typewriter so he could write a column from his cell. They were released after five hours. The case went to the Texas Court of Criminal Appeals, which upheld Judge Browning, ruling that newspaper coverage was "calculated to obstruct and impede the administration of justice and embarrass the judge." Robert Jackson, the paper's editor, wrote that, "We have every right to report to the people what is happening in their court without any editorial direction from the bench."

The case styled Craig v. Harney reached the U.S. Supreme Court, the court of last resort. On May 28, 1947, the high court reversed the findings of Judge Browning and the Court of Criminal Appeals in a 6-3 opinion written by Justice William O. Douglas.

The main points in the decision noted that a trial is a public event, that what happens in a courtroom is public property, and that a judge cannot use the power of his office to shield himself from criticism, even unfair criticism. Craig v. Harney was a landmark decision in constitutional law that remains one of the bedrock foundations of the freedom of the press.

Claude D'Unger recently told me he found a batch of trial transcripts from this old case in his attic. His father, Jerry D'Unger, represented Sheriff Harney and Judge Browning. Like many cases, the big winners were also big losers. The Caller-Times won its case but spent $36,000 in legal fees. "We don't want to win any more lawsuits like that one," the editor said. Joe Mayes, another "winner," did not get a new trial and lost his lease of the Elks Building. The big loser was Joe Browning defeated for re-election and never serving another term as judge.

—*Oct. 11, 2017*

Column 93

Angle led to wedge-shaped structures

Buildings on Schatzel Street were apparently designed to conform to the unusual angle of the street.

A "Doc" McGregor photo from May 26, 1935 taken from the White Plaza Hotel shows the blocks between Schatzel and Peoples that are fan-shaped, with the small end under the bluff and the large end on the bayfront. This led to irregular-shaped buildings on Schatzel Street.

The street on the left side of the photograph is Peoples while the one on the right is Schatzel. On Peoples all the buildings appear to be standard in shape. At bottom left, barely visible, is the Lovenskiold Building followed by the Furman Building, City Bank, and Nueces Hotel. On the south side of Peoples, looking east, is the Seeligson Building, partly visible, followed by the Bonner Building, Montgomery Ward and Sherman/Jones Building. The Pleasure Pier extends from Peoples ou into the bay.

The right side of the photograph shows Schatzel Street and five oddly shaped buildings. These five buildings include City Hall at lower left, built in 1911, the State National Bank Building at the corner of Mesquite Street, with the round tower front, built in 1908, the four-story Gugenheim-Cohn Building, built in 1907, the Corpus Christi National Bank and, across Chaparral, Lichtenstein's third store, built in 1911. All five of the buildings along Schatzel Street are wedge-shaped, apparently designed so that the buildings would conform to the unusual angle of the street.

A 1935 "Doc" McGregor photo shows Peoples Street to the left and Schatzel Street angling off to the right. The five major buildings along Schatzel were apparently designed to conform with the variant angle of the street.

The Priours of Salt Lake

One prominent natural feature near Corpus Christi was the Salt Lake a mile west of town, between today's Winnebago and the port turning basin. The lake disappeared in a drought and became known as the salt flats.

Robert Adams in his memoirs noted that "Old man Priour lived at the Salt Lake west of town, where he grew vegetables to sell. His wife was the daughter of old lady Hart, who had a store." The story of the Salt Lake begins with the Priours.

Rosalie Bridget Hart's family left Ireland in 1833 as part of the Power-Hewetson Colony. They landed at Copano in 1834. Rosalie's father died of cholera and was buried on the beach.

Mrs. Hart and her two daughters traveled by oxcart to Refugio. There they built a lean-to against the old mission walls. Most of the colony came down with fever and Mrs. Hart nursed the sick. Rosalie, age nine, did the cooking. Many died and were buried in blankets; there was no wood for coffins.

386

During the Texas Revolution Elizabeth Hart and daughters evacuated to Mobile, Ala. Rosalie's younger sister died of fever. Rosalie went to a convent school and later married Jean Marie Priour, a Breton. Mrs. Hart moved to Corpus Christi and opened a store in 1848 and Rosalie and her husband joined her.

Rosalie's husband ("Mr. Priour," she called him) bought a tract of land at the Salt Lake where he could indulge his passion for gardening. He grew vegetables that he sold in the town. In the Civil War, Mrs. Hart closed her store and moved to her ranch on the Aransas River. Rosalie and children moved to the ranch while her husband remained at the Salt Lake.

Elizabeth Hart died in 1863 and Rosalie brought her children back to Corpus Christi. She taught school in her mother's store while the family lived in a house on the edge of the Salt Lake. Confederate soldiers drove cattle there to slaughter.

There was a terrible drought during the war. Rosalie in her memoirs wrote, "To augment the misery of the country we had a drought that lasted seven years. Nothing could be raised west of the San Antonio River." The Salt Lake dried up during the worst of this long drought. After the war, when the rains came back, Priour planted 10 acres of cabbage, cauliflower and melons. Rosalie noted that "It was the first crop he had been able to raise since the beginning of the war on account of the drought."

In the summer of 1865, Corpus Christi was occupied by Union colored troops. One unit was the 28th Indiana commanded by Gen. Charles S. Russell. While the Union troops were bivouacked in town, there was a lot of nighttime activity at the Salt Lake. The Union troops made moonlit forays on Priour's fields and he had to keep his vegetables under close scrutiny.

Rosalie said, "Mr. Priour went into town and informed the general (Russell) of the way we were annoyed by his troops. He had a guard of five men stationed on our place (at the Salt Lake)" and that stopped the nighttime raids on the Priours' garden.

Although Rosalie said the colored troops had plundered their garden and humiliated local citizens, she became friends with the wives of the white officers. When the occupation troops were ordered to Brownsville, Mrs. Priour wrote that "it was like parting with a part of my own family. Before leaving, they gave me a white cat and two white chickens . . . They were counted among my greatest treasures."

Jean Marie Priour died on the last day of the year, 1880, and Rosalie died in 1903. They left a large family, including John M. Priour, hunting guide and naturalist who was the subject of the book, "A Man From Corpus Christi."

The Priours' lake was there in the 1870s, said Andrew Anderson. "It was very pretty. We used to go there and shoot ducks. The water was four or five feet deep and the shores were beautiful with green shrubs growing down to the water's edge." Then the lake dried up again. Where it had been there were salt flats, which were used as a municipal dumping ground until the city got a garbage incinerator in 1913.

When the new high school was built on Carancahua, a wooden building on the site was moved to the salt flats for use as an elementary school. In 1913 the Salt Lake School had 78 pupils and one teacher, Geraldine Dunne, who rode a horse out there from her home in town. The school was closed after the 1913 school year.

The Salt Lake dried up. It was there and then it was gone. It has been dead nearly 150 years and exists now on old maps and in old archives. When the lake lost its water, it all but lost its history, which is so closely linked to the history of the Priour family.

—Oct. 18, 2017

Perkins opened in October 1929

The corner of Leopard and Carancahua, across from the
R.R. Savage home was the site where Perkins Brothers
department store was built. It opened in October 1929
about the time the stock market crashed.

The corner of Leopard and Carancahua, across from the R.R.
Savage home, was the site where Perkins Brothers department
store was built. It opened in October 1929 about the time the
stock market crashed.

The newspaper at the time said that the Perkins store was
erected at a cost of $150,000 and represented "one of the most
modern buildings in the city." The building was designed by Fort
Worth architect Wyatt Hedrick. One noted feature of the store
was its terrazzo floors.

Perkins was Corpus Christi's second largest department store,
after the famous Lichtenstein's. Perkins was part of a chain
established in North Texas by Sam B. Perkins. The local store
was managed by his son, Willard Perkins, who married Mabel
West, the daughter of South Texas cattle rancher George West.

After 26 years in business, Perkins Brothers' Corpus Christi
store was sold to its competitor, Lichtenstein's, in 1955. Janice
Edison wrote me a note about that sale. "My father was Nathan
Friedman, the last president of Lichtenstein's. I remember the
night he came home and said they had just bought the old Perkins
store on the bluff. We got in the car and drove up the bluff to see
it that night. Dad went into the store and started flipping on lights
and going through the stockrooms. He would pull stuff out for
us to see, laughing, amazed to find such old

Perkins Brothers Department Store at the corner of Carancahua and Leopard was 11 years old when "Doc" McGregor snapped this photo on Nov. 22, 1940. It survived another 15 years as Perkins before it was sold in 1955 to become Lichtenstein's Uptown Store until it closed in 1968

merchandise still in the stockrooms. He found a treasure trove of old shoes, still in their boxes, in the stockroom. Some of the merchandise was more than 50 years old."

In 1968 Lichtenstein's closed its uptown operation, the old Perkins Brothers store, and the building was torn down to make way for a bank parking garage.

The Battle of Laredo

Edmund Jackson Davis, a Corpus Christi judge, opposed the move toward secession. When the issue came up for a vote in February 1861, Davis spoke at the Nueces County Courthouse against Texas leaving the Union. Like his father-in-law, Forbes Britton, who died two months before, Davis was an ardent Unionist.

When the Civil War broke out, Davis went to Matamoros to organize the First Texas Cavalry, U.S.A., which was composed of Unionists like himself. Confederates called them renegades. Davis was commissioned a colonel of volunteers.

After the Union invasion of the Texas coast in 1863 by an army under the command of Gen. Nathaniel P. Banks, Davis was ordered to disrupt Confederate supply lines in South Texas.

With Union forces in control of Brownsville and the mouth of the Rio Grande, the Confederacy's vital cotton trade shifted upriver to Laredo and Eagle Pass, where trains of wagons loaded with cotton made their way downstream on the Mexican side of the border, safe from attack.

In March 1864, Davis led an expedition up the Rio Grande to capture Laredo, 210 miles from Brownsville. The intent of the expedition was to seize Laredo and eventually Eagle Pass to stop the cotton traffic. Davis's Second Texas Cavalry and other troops left Brownsville in the middle of March. Some troops were carried on the steamboat Mustang while the cavalry rode along the river.

. At Laredo, Confederate Col. Santos Benavides, the highest ranking Mexican-American in the Confederate Army, learned of the federal expedition. He took his regiment and three other companies out to intercept Davis's force.

When the river became too shallow for the steamboat Mustang to proceed past Guerrero, Davis sent an advance guard of 200 men ahead to Laredo, with plans to bring up the main body as quickly as possible. The advance guard was under the command of Maj. Alfred Holt, who was ordered to capture Laredo and seize 5,000 bales of Confederate cotton stacked in Laredo's main plaza.

Laredo was lightly defended because Col. Benavides had deemed it unlikely that Union forces at Brownsville would venture so far from their home base. Benavides' forces were scattered in other places to protect the cotton routes.

With the help of local guides, Davis's advance force under Major Holt were able to ride over little-known roads and were almost to the outskirts of Laredo when a ranchero sounded the alarm. With few Confederate soldiers around, Laredo citizens were mustered to defend the town and they built barricades in the plaza.

Col. Benavides took 42 men to the outskirts of Laredo, divided them into squads and posted them in houses on both sides of the main road. Maj. Holt's 200 men arrived at three in the afternoon. When skirmishers were in range, Benavides' men posted in the houses began firing, forcing the federals back. The federals dismounted and advanced on foot.

"My men maintained a steady fire," Benavides wrote in his report to Brig. Gen. Rip Ford. "The brave Major Swope and Juan Ivara charged right upon an advancing squad of 40 Yankees and compelled them to retreat. Major Swope stood there until he emptied the last shot of his six-shooter, which compelled him to retire for the purpose of reloading. While doing so his horse was shot three times and also Juan Ivara's.

"The enemy advanced again but were repulsed by the vigorous fire of my gallant men, who were full of fight. The firing was kept up until dark when the Yankees thought best to skedaddle in their own peculiar style and give up the intention of walking into Laredo that day."

That ended the battle of Laredo on March 19, 1864. Maj. Holt was forced to retreat and rejoin E. J. Davis's main body. They made their way back to Brownsville. Laredo celebrated the victory with the ringing of church bells throughout the city. That ended the battle of Laredo on March 19, 1864.

E. J. Davis was promoted to brigadier general in the Union Army. At war's end, he returned to Corpus Christi and opened a law office. He was elected governor in 1869, with Texas under military rule, and became governor during Reconstruction. He died in 1883. Col. Santos Benavides, the victor in the battle of Laredo, returned to his ranch outside Laredo after the war. He was elected to the Legislature and served as an alderman in Laredo. He died in 1891.

—Oct. 25, 2017

Sitting on the porch

"Doc" McGregor's photo of porch sitters has several
points of visual interest: the flowers in the foreground,
the washtub, the little girl with hands clasped in her lap,
the woman's dress with a lace collar, the man's shirt
buttoned at the top.

Among the hundreds of copies of photos that I have is one I
call the Porch Sitters, which shows two adults and two
children sitting on the steps of a house, probably the
front porch judging by the flowers in the yard. It is one of "Doc"
McGregor's photos.

John Frederick McGregor moved to Corpus Christi from
Pennsylvania in 1929. He had been educated as a chiropractor at
the Palmer School of Chiropractic in Davenport, Iowa, which led
to the honorific of "Doc". He opened an office in the Furman
Building but it was the Depression and his patients couldn't pay.
He was an amateur photographer and began to sell photos. He
moved the family from the Vaky Apartments to 1015 Chaparral,
which became the family home, photo studio, and medical office.

McGregor took photos for the Caller, not for pay but a credit
line. His name became famous and his hobby became his
mainstay. He took thousands of photos in the 1930s, '40s and
'50s. McGregor died in 1986. He left an estimated 250,000
negatives that are archived at the Museum of Science and
History. This splendid collection reflects much of the history of
Corpus Christi, though they do require some filling in the blanks.

The corresponding information behind most of McGregor's
photos has been lost. In the case of the Porch Sitters, we do not

What appears to be grandparents, or maybe even parents who have had a hard life, sit with two children on the steps of a porch in this "Doc" McGregor photo taken on Jan. 31, 1930, in the second year of the Great Depression.

know who they are or where the photo was taken. We do have the date. Chelsea Aldrete at the museum tells me it was taken on July 31, 1930, but nothing else is known.

The man and woman sitting on the steps may have been the grandparents or the parents of the two children. They look as if they had had a hard life. The photo has several points of interest for the eye. The flowers in the foreground. The washtub under the porch. The little girl with her hands clasped in her lap just like her daddy's or granddaddy's. The woman's dress with a lace collar, her Sunday shoes. The man's shirt carefully buttoned at the top. They sit serious and dignified, accommodating and looking at the photographer. You find yourself wondering how they lived, what troubles they had, and how they died.

The anonymous porch sitters remind me of Walker Evans' photos of sharecroppers in 1936 Alabama that became the basis of "Let Us Now Praise Famous Men." While all photos capture light, McGregor's old photos capture the light of other days, the light of times long past.

A long trip for a good cigar

War fever gripped South Texas, like the rest of the U. S., when the American cruiser Maine exploded in Havana Harbor on Feb. 16, 1898. War against Spain, the colonial power in Cuba, was declared on April 25.

In Corpus Christi, a volunteer militia company called the Kenedy Rifles marched through town on their way to Austin. They had been organized in May 1889. Other volunteer units forming across the state included the Belknap Rifles and the O'Connor Guards of Victoria. The First Volunteer cavalry, commanded by Gen. Leonard Wood with Theodore Roosevelt second in command, was in training in San Antonio. They were called the Rough Riders, a name Roosevelt hated.

In Corpus Christi, 38 members of the Kenedy Rifles left town on May 3, departing for Austin from the SAAP Depot. Jose Crixell's brass band played the national anthem as they boarded the train. The Kenedy Rifles picked up volunteers on the way and arrived in Austin with 84 men. At Camp Mabry, they were mustered into U.S. service as Company E of the 1st Regiment, Texas Volunteers. The captain of the company was Augustus MacManus, first lieutenant was Tobe FitzSimmons. Another was Robert Hall, for whom Bob Hall Pier was later named.

While Company E was in training, Admiral Dewey destroyed the Spanish fleet at Manila, the battle of El Caney was fought in Cuba, the Rough Riders stormed up San Juan Hill, afoot. The fighting was over by August 1898. Company E was moved to a camp at Mobile and Jacksonville before being sent to Savannah and issued Krag-Jorgensen rifles for duty in Cuba.

On Christmas Day 1898 Company E boarded a transport ship and arrived at Havana on Dec. 30. They could see the smokestacks of what was left of the Maine in the harbor. They waved at departing Spanish soldiers who waved back, glad to be going home.

Tobe FitzSimmons wrote his parents in Corpus Christi: "We were expecting trouble but there was nothing but cheers from the natives for los Americanos." FitzSimmons described Cuba as being like Mexico with cobbled streets and no sidewalks. Robert Hall in a letter to his parents said the Cuban people were very friendly when they marched through Havana on their way to the camp. "They waved and threw us cigars."

The soldiers of Company E were stationed at a camp at the base of a mountain on the Atlantic side of the island. They soon discovered rum. Sgt. Arthur Dear, from Corpus Christi, wrote home that, "There is a drink here that will set a person wild. Some of the boys got hold of some and nearly went crazy."

Company E was assigned garrison duty all over Cuba. Almost a year after they had marched out of Corpus Christi, Company E left Dry Tortugas for Galveston, where they were inspected by a health officer to make sure they were not carrying an infectious disease. They turned in their Krag-Jorgensen rifles and were discharged. Their pockets were filled with Havana cigars and Spanish army buttons they obtained in trade.

They arrived at the train depot in Corpus Christi on Sunday night, April 16, 1899. They were greeted by a cheering crowd and Jose Crixell's brass band playing patriotic tunes. They were supposed to march through town to Market Hall but, said the Caller, "it was impossible to form them into procession as parents would not give them up."

Three days later Market Hall was draped in bunting and decorated with a large portrait of Mifflin Kenedy, namesake of the Kenedy Rifles, as the returning heroes were showered with laurel leaves and given the freedom of the city. There was dancing and a banquet was served at midnight. For the Kenedy Rifles, or Company E, their part in the Spanish-American war was over.

—Nov. 1, 2017

Column 96

City swallowed small communities

The old communities on the outer reaches of the city
were swallowed as the black hole of the city spread out
from its downtown core.

When Corpus Christi was contained in the constricted area of
what is now downtown and uptown, it was surrounded beyond its
perimeter by smaller communities, most of them with their own
post offices and schools. Besides Calallen and Flour Bluff,
familiar to all, others were Aberdeen, Brighton, Gardendale,
Kostoryz and Sunshine.

Aberdeen was five miles south of downtown. It was past the
Alta Vista Hotel, past the Chautauqua Grounds, and situated
around where the Seaside Cemetery is today. Aberdeen was big
enough to have a post office but since there was already
an Aberdeen, Texas, the name was changed to Alfred, after the
son of postmaster Oliver Watson. (Another community named
Alfred was near Orange Grove.)

A news item from Feb. 28, 1896 announced that a phonograph
concert would be given at Aberdeen and all who rode the
streetcar from Corpus Christi to Aberdeen would be admitted
free. The Aberdeen school was later consolidated with the
Sunshine school to become the Sundeen district.

Annaville began in 1940 when Leo Stewart and wife Anna
bought 40 acres west of Corpus Christi. They put lots up for sale,
built a store, and erected a sign that read, "Annaville." Like its
neighbor Calallen, Annaville was absorbed by the spreading blob
of Corpus Christi but kept its separate identity.

397

Brighton, on the shore of Laguna Madre opposite Pita Island, was named for Brighton, Tenn. The Corpus Christi Crony on June 21, 1902 reported that, "Postmaster C. L. Barnes of Brighton proves that this is grape country, even when it doesn't rain. He disposed of a wagon-load in town last week. They are fine."

The late Bill Duncan, a Caller-Times editor who grew up in that area, said Brighton was often called Flour Bluff Two while the area around the Point, where NAS was built, was known as Flour Bluff One.

Brooklyn in the 1870s was what we know as North Beach. A wooden bridge across Hall's Bayou was called — what else? — Brooklyn Bridge. When the railroad came, Brooklyn was dropped in favor of Rincon, the historic name for North Beach.

Calallen was founded by Calvin J. Allen. He convinced the St. Louis, Brownsville and Mexican Railroad to bypass Nuecestown and run its line across his ranch. A town called Calvin grew up around the depot but since there was already a Calvin, Texas, the name was constricted to Calallen.

A news item in the May 23, 1908 Caller reported that the first carload of watermelons of the year was shipped from the Calvin depot. The 974 melons sold for $400.

Roy Terrell recalled traveling by auto to Calallen. "There were no paved roads, not even the streets in town were paved. The only road that could be traveled in bad weather was a shell road from Corpus Christi to Calallen, following the old stagecoach road. I made this trip several times with my uncle Cal Allen who had one of the first automobiles. This road was made from oyster shells dredged from Corpus Christi Bay."

Clarkwood was first called Woodland Park, which was platted but never built. In 1909, Z. H. Clark filed a plat for the same site west of Corpus Christi and began selling lots. The town was named after Clark and the earlier Woodland Park.

A post office for Clarkwood was authorized in 1914. The first business was a cotton gin, not surprising since this was among the county's top cotton-growing areas.

Flour Bluff's name dates back to 1838. During the Pastry War between France and Mexico French ships blockaded Mexico's

Calvin J. Allen, founder of Calallen, served on a grand jury around the turn of the 20ᵗʰ Century. Allen, shown with other jury members sitting on the steps of the 1854 Courthouse, was in the center of the bottom row holding his hat.

ports and smugglers landed supplies on the Texas coast. When the Republic of Texas tried to stop the smuggling, Texas militia interrupted a band of smugglers and they fled, dumping barrels of flour as they escaped, and thus the name Flour Bluff.

Corpus Christi annexed Flour Bluff in 1961, over almost unanimous opposition, and after a long and bitter legal struggle that reached all the way to the U.S. Supreme Court.

Gardendale, in the vicinity of today's Rodd Field Road and Everhart, was founded in the early 1900s. It was in no position to object when it was annexed by Corpus Christi in 1954.

Juan Saenz was seven miles west of Corpus Christi where Shell (UpRiver) Road crosses Clarkwood Road. The community took its name from a ranch-hand of Henry Kinney, Juan Saenz Garcia, who settled there. In the Nuecestown Raid in 1875 bandits plundered George Frank's store at Juan Saenz.

Kostoryz was founded in 1906 after Stanley Kostoryz bought 7,000 acres of ranch land west of Corpus Christi. Kostoryz, originally from Czechoslovakia, advertised farms for sale in Czech newspapers around the country and Czech farmers and their families moved into the area beginning in 1906. The Kostoryz community was swallowed by Corpus Christi.

Nuecestown was originally known as The Motts. It was founded in 1852 by Henry Kinney, who agents to England to attract settlers and established Nuecestown as a farming community. A post office was established in 1854. Bandits raided Nuecestown on Good Friday 1875 and burned Thomas Noakes' store.

Noakes rebuilt his store a mile west of the original site and the town followed. Nuecestown withered away after Calvin J. Allen enticed the railroad to build across his ranch, creating Calallen.

Sunshine was two miles west of Oso Bay. The larger area around it was known as the Encinal. Sunshine had a post office from 1903 until 1911. The Sunshine school, started in 1887, was merged with the Aberdeen district to become the Sundeen district.

After the turn of the century the annual Encinal barbecue and dinner on the ground at the Sunshine school was famous throughout Nueces County.

The old communities on the outer reaches of the city were swallowed as the black hole of the city spread out from its downtown core. Except for Flour Bluff, Calallen and maybe Annaville, which were able to hold on to their own identity, very little is left of the older communities like Aberdeen, Brighton and Sunshine.

The historical memory has all but faded away. There is an Aberdeen Avenue, a Kostoryz Street and a Brighton Street. But not much else.

—Nov. 8, 2017

Column 97

Bascule had its ups and downs

People were pleased with the bascule bridge at first, before it became a bottleneck to traffic and a menace to navigation. The 90-foot opening was a tight squeeze for the ever-larger oil tankers and freighters visiting the port.

The bascule bridge opened to auto traffic on July 30, 1926. Riding across in the first car, a new Buick Touring Sedan from Reed Auto, were Mayor P. G. Lovenskiold and Navigation District Chairman Robert Driscoll.

Six weeks later, on Sept. 14, 1926, the port was opened with a great celebration. Flags waved, bands played, and crowds gathered to marvel as the bascule rose to the occasion to allow the first commercial ship, the SS Ogontz, to enter the port's turning basin.

Well, not the first. The bascule had to be opened before the port was ready so that a temporary wooden bridge across the entrance could be dismantled. That allowed the dredge boat Texas to enter the turning basin and finish dredging work on the western shore.

The bascule was not given a formal name. It was simply the bascule, the French word for seesaw. It weighed 1,500 tons, was 121 feet long and 52 feet wide, and so delicately counter-balanced that it could be raised 141 feet in the air by two small electric motors. There was a walkway on one side, streetcar tracks in the middle, and railroad tracks on the port side. It cost $406,000 and took the Wisconsin Bridge & Iron of Milwaukee a year to build.

401

The bridge was too small and the port entrance too narrow, the U.S. Corps of Engineers warned before it was built. But the city, which was paying for the bridge, said that the bascule was all it could afford.

People were pleased with the bascule, at first. The siren that signaled the raising of the bridge invariably summoned those who would park their cars and watch the arrival of a great ship coming in from the sea.

Despite the fascination, within five years the bascule came to be seen as a bottleneck to traffic, a menace to navigation, and a handicap to the port's growth.

At any time, convenient or not, the siren would sound and the massive bulk of the bascule would raise to its towering height of 141 feet. In the 12 to 30 diverting minutes it took for a ship to slowly, slowly make its way under the upraised bascule and through the entrance to the port, motorists were stalled on both sides of the bridge.

Stalled and often fuming. One bridge operator said that resentful motorists called them names you didn't hear in Sunday school.

The bridge was dangerous for ships. The 90-foot opening was a tight squeeze for the ever-larger oil tankers and freighters visiting the port. Ship captains called it threading the needle. A Norwegian captain, O. Nillson from Olso, told a reporter in 1954 that he had entered the port countless times, beginning in 1931 when he was a seaman, "and every time I hated it." John Peter Dekker, master of a Dutch freighter, said it "scared the hell out of me."

Ships trying to navigate through the narrow opening often collided with the bascule. One of the worst incidents occurred in 1931 when the steering mechanism jammed on a cargo vessel, the Youngstown, and it smashed into the concrete control house of the bridge. Max Luther, the tender, realized something was amiss and ran just before the collision. The bascule was locked in the up position for 10 days, forcing motorists to detour by way of Calallen.

A bit of the wooden hull of the USS Constitution was scraped off when it smashed into the bascule in 1932. The SS Liberty

The USS Constitution, Old Ironsides, approaches the bascule bridge as it leaves the port turning basin on Feb. 23, 1932 after a nine-day visit. The 1812 warship scraped the sides of the bascule bridge as it passed through when it arrived on Feb. 14, 1932. Photo by "Doc" McGregor.

Bell plowed into the control house in 1940 and a British ship, the Greenwich, slammed into the north side of the bascule structure in 1957.

At least 183 wrecks were recorded, but there were more. The city operated the bascule in the first four years, from 1926 to 1930, and its records were lost. After 1930 the city turned over the bascule to the Nueces County Navigation District for $1 a year; the district paid the salaries of the bridge tenders and maintenance costs.

Beginning in the early 1930s, city, port, and Navigation District officials began looking at options to replace the undersized bascule. In 1933, New Deal funding was sought, unsuccessfully, to build a larger lift bridge with a wider opening

403

to the port. In 1936, the city tried to get the federal government to participate in digging a toll tunnel. In 1941, plans for a $4 million toll tunnel were put on hold because of the war.

The subject returned in the 1950s. An industrial-sized dispute raged over whether to dig a deep tunnel under the port entrance or build a high bridge over it. The town was split between the two factions. At a heated session of the City Council, Mayor Albert Lichtenstein, who favored a tunnel, resigned in a huff and took a seat in the audience. In the end, it was not the city's decision to make. The Texas Department of Highways offered $9 million of the $22 million it would take to build a high bridge but nothing for a tunnel. That ended the debate. The tunnel was dead.

Work began on the new bridge in June 1956. They started building it from both sides. The north and south ends were joined on March 13, 1959. It took three years and four months to build Harbor Bridge. The finished structure included 21 million pounds of steel and 134 million pounds of concrete for a total weight of 155 million pounds. It was 5,818 feet long and rose 250 feet above the water. Because of its shape, sailors called it Napoleon's Hat.

Harbor Bridge opened to traffic on Oct. 23, 1959. In the excitement of the new bridge for the next few months, few paid much attention as wreckers dismantled the old bridge. After it was cut up and scrap iron hauled away in railroad cars, after the concrete foundation was broken up and dumped at the Glasscock Fill breakwater, a long familiar scene was gone. Now, nearly 60 decades later, we will get a new high bridge and Harbor Bridge will follow the unlamented passing of the old bascule.

—Nov. 15, 2017

Power and Light

The electric power business in Corpus Christi started in
1890 with the Corpus Christi Electric Company plant in
a corrugated tin building on Water Street.

The police department and municipal court building on
Chaparral served as the main headquarters of Central Power &
Light for half a century. The ice house and power plant were
behind it, on Water Street. Besides selling electricity, CPL in its
early years delivered ice door to door and ran the streetcar line.

The electric power business started here in 1890 with the
Corpus Christi Electric Company plant in a corrugated tin
building on Water Street. It went broke and in 1898 was sold to
E. A. Born and Royall Givens, who purchased a 20-ton ice plant
and renamed it the Corpus Christi Electric and Ice Company.
Electricity was provided only at night.

A competing firm — the Peoples Light Company — was
formed in 1907 and promised to provide electricity full-time with
a new 125-horsepower gas engine.

Daniel Hewitt started an electric streetcar operation in Corpus
Christi in 1910. Streetcars and ice manufacturing both needed
cheap power to operate, so there was a conjunction of interests
with power companies. Hewitt purchased power from the
Peoples Light Company. He ran four cars and charged a five-cent
fare. After a year he sold to the Heinley brothers of Denver, who
built their own power plant, added three cars and still charged
five cents a fare.

A Philadelphia consortium purchased the streetcar line and
electric system in 1914 to comprise the Corpus Christi Railway

Central Power & Light's main office building at Chaparral and Laguna (renamed Sartain), shown in a photo by "Doc" McGregor taken on Sept. 4, 1940.

Central Power & Light's main building was enlarged and remodeled, as shown in a photo by Sammy Gold taken on Aug. 9, 1957. After CPL moved to new headquarters on Carancahua, the city purchased the building in 1988 to house the police department and municipal courts.

and Light Co. The streetcars lost money until the Army established Camp Scurry in 1916. With thousands of soldiers at the camp, the trolley business entered its golden age, which lasted until Scurry was closed, after the end of World War I, and the hurricane of Sept. 14, 1919 wrecked the power plant, located on the shoreline of Corpus Christi Bay, and virtually destroyed the streetcar system.

Power was restored a week after the storm, but the streetcars sat idle for two months. While they were out of service, a Jitney service with automobiles ran fixed routes. The streetcar system went bankrupt and was purchased in 1921 by Texas Central Power, which was formed in 1916 by Ralph Morrison and Warner McCall, who bought small electric companies across South Texas.

A fire destroyed the power plant on Water Street on Nov. 20, 1921, leaving the city dark. When temporary service was restored, the damaged plant couldn't meet peak demand so a section of the city was cut off each night.

The electric company was reorganized as Gulf Coast Power Company, a new steam generating plant was installed and the streetcar system was restructured as the Nueces Railway Company. In 1925, it was sold to the Middle West Utilities. The operating name in South Texas was Central Power and Light. The power plant and ice plant were remodeled; a fleet of ice delivery trucks operated from the plant.

CPL shut down the streetcar line on Jan. 31, 1931 and instituted a bus service with routes to North Beach, Hillcrest and Del Mar until 1933. CPL sold the bus line to Edwin and Bob Ekstrom, who founded Greyhound. The bus system was still charging a five-cent fare.

In 1932, a two-story brick building was constructed at Chaparral and Laguna (now Sartain) to house CPL's main offices. A third story was added in 1937 and two floors built on in 1954. The building was remodeled in 1957 with one of those unattractive modern facades. The old power plant and ice house were leveled in the 1960s.

In 1987, before it merged with American Electric Power in 2000, Central Power & Light moved to a 16-story tower on

Carancahua. In 1988, the city purchased the five-story CPL building to house the police department and municipal courtrooms. The city also ended up with the bus system, which evolved into the RTA.

Jail History

Nueces County was three years old on Feb. 21, 1849 when county commissioners discussed the need for a jail. When the sheriff made an arrest, he put the prisoner in a boarding house, at county expense. A special meeting of the commissioners' court was held to discuss whether the county could afford to build a jail. The issue was postponed.

The following year the county ordered a courthouse and jail built. The courthouse was finished in 1857 at a cost $4,000. There was not enough money left to build the jail. The sheriff was back to lodging prisoners in boarding houses.

The lack of a jail became a critical issue in 1860.

A man named John Warren got drunk, started a fight in a saloon, and was taken by Sheriff Mat Nolan to sleep it off at his boarding house. He returned to the saloon, stabbed the bartender, and then shot and killed the sheriff's brother, Tom Nolan, when he tried to arrest him. After Tom Nolan's death the Ranchero newspaper wrote about the county's need for a jail and a jail bond issue was passed on Nov. 6, 1860, but the plans were scrapped when the Civil War began.

The county still had no jail after the war. Commissioners bought an iron cage and installed it on the top floor of the 1854 courthouse. They called it a "jail." After it was installed, three prisoners picked the lock on the iron cage and escaped.

The county built a new courthouse in 1875, called the Hollub Courthouse after the builder. The old 1854 courthouse next door was used for a jury room and a jail. Two killers convicted of a notorious massacre at the Morton store on Baffin Bay were hanged from a scaffold built out from the gallery of the old courthouse.

After four decades of talking about a need for a jail, they finally built the county's first real jail on Mesquite Street near

The first real jail, with the steeple, was located next to the 1854 courthouse And conveniently down the block from the 1875 Hollub courthouse. Photo from Jim Moloney.

the courthouse in 1892. It had its own gallows at the rear of the building. When the county outgrew the 1875 Hollub courthouse, it built a six-story structure in 1913. The jail facilities on the fourth and fifth floors had padded cells for a lunacy department and hot boxes to punish unruly prisoners.

The specially built gallows on the fifth floor were never used. The state took over the task of conducting executions and the hangman's trap door was welded shut.

—Nov. 22, 2017

The ship Japonica

The bay excursion vessel made daily trips between
Corpus Christi, Ingleside and Port Aransas. It was
stranded next to the bluff in the 1919 storm. It was
repaired and later burned off the Texas coast in 1946.

The japonica, a flowering shrub that originally came from
Japan (I looked it up), was fashionable in the South in the 1930s
and 1940s. But the word Japonica, with a capital J, takes on
another meaning here. It was a pleasure and passenger craft that
figured prominently in Corpus Christi history for more than three
decades in the early part of the 20th century.

The steam yacht, built in 1906, was 80 feet long with a beam of
14 feet and had triple screws and three 90-horsepower engines. A
man named E. E. Jenkins sailed it from New Orleans to Corpus
Christi in 1911 and put it into daily service between Corpus
Christi, Ingleside and Port Aransas. Capt. Andrew Anderson of
the family of bar pilots paid Jenkins $3,000 for the Japonica in
1913. Anderson's younger brother Ben operated the vessel.

In the 1919 storm the Japonica ran aground and was stranded
next to the bluff below the W. W. Jones home. The ship was
repaired and Capt. Ben Anderson ran the ship for bay excursions
for many years. When not on the bay it was usually docked on
the T-head of the Pleasure Pier.

People would take a trip on the Japonica to go fishing at Port
Aransas or to Rockport for picnics and outings. Corpus Christi
High School's graduating class of 1924 took a bayfront ride on
the Japonica. Mrs. A. R. Yeargen, who operated a grocery,

The Japonica, a local pleasure and passenger cruise yacht which operated out of Corpus Christi from the end of the Pleasure Pier. It was owned by Capt. Andy Anderson. It burned in 1946.

recalled taking family excursions to Port Aransas to fish. "We went on the Japonica and it took about two hours."

Capt. Andrew Anderson sold the Japonica in the mid-1930s. It was moved to New Orleans where it was used to transport beer up the Mississippi River until it sank in a river accident in 1935. It was salvaged, repaired, and returned to the Texas coast where it burned in another accident in 1946.

Captains of the Sea

The John Anderson family of sea captains were witnesses to the great events in Corpus Christi history, from the days when Zachary Taylor's army landed to prepare for war with Mexico, to the bombardment of the city during the Civil War, to the building of the seawall eight decades later.

John Anderson came from Sweden. He landed in Mobile, Ala., in the 1830s and within a few years owned his own schooner.

When Zachary Taylor's troops moved from Louisiana to Corpus Christi, Anderson transported supplies for the army. He would anchor his schooner off North Beach while stores were offloaded onto small skiffs and ferried ashore.

In 1852 Anderson married widow, Hannah Bowen Yung, and returned to Corpus Christi. He built a house on Water Street for his family and worked as a bay pilot. His son Andrew was born that year. The captain built a scow schooner in 1860 and named it the Flour Bluff. It was constructed with a shallow draft to sail on the shallow waters of the Laguna Madre and Corpus Christi Bay and used it to lighter goods from larger vessels at the Aransas Pass.

In 1860 Capt. John and his oldest son Andrew hauled a load of lumber to Padre Island. John Singer, brother of the man who invented the sewing machine, lived on the island and he was convinced there was oil under the dunes. Timber to build a derrick was shipped in and taken to the island on the Flour Bluff. Singer's oil-drilling operations were disrupted by the outbreak of the Civil War.

In the summer of the second year of the war, Lt. John Kittredge, commander of the Union forces blockading the coast, sailed into Corpus Christi Bay and, under a flag of truce, threatened to bombard the city. The Andersons buried the household silver and evacuated west of town. They could hear the bombardment. When the Andersons returned, their house had been hit and their gray cat was missing an ear.

After the bombardment, the Andersons moved to Flour Bluff and lived in a building used to store salt near Anderson Point. Capt. John was nearly lynched during the war. He was taking a French couple on his boat down the Laguna Madre when they were captured by Union forces. The Frenchman and his wife were sent on to New Orleans while Anderson was held at the federal outpost Port Aransas. He was freed and given provisions for his trouble.

When Anderson returned to Corpus Christi he was suspected of aiding the enemy. A friend overheard Confederates discussing their intention to "string up old man Anderson." Anderson escaped and went over to the other side. Capt. John worked as a pilot for Union ships and when the war ended he was the captain of the steamer Planter that brought three regiments of Union soldiers as an occupying force for Corpus Christi.

Capt. John built a windmill next to his home on Water Street. He used old cannon balls from the Kittredge bombardment as ball bearings to shift the windmill to face the prevailing wind. The mill was used to saw wood and grind salt. During this time, Capt. John and Capt. Andy worked for Mifflin Kenedy, hauling supplies to the ranch and transporting hides and tallow from Kenedy's packing house at Flour Bluff to Rockport.

John Anderson and each of his sons, Andrew and William, were called "Captain." When the San Antonio and Aransas Pass Railroad planned to build a bridge across Nueces Bay, Capt. Andy made the soundings. In 1880, when the jetty was being built at Aransas Pass, the contract to haul rocks went to Capt. John, who hired men and leased a fleet of schooners to transport rock from Point of Rocks in Baffin Bay. Capt. John died in 1898. His old windmill was torn down two years later.

Capt. Andy in his last years made sailboats and spent his time in a waterfront warehouse where he could watch ships coming and going. His company included various cats and a brown pelican named George William. The warehouse was torn down in 1938 to make way for the seawall. Capt. Will died in 1939 and Capt. Andy in 1949, three years shy of his 100th birthday.

—Nov. 29, 2017

City was booming during the war

Corpus Christi was humming with activity. Hotels were packed. The downtown was a maze of torn-up streets as sewer lines were laid, ditches dug, roadways paved. Dredge soil from the bay was piled up as the seawall was being built. With all that construction going on and the naval air station in full gear. Corpus Christi was called "Zoomtown!"

Flour Bluff was chosen in 1939 for a new naval air station and construction soon began on a 2,050-acre site bounded by Cayo del Oso, Corpus Christi Bay and Laguna Madre. By June 1940 some 9,000 construction workers were hard at work.

With war threatening in Europe and the Pacific, they raced against time. Fishing shacks, homes and trailers located on the site were moved or demolished. Sand dunes were leveled, a ship channel was dredged, and docking facilities built. Roads, runways, and hangars were constructed. Barracks, mess halls, repair shops, and administrative and school buildings followed. A 13-mile water line and 19-mile railroad spur were completed from the city to the base. And all of it was done at a frenzied pace.

The base was nearly completed a year ahead of schedule when it was dedicated on March 12, 1941. Frank Knox, the Chicago newspaper tycoon who had been appointed Secretary of the Navy, was the main speaker. A dinner banquet was held at the White Plaza Hotel. Lyndon Johnson, whose political influence with President Roosevelt helped locate the base at Flour Bluff, was on hand.

A week later, on March 20, the first class of 52 cadets started classes. They were trained in an open cockpit biplane called the Yellow Peril for its canary yellow color. In coming months Rodd Field, Cabaniss and Cuddihy auxiliary fields were rushed to completion.

The city was humming. Almost overnight Corpus Christi jumped from a small languid town to a large bustling city. With all the construction in town and at the base, hotels were packed. The Nueces Hotel put beds in its famous Sun Room and people in town rented out extra rooms to the influx of workers. A migrant camp of tents on North Beach filled with workers and their families hoping to find jobs at the naval air station.

Downtown Corpus Christi was a maze of detours and torn-up streets as new sewer lines were laid, ditches dug, roadways paved or dug up. Dredge soil from the bay was piled up to use in raising the grade as the seawall was being built. While the bayfront was being transformed, the 20-story Robert Driscoll Hotel was rising on the bluff. With all that construction going on and the naval air station in full gear, an article in Collier's called Corpus Christi "Zoomtown!"

Seventy-six years ago, on Sunday, Dec. 7, 1941, it turned out to be a cool and placid day. Shortly after noon people heard on radio that Japanese planes had attacked the U.S. bases at Pearl Harbor. At the Naval Air Station, leaves were cancelled. On Monday at the Assembly & Repairs hangar, sailors and workers listened to President Roosevelt's day of infamy speech. In following days local men crowded recruiting offices on Starr Street trying to enlist.

The city's first casualties of the war were Billy Jack Brownlee, killed in the bombing of Hickam Field, and Warren Joseph Sherrill, killed on the USS Arizona.

Beginning in 1942 the Navy operated a hush-hush radar training school on Ward Island. People in town had no idea what the big secret about Ward Island was until after the war. From the summer of 1942 until the end of the war, 10,000 Navy personnel were trained on "Radar Island."

The city's first blackout drill was held on Jan. 19, 1942. The next blackout, 10 days later, was the real thing when a U-boat

A sailor leaves the Driscoll Hotel one day in 1943. Photo by John Vachon, the Library of Congress.

was sighted near the Aransas Pass channel. To prevent ships from being silhouetted against city lights, a blackout was strictly enforced. Air-raid wardens patrolled the streets looking for signs of light.

U-boats menaced the Gulf, especially in 1942, sinking U.S. and allied ships, mostly tankers carrying oil and gasoline. No more dangerous job existed than being on an oil tanker tracked by a U-boat. A torpedo could transform a tanker and sea around it into a flaming inferno. In May and June of 1942 U-boats operating in the Gulf claimed the highest total of ship losses for any two-month period of the war.

The campaign against U-boats was conducted by the Eighth Military District headquartered in the federal building on Starr Street. Eventually, the increased activity by anti-sub planes and ships made it too hot for U-boats, which returned to the Atlantic before the end of the war.

Here, as elsewhere, women filled jobs left vacant by men who went off to fight. At the Naval Air Station many worked in the Assembly and Repair Department. At the mid-point of the war, 20,000 civilians were employed at the base, and many were women who repaired Navy planes and kept them flying.

On April 21, 1943, President Franklin D. Roosevelt and Mexico's President Manuel Avila Camacho arrived from Monterrey, where they had conferred for several days, to visit the Naval Air Station. They were welcomed by the base commander and had lunch with cadets in the mess hall.

In 1944, two German POWs escaped from a camp at Mexia and fled to Corpus Christi. This set off a manhunt and people began to see Nazis everywhere. Two Russians, here to study refinery operations, were arrested when they were heard "talking foreign." The POWs were captured at a tourist court on North Beach. Eugene Kurz and Heinz Grimm, Luftwaffe pilots, were returned Mexia.

Corpus Christi celebrated when the war in the Pacific ended on Aug. 15, 1945. Cars drove down Chaparral, horns blaring, bands playing, as people jammed the streets and danced in Artesian Park. The joy of long-awaited peace exploded and for that brief moment in time, one reporter wrote, "everybody in the city loved one another."

With the war over, the base took on one new function when German POWs were housed in a barbed-wire compound near the South Gate. The POWs worked at manual labor jobs around the base. Then auxiliary fields were closed, Navy planes were mothballed, and it was more gloom than zoom at the Naval Air Station, which became a ghost of its wartime self. But the base had served its purpose in helping to win the war. Many aviators who fought and died in the great naval battles of the Pacific, the battles that ultimately won the war, were trained at Corpus Christi NAS.

In December 1945, for the first time since 1941, Corpus Christi streets were lit up with Christmas lights, at peace with the world.

—Dec. 6, 2017

Column 101

Bay View College opened in 1894

"This was ranch country then and there were practically
no schools, so Bay View flourished." —Madelyn
(Fisher) Stone

The Portland Hotel opened in December 1891. Twenty-five
couples from Corpus Christi took the train across the bay to
Portland where they were met at the SAAP depot by hacks which
took them to the handsome new hotel at Elm Street and First
Avenue.

This was during the Ropes boom. Elihu Ropes arrived in 1889
and bought large tracts of land, built a resort hotel on Ocean
Drive, began dredging a pass across Mustang Island, and
projected building a railroad to Brownsville. Portland emerged as
part of the general boom.

John Willacy bought 640 acres from the Coleman-Fulton
Pasture Company, a site by the bay on both sides of the SAAP
Railroad line. Willacy established the Portland Harbor &
Improvement Company and began selling lots. Expectations
were high, if not exalted. A map showing Portland, Maine,
Portland, Oregon, and Portland, Texas at the bottom of the large
triangle demonstrated the reach of their ambitions. The townsite
had a planned grid of streets with an open square reserved for a
courthouse.

The Ropes boom fizzled in 1893 during a nationwide
depression. Ropes Pass on Mustang Island silted in and other
Ropes' endeavors were stopped in their tracks. Land values
plummeted. The Portland Hotel was closed, unsold lots were

repossessed by the Coleman-Fulton Pasture Company and turned back into pasturage or farmland.

This was not a promising time to start a new college. It happened this way. Thomas Marshall Clark, better known as T. M., was asked to start a private boarding school in Portland. Clark was one of the founders (with his father and two brothers) of Add Ran College in Hood County in 1873. Add Ran was later moved to Fort Worth to become TCU. Professor Clark taught at Add Ran and married Alice Yantis of a prominent local family.

The connection seems to have been established by Molly Allen, who had been a teacher at Add Ran and knew Professor Clark. She married R. E. Turner and returned to teach in San Patricio County.

After Turner wrote Clark, the professor visited Portland in December 1893. The vacant Portland Hotel was offered to house the college and the local school trustees "agreed to apply school funds to the college, which would allow town students to attend there. This was a valuable nest egg," said Wallace Clark, son of T. M. Clark. The professor accepted the offer, in part because his wife Alice needed to move to a warmer climate for her health.

Professor Clark traveled with the household furnishings and goods — including a milk cow and the family dog Brom — in a freight car, which took several days to make the trip. Wallace and his mother took the passenger train.

"The train from San Antonio to Corpus Christi, the San Antonio and Aransas Pass Railroad (SAAP), took all afternoon," Clark wrote. "Late in the afternoon the conductor (his name was Goode, I found out) sat down beside me. 'So, you are going to Portland,' he said. 'Well, you'll just about be in time. They are moving most of the houses away from Portland, taking them to Sinton, the new county seat. What are your folks going to do in Portland?'

Wallace told him. "My father and mother are starting a private boarding school there."

The conductor said, "School? What will they have for pupils? Jackrabbits?"

The school opened in September 1894. It was called Bay View College. There were three teachers in the beginning, Professor

Professor T. M. Clark and his wife Alice (lower right) with the 1901 class at Bay View College in Portland.

Clark, Alice Clark, and Molly Allen Turner. Professor Clark taught music, elocution, and higher English. He was called the Professor. Mrs. Clark served as matron and principal of the art department. The students called her Aunt Alice. Molly Turner taught Greek, Latin, and higher mathematics.

There were day students from Portland (no jackrabbits) and boarding students from area ranches. "This was ranch country then," said Madelyn (Fisher) Stone, a pioneer resident, "and there were practically no schools, so Bayview flourished."

Wallace Clark wrote that his father began making cement blocks and no one knew what they were for. He would spend an hour or two a day, all the spare time that he had, making cement blocks. They were later used to build new structures for the college. The original building, the old Portland Hotel, was converted into the girls' dormitory, dining hall and family residence. Professor Clark's cement blocks were used to build a boys' dorm and chapel. A one-story gymnasium was added to give the college four main buildings.

Shirley Taylor, whose family lived at Gregory, attended Bay View. "We had our meals at the house. The meals were pretty good. A black man named Richard Ware did the cooking. The Professor was a great old man, very educated, and he could do all kinds of work, everything from crocheting to making cement blocks.

"Some of the rules of the college were very strict," she said. "We didn't leave the school grounds without being accompanied by one of the teachers. We went swimming sometimes when we weren't in school, but one of the teachers always went with us." Three things would not be tolerated on campus: drinking, gambling, and cursing. "Pupils guilty of any one of these need not wait to be dismissed," warned a college catalog, "but may pack their trunks and go at once."

"I was a day student at Bay View," Nellie (French) Sutherland said. "The girls' rooms were upstairs in the original building. The boys' rooms were over by the chapel which was built of bricks. Bay View, when I attended, was equivalent to a junior college. We studied algebra, trig, word analysis, Latin, Spanish, advanced geometry and bookkeeping. I received a diploma from the college.

"I never paid a dime to attend Bay View," Mrs. Sutherland said. "The children of Portland were admitted free because Portland's tax money went to the school college. The children from out of town who lived there had to pay. Bay View was considered a culture center of this part of the country. We had students from Mexico and all parts of Texas."

—Dec. 13, 2017

Column 102

Bay View College closed in 1917

Greater competition from public schools, the death of
Alice Clark, matron and guiding light of the college, and
the hurricane of 1916 led to the closing of the institution.

Portland was three years old (the original townsite was platted
in 1891) when Bay View College began classes on Sept. 1, 1894.
Portland was a college town with more college than town. Even
though the town fell on hard times after the financial panic of
1893, Bay View prospered, attracting students from Beeville,
Portland, Rockport, Corpus Christi, and surrounding ranch
country.

Tol McNeill, a rancher on Ramireña Creek in Live Oak
County, sent his daughter Alma and son Oliver ("Ollie") to Bay
View. McNeill wrote Professor Clark. "We are well-pleased with
Alma's progress in your school," McNeill wrote, not mentioning
Ollie's progress.

Alma also wrote after she graduated in 1899. "We reached
home Saturday at supper time. Papa met us at Beeville. How
pleasant it is to be home. But already I am homesick for Bay
View. Papa thinks I have done fine work and he also thinks, as I
do, that the Professor is the only teacher." Both letters were
printed in Bay View catalogs, which are now stored at La
Retama Library.

Calvin J. Allen, a rancher at Nuecestown, who would establish
the town of Calallen, wrote Professor Clark. "We are glad to
have Frank and Lula (his son and daughter) at home again and
are well-pleased with their work in Bay View College." (After

423

Frank Allen left Bay View he managed the family store at Calallen and Lula married "New" Noakes.)

The first Bay View catalog from the 1897-'98 school year lists students from the previous year. They came from Sharpsburg, Goliad, Rockport, Kalita, Dinero, Gregory, Lagarto, and Ingleside. Students from Portland and Corpus Christi were listed as "local." Among the students were the McNeills from Ramireña Creek, the Bordens from Sharpsburg, the Rachals from White Point, the Baylors from Kalita, and Caldwells from Corpus Christi.

A state charter in 1897 allowed Bay View to grant degrees. The first three graduates of the school, two years after its founding, were Lucile Long, E. R. Rachal Jr., and Wallace Clark. Rachal and Wallace Clark joined the faculty. Clark taught music and math while Rachal taught bookkeeping and Spanish, subjects valuable to ranchers' children.

Wallace Clark in an article about the school named some of the students who were educated at Bay View. Zula Hill of Corpus Christi, who married Conrad Meuly Blucher, went to Bay View, and so did Ralph Bradford, who was appointed director of the Corpus Christi Chamber of Commerce in 1924; he later became director of the national Chamber of Commerce. Nannie Caldwell studied at Bay View; she taught at David Hirsch Elementary for many years. Alice Borden was a Bay View grad; she married Russell Savage, lawyer and state legislator; the Alice Borden Savage Elementary on Shell Road was named for her. Tom Powers, a well-known actor on Broadway, attended Bay View.

The college was a cultural center for the area. Mrs. Adele Fisher said the students at Bay View would present three-act plays, which were "a special treat for the people of Portland." Bay View's baseball team, which had a local following, was coached by Raymond Mullen, who later married the school's music teacher, Blanche Lyons.

Roy Terrell of Corpus Christi recalled when his team played the Bay View team. They must have had strong views about how the game was played. "We went by train, which ran over a trestle across the bay," Terrell said, "We beat Bayview and they told us to get out of town — they were going to run us out if we didn't

Bay View College in Portland, about 1913, included the main building and girls' dormitory (left), a one-story gymnasium, a two-story boys' dormitory, and a two-story chapel. The boys' dormitory and chapel were built of bricks made by Professor Clark.

leave. We told them we had to wait for the train, and they told us we didn't need to wait — so we walked the railroad trestle from Portland to Corpus Christi. We didn't meet a train or I wouldn't be here to tell this tale."

What happened to Bayview? Wallace Clark explained the circumstances that led to the institution's closing.

One was the land rush and population growth, which resulted in new public schools opening throughout the area. The schools "presaged something ominous to the private college."

Another was the death of Alice Clark, whom the students called Aunt Alice. When she died in San Antonio in 1913, Wallace said, the school lost its guiding star.

Still another was the hurricane of 1916, which ripped off the top floor of the main building and destroyed the boys' dorm. Only the chapel building was left intact.

Bay View struggled to stay open before the end came in 1917, a century ago. Professor Clark went on to teach at several colleges around the state. He retired to Portland in 1935. Failing eyesight kept him from doing his crocheting and he was cared for by Richard Ware, the former college cook who remained loyal to the end.

Professor Clark died in 1943 and was buried next to his wife in the Gregory Cemetery. In honor of his memory, a school in

Portland was named the T. M. Clark Elementary in 1953. A historical marker was unveiled at the school was unveiled on March 1, 1973. The last remaining structure of Bay View was destroyed by Hurricane Celia in 1970.

To place it in its historical context, Bay View College was preceded by other well-known education institutions in the region. One of the oldest was the Nold Academy founded by Henry and Elizabeth Nold at Ingleside in 1857. It was closed during the Civil War. The Hidalgo Seminary in Corpus Christi, run by the Catholic Church, attracted students from all over in the 1860s and 1870s. Robert Dougherty, who once taught at Hidalgo, opened his own boarding school at Round Lake near San Patricio in 1877. It closed in 1881. One of the most famous was Lagarto College, which was founded in 1884 and flourished for a few years before it was forced it to close.

Professor Clark's Bay View College was perhaps a measure above its predecessors. For more than 20 years it nurtured and educated — no, not jackrabbits — but a generation of town kids from Portland and Corpus Christi and ranch kids were flushed from their natural habitat and introduced to classic Greek and Latin aphorisms.

—Dec. 6, 2017

Barrileros filled water needs

Water vendors, called barrileros, filled barrels at the
Nueces River or at wells in the arroyo and went door to
door shouting "Agua! Fresca! Agua!" Water sold for 25
cents to $1 a barrel, depending on the severity of the
drought.

Henry Kinney landed at the mouth of an arroyo on Corpus
Christi Bay in 1839. This natural watercourse flowed from
Chatham's Ravine. The Chatham it was named for has been
forgotten. Kinney built his home on the bluff and behind it was a
pond called Kinney's Tank, which was a source of water for the
settlement. (Today the ravine runs through culverts from
Blucher Park and drains to the bay near the Yacht Club.)

Lack of fresh water was always a recurrent problem. Zachary
Taylor's soldiers in 1845 dug shallow wells on the shore and a
deep artesian well in Artesian Park. Water from the seep wells
could be used only for laundry and the artesian well water
smelled of sulfur. The army hauled drinking water from the
Nueces River.

Henry Kinney hired a well-digger from Alabama named J. M.
Cooper. The Corpus Christi Star noted his arrival on Oct. 17,
1848 and said his fame for finding water was known far and
wide. "If there is a vein of water in the earth, we feel certain he
will find it." In those years, a good well-digger was highly
esteemed. Cooper began drilling wells in the arroyo.

Felix Blucher bought property from Kinney west of the arroyo
and the old Chatham's Ravine became known as Blucher's
Creek. Maria Blucher could watch the well-digger Cooper at

work. She wrote her parents in 1852. "Drought has depleted the grass and our pond is half dried out. The town's artesian well is always being dug, dug, dug. The digger gets $2 a day and free board in Kinney's house. This fellow has been digging four years and always says, 'In a fortnight there will be water!' "

Felix Blucher was hired to build an earthen dam in the arroyo to form a water reservoir for the town's needs. To keep it moderately clean, the city adopted an ordinance banning hogs from running loose.

The reservoir wasn't the only source of water. Most residents had cisterns to store rainwater. Older cisterns were made of shell concrete and were usually built underground with a plank top to keep out small boys and idle dogs. Later, round cypress cisterns were built aboveground.

Andrew Anderson recalled that their cistern was square and was eventually made useless by the penetration of roots. "Many persons purified their cisterns by keeping a bag of charcoal under the spout leading to the cistern so the water going into the cistern would be clear and pure. Some built boxes for this purpose."

When cisterns ran low during droughts, water-sellers called barrileros filled barrels at the Nueces River or at wells in the arroyo and went door to door shouting "Agua! Fresca! Agua!" Water sold for 25 cents to $1 a barrel, depending on how bad the drought was. Two pioneer residents recalled the arroyo wells and 'roly' barrels used to haul water.

Mamie Jones' grandparents, Rachel and Thomas Parker, arrived in Corpus Christi in 1845. Parker had a beef contract for Taylor's army. Mamie Jones recalled her grandmother telling her of the Parker wells, which were north of where Kinney Avenue and Tancahua intersect today.

She said the wells furnished good sweet water, which was drawn up in buckets, and there were troughs there to fill for horses. Jones said her grandmother told her that "Indians were often seen filling the troughs to water their horses. Little Frank Vasquez was there alone when Indians stole him in 1855." Until then, she said, children were allowed to roam on their own but after little Frank was stolen "people were more careful about letting their children go down to the arroyo wells alone."

Water-vendors known as barrileros wait in line to fill their casks with the city's new drinking water at a standpipe on the bluff, about 1895. The barrileros used 55-gallon barrels on two-wheel carts, pulled by mules or donkeys. This standpipe was at Sam Rankin and Mestina.

Frank Gay, who lived near the arroyo, said "people hauled water home in 'roly' barrels, pulled by a rope fastened to a short length of chain attached from one end of the barrel to the other. Chain had to be used close to the barrel as rope would have been cut by the edges of the barrel as it rolled."

The city began searching for a source of fresh water in the 1880s. They drilled wells west of town but the water was salty. They re-drilled Zachary Taylor's well in Artesian Park but the water was still odorous. They said it had a horrible smell and tasted even worse, but some people prized it for its medicinal qualities. George Washington Grim drank a gallon a day and swore that it was keeping him alive.

Most homes still had a cistern to store rainwater and when the cisterns dropped to the fetid sludge at the bottom, barrileros hauled water from the Nueces River.

A fire on July 14, 1892 burned homes and stores in the 200 block of Chaparral. To fight the fire, volunteer firemen had to fill their water wagons from box wells on the bay. After the fire, the city got serious about establishing a municipal water system.

The city celebrated its new water system on May 26, 1893. Some 200,000 gallons of untreated water were piped in daily from the Nueces River. The water wasn't pumped directly from the river but from a well 50 feet away, where it was naturally filtered by sand and gravel.

City water lines did not extend to most homes. People continued to depend on their cisterns and the barrileros. One difference was that barrileros didn't have to travel 12 miles to the Nueces River for water; they could fill their barrels at standpipes in town.

Roy Terrell, born on a ranch on the Oso in 1896, said in his memoirs that the water supply was limited when he was young. "We couldn't turn on a tap to get cold water. Everyone had a cistern to catch rainwater. When a long dry spell hit, the cistern would be nearly empty and we had to put potash in the water to kill wiggletails so we could use it. And we bought water from a barrilero who came by in an old two-wheeled cart."

The barrileros were still making their rounds — Agua! Fresca! Agua! — well into the second decade of the 20th Century. They were a colorful part of the city's water history — well, maybe not colorful — but certainly reminders of a vanished world.

—Dec. 27, 2017

A long way from a lemon

Rancho Perdido, in the Penitas Valley, was known as the
lost ranch. Ruth Dodson, who grew up on the ranch, said
a woman similarly situated said she was 50 miles from a
lemon, which could be found in Corpus Christi.

Ruth Dodson grew up on a ranch on the north side of Penitas
Creek, six miles south of Lagarto and 50 miles from Corpus
Christi. A woman similarly situated, Ruth once wrote, said she
was living 50 miles from a lemon. The Dodson place was called
Rancho Perdido, or lost ranch, and was said to have gained its
name from the cry of a whippoorwill – per-di-do – or perhaps
from the hidden nature of the site in the Penitas Valley.

Ruth Dodson's father was Milton Milam Dodson. He once told
her about crossing the Nueces River in a wagon loaded with
family belongings in 1858 when he was 19 and the family was
moving west from the Brazos River. They settled at Barlow's
Ferry, which later was renamed Dinero. Milton Dodson's father,
Archelaus Dodson, was a first lieutenant in Sam Houston's Texas
army. He named a daughter Harriet Houston Dodson after the
general.

After the Civil War, in 1866, Martin Culver, a young man from
Oakville, bought a herd of cattle and 600 acres in the Penitas
Valley. Culver hired Milton Dodson as foreman and vaqueros to
work the cattle. Though few of the vaqueros knew English, they
learned enough and Culver and Dodson learned enough Spanish
to communicate in a mix of cow-camp English and Spanish.

Within a few years Culver was a wealthy cattleman, employing
as many as 100 vaqueros, and he was sending herds of 1,000

head or more up the trail to Kansas with Culver's KL brand (for wife Kate and daughter Lizzie). The size of his trail herds rivaled those of King Ranch.

In 1868 Culver's half-sister, Mary Susanna Burris, came to visit and within a year she married Culver's range foreman, Milton Dodson.

In 1870 Culver built a ranch house around the nucleus of an older structure in a valley on Penitas Creek. A former sailor named Stephenson designed and built the house, which included nine rooms and a wide front porch. Though it was called the lost ranch, Stephenson made sure that the house wasn't lost. He had it painted London purple with white trim. (The painter was David Gambel who drew a sketch of the battle of Corpus Christi in 1862. Gambel, as an artist, would create ranch scenes on interior walls of some of the houses he painted. He died after consuming wood alcohol.)

In 1876, with the spread of barbed wire presaging the end of free grazing, Martin Culver sold Rancho Perdido to his half-brother, Basil Burris, who in turn sold it to Milton Dodson for $5,000. Culver moved to San Antonio and then Kansas. Milton Dodson moved his family into the Culver ranch house on Penitas Creek.

Viola Ruth Dodson was born on the ranch on Sept. 3, 1876. Her older sister Miranda, called Nannie, was born in 1869. Over the years, other Dodson children were Martin, Archie, Kate, Edgar, Susan, Kilmer, Harriet, Sarah, and Thadeus.

Growing up on the ranch, Ruth learned Spanish as well as English and once recalled that of all the ranch hands employed by her father, only one spoke English. She later wrote that the ability to converse in Spanish with the vaqueros and their families on her father's ranch "was the most important attainment of my young life."

She remembered having her photo being taken by F. L. Whipple, a photographer who had moved from Corpus Christi and opened a studio in Lagarto. She was photographed with Whipple's daughter Ethel, who was a friend.

"The picture is still in existence," Dodson wrote. "I am a little girl about six years old. I am sitting on a low chair with my legs

Ruth Dodson's family on the porch of the ranch house at Rancho Perdido in 1890.

crossed and Ethel is standing at my side with one hand on my shoulder. She was instructed to cross one foot over the other, which awkward position leaves her standing stork-like on one leg. I have on buttoned shoes which didn't fit, as shoes usually didn't in those days." This story is told in "Lagarto, A Collection of Memories," by Hattie Mae Hinnant New. (Whipple took one of the few existing photos that shows a class photo in front of the Lagarto College building.)

When Ruth was eight, she and her brother Archie and older sister Nannie would ride six miles up the Lagarto Road to attend school at the Lagarto College, which had just opened in the fall of 1884. "I rode a small gray horse with a small side-saddle that had been my mother's. I had to get all possible speed out of the little gray horse. My sister was a fast rider and to keep up with her for the sake of being there when she opened the three pasture gates on our way, I had to ride as fast as she did.

"My teacher was a young woman with yellow hair. I thought her very beautiful. If she ever spoke a word to me, I don't recall it." Though it was called a college, Ruth joined the younger students who studied from McGuffey's First Reader — "Ned has fed the hen. She is a black hen. She has left the nest. See the eggs in the nest! Will the hen let Ned get the eggs?"

433

The books in her home in those years had been lugged along with the Dodson family belongings by wagon from east Texas in 1858. There was a Bible, "which functioned in our home as a source of interesting reading" and a thick volume titled "The Speeches of Clay, Calhoun and Webster," which her father had had to read in school. And there was a four-volume set of Gibbons' "Decline and Fall of the Roman Empire" that looked almost new since it didn't get much use. Years later, Ruth wrote, her brother Kilmer asked her for something to read and she asked him what he liked. "I don't know what I like," he said, "but I know what I don't like — the Decline and Fall of the Roman Empire."

—Jan. 3, 2018

The lost world of Ruth Dodson

"When we would see Dr. Heaney pass in his buggy, we would not be sure whether he was calling on some patient at a ranch or paying a social call on Judge Gilpin. He and the judge were the only two people in the settlement who knew how to play chess." —Ruth Dodson

Ruth Dodson grew up on Rancho Perdido, the lost ranch, that had been established by her uncle, Martin Culver, and then sold to her father, Milton Milam Dodson. The ranch was on Penitas Creek was south of Lagarto and north of Casa Blanca. It was in Nueces County then, but now would be part of Jim Wells County.

Two miles to the east was Loma Prieta (Black Hill), a horse ranch owned by Theodore Dix. To the west was the Penitas Ranch owned by H. A. Gilpin. The Penitas Ranch, Ruth Dodson wrote, "took its name from the creek and the creek took its name from some rocks in it some place that I have never seen."

To the west of Gilpin's place was the F. W. Shaeffer Ranch, known to have some of the finest horses around. To the south of Penitas Ranch was George Reynolds' Rancho Ventana (Window Tree), which was named for a local landmark. The limbs of two trees intertwined to form an open square, or window — a ventana.

To the northwest was Ed Killmer's place with a ranch house on a hill overlooking Barbon Creek. Henderson Williams had a ranch on Lagarto Creek; Mrs. Williams had once been attacked by a panther and would show the scars on her shoulder.

435

A mile below Lagarto was Dr. A. G. Heaney's Valley Ranch. Dr. Heaney later moved to Corpus Christi to practice medicine with Dr. Arthur Spohn.

"When we would see Dr. Heaney pass in his buggy," Ruth wrote, "we would not be sure whether he was calling on some patient at a ranch or paying a social call on Judge Gilpin. He and the judge would spend hours playing chess. Probably they were the only two people in the area who knew how to play chess."

Judge Gilpin was the most exotic of Dodson's neighbors. He was a former Corpus Christi merchant and judge who had retired to his Penitas Ranch. His father had been a British ambassador in Rhode Island and retired to Nova Scotia. Gilpin was a scholarly man who could quote law, history and science with equal felicity. At Penitas he devoted his time to the study of weather and astronomical observations. He would sit on his front gallery and invite neighbors in for tea.

He was an old man with kindly eyes when Ruth Dodson knew him. She once wrote that some Sunday mornings her father would say, "Do you girls (Ruth and Nannie) want to walk with me to see the Judge?" They would cross the Penitas Creek before they reached a white paling fence, with cedar and mesquite trees behind it which almost hid the judge's house. "In our little world, there were no roses, but here they grew to perfection." After the visit, the judge would "walk out into the yard with us. If the roses were in bloom we were given a bouquet, to be enjoyed to the last wilted petal." On a bitterly cold night on Nov. 11, 1895, Judge Gilpin died. He was buried in Old Bayview Cemetery.

When Ruth Dodson was 25, she moved to Alice to help care for her sister's children. She later lived in Catalina, Calif., with an aunt and then with another sister in Kewanee, Ill. She returned to Texas and moved back to the ranch to care for her aging parents, until they died, then moved to Corpus Christi. She wrote articles for Southwestern Review, Frontier Times, and other periodicals about the history and folklore of her patch of Texas. She had the style of a front-porch talker with a gift for anecdote and detail.

She was interested in everything. She wrote about the vaqueros on Rancho Perdido who would pick mesquite leaves which they

436

Ruth Dodson, who grew up on the Perdido Ranch on Penitas Creek, six miles south of Lagarto, wrote about her neighbors and life on the ranch. Her best-known work is the story of Don Pedrito Jaramillo, a curandero, or faith healer, who lived on the Los Olmos Ranch between Falfurrias and Premont.

used to line their hats to keep from overheating in the hot sun. She made a list of the colors of horses and mustangs; one relative said he stopped visiting her until she quit pestering him about horse colors. She recalled the black-maned mustang owned by her mother. "Penning him was always a trial, but once in the pen he was as gentle as a dog." Dobie wrote about the horse in "The Mustangs."

Dodson's most famous work is the story of Don Pedrito Jaramillo, a curandero, or faith healer, who lived on the Los Olmos Ranch between Falfurrias and Premont. She talked to many people who knew Don Pedrito or had family members who were cured by him. "I became so intent on finding information that I would stop people on the street and start talking to them. But when I had enough information, I wrote the book in Spanish because I wanted it to be for the Spanish speaking people." Her book was published in 1934. She later translated it into English, which was published in 1951.

Pedro Jaramillo, a native of Guadalajara, moved to a ranch on Los Olmos Creek, in Starr County, in 1881. He became famous as a healer, though he claimed no special knowledge or power. His prescriptions were simple, often involving water, or coffee, or native plants. He believed people could be cured through their faith and his advice always included — *En el nombre de Dios,* in the name of God. The San Antonio Express wrote of his cures and his wide following in 1894 in an article titled "Miracles of Don Pedrito." He died on July 3, 1907 when he was 78. He was buried on Los Olmos Ranch. A reporter who visited the cemetery, near La Gloria School, in 1957 found his tomb covered with flowers.

Viola Ruth Dodson died in Corpus Christi on July 19, 1963 when she was 86. The ranch she grew up on in the valley of the Penitas was known as the lost ranch. It is part of that lost world when life must have seemed simpler, the sun brighter, the thunder louder, the rain heavier, and the mesquite leaves, which the ranch vaqueros used to line their hats, were so much greener.

—Jan. 10, 2018

A real loss for Rockport

Aransas County's striking Moorish-style courthouse —
designed by famous San Antonio architect J. Riely
Gordon and built in the boom times of 1890 — was
demolished in 1956.

Looking through a bank of photos, I lingered over the old
Aransas County Courthouse, a celebrated landmark with
horseshoe arches and Moorish-style embellishments. It
represented progress when it was built in 1890 and it succumbed
to progress when it was knocked down in 1956.

To begin at the beginning (a subjective call), the thread of this
story goes back to before Aransas County was created, when it
was still a contentious part of Refugio County.

The state constitutional convention in 1869 passed an
ordinance urging Refugio County to move the county seat to St.
Mary's on the coast, but no effort was made to follow the
recommendation. The court and court records remained at the
town of Refugio.

The following year, coastal residents signed petitions seeking
the removal of the county seat from Refugio to St. Mary's or
Rockport. The population of Refugio County was 2,320, with
most of it on the coast. The newly incorporated town of Rockport
contained more than half the population of the entire county.

There was a tug of war between Refugio of the cattle ranches
and coastal Refugio over the location of the county seat. Finally
bowing to the wishes of coastal voters, the Legislature in 1871
ordered Refugio County to move the county seat to Rockport.
County commissioners met there on May 1 and in July the court

rented space on the second floor of a building owned by S. C. Skidmore to serve as a courthouse.

What happened next was detailed in Hobart Huson's "History of Refugio County." He quotes Judge W. L. Rea, who said, "Until the offices and records were actually moved away from the Mission, the old settlers of the county had been in a lethargy. Removal of the records brought the old-time leaders back to life."

Meetings were held between inland and coastal leaders to iron out differences and the result was an agreement that the county should be divided to give Rockport and the coastal area their own county.

The agreement was endorsed by the Legislature on Sept. 18, 1871 and a new county, Aransas, was carved out of old Refugio. With the news that a new county had been created and that seat of government would be moved back to a smaller Refugio County, spirits soared in Refugio. They considered it a fair trade. They could do without that part of the county with its coastal malcontents in return for getting back the county seat.

Huson quotes Rea again. "The people of Refugio held a spontaneous celebration and it was plenty wild. It was the biggest Irish wake ever held in this county. As the ranchmen and cowboys in the outlying area heard the news, they saddled up and rode into town and joined the party at Bill Doughty's Saloon. The celebration lasted all night and into the next day. As the evening wore on and the men began to get mellow, there were many speeches, eloquent and otherwise. Those who had ruffled the complacency of easy-going old Refugio were roundly cussed, individually and collectively."

The outcome was considered a win for both sides. Rockport was happy with Rockport and Refugio was happy to be left alone. In Rockport, the seat of government of the new regime was on the second floor of the Skidmore building rented by Refugio six months earlier.

Ten years later, in July 1881, Aransas County purchased Mehle Hall to use as a courthouse. The county agreed to pay C. Mehle $1,000 for the two-story building on Main Street. The commissioners were $115 short of the sales price; several of the

The Moorish-style Aransas County Courthouse in Rockport, built in 1890, was much admired by residents and visitors alike. It was torn down in 1956.

commissioners loaned the county from $5 to $20 to make up the shortfall.

The ground floor of Mehle Hall was occupied by a dry goods store owned by John Caruthers. County offices and courtroom occupied the second floor. Old stories say that the second floor doubled as a dance hall and that on Saturday nights the judge's bench was pushed back against the wall to make room for fiddlers and dancing couples.

In 1889, a contract was let to construct a new courthouse, their first built for the purpose. It was completed in 1890. The new courthouse cost $19,494 and was designed by San Antonio architect J. Riely Gordon, known for his design of Texas courthouses. With its striking features suggestive of the architecture of the Moorish cities of Cordoba or Seville, it was

441

probably the most unusual courthouse in Texas. It was featured in an article in Frank Leslie's Illustrated Weekly on Oct. 18, 1890.

Building the courthouse was undertaken and completed during Rockport's boom years, when many believed it would become the metropolis of the coast. The city expected to gain a deepwater port and changed its name briefly to Aransas Pass, named for the ship channel.

The city boasted that it was "the unrivaled Gulf port of Texas, the coming city of 200,000." An electric light plant and ice factory were built and mule-drawn streetcars ran to Oklahoma, a nearby community. John Traylor built the Aransas Hotel, one of the largest resort hotels on the Gulf, which covered a city block.

Sixty-six years later, the stylish Moorish courthouse was doomed when Aransas County decided it needed to build a new courthouse on the site.

Workers pulled down the old building in early 1956. The demolition crew found a few things in the cornerstone — a Sept. 12, 1889 copy of the Aransas Pass Beacon, a Sept. 10, 1889 copy of the San Antonio Express, a list of names believed to have been the employees of the builder, and 67 cents in old coins, including two quarters minted in 1856 and 1877, three "V" nickels minted in the 1880s, an 1884 Indian-head penny, and a quarter-size one-cent piece dated 1882. The contractor added the coins to his collection and turned the papers over to the county.

How many remember this exotic and distinctive Moorish-style courthouse? While buildings come and go, this one was not forgotten. I never saw it. It was demolished long before I moved here. But as I looked at the photo, this one was a real loss.

—Jan. 17, 2018

U.S. Grant fell into Corpus Christi Bay

The young lieutenant Grant, in the 4th Regiment, was among the soldiers in Zachary Taylor's command who trained at Corpus Christi in preparation for the coming war with Mexico.

Ulysses S. Grant, a second lieutenant in the 4th Regiment, thought he knew how the rope pulleys and winches worked on the transport ship Suviah. As soldiers were being transferred to lighters to cross Corpus Christi Bay, Grant jumped up on the rail, grabbed a rope, and to his surprise plunged head over heels into the waters of Corpus Christi Bay.

Grant swam around until he could grab a rope dangling from the side of the ship and sailors pulled him back up on deck. Grant thought it a good joke and laughed with everyone else.

Grant was among the soldiers who trained at Corpus Christi in 1845 in Zachary Taylor's command. Taylor chose Corpus Christi to concentrate the army in the event of war with Mexico. Grant described Corpus Christi as "a small Mexican hamlet." It was a trading post, hardly a village, but it became an armed camp with 4,000 soldiers — half the U.S. Army — in training for the coming conflict.

On his way across the bay Grant saw the wrecked remains of the Dayton, a sidewheel steamer which exploded on Sept. 13, 1845, killing nine men. Grant wrote about the accident to Julia Dent, his fiancé in Missouri. Two of the men killed were lieutenants he had known at West Point.

In Corpus Christi in 1845 half-wild mustangs could be purchased for a pittance and Grant, who loved horses, bought four of them. The servant Grant hired to cook his meals and clean his tent, a free black man from Louisiana named Valere, was taking the horses to water and they ran away. "I heard that Grant lost five or six dollars' worth of horses," Taylor's adjutant, W. W. Bliss, joked. Grant said that was a slander, that they were worth $20.

Grant and other officers joined a paymaster's expedition to San Antonio. Grant wrote that wild game abounded but they saw no inhabitants until they approached San Antonio. Three weeks later, afraid they would be late and listed as absent without leave, Grant and another officer started back by themselves. One night they heard wolves howling and Grant thought there were at least 20 in the pack. When they got close enough to see them, there were only two. Grant later joked that members of Congress were like wolves — "There are always more of them before they are counted."

In December 1845 officers decided to stage "Othello." Grant's girlish good looks had earned him, from his fellow officers, the sobriquet of "Beauty" and he was urged to play the part of Desdemona. In rehearsals the officer playing the Moor couldn't look at Grant in a dress without breaking into fits of laughter. They had to send to New Orleans for a professional actress to play the part.

Henry Berry, who would later become sheriff of Nueces County, competed with Grant for the attentions of a young girl named Elizabeth Moore. Berry would take her riding on his black pacing mare. One day, Grant asked to borrow the mare and Berry saw him riding with Elizabeth along the beach, though Grant at the time was engaged to Julia Dent, whom he would marry.

Berry later said that Grant came a second time "and I loaned him my mare again, but not the third time. I told him I needed the animal. The fact was, the young lady scarcely talked to me when I went to call on her. I saw at once that the gallant lieutenant was winning my girl away. I offered to take her out riding and she consented to go. But my mare was nowhere to be found. Riding out with Capt. McCook, he said, 'There is your mare, standing over there.' I did not recognize her, she was so

444

U.S. Grant was in the 4th Regiment of Infantry in Corpus Christi in late 1845 and early 1846. When his regiment arrived on board the Suviah, Grant got a good soaking when he fell into the bay.

disfigured. Her mane and tail had been shaved, a trick of Grant's. When I went to see the young lady to go for the ride she refused to go, saying she would not ride such an ugly horse." Berry eventually married the young lady.

In March 1846, Taylor's army left, in high spirits, for the Rio Grande. The march south covered 174 miles over prairies with high grass and sands glistening with salt. Grant one day rode out to see herds of mustangs so vast they blotted out the horizon. On the way south, Grant joked with his servant Valere that he would have had a mount to ride if he hadn't let the horses escape. After a three-week trip, the army reached the Rio Grande.

Grant was in the first battles of the Mexican War, at Palo Alto and Resaca de la Palma. He led one charge and captured a Mexican colonel who, it turned out, had already been captured. The battles would have been won, Grant realized, if he had not been there. Grant thought it a most unjust war. "I know the struggle I had with my conscience during the Mexican War," he wrote in his memoirs. "I have never forgiven myself for going into that. I had very strong opinions on the subject. I don't think there was ever a more wicked war than that waged by the United States on Mexico. I thought so at the time, when I was a youngster, only I had not the moral courage to resign."

Besides Grant, there were several future Civil War generals, Union and Confederate, with Zachary Taylor at Corpus Christi, including James Longstreet, George Meade, Braxton Bragg, John Magruder, and E. Kirby Smith. Robert E. Lee was not at Corpus Christi; he joined Taylor's army at Monterrey. At the time, there was little to suggest that an obscure second lieutenant named Ulysses S. Grant would one day become the most acclaimed military leader of his time, the winning general of the Civil War, and president of the United States. I doubt if anyone called him "Beauty" since the time he tried out for Desdemona in the winter of 1845 in Corpus Christi.

—*Jan. 24, 2018*

Column 108

Hitchcock at Corpus Christi

"Colonel Kinney thinks there are 2,000 people here besides the army. They are nearly all adventurers, brought here to speculate on events growing out of the presence of the troops." —Ethan Allen Hitchcock in 1845

Ethan Allen Hitchcock, a grandson of Revolutionary War hero Ethan Allen, was in Zachary Taylor's command at Fort Jesup, La., in July 1845 when the army was ordered to move to Texas. Col. Hitchcock's 3rd Infantry boarded the steamboat Alabama at New Orleans and arrived off St. Joseph's Island on Friday July 25, 1845.

Early Saturday Hitchcock sent Lt. D. T. Chandler ashore and Chandler planted an American flag on a sand dune, the first to fly over Texas. All eight companies of the Hitchcock's 3rd were landed on the island by July 28. Gen. Taylor ordered companies K and G of Hitchcock's command to board the lighter Undine, sail across the bay, and set up camp at Corpus Christi. After some difficulty in crossing the mudflats between Aransas and Corpus Christi bays, fishing boats were hired to transport the companies. They landed on North Beach at sundown on July 31, 1845.

Next morning, a delegation of local inhabitants visited Hitchcock and offered assistance and information. Taylor arrived on Aug. 15. Hitchcock had defensive embankments thrown up since no artillery had arrived and borrowed two old cannons from the town's founder, Henry Kinney. Tents were erected in neat squared lines along the sandy shore.

447

A violent thunderstorm hit on Sunday, Aug. 24. Tents were blown down, they heard a deafening crack of thunder and saw a vivid flash of light. "In a moment I saw Lt. (W. H.) Henry running past my tent calling for a doctor." The lightning struck Lt. Braxton Bragg's tent pole, killing one slave and injuring another.

On Sept. 7, 1845 Hitchcock went to see Henry Kinney, who was in bed sick. He found Taylor and William Mann, a prominent trader, also there visiting. He met Chipito Sandoval, Kinney's spy, who came from the Rio Grande with reports of army movements in Mexico.

On Sept. 12, boilers on the Dayton, an old steamer contracted to ferry troops across the bay, exploded. Ten men were killed and 17 wounded. Hitchcock picked a burial site with a view of Nueces and Corpus Christi bays, "a very beautiful spot," which later became known as Old Bayview Cemetery. The victims were buried at sundown as the 4th Regimental Band played Handel's Dead March in Saul.

Ships continued to arrive with troops. Hitchcock noted in his diary that the 3rd, 4th and 7th regiments were at Corpus Christi, along with the 2nd Dragoons, a company of regular artillery and two companies of volunteer artillery.

The settlement, he wrote, began along the shore to the south. The first house was a store owned by Kinney, rented by the government for use as a hospital. Next was William Mann's store followed by a saloon and eating house "for loafers," a bakery and store, and several more drinking houses, some of them wood frames covered with cloth.

After the stores and saloons came the volunteer camp, which consisted of two artillery companies from New Orleans, then the 4th and 3rd regiments, Braxton Bragg's artillery company, followed by a fieldwork thrown up by Hitchcock's 3rd when it first arrived. Behind the fieldwork was a cluster of tents that housed the supply depot. Next came the 5th and 7th regiments, then a small lagoon followed by the 2nd Dragoons. Beyond an inlet from Nueces Bay was the 8th Infantry, followed by three or four companies of artillery serving as infantry. The camp stretched a mile and a quarter.

Col. Ethan Allen Hitchcock, shown in 1851, commanded the 3ʳᵈ Infantry when Zachary Taylor concentrated half the manpower of the U.S. Army at Corpus Christi in the second half of 1845 and early 1846. Hitchcock kept a diary during his time at Corpus Christi.

After a review of the troops in mid-September, Hitchcock, in his role as nagging martinet, wrote that none of the senior officers could form the men into line and that Taylor knew nothing about moving an army on the battlefield. Hitchcock thought he was the only officer of field rank who could maneuver the troops. He had no respect for Taylor, writing that "The general is instigated by ambition, or so it seems to me." Of the commander of the Dragoons, Col. David Twiggs, Hitchcock described him as a lecher known for "shocking licentiousness in open defiance of public opinion."

October and November were wet and cold and most days it rained with a steady drizzle. A freezing norther hit the camp on Nov. 30 and troops made a windbreak of chaparral brush to shield the encampment. Hitchcock stayed in his tent reading the works of mystic Emanuel Swedenborg and writing a legible copy of Spinoza's Ethics.

New Year's Day 1846, Hitchcock wrote in his diary that the day would go as other days, with drinking, horse-racing, and gambling, but he would remain in his tent consoled by Swedenborg and Spinoza. "Colonel Kinney thinks there are 2,000 people here besides the army," he wrote in his diary. "They are nearly all adventurers, brought here to speculate on events growing out of the presence of the troops."

On Feb. 6, Hitchcock noted that Taylor had received orders to move the army to the Rio Grande. "This will make a considerable stir." On Feb. 14 a freezing norther passed over the camp. "I have had a headache most of the morning," Hitchcock wrote, "and having completed my copy of Spinoza I am out of employment and restless."

On March 8, 1846, the army took up its line of march to the Rio Grande. Hitchcock's 3rd, which had been the first to arrive, was the last to leave. Hitchcock was sick and while on the trip south he rested on boxes of ammunition in a wagon pulled by oxen. At the end of the trip he recovered enough to ride a horse, though he was "excessively fatigued and weak to the last degree."

Later in the war Hitchcock served as an adviser to Gen. Winfield Scott and was put in charge of covert operations and formed an organization of spies. In the Civil War, he served as military adviser to Abraham Lincoln and was offered command of the Union Army in 1862 but turned it down. He died in Sparta, Ga., on Aug. 4, 1870.

—Jan. 31, 2018

Daniel P. Whiting at Corpus Christi

"One day I was attracted by hearing a noise in my campground and looking out I saw her (the Great Western) pick up a man who had offended her and, as if he were a child, set him down in her wash tub." — Daniel Powers Whiting

Capt. Daniel Powers Whiting of the 7th Infantry was with Zachary Taylor's forces at Corpus Christi in 1845 and early 1846. Today, he is known for his sketch of the encampment at Corpus Christi, with rows of tents squared in neat lines along the beach.

Whiting, the son of a judge in Troy, N.Y., entered West Point in 1828 and after he graduated in 1832 was ordered to Fort Gibson in Indian Territory. Whiting's regiment was sent to Florida during the Second Seminole War. In August 1845 Whiting's 7th Infantry was ordered to Texas to prepare for an expected war with Mexico over the admission of Texas to the Union.

On the 24th of August, Writing wrote in his memoirs, orders were received for the movement to Corpus Christi and they departed in the steamer Creole. They landed at St. Joseph's Island on Aug. 28 and three days later took the steamer Dayton to Corpus Christi. Whiting wrote later that the Dayton was "an old and unsafe boat which a few days afterward blew up, killing several officers and men."

Whiting's regiment made camp on Aug. 31. "On clearing the ground for our camp, which was covered with scrub, we found the place infested with rattlesnakes; many were killed. I was awakened one night by the rattle of one in my tent, close to where I was lying, that had its head outside, alarmed by a dog barking at it. Gathering myself up, I called some men and sprang out. When the snake was killed, I found it to be six feet in length. These and other vermin prevailed at the camp. We found scorpions in our clothing and boots when about to put them on."

After the grounds were cleared, Whiting thought the encampment a fine esplanade and noted that the camp stretched almost two miles along the shore of the bay, extending from the village of Corpus Christi to the point of land made by the junction of the Nueces Bay with Corpus Christi Bay. "Here were 3rd and 4th regiments of Infantry and the artillery. Our own regiment was commanded by Lt. Col. Hoffman who soon after was taken sick and died on the 26th of November. I made a sketch of the camp about this time, which was afterwards published in my Army Portfolio."

Whiting said there was "much good music" in the camp, with several fine regimental bands. "I used to have frequent musical soirees at my tent with various amateur and professional performers. Such recreations as billiards, bowling alleys and a theater composed our amusements while regimental brigade drills made up our official occupation."

Winter arrived early and cold that year. "Our camp was defended by hedges and embankments with chimneys to our tents, generally of casks of different sizes diminishing towards the top. I had a mess composed of the officers of the company, conducted by the wife of one of my sergeants. 'The Great Western' she was called from being a gigantic woman of great strength and hardihood who afterwards became famous. One day I was attracted by hearing a noise in my campground and looking out I saw her pick up a man who had offended her and, as if he were a child, set him down in her wash tub."

A terrific norther visited the camp one night, Whiting wrote, raising the tide of the bay and overflowing the low flats on North Beach. "After it subsided, vast numbers of fish of the best species of the Gulf were found stranded in a frozen and benumbed state. Wagonloads of fish were procured and distributed throughout the camp."

Capt. Daniel Powers Whiting served in the Second Seminole War in Florida when his regiment, the 7th Infantry, was ordered to Corpus Christi to prepare for an expected war with Mexico.

Capt. Whiting was trained at West Point in topographical drawing. He published five lithographs of the Mexican War, including his scene of the army encampment at Corpus Christi in October 1845.

About the beginning of March 1846, Whiting noted, the army begin preparing for its movement to the Rio Grande and their appointment with manifest destiny. Whiting's 7th was among the first to depart in the general exodus. The eight months spent at Corpus Christi, Whiting wrote, contributed to the esprit de corps that would prevail throughout the coming war.

"Leading off on foot at the head of my company, I was sorely fatigued on the first day's march," Whiting wrote in his memoirs. "In fact, I was almost broken down by the time we reached Twelve-Mile Motts, where we camped. The next day I was less so but very sorry I was only a captain of foot. We marched 16 miles to Agua Dulce. By the third day, I began to believe I could succeed in the exercise if I continued judiciously. We marched 14 miles to Santa Gertrudis Creek. On the fourth day, I arrived at camp quite efficient and elastic and afterwards, and throughout the war, I continued my pedestrianism, never mounted, without fatigue or weariness, and many a stout man succumbed where I never faltered."

On March 19, when Whiting's company halted to rest, wild cattle were seen in the distance and several riders gave chase. A soldier mounted on a pony, servant to one of the captains, chased a longhorn bull which ran toward the resting men. The man chasing him "fired his gun and, missing the beast, the ball struck the ground amidst the soldiers, miraculously hitting no one. After we were camped that night, an altercation was heard in this man's tent between himself and his Irish wife. She was heard to say, 'You're a pretty soldier! Shoot at a bull and miss a regiment!' "

Whiting's regiment raised the flag on the north bank of the Rio Grande and occupied a makeshift fort called Fort Texas. Whiting's commanding officer, Maj. Jacob Brown, was killed in the bombardment of the fort by Mexican batteries across the river. The fort was renamed Fort Brown. Whiting could hear the noise of battle from Resaca de la Palma and watched Mexican troops rushing toward the river chased by Americans. Capt. Whiting went on to fight at Monterrey, Veracruz and Cerro Gordo. He died on Aug. 2, 1892 in Washington. He was 85.

—Feb. 7, 2018

Column 110

Cowboys could do more than rope and ride

A good cowhand had to understand the nature of cattle and make them understand him. A good cowhand was known for intelligence, determination, independence, and self-sufficiency.

W. G. Sutherland was a school-teacher and historian who lived in the Bluntzer community. In an article in the Caller in the 1920s he wrote that the old-time cowboy was sometimes described as ignorant and uncivilized.

That was a libel and a slander, Sutherland said. Some may have been un-schooled but others were well-educated, some the products of great universities. Many cowboys who worked on ranches and went up the trail on cattle drives became bankers, lawyers, judges, businessmen and ranch owners.

Sutherland was right. I thought of a few off the top of my head. Shanghai Pierce worked as a cowboy for the Grimes Ranch near Indianola before he became one of the great cattle barons of South Texas.

W. W. Jones trailed cattle to Kansas before he started his own ranch in Jim Hogg County south of Hebbronville. In 1905, Jones moved to Corpus Christi and turned to banking and real estate. He invested in building the 278-room Nueces Hotel, which opened in 1913, and later bought out the other investors. As sole owner, he became a fixture in the lobby and hotel employees learned not to notice his tobacco-chewing and errant aim. Besides the hotel, he bought the Jones Building (first called the Sherman Building) across the street.

D. C. Rachal of White Point was a cowboy before he became a rancher. He and his brother Nute trailed huge herds to Kansas. The Rachal brothers were known for pushing their herd at a fast pace and then let the cattle eat and fill out after they reached Kansas. The technique became common. A trail boss hurrying his herd similarly would say, "Rachal 'em, boys, Rachal 'em."

Tom Coleman, one of the founders of the Coleman-Fulton Pasture Company, got his start as a ranch hand and so did Thomas Beynon, who bossed trail herds for King Ranch. He served as sheriff of Nueces County and established a successful livery business in Corpus Christi. Archie Parr of Matagorda Island worked as a ranch-hand when he was 11 years old and became a full-fledged cowboy. He was hired as foreman of a ranch in Duval County. He was elected to the state Senate, established a political empire, and known far and wide as the Duke of Duval.

Josiah "Si" Elliff ran away from his home in Tennessee as a teenager when his father died and his mother remarried. He got work as a cowhand, for $10 a month, on Martha Rabb's "Bow and Arrow" Ranch. Years later, he started his own ranch and bought land until he had some 50,000 acres, one of the larger ranches in Nueces County.

One of the most famous cowboys was Charlie Siringo, who also came from Matagorda Island. Siringo's father was an Italian immigrant and his mother Irish. After his father's death, Siringo worked as a cowboy for "Shanghai" Pierce and went up the trail to Kansas. After that, he worked on a Panhandle ranch and led a posse chasing Billy the Kid. Siringo later became a Pinkerton detective and tracked down wanted men all over the West.

It was said that a good cowhand, besides being a good roper and rider, had to understand the nature of cattle and make them understand him. A good cowhand was known for intelligence, determination, independence, and self-sufficiency. Not bad traits for any other profession.

Photo by Erwin E. Smith shows a cowboy breaking a wild bronc on the LS Ranch in Texas in 1907. From the Library of Congress.

Cowboy Words

Cowboys are not remembered for their literary efforts but they certainly had a way with words. They were specialists and like other specialists created their own colorful and piquant language. Walter Prescott Webb wrote that cowboy sayings took on the character of the land, close to primal elements.

Some years ago, in preparation for some project that was never finished, I created an index file of cowboys' pithy expressions. I relied on Ramon Adams' "Western Words" and on my own gleanings from Western literature, such as there is. Here are a select few, revisited.

Angry: Someone in a bad mood was "all horns and rattles" or "touchy as a teased snake." Bath: "Wash out the canyon." Clumsy: "Always saddling the wrong horse." Confused: "Spurs tangled up." Confusing others: "Clouding the trail." Cow manure: "Compressed hay," "Prairie pancakes." Cowboys talking about the weather: "A hard-winter bunch." A reliable cowboy: "Good to ride the river with."

Delicate situation: "Hair in the butter." Depressed: "Down in the boots." Emergency: "Requiring all hands and the cook." Evade responsibility: "Beat the devil 'round the stump." Experienced hand: "Bone seasoned" and "Wrinkles on his horns." Farming: "Turning grass upside-down." Flexible: "Can ride any horse." Friends: "Made of the same leather" and "Chews tobacco from the same plug."

Hanging: "To decorate a cottonwood," "trim a tree," "hang out to dry." Hungry: "Narrow at the equator" and "Empty as a banker's heart." Opinionated: "Has a saddle to fit any horse." Opportunity: "Take advantage of a situation while the gate is still open." Ready to fight: "On the prod." Ride a bucking horse: "Waltz with the lady." Roll a cigarette: "Fill the blanket." Rustler: "Brand artist with a long rope."

Small outfit without a chuckwagon: "A greasy sack bunch." A flock of sheep: "Herd of underwear." Shootout: "Powder-burning contest." Shoot up the town to make a cheerful departure: "Wake up the sheriff." Shooting victim: "Leaned against a bullet going by" or "Got sawdust in his beard." Six-gun: "Black-eyed Susan," "Smoke Wagon" or "Artillery." Someone religious "Raised on prunes and proverbs." Shut up: "Hobble your tongue."

Tough customer: "A curly wolf." Unloaded gun: "No beans in the wheel." Useless: "As socks on a rooster" or "Lipstick on a pig" or "A three-legged horse." Welcome: "As hard rain in dry country." Whisky: "Tarantula Juice," "Coffin Varnish," "Who-Hit-John," "Kill-Me-Quick" and "Whoop-'Em-Up-Liza-Jane." Wine drinker: "Has an educated thirst." A saloon drunk: "Had blisters on his elbows."

Work: "Every bull has to carry his own tail." A full day's work: "Entitled you to a warm place by the fire."

I still have an index box filled with cowboy sayings just in case I ever get around to writing whatever it was that I was going to write.

—Feb. 14, 2018

Underwater road across the bay

A raised oyster reef between the bays connected Rincon Point and Indian Point. At low tide, the water over this reef was no more than knee-high. The passageway was known to generations of travelers as the reef road.

The underwater reef road was a natural oyster shell ridge between Nueces and Corpus Christi bays, stretching from Rincon Point on North Beach to Indian Point on the Portland side. It was used a roadway by riders on horseback and in wagons and buggies by travelers for generations.

Corpus Christi's first settlers did not know it was there until one day in the early 1840s. Historic legend records that Comanche warriors on a horse-stealing raid were chased to Rincon Point by a company of Rangers under the command of a Capt. Crouch. There was a standoff at sundown.

Capt. Crouch decided it would be best to keep the Comanches pressed up against the bay while he sent to town for reinforcements and, next morning, they would attack the Indians at first light.

At dawn, Capt. Crouch's men discovered there was no one there, not an Indian in sight, not a pony, not a fallen feather from a war bonnet. The Rangers followed the tracks which led into the bay. The water was barely knee-deep.

The Indians had decamped in the night, stealing silently across the water by following the raised natural reef that divides Corpus Christi Bay from Nueces Bay. The Indians knew, perhaps they had always known, of this underwater passageway between

Rincon Point and Indian Point, which was an ancient Indian campsite.

The discovery by Crouch's Rangers was to have a long and useful life. The reef was a natural sandbar between the two bays. Tides carried silt that built it up over eons and oyster beds developed on the sandbar. At low tide, the water over this reef was no more than knee-high. By twists and turns, the reef connected two sand spits, like outstretched fingers, from the northern and southern shores. They called it the reef road.

When Zachary Taylor's army was concentrated in Corpus Christi in 1845 and early 1846 preparing for the coming clash with Mexico, Lt. Jeremiah Scarritt, an army engineer, used a squad of soldiers to cut an opening through the reef. This allowed small boats to cross into Nueces Bay and sail up the Nueces River to carry supplies to an outpost stationed at the village of San Patricio.

Lt. Scarritt's cut in the reef was made on the south end near the Corpus Christi shore and for years afterwards, at high tide, horses would have to swim across that gap.

The first Nueces County Commissioners Court, which met at Henry Kinney's house on Jan. 11, 1847, named John Owen as road overseer and instructed him to "mark and designate by strong and substantial stakes" the reef. From that time on, the reef was considered a public roadway and maintenance of the post markers a county responsibility.

They must not have been over-zealous in seeing to that responsibility for within a year, the .stakes on the reef were knocked down or displaced. The Corpus Christi Star reported that the problem was fixed by two enterprising citizens, Henry Gilpin and Thomas Parker, who crossed the reef in a wagon and drove in stakes at the points where they were needed. The stakes, actually cedar posts, were placed 12 to 14 feet apart and stuck up above the water by three or four feet. They marked the twists and turns, which zigzagged back and forth in an irregular pattern.

A sharp bend near the center forced traffic to go a mile out of the way. Those who tried to take a shortcut to avoid this dogleg were making a big mistake. They would get a good soaking or their teams and wagons would bog down in the bay bottom.

J. Williamson Moses, a Texas Ranger and mustanger who lived in the area in the 1850s, said the road across the reef looked very much like going to sea without a boat. Wagons and horses seemed, in the distance, to float upon nothing. At times when the stakes were washed away by a storm an unwary traveler would stray off the reef, get stuck in the mud and his horses' legs would be lacerated by the razor sharp edges of oyster shells.

The stakes were removed for security purposes during the Civil War. A Confederate schooner, the Elmer, was set afire and burned on the reef to prevent its capture by Union ships. After the war, one of the first acts of the new county government was to order the replacement of the stakes on the reef.

George C. Hatch made a regular trip from his place at Ingleside to Corpus Christi. He was ambushed and slain by bandits at Indian Point at the northern terminus of the reef road. "Red John" Dunn gives an account of this crime in "Perilous Trails of Texas."

"On the 7th of June, 1872, Mr. George Hatch was shot to death in his buggy on the north side of the reef. Mr. Hatch was an early settler who owned a splendid vineyard at Ingleside. His habit of making a weekly trip to Corpus Christi for mail and supplies was undoubtedly known to his assassins, who laid in wait and shot him on one of these occasions. The murderers cut out his pockets and robbed him, after which they took his horses and fled. Mr. Hatch was 83 years of age when he was murdered."

E. H. Caldwell, a young bank clerk, was returning from Refugio when he reached the reef at Indian Point, where Hatch had been killed. It was turning dark and he saw two riders behind him. He was sure that they were bandits. He rode into the bay, following the stakes that marked the reef and looking behind him as the riders drew closer. They were some distance behind him when he eased his horse off the reef and waited, with only his head showing above water. The riders passed without seeing him. He was convinced they were bandits. Caldwell contracted pneumonia and was in bed for two weeks with reef road fever.

—*Feb. 21, 2018*

Reef road replaced by causeway

People traveled over the reef into the second decade of the 20th century until Nueces County built a modern causeway from Corpus Christi to Portland. It was opened for traffic in January 1916.

The reef road was two to three feet under water and from a distance it must have looked like a mirage, with wagons and buggies moving across the bay, as if the horses and mules were walking on water. It was a familiar sight from the 1840s into the 20th Century.

The stage to San Antonio crossed over the reef except when high tides made it too dangerous. Then the stage would travel up the south side of Nueces Bay and cross the river at Borden's Ferry.

Leona (Gussett) Givens took the stage hack to reach the end of the railroad line (before the SAAP reached Corpus Christi). The driver was following the stakes across the reef and the horses fell into a hole and turned the hack over. This caused a great deal of commotion. "Dr. Harry Hamilton carried my sister and Mrs. Susie Brooks out of the water," she recalled. "I don't know who rescued me, but whoever it was had an armful. It was quite a feat."

Pioneer resident William Rankin said, "When I was a boy, there was no way to get across to Portland except to drive through the water. The route was staked out, but sometimes it was hard to see the stakes. First you would start out straight, then you would zig-zag left, then zig-zag right, then go ahead again. If

Bicycles with modified wheels were used to cross the bay by hunters going to shoot ducks at Gum Hollow. Photo from Jim Moloney.

you didn't turn at the right places, you would end up in 15 feet of mud." Those who tried that once never did it twice.

When the San Antonio and Aransas Pass Railroad prepared to build a trestle bridge across Nueces Bay in 1886, Capt. Andrew Anderson made soundings. The plan was to build the bridge from White Point to where the turning basin is today, but Anderson found deep mud with no solid footing on that route. The bridge was built next to the reef.

When Clarence Vetters would walk over the railroad trestle to hunt ducks at Gum Hollow, he would sometimes meet a train, which forced him to drop down below the tracks and hold on to a crossbeam as the train passed above him.

While the SAAP offered travelers another way to cross the bay, traveling by train involved at least a two-day visit and many San Patricio residents who bought supplies in Corpus Christi continued to use the reef road. The route to Corpus Christi from the northeast was a 40-mile trek around Nueces Bay.

The first causeway across Nueces Bay was built in 1915 over the old reef that had been used as an underwater passageway since the 1840s. This first causeway opened to traffic in January 1916 and lasted until it was destroyed by the 1919 hurricane. Photo by Karl Swafford from Jim Moloney.

Families coming to shop in Corpus Christi would time their trip so they would cross the bay before dark. After nightfall, the only way to see the stakes was by the faint glow of phosphorous kicked up by the horses. Someone would lie in the wagon bed trying to make out the dim outline of the stakes.

Wallace Clark, who taught at Portland's Bay View College, founded by his father, recalled one Saturday when he traveled over the reef with several of his students. They rode over the reef with two mules and a wagon.

"After reaching Corpus in the forenoon, we left our team and wagon in Blossman's wagon yard. We agreed to meet for the return trip about three o'clock at Lichtenstein's. One of those old-time northers blanketed the area and by the time we were ready to start back it was wet and quite cold.

"Mr. Morris Lichtenstein saw us boys huddled at the front of the store talking. 'Wallace,' he said, 'you surely can't be thinking about going back to Portland across the reef in this norther.' We said that we were. 'Well, if you insist on doing such a foolish thing, all of you come back here with me.' That fine gentleman outfitted every one of us with a slicker and a blanket. Now there was a gracious, fine old man."

May (Mathis) Watson recalled traveling across the reef. "Trips were made by wagon to bring back supplies and if the tide was in it would be dangerous crossing the reef, with occupants of the wagon having to stand up in their seats while the team was forced to swim." This was over the old cut made in the reef by Zachary Taylor's men.

Madelyn May Fisher (she later married Arthur Stone) of Portland said when her father, Edwin Fisher, planned to cross the reef he would send one of his employed men down to the bay to see if the tide was in or out. "He would take a spring wagon and drive across the reef following the posts. When we would get just north of North Beach, that was the mouth of the Nueces River, and it was deep there and the horses would have to swim. If we had packages on the way back, we would put them on the seat and put our feet up. The water would come in through the wagon bed."

Though it could not be crossed in low-slung automobiles, people still traveled over the reef well into the second decade of the 20th century. The beginning of the end came in August 1914.

Nueces County let a contract to build a causeway adjacent to the railroad trestle. When it was completed, the north end near Portland was oyster shell fill with a roadway and the bridge portion from Corpus Christi featured concrete spans with open arches to let the tide through. The causeway included a small lift bridge to accommodate fishing boats.

The first trip across the new causeway was made by Mr. and Mrs. Walter Timon and Mr. and Mrs. Russell Savage in a seven-passenger Cadillac on Dec. 10, 1915. "It is now possible to make the trip across the causeway," the newspaper reported, "but the road will not be opened until paving has been completed. The work will be started at once and should be finished by the first of the year."

It was not, however. The causeway was not opened to traffic until late January 1916 after the paved roadbed was covered with tar in a process called "tarviating." The delay was caused by a long wait for the arrival of the tarviating machine.

—*Feb. 28, 2018*

Temporary causeway lasted three decades

After the 1919 storm destroyed the first causeway across
Nueces Bay, a temporary structure was built in 1921. It
was still in use when the first span of the two modern
causeways was built in 1950.

A hurricane on Aug. 18, 1916 knocked out the new causeway
built over the old reef road. The causeway was repaired only to
be destroyed three years later in the great storm of 1919. Heavy
timbers from Harbor Island crushed the causeway and its
concrete girders were knocked up to 200 feet away. Only the
small lift bridge was left standing.

For two years after the storm, people of Portland, Gregory and
Taft were forced to travel 40 miles around Nueces Bay to reach
Corpus Christi, unless they came by train.

In 1921 a temporary causeway was built by the Austin Brothers
Bridge Company. It was opened to traffic on Oct. 8, 1921 with a
celebration led by County Judge Hugh Sutherland. The
celebration included band concerts at Artesian Park, rodeo
events, a parade across the causeway, a street dance and banquet
at the Nueces Hotel.

The temporary causeway was a wooden bridge a few feet
above water level. During storms and high tides, the splashing of
waves would impede traffic. The draw span from the 1915
causeway was re-used in the new causeway.

Another drawbridge across the railroad trestle allowed small
vessels to pass between the bays. (The first watchman on the
railroad drawbridge was Frank Rodriguez; when he died in 1892
his son John took over the position.)

A hurricane on Sept. 4, 1933 destroyed the roadbed of the temporary causeway, though it left the pilings intact. This severed the direct link between Corpus Christi and the northeast.

As a makeshift solution, it was proposed to operate a shuttle train with automobiles carried on flatcars across the railroad trestle, which had survived the storm. That proved to be too costly. Another idea was to get the U.S. Army to build a pontoon bridge across the bay, which also turned out be too expensive.

The solution was to move a ferryboat from Port Aransas to carry cars across Nueces Bay. The ferry carried 18 cars a trip, at 50 cents per car, and made the trip every hour. Mrs. Raymond Dugat of Portland said she would never forget crossing that ferry one night about nine o'clock. "We came back around by Calallen. I think that was the only time I rode that ferry." The ferry operated for three months until the causeway was repaired.

The temporary causeway carried traffic across Nueces Bay from 1921 until the first of two modern concrete spans was built in 1950, proving to be more durable than its predecessor, the permanent causeway that didn't survive four years.

The new elevated causeway was constructed by the Austin Bridge Company, which also built the temporary causeway. (It is worth noting that an early engineer for the Austin Bridge Company was William M. Goldston, known generally as the colonel, who founded the Goldston Company.)

The new causeway cost $2.4 million, a little more than the $166,000 it cost to build the first causeway and the $412,000 it cost to build the temporary causeway. There was no ceremony to mark the occasion when traffic began to flow over the new causeway on Nov. 28, 1950.

The first person to drive across was Dr. John Tunnell of Taft. He was going home after delivering a baby (one of almost 10,000 he delivered before he retired). "That causeway sure looked good to me," the doctor said. "I guess I was pretty tired after that all-night ordeal at the hospital." Wes Tunnell of Texas A&M-Corpus Christi, the doctor's son, told me his father made some people mad that day. "He was on an emergency run to Spohn and came upon a long line of people waiting in their cars to be first, or one of the first, to cross the new causeway. He

The second causeway across Nueces Bay, built in 1921, was intended to be a temporary fix. On the right was the railroad bridge built in 1886. The photo was probably taken while the causeway was under construction. The sign at right put the cost at $300,000 but it ended up costing $412,500.

went alongside of them with his lights flashing and got to the front of the line just as they cut the ribbon and drove across as the first person to make the trip."

The old temporary causeway was left open to traffic for a week, just to allow motorists to get accustomed to the new elevated causeway. After it was closed, the old wooden causeway became a favorite loitering place for fishermen until it was dismantled in April 1951.

Work began on a second causeway on Sept. 30, 1961 and was completed two years later. The second causeway provided double spans across the bay, allowing one-way traffic.

The first new causeway had a bascule lift bridge to allow boats to pass from Corpus Christi Bay to Nueces Bay. Motorists had to wait when the lift bridge was raised. When the second causeway was constructed, an elevated "hump" near the south end gave a 50-foot vertical clearance for barges and boats. The 1950 causeway was remodeled to add a similar "hump" adjacent to the same location.

The new causeway was opened to traffic on Aug. 1, 1963 and dedicated in a ceremony two weeks later. The ceremony included officials pouring jugs of water from Corpus Christi Bay, Nueces

Bay and the Nueces River over the concrete at the top of the hump, followed by a luncheon at the Driscoll Hotel.

Work began in 1966 to dismantle the old railroad trestle. Southern Pacific, which acquired the old SAAP line, stopped regular traffic across the railroad bridge after 1961. When the Tule Lake Lift Bridge was opened, Southern Pacific rerouted its trains to enter Corpus Christi from the west instead of over the old trestle across the bay.

Work on removing the pilings was stopped due to some complication and was not resumed until the state sued the railroad, arguing that the pilings represented a danger to boat traffic. The pilings were not removed until 1977 when the Goldston Company was hired to do the job. William Goldston, whose grandfather, the colonel, founded the company, said many of the pilings were good "below the mud line" and some were used in building Snoopy's on the Laguna Madre.

Today's modern causeway crosses over and above the old reef. It is a lineal descendant of that twisting underwater road, which was so rich in history and so unlike any other roadway in the world.

—March 8, 2018

Column 114

Fred Roberts' murder linked to Klan activity

"You're a Kluxer, aren't you, Warren? By God, you
know you are." —Sheriff Frank Robinson to storeowner
G. E. Warren

Fred Roberts, a real-estate dealer and farmer, was shot to death
in front of a grocery store on Railroad Avenue at Staples Street
on Oct. 14, 1922. The crime was related to the growing power of
the Ku Klux Klan in Nueces County and the forces arrayed
against it.

In the 1920s the KKK was a growing movement not only in the
South but around the country. Many joined the Klan as an agent
of political reform, overlooking the invisible empire's violent
opposition to blacks, Catholics and Jews.

In Nueces County and Corpus Christi, the Klan was opposed
by the political machine of former County Judge Walter Timon
and many other prominent Catholics.

The Klan held initiation meetings and burned crosses in a
pasture near Savage Lane and a vacant lot at Doddridge and
Ocean Drive. Meetings were also held at David Peel's funeral
home at Taylor and Lower Broadway, where the Caller-Times is
today. Peel was known as an active supporter of the Klan.

In a story for the Caller-Times Centennial edition in 1983, C.
W. Carpenter wrote about the march of hundreds of Klan
members in their white sheets in Sinton. David Grossman, who
owned a store in Sinton, said, "I knew every one of those
Klansmen. I sold them shoes and I could look at their feet and
tell who was who."

Keith Guthrie ("History of San Patricio") wrote that the Klan held a big meeting at Sodville and while it was underway opponents of the Klan spread roofing nails over the roads and under car tires. "There were lots of flat tires and swearing that night."

The Klan planned a march in Corpus Christi but when robed members arrived at the Tex-Mex Depot they were met by Police Chief Monroe Fox. He ordered them not to get off the train. Expecting trouble, Fox had men stationed on the roof of City Hall and State National Bank armed with submachine-guns.

The City Council passed an ordinance prohibiting parades by two or more masked persons, obviously aimed at the Klan. Armed volunteers patrolled, night and day, around Incarnate Word and the bishop's residence on the bluff in fear of Klan violence. Across the region, crosses were burned, threats made, guns were carried as a matter of course, and violence was more than an abstract possibility.

It was against this highly charged atmosphere that the events of Oct. 14, 1922, a Saturday, unfolded.

Sheriff Frank Robinson and deputy Joe Acebo stopped at G. E. Warren's grocery store to buy tobacco. Warren was thought to be a Klan member. Sheriff Robinson barely won election that year against W. F. "Wildfire" Johnston, the Klan-backed candidate. Robinson was an ally of the Timon clique and hated the Klan.

The sheriff bought tobacco and asked Warren how business was going. Warren said it was slow. "That's how it is with you Kluxers," said the sheriff. Acebo piped in, "Warren is a Kluxer; everybody says so." The sheriff said, "You're a Kluxer, aren't you, Warren? By God, you know you are."

The sheriff slapped the storekeeper, who shouted, "Don't hit me. Get out of here." Robinson and Acebo strolled across Staples Street to Blake's Drug Store, where they stood leisurely watching Warren's store.

The storekeeper's wife, Dove Warren, called Police Chief Monroe Fox. He showed up with constable Lee Petzel and another man, Cleve Goff. Fox found Sheriff Robinson and Acebo talking across the street. Fox told the Warrens the sheriff was minding his business and he could do nothing unless the

David Peel's funeral home at Taylor and Lower Broadway (where the Caller-Times is today) was a meeting place of the Ku Klux Klan. After Klan leader Fred Roberts was slain, his body was taken to Peel's to lie in state. Photo by Doc McGregor from the Museum of Science and History.

Warrens signed a complaint. The police chief returned to his office while Petzel and Goff stayed behind.

Warren called his friend Fred Roberts, a known Klan leader, who came to the store, talked to the Warrens, then went out to his car. He started the engine and Sheriff Robinson walked over, reached in, and turned off the ignition.

As witnesses related, the sheriff fired three shots at Roberts from his .45 caliber Colt revolver while Acebo, from the passenger side of the car fired one shot. Petzel in turn fired a volley of shots at the Warren grocery and Goff was somehow involved. Roberts was killed instantly, shot dead in the front seat of his car. His body was taken to David Peel's funeral home to lie in state.

Feelings were strong. The paper ran an unusual front-page editorial urging people to stay calm and to let the judicial system run its course. Mayor P. G. Lovenskiold and County Judge Hugh Sutherland asked Gov. Pat Neff to send Texas Rangers to prevent further violence.

Ranger Capt. Frank Hamer arrived with four men. There is some dispute about whether "the murderers" and some 30 or 40 armed henchmen barricaded themselves in the courtroom and whether Hamer kicked in the doors of the courthouse when he arrived, declaring, "I'm Frank Hamer, Texas Ranger. I have warrants for the arrest of those involved in the murder of Fred Roberts. The rest of you put up those guns and get the hell out of here." This colorful version in Hamer's biography is not supported by local accounts.

Sheriff Robinson, Acebo, Petzel and Goff were indicted for murder. The trial was moved to Laredo on a change of venue. Eyebrows must have been raised over the fact that the presiding judge was Walter Timon, the former county judge who had been appointed district judge by the governor. Timon was a political ally of Robinson and both men were viscerally anti-Klan.

The former sheriff (he resigned after the shooting) testified that he shot Fred Roberts because he thought he was going for a gun, though no weapon was found in the car. The jury brought back its verdict on Jan. 13, 1923. All four defendants were found not guilty.

Former Sheriff Frank Robinson, fearing Klan retaliation, left the country and lived in Mexico for a decade. In Corpus Christi, a new hospital was named in honor of Fred Roberts. The Ku Klux Klan became increasing negligible as a political force in Nueces County and the general area. Its power began to ebb after the slaying of Fred Roberts and mostly had disappeared by the 1930s.

—*March 14, 2018*

Column 115

Blacksmith Bob trained on North Beach

The boxer ran wind sprints on the beach with one of his
pet lions loping beside him. When the alarm spread that
one of the lions escaped, mothers kept their kids close
while a search was mounted. The lion was sleeping under
a house.

Blacksmith Bob Fitzsimmons set up a training camp in Corpus
Christi in 1895 to prepare for a much-anticipated heavyweight
match with Gentleman Jim Corbett.

Fitzsimmons rented a house on North Beach (it was later the
W. E. Carruth home) and erected a training barn. One of his
training exercises was to run holding on to the back of wagon
moving at a fast clip. He ran wind sprints on the beach, with one
of his two pet lions loping along beside him. When the alarm
spread that one of the lions had escaped, mothers kept their kids
inside while volunteer lion-hunters combed the area. After four
days, the lion crawled out from under a house on North Beach
where he had been hiding.

Local boys would hang around the barn-room gymnasium on
North Beach to watch Fitzsimmons work out with his sparring
partner Duncan Ross. In September 1895, Fitzsimmons issued a
challenge for any citizen in town to spar with him at his training
camp.

"He will not hurt anyone," the paper said, "but they are
welcome to pound him as much as they like. He spars with
members of his own party, alternating with them as the wind
plays out." The only local man to take up the challenge was

"Blacksmith Bob" Fitzsimmons trained on North Beach in 1895 for a championship fight with "Gentleman Jim" Corbett. There was a panic in town when Fitzsimmons' pet lion escaped and fearful mothers kept their children indoors until the lion was found under a house on North Beach.

Walter Timon, who later was elected county judge of Nueces County and then was appointed district judge.

"Fitzsimmons was a great fighter," Timon said later. "He never weighed more than 170 pounds but won the world's heavyweight title. First time I boxed Fitz, I said to myself, anybody who shuffles around like that I'll whip. But I didn't. He was a fast man and a terrible puncher. He just looked slow."

Blacksmith Bob's fight with Gentleman Jim Corbett was set for Dallas, but the Texas Legislature passed a bill, signed into law, that made prize-fighting illegal in Texas. So the match was called off. Judge Roy Bean, the famous character who was called "the law west of the Pecos," arranged to stage a fight between Fitzsimmons and Peter Maher on a sandbar in the Rio Grande, which was outside Texas' jurisdiction. It wasn't much of a fight. Maher went down in less than two minutes.

476

That summer Corpus Christi got the news that Fitzsimmons' lion was killed in Chicago when he somehow got entangled in electrical wires.

Finally, the long-waited and much-ballyhooed fight between Blacksmith Bob Fitzsimmons and Gentleman Jim Corbett was held in Carson City, Nev., in 1897.

A crowd gathered in Corpus Christi outside the Caller office where results came in by telegraph. At the end of each round the results were relayed to the waiting crowd.

A great cheer went up when it was announced that Blacksmith Bob, in the 14th round, knocked out Gentleman Jim Corbett to become the heavyweight champion of the world.

Sheriff in troubled times

Pat Whelan, one of Nueces County's long-serving and outstanding sheriffs, emigrated from County Wexford, Ireland with his three brothers. Patrick, the oldest, was born in 1840. He arrived in New York in 1864 and moved on to Corpus Christi. His brother Thomas, born in 1846, followed and another brother, John, born in 1850, arrived in 1875.

Pat Whelan was listed as a bricklayer in the 1870 census. He was appointed to the State Police Force created by Gov. Edmund J. Davis to replace the Texas Rangers. He also served as city marshal, beginning in 1871, when he was elected over Thomas Murphy. He requested that the City Council purchase a horse for his use so that he might "better discharge his trust."

Whelan led a posse searching for the bandits who killed four men at Peñascal on Baffin Bay in May 1874. He was on the posse that chased the bandits in the Nuecestown Raid in March 1875.

Whelan was a close friend of John McClane and when McClane's last term as sheriff was coming to an end, the books were audited and a shortage discovered. McClane sent Whelan to seek help from rancher Richard King, another longtime friend. King got expert help and found the books balanced to the penny. Whelan was chief deputy under Sheriff Thomas Beynon, from 1876 to 1882.

Pat Whelan was elected sheriff in 1882 and served until 1896, nine terms in all. In one episode during his tenure, Whelan picked up a prisoner at Brownsville and it was feared a lynch mob might waylay him on the return trip. Whelan brought his prisoner by boat and had him safe in the county jail before any lynching party could be organized.

In another story that showed his independence, Whelan had a female prisoner in the county jail and Mexican authorities were demanding her extradition. Whelan refused. The governor joined the Mexican authorities and ordered Whelan to turn over the prisoner. Whelan still refused and cited some technical legal points. It was later determined that Whelan was right, from a legal standpoint, and the demands were withdrawn. The prisoner was found to have been wrongfully charged.

After his last term as sheriff, Whelan was elected justice of the peace and served in that capacity until he died on May 29, 1921.

An obituary in the Caller said of Whelan: "During the tenure as sheriff, Mr. Whelan maintained the reputation of a cool, calculating and capable officer . . . he had been in many close and dangerous and places, but never under any circumstances had he been known to falter in his duty. His term of office was during the period when the Southwest was the rendezvous of such bad men as Ben Thompson, King Fisher, John Wesley Harden, Sam Bass, Bill Longley, and others, but Nueces County was not one of the counties these men selected to perform in. The policy of Pat Whelan the officer and Pat Whelan the private citizen was to save life and not take it, nor have it taken."

At the time of his death, he lived at his home on Mesquite Street, near the courthouse. His wife Johanna preceded him in death. Pat Whelan was survived by a daughter and his brother Thomas. He was buried at Holy Cross Cemetery with Rev. Claude Jaillet officiating.

—March 21, 2018

Column 116

The Ladies Pavilion

The ladies of the Woman's Monday Club sold shares of stock to raise funds to build the Ladies Pavilion. It was constructed in 1902 over the water off Water Street, below Peoples Street. The Ladies Pavilion opened on Aug. 7, 1903 and it soon replaced Market Hall as the town's main social center.

Corpus Christi's Market Hall, built in 1871 between Peoples and Schatzel on Mesquite, was the social center of the city. It had market stalls for vendors and butchers, room for city offices, and an auditorium on the second floor where meetings and dances were held. But by the turn of the century, the town had outgrown the space available at Market Hall.

The Woman's Monday Club did something about it. The women sold shares of stock to raise funds to build the Ladies Pavilion. It was constructed in 1902 over the water off Water Street, below Peoples Street, near where the Peoples Street T-Head is today.

The Ladies Pavilion opened on Aug. 7, 1903 and it soon replaced Market Hall as the town's social center, where plays and dances were held. The dance floor was sometimes converted into a skating rink for youngsters.

One memorable tableau presented at the Ladies Pavilion was called "A Dream of Beautiful Women." The town's most fashionable women — Mrs. Leo Kaffie, Mrs. Moise Weil, Mrs. Roy Miller, Mrs. Walter Timon, among others — struck fixed poses of famous women. Clara Driscoll reclined on a couch as Cleopatra.

The Ladies Pavilion was also where the city's first conventions were held. The Texas Bankers Association, the Texas Medical Association, and the Texas Press Association held conventions at the new Ladies Pavilion.

479

The Ladies Pavilion was built off Water Street between the end of Peoples and Schatzel streets. It opened on Aug. 7, 1903 and quickly supplanted the old Market Hall as the town's social center. It was destroyed by the 1916 hurricane.

Most important was a reception given at the Ladies Pavilion in 1904 for members of the Methodist Epworth League. They were looking for a place to hold an annual summer encampment and had narrowed the choices down to Corpus Christi and Rockport.

The Epworth League representatives were delighted with Corpus Christi and when the city sweetened the deal by offering 18 acres, free of charge, on North Beach, the result became the encampment of Epworth by the Sea.

The first encampment was held in August 1905. Roy Terrell, a Corpus Christi resident, remembered the encampment. "A frame building, called Epworth Inn, was constructed and contained both lodging places and a large auditorium. Smaller buildings went up and the overflow lived in tents stretched along the sand. Preaching took place night and day, but there was time for games and bathing. There was a big tent where they served meals. The first time I ever tasted ice tea was at one of these Epworth meetings."

Epworth by the Sea was held every year for a decade. Each summer, hundreds of Methodist families and missionaries from around the world gathered on North Beach.

The beginning of Corpus Christi as a tourist destination can be traced to two events. One was in 1895 when heavyweight champion Blacksmith Bob Fitzsimmons trained on North Beach for his prize fight with Gentleman Jim Corbett. Corpus Christi got a lot of national attention that year. The other was the annual Epworth by the Sea

480

encampment, which introduced many Texans to North Beach and the summer pleasures of Corpus Christi Bay. It was one of the turning points in the city's history, though they probably didn't recognize it as such at the time. The Ladies Pavilion didn't last long. It was destroyed in the hurricane of 1916.

From the Land of Plenty

A special excursion train called the Black Land Special pulled out of Corpus Christi on Nov. 9, 1924. On board were 110 farmers and businessmen from the Corpus Christi area, all wearing pearl-gray Stetsons.

The group toured central and north Texas to promote the black land farming region of South Texas. They would parade through a town and rent a movie house to show a film called "Land of Plenty."

The Black Land Special included three railroad cars carrying exhibits of cotton, grain and other crops grown in the "black soil" of Nueces, San Patricio, Jim Wells and Kleberg counties.

It was the idea of Maston Nixon, who would later build Corpus Christi's first towering office building on the bluff. Nixon had a survey run on black land farm acreage unfarmed but available for sale in the four counties of the Coastal Bend. His survey showed that hundreds of thousands of acres were available for farm tracts. The question was how to get that message out. The idea at first was to hold a county fair and send out invitations to farmers throughout Texas. Then someone thought of hiring a train and rather than bring people here take farmers and farm products to show them what could be grown here.

Nixon enlisted the help of Missouri Pacific, Southern Pacific and Tex-Mex Railroads, which helped cover expenses for the 12-car excursion train. Texas A&M University helped to prepare the exhibits. The 20th Infantry Army Band at Fort Sam Houston provided the music.

The train departed the San Antonio & Aransas Pass depot on Sunday, Nov. 9, 1924. At the first stop on Monday morning at Lockhart, 800 people visited the Black Land Special. At Taylor on Tuesday, 1,500 people saw the film and visited the exhibits.

At each stop, the 20th Army Band, followed by the delegation in their pearl-gray Stetsons, would parade through the downtown to the theater where people would see the film "Land of Plenty" about farming techniques and products of the Coastal Bend, then they would visit the exhibit cars.

On Nov. 9, 1924, a train called "The Black Land Special" pulled out of Corpus Christi with farmers, businessmen and civic boosters on board. The train would stop at towns in central and north Texas to promote black-land farming in the Corpus Christi area.

The first was the cotton car. One end was a miniature cotton field, with real stalks and a typical cotton wagon. The other end featured cotton products with the placard, "From the Realm of King Cotton."

The second exhibit was the grains car, with all the varieties of corn and grain and a map of the four counties made of various grain seeds.

The third included pecans, date palms, among other trees. The fourth car showed varieties of fruits and vegetables grown in the region, including flapper cabbage, Bermuda onions, and "carrots that made your hair curl and beets that put roses in your cheeks."

The men in pearl-gray Stetsons returned after two weeks. Everywhere they went — Sherman, Paris, Ennis, Mexia, Corsicana, Waco — they were greeted by large and enthusiastic crowds. The Black Land Special was called the greatest promotion ever launched for any one section of the state. Some 55,000 Texans saw the movie, "Land of Plenty," 65,000 viewed the exhibits, and within five years 100,000 new acres were brought into production, in large part as a direct result of the Black Land Special.

—March 28, 2018

Cranking up a new era

George Blucher met Ransom Olds in the summer of 1901 and bought the first automobile seen in Corpus Christi. It was shipped in a wooden crate with a mechanic to assemble it. Dr. Heaney and Dr. Spohn soon followed by buying their own cars, both Cadillacs.

George Blucher, who owned an ice house on Water Street, met Ransom Olds, manufacturer of the Oldsmobile, at the Pan-American Exposition in Buffalo in the summer of 1901. Blucher bought one and had it shipped to Corpus Christi from Detroit. It arrived in October in a wooden crate accompanied by its own technician to assemble it.

Blucher's Oldsmobile was the first car in Corpus Christi. It cost $650, had a motor under the back seat and a tiller instead of a steering wheel. It would get 40 miles for a gallon of gas.

In 1902, Dr. Alfred Heaney bought a one-cylinder Cadillac. Not long afterwards, Dr. Heaney's friend and rival, Dr. Arthur Spohn, bought his own automobile, a red Cadillac.

Peter McBride was in a mule cart to make his early morning milk deliveries when he encountered Dr. Spohn in his new automobile. "I kept holding the mules back," McBride said, "but they were scared and there was no stopping them. Automobiles could go 25 miles an hour and we thought that that much speed could kill people."

Corpus Christi got its first taxicab in 1906, operated by Pitts Livery Stable and Funeral Home. A man named Dan Darby was the driver. Roy Terrell got his first automobile ride in the Pitts taxi. "My father sent the taxi to our house to pick us up and take

George Blucher's Oldsmobile was probably the first car in Corpus Christi. It cost $650 and would get 40 miles for a gallon of gas. It had a tiller instead of a steering wheel and the motor was under the back seat.

us to the railroad station, a distance of four blocks, but what an experience!"

A Caller reporter took a spin around town on Dec. 21, 1906 in E. R. Oliver's new car. "The auto is a rapid mover, yet it can be stopped in a few seconds, even in going up or down the bluff."

One of the first auto ads in the Caller ran in 1906 for Noakes Brothers. They were selling Cadillacs and Noakes promised to keep the machine in repair for six months, barring accidents or punctured tires. The ad said Cadillacs were so popular there were already four in town. "The Cadillac Motor Car," said the ad, "needs no recommendation. The merit of the four cars used in this city is good enough. The Cadillac is past the experimental part, and is sold in Corpus Christi by Noakes Bros."

In March 1908 the Caller reported that John D. Barnard and Dr. W. E. Carruth were on Broadway at night when an automobile collided with their buggy, throwing both men out, and knocking the horse down.

Dr. Arthur Spohn in his new Cadillac in front of the Mifflin Kenedy mansion where he and his wife Sarah Josephine Kenedy Spohn lived. In the back seat is his wife's niece from Brownsville. It was about 1905, the year he opened Spohn Sanitarium on North Beach.

Following the accident, the Caller started an editorial campaign pushing for a vehicle ordinance to deal with "reckless auto-ing." An ordinance was passed requiring motorists to sound a horn, bell, gong or trumpet as the driver approached intersections. After the new ordinance went into effect, the Caller editor complained that drivers were "blowing their horns louder and longer than ever; if they can't be a nuisance one way, they will another."

South of town, farmer Herman Poenisch bought his first automobile, a Ford sedan, equipped with carbide lights. A tube ran from the carbide system to the lights. One night, coming back from town, they hit a bump, which knocked the tube loose, and Poenisch hit a cow; the family helped to pull the scared but unhurt cow from under the car. Their next car had magneto lights; the faster the car went, the brighter the lights.

Carlyle Leonard, whose grandfather Will Leonard opened one of the town's first barber shops, noted that people in town knew everyone who had a car. "If we saw a Hudson coming down Chaparral, we knew it was Mrs. Maude Miller. If we saw an open Benz with the brass shining, we knew it was Mr. Driscoll. If you were near Artesian Park and heard a Cadillac moving slowly, you would know it was Judge McDonald."

Before highways sliced across the land, traveling by car was tough going. The automobiles were under-powered and streets of shell or dirt turned to gumbo-like clay after a heavy rain. They were all but impassable. Country roads were even worse. Mrs. A. R. Yeargen, who ran a grocery store on King Street, remembered taking a trip to San Antonio in their first car, an Overland, across the 1915 causeway. "We left at sun-up and by noon we were at Kenedy and by sundown at San Antonio. We traveled 25 miles an hour over roads that were not paved. We got stuck in the sand and had numerous flats."

POWs in Corpus Christi

In February 1944 two German prisoners of war escaped from a POW camp at Mexia, 360 miles to the north, and fled to Corpus Christi, hoping to find a boat and reach Mexico. They were captured were captured without mishap at a tourist court on North Beach, posing as "Free French" soldiers.

Before they were caught, the police switchboard was flooded with tips. Someone reported a merchant seaman with an accent; he was arrested and held briefly. One man called and said he knew a dive where the Germans hung out; it was a local bar. Two Russians in Corpus Christi studying refinery operations were arrested after they were heard "talking foreign" in a restaurant.

After the POWs were arrested, Bob McCracken, the Crow's Nest columnist in the Caller-Times, interviewed the POWs and reported what they had in their pockets when they were captured. They had ID cards, dog tags, ration books, combs, mirrors, French invasion currency, good luck charms, and one had an Iron Cross made of cheap metal.

The following year, in 1945, German POWs were housed at the Naval Air Station. They were kept in a 10-acre garrison enclosed by barbed wire near the station commissary. The POWs worked 48 hours a week at manual labor jobs, for which they were paid 80 cents a day. In one assignment, they dug up hackberry trees from along the Nueces River and transplanted them around the Naval Air Station. They were shown movies in the evenings and particularly liked Disney films. People in Corpus Christi found the POWs to be cheerful, good workers. The POW camp was in operation from August 1945 until March 1946.

—April 4, 2018

First teacher, first school

Amanda Brooks, who was 17 at the time, taught 40 students in a room of John P. Kelsey's store on Water Street in 1846. She was Corpus Christi's first teacher and her school was the city's first.

Amanda Brooks taught classes in a room of John Kelsey's dry goods store on Water Street. That was in 1846. She was a graduate of Marietta Seminary in Marietta, Ohio who came to Corpus Christi with her parents, Abidja and Laura Brooks. She was 17.

Amanda Brooks' father was killed soon after they arrived when he was thrown from his horse. A delegation of businessmen led by Kelsey urged Miss Brooks to open a school and free space was offered in Kelsey's store.

Amanda Brooks taught 40 students. Tuition was $2 per child per month. The teacher and storekeeper married in October 1847 and lived in Kelsey's home on Chaparral. They moved to Rio Grande City in 1848.

Kelsey sold his store to D. H. de Meza and his wife, who came to Corpus Christi from the Dutch West Indies. The Corpus Christi Star said Mrs. De Meza would open a school on Oct. 9, 1848 in the store where Amanda Brooks had taught. She would teach English, Reading, Writing, Grammar, Geography, History, French, Spanish, and Needlework.

The school was short-lived. Within a month the Star lamented that Corpus Christi had neither church nor school. In 1849, C.C. Farley and W.W. Whitley opened the Corpus Christi Academy in

Early educators in Corpus Christi: Amanda Brooks, shown in later years, taught students in the room of a store on Water Street in 1846. She was Corpus Christi's first school teacher. Charles Lovenskiold, from Denmark, opened the Corpus Christi Academy in 1853 in an adobe-brick building on Mesquite Street.

a small building at Chaparral and Lawrence. The school closed when Farley departed to teach in Austin.

Four years later, Charles Lovenskiold, from Denmark, opened the Corpus Christi Academy. Lovenskiold, a lawyer, moved from New Orleans to Corpus Christi with the encouragement of Corpus Christi founder Henry Kinney.

Lovenskiold arranged to bring three instructors from Illinois to teach in his academy, including M. P. Craft, Mary Gordon and Julia Marsh. The school was in an adobe-brick building on Mesquite Street across from where Spohn Park is today. Andrew Anderson recalled that the school had small wooden desks and benches.

The Nueces Valley on Jan. 2, 1957 reported that the school would begin its new term on Jan. 11 and remain in session for 11 months. The cost was $30 per year per student. Trustees of the academy were merchant Frederick Belden, Capt. S. W. Fullerton, and Judge M. P. Norton.

It was a private school, tuition was paid by the parents, but it did have public money. Teachers submitted tabular statements showing the number of days attended by students who could not afford to pay tuition. The amounts were reimbursed by the county from its free school fund.

Lovenskiold stressed habits of order and cleanliness and insisted that students come to school clean. They lined up in military order for inspection and those with improper clothes or dirty fingernails were sent home. Unruly students were fitted with a dunce cap.

When Lovenskiold left to practice law, he named M. P. Craft as principal. At the beginning of 1860 the school held exercises, including declamations and dialogues, to show that the students had learned all the things that couldn't be of the slightest use to them. The academy struggled during the Civil War before it closed in 1862.

Rosalie Priour taught elementary age students in her mother's old store on Water Street during the last two years of the war.

The Catholic Church opened the Hidalgo Seminary in 1863. It was a school for boys in a two-story concrete building at Lipan and Tancahua. The Hidalgo Seminary was founded by Father John Gonnard, a missionary from France. Father Gonnard loved boats and would run down to the waterfront when a ship came in.

Eli Merriman, who attended the Hidalgo Seminary, said it was one of the best schools in Texas. Pupils came from Laredo to Victoria and points in between. Most of them boarded at private homes in town while a few boarded at the school. Students were taught moral and spiritual lessons and academic subjects.

The school was managed by the Catholic Church with Father Gonnard at the head. He employed two teachers, William Shakespeare Campion and William Carroll, known as "Little" Carroll. (Carroll's niece, Mary Carroll, would one day become superintendent of Corpus Christi's public schools.) Campion, from Galveston, was educated in Switzerland and taught school in San Antonio before he moved to Corpus Christi.

When Thomas Noakes was preparing to teach school at Nuecestown in 1865, he spent a day at the Hidalgo Seminary observing how William Carroll conducted his class. Noakes noted in his diary that the teacher copied the writing lesson on the board and pupils recopied it on their slates. Every student would recite what he had written. This was followed by spelling, geography and arithmetic, in which the students went over the multiplication table with Carroll copying sums on the blackboard. When the sums were completed, the students took their slates up for the teacher's inspection.

Maria Blucher in a letter to parents dated Oct. 4, 1866 said her children were back in school. "They go to Hidalgo Seminary, an excellent school. They are at lessons from 8 in the morning to 5 in the evening. Their studies are English, Spanish, French, arithmetic, geography, history, writing, reading, drawing, etc. they all make excellent progress and are eager to learn."

Father Gonnard died in the yellow fever outbreak of 1867. The church hired Robert Dougherty to run the school. Kate Dougherty (later Mrs. Vincent Bluntzer) said her father taught older boys in the large hall upstairs while her mother taught smaller boys in a room downstairs.

Dougherty left in 1874 to establish his own school at Round Lake near San Patricio. One of the original teachers, William Shakespeare Campion, was hired to teach and supervise the Hidalgo Seminary. It remained open for another three years until 1877 when it was closed.

Eli Merriman speculated that if Father Gonnard hadn't died in 1867 the Hidalgo Seminary "would probably have grown to be one of the great educational institutions in the state." As it was, from 1863 to 1877, the Hidalgo Seminary was the most important school in Corpus Christi.

—Dec. 6, 2017

Private schools flourished after the war

Mary Dix ran one school in her home on Water Street. It
was later run by Jane Marsh in the post office building.
Another school was conducted by Mr. and Mrs.
Carpenter on the bluff and others were run by Professor
Brooks and Professor McOmber.

After the Civil War a school for girls was operated in the John
Dix home on Water Street (where the Seaside Hotel was later).

It was said that Mary Eliza Hayes Dix was the very image of
Queen Victoria. She taught daughters of former slaves in the
morning and white girls in the afternoon. Black girls were taught
sewing and white girls academic subjects.

Instead of desks the school had small chairs arranged in a semi-
circle and students wrote on slates, copying lessons from a
blackboard. The school had two books, McGuffey's Reader and
Blue-Back Speller.

Jane Marsh took over when Mrs. Dix became ill. Marsh was a
Connecticut Yankee who was appointed postmaster. She raised
tuition from $1.50 a month to $2 and moved the school to the
post office on Mesquite Street. The post office and school were
on the first floor and she lived on the second. When Jane Marsh
became ill in the yellow fever epidemic of 1867, she sent for
material to make her shroud and died soon afterwards.

Anna Moore Schwien recalled that after the war Cora Cook
taught young children in the Richard Power home on Broadway.
Cora and her brother were taken in by Mr. and Mrs. Power after
their parents died.

J. B. Carpenter and his wife ran a school for boys and girls beginning in 1867. It was in the old Chapman house on Broadway. Andrew Anderson recalled that the rules of conduct were hung up inside the front door. "Mr. Carpenter did not whip anybody, but if a pupil would not obey the rules he had to go home." The school closed in 1869 when Carpenter opened a law office.

In 1867 the Corpus Christi Eclectic School, with J. T. Easterline as president and A.F. Cox his assistant, opened for classes but did not last long. Neither did a school run by a Mr. Allen, a graduate of West Point, who taught boys on the first floor of the Meuly home on Chaparral.

"For a while I went to Allen's school, in the downstairs part of the Conrad Meuly building on Chaparral," Eli Merriman wrote. "Another school I went to was Professor McOmber's in the Methodist Church building." Professor McOmber was not shy about using the rod and if parents objected they could take their children home.

Hannah Conklin conducted a school for girls in 1870. Mrs. Conklin, who always wore a hoop skirt with a large bustle, was a devout Episcopalian and opened every class with a prayer. She was the daughter of John M. Moore, a former Confederate officer, prominent businessman and mayor at one time.

She first held classes in a small adobe cottage behind the Moore home on the north end of Water Street. Mrs. Conklin was later hired as a teacher for the new public-school system. After her husband died in 1878 she conducted a boarding and day school for girls in a converted home on Carancahua. She returned to teach in the public schools after 1880.

The Incarnate Word Academy was founded by the Sisters of the Incarnate Word in 1871. Classes were conducted in the old Hidalgo Seminary building at the corner of Lipan and Tancahua by four nuns of the order, who came from Brownsville. In 1885, a three-story building was erected at the corner of Tancahua and Leopard. In time, with a new building constructed in 1925, the academy took up most of the block between Carancahua and Tancahua. Besides the main three-story brick building facing Carancahua, the complex included two wooden buildings that

Rosa Beynon, known as a strict disciplinarian, was one of three teachers when Corpus Christi's first public schools opened in 1871. The other two were Rhoda Burke and Hannah Conklin.

were part of the original academy and convent built in the 1880s. St. Joseph's parochial school for boys began in 1888 next door to the convent.

The sisters of the Incarnate Word lived cloistered lives until early in the 20th Century when they were given dispensation to go sea-bathing. One article said the sisters went to the beach every morning at 5:30, before the rest of the town was awake. The cloister was abrogated in 1915 and the high wall around the convent destroyed by the 1919 hurricane. The school and convent were moved to modern new facilities on South Alameda in the 1950s.

The Corpus Christi Female Academy, run by Professor J. D. Meredith and his wife, was in operation from 1880 to 1896. Meredith's school was in a tin-roof two-story building, painted black, between Lower Broadway and Mesquite, where the State

Hotel was built later. One account said that large stoves heated the classrooms, coal supplies were stored under the house, and the school toilets were outdoor privies.

Professor A. A. Brooks moved to Corpus Christi from Goliad, where he had a boarding school, and built a large house at Buffalo and Carancahua where he started a finishing school for young women called Kensmar Seminary.

The town's most prominent young ladies attended his seminary. Among the students in 1890 were Lulu and Blanche Rivera, Eva McCampbell, Selma Lichtenstein, Lottie Savage, Katie Ricklefsen, Nellie Chapman, May Ward, and Anna Mussett.

The year 1871 was a time of transition from private to public education. Classes for white students were held in the shellcrete Methodist Church where Professor McOmber formerly had his school. This was the original Methodist Church built in 1854 at the corner of Mesquite and Mann. It was used as a school during the week and for church services on Sunday. Classes for black students were held in Mann's old "Virginia House" on Water Street. Anna Moore Schwein, who was born a slave in 1856, attended this school.

William Hanna was the first public school principal, at the old Methodist Church, and his teachers were Rosa Beynon, Rhoda Burke and Hannah Conklin, who were each paid $50 a month. Lilly Rankin said Professor Hanna's teachers were very strict. One day she went to school with a cough which she tried to stifle. Rosa Beynon, her teacher, warned her that if she didn't stop coughing she would get a spanking. She said that cured her for the rest of the day.

—April 18, 2018

First public schools built in 1872

The first high-school commencement was held at Market
Hall in June 1893. The four graduates sang "Upidee," a
song about a Confederate bugle boy's yearning for
peace, followed by a piano recital titled "The Waves of
Corpus Christi."

After Corpus Christi got its first public schools in 1871, for the
fall term of 1872 the school board rented an old building on
Mesquite until two new buildings could be constructed.

It's not clear, based on the newspaper accounts, but it's
believed that the building rented was Lovenskiold's old Male and
Female Academy in the 200 block of Mesquite, across from
today's Spohn Park.

Two new school houses were constructed in 1872, one for
white students and one for blacks. They were built on land
donated by Richard King between Carancahua and Tancahua.
These were the city's first public school buildings constructed for
the purpose, which began a new era in which people believed
that education was a public responsibility.

Anna Moore Schwein said a two-story building, with floor
rooms on each floor, was built for the white students and south of
this was a smaller two-room building built for colored pupils.

The Weekly Gazette on Jan. 25, 1873 said the school for
colored children was completed and in use that the school for
white children was almost finished. It opened in May and was
known as the Central School.

The board of directors of the public schools of Nueces County
met on June 14, 1873. Members were Perry Doddridge, Horace

Students gather in front of the Central School on the bluff. The school, built in 1872, contained four classrooms on each floor. A wooden fence extended from the front porch across the schoolyard, which separated the boys' and girls' playgrounds.

Taylor, William Headen, and John J. Dix. Professor William Hanna was appointed principal at Corpus Christi with teachers Hannah Conklin, Rosa Beynon, Ellen Clark, and W. B. Lacy. The first school-board members elected in September 1873 were William L. Rogers, Nelson Plato and John M. Moore.

The new school system soon ran out of money; the state paid for only four months of operations. With no money to pay teachers and principals, the schools closed in 1873 when educators refused to work without pay. The four teachers and principal resigned in October 1873.

Trustees appealed to parents to pay "subscription" money to operate the schools. Those who signed a "subscription" were obligated to pay two or three dollars a month for six months. With funds in hand from this infusion, schools were reopened the following year.

After an enabling act was passed by the Legislature, the city took over the public schools inside the city limits in 1874. City Council members asserted their new authority by passing an ordinance intended to remove any religious flavor in the schools.

Professor Moses Menger was lured from Austin to become principal of Corpus Christi High School.

The ordinance said that "all religious exercises must cease from this time in the public schools." There was an outcry and the council backed down.

Solomon Coles was an ex-slave who was educated at Lincoln University and Yale Divinity School and ordained as a minister in the Congregational Church. When Coles arrived in Corpus Christi, the children of former slaves were being taught in the old Mann place on Water Street. Coles was named principal of the black public school on the bluff, with a salary of $42.88 a month.

Coles was described as quiet and unassuming, but "an exacting teacher and fine disciplinarian." One student recalled that "you had to be in your seat by 9 a.m. or you would get a whaling."

Coles left for San Antonio in 1894 where he taught school until he retired. The colored school was moved from the house next to the Central School to a four-room frame building on Winnebago, which had been a broom factory. In later years a new school was built on this site and named for Solomon Coles.

A campaign to improve education began in 1889 when Professor C. W. Crossley was named principal of the schools and the following year was appointed superintendent, the first to hold that position.

The city's first high school was a two-story building painted yellow. It was constructed in 1892 at a cost of $1,563, built next to the two elementary schools on school grounds in the block between Carancahua and Tancahua south of Leopard Street. The building housed the three high-school classes: juniors, sub-seniors, and seniors.

Professor Moses Menger was hired as principal of the high school. Menger was born in Toronto and educated at the University of Toronto. He taught at the Bickler Academy at Austin and schools in Flatonia and Halletsville. It was said that he had no superior as a teacher.

Under Menger's guidance, the high school established a reputation for excellence and was one of the few schools in the state whose graduates were accepted at the University of Texas without taking an entrance examination.

The first high-school commencement exercise was held at Market Hall in June 1893. The four graduates were Irving Westervelt, the valedictorian, Harry Ropes, Willie Blanton (a young woman), and Hattie Evans. As part of the program, the grads sang "Upidee," a song about a Confederate bugle boy's yearning for peace. This was followed by a piano recital titled "The Waves of Corpus Christi."

A room was rented in the Grande Building on Leopard Street for use as a classroom to teach first, second and third-grade Mexican-American pupils. Rose Dunne (later Shaw) was hired in 1896 to teach at what was called the Fourth Ward School. The school's main purpose was to teach children English so they could attend the Central school where they would go after completing the course of study at the Fourth Ward School. As a student progressed from one grade to the next, he or she would move from one side of the room to the other. An innovation was to place water coolers in the classrooms to reduce trips to water jars in the yard.

Rose Dunne Shaw said her first rule was order. "I would tap a bell for just about everything. One tap meant one thing and two taps meant something else and three taps meant to march outside for recess." Rose Shaw quit teaching for a time but she went to the 1902 graduation ceremony to see Julia Pena become one of the first Hispanic students to graduate from Corpus Christi High School.

—April 25, 2017

Mary Carroll started teaching in 1901

The new high school built in 1911 was called the Brick
Palace. "It had an auditorium, balcony and stage," Mary
Carroll said. "We thought it was so elegant."

Mary Carroll was hired to teach Spanish to students from the
sixth through 11 grades in 1901. Her father had designed St.
Patrick's Church and her uncle taught school in the Hidalgo
Seminary. She was raised in Mexico and spoke fluent Spanish.

Mary Carroll was 18 years old in 1901. She divided her school
days between the Central School and high school, teaching
Spanish to students from grades 6 through 11. She was paid $50
a month, which was less than what male teachers were paid.
"They explained the difference," she said later, "by saying that
men had dependents to support, but many women teachers did,
too, with younger brothers and sisters."

An act of the Legislature created the Corpus Christi
Independent School District in 1909. The new district had 1,296
students, 29 teachers and principals, four elementary schools and
one high school. One of the first acts of the district trustees was
to build a new high school. While it was being built, classes were
held in an old frame building on Staples which the students
called "the chicken coop."

Students moved out of the chicken coop into the Brick Palace in
1911. Some in town called it the new high school, although it
housed all the grades above the fourth grade before the new ward
schools were built. Because it cost $85,000 to build, a prince's
ransom back then, people in town called it the Brick Palace.

501

Mary Carroll, shown when she was 21, began teaching Spanish to grammar and high school students when she was 18, in 1901. She later became school superintendent.

It had an auditorium, balcony and stage," Mary Carroll said. "We thought it was so elegant."

Herman Behmann, whose family operated a grocery on Staples Street, attended school in the Brick Palace. "We didn't have any of this cafeteria set-up like today and we had to walk home to eat dinner and then back in the hour they gave us."

Three new ward schools — David Hirsch, Edward Furman, and George Evans — were built in 1912 at a cost of $11,000 each, all constructed using the same floor plan to save money. Theodore Fuller, who was a student at David Hirsch, wrote in his memoirs that the new schools "were the last word in modern school architecture."

One of the vacated old wooden buildings on the school grounds was moved to the Salt Lake to become the Salt Lake School. After one year the building was moved to North Carrizo

Corpus Christi High School, built on Carancahua in 1911, was generally known as the Brick Palace. It later became Northside Junior High.

and renamed the Mexican Central School with Rose Shaw as teacher. After the death of Cheston L. Heath, a longtime school-board member, the school was named for him.

In 1914, a new school superintendent was hired from Oklahoma. Joseph Tucker followed C. W. Crossley, who retired in 1913, and Moses Menger, who held the job for a year. Tucker did away with outdoor privies and moved restrooms indoors. He added vocational classes at the high school, including cooking and sewing for girls and metalwork and masonry for boys.

The cooking class was called domestic science. It was held in the basement of the high school. After the 1919 storm struck on Sept. 14, the domestic science lab was turned into a soup kitchen for the homeless survivors of the hurricane. "We got plenty experience cooking and cleaning up," one student recalled.

The entire city mourned when Professor Moses Menger died on April 1, 1920. An obituary in the Caller said "it was due as much to his efforts, more than those of any other individual, that the city has a school system of which it might well feel proud."

Mary Carroll, who began her career teaching Spanish, was named principal of the high school in 1921 and then school superintendent the following year. During her tenure as superintendent, the district got its first paid football coach. He was Charles Coleman, a teacher who had resigned to open a

503

produce business. Mary Carroll asked him to coach football for half of the season's gate receipts from football games. He made $301 for the season. The following year, in 1926, Nixon Askey was hired as a full-time football coach. The custom had been for a male teacher to coach for nothing on his own time.

When fire escapes were added to the upper floors of the Brick Palace, school officials conducted sliding drills and older boys stationed to help girls onto the slides. After a week of ruining shoes and snagging clothes, the thrill of the exercise wore off.

Lunchrooms were also added to the schools during Mary Carroll's tenure, Crossley Elementary was built in the Hillcrest addition in 1926, and Menger Elementary was built on South Alameda in 1928.

In 1929, with the city growing after the opening of the Port of Corpus Christi, the district built a new high school "out in the country" near the end of Leopard Street. School officials expected the city to grow to the west. The new high school cost $320,916, about four times what it cost to build the Brick Palace.

The school district opened its new three-story high school on Fisher Street. Corpus Christi High School (later renamed in honor of Roy Miller) had 26 larger-than-normal classrooms and a huge auditorium that would seat 1,600. A brick structure was built for the Cheston L. Heath School and the Brick Palace became the Northside Junior High School.

Corpus Christi's early school history is contained in the period from 1846, when Amanda Brooks began teaching in John Kelsey's store, to 1929, when the modern Corpus Christi High School was built off Leopard Street. In between were the major developments in education, including Charles Lovenskiold's academy in the 1850s, the Hidalgo Seminary in the 1860s and 1870s followed by the Incarnate Word, the beginning of public education in 1871 and the building of the first public school structures in 1872.

—May 2, 2018

Column 122

Farewell

I started writing a column on history in 1998. After more than 1,000 columns and about a million words, it seemed like a good time to call it quits.

I was doing research on Walter Timon, county judge and political boss in the early 20th Century, and suddenly it didn't seem to matter. I had written about Timon before, about his sparring match with the great Bob Fitzsimmons, about his father's mysterious death, and about his trial for election corruption in 1915. I put down my pen and closed my notebook.

Writing a column on history has gotten harder. Maybe because I have been doing it so long and there are few new topics to explore. And maybe, in these times of anxiety, stress and despondency, with the world about to blow up and the present so insistently in your face, it has become harder to concentrate on the past. They didn't study history during the Dark Ages.

I started writing a column on history — what seems now like a hundred years ago — in 1998. Nick Jimenez was editorial page editor and I was on the staff, with Brooks Peterson. When I mentioned writing a history column, Nick said he assumed I meant one column. I had more than that in mind though I would not have expected it to continue for 20 years.

I haven't counted the number of columns written since then, but I figure I wrote 1,000 columns over the years which, at more than 1,000 words per column, would be at least one million words. A million is a nice round figure. It seems like it is a good time to quit.

The way I remember it, what prompted me to start writing a history column was the void left when the late Bill Walraven retired. He was the paper's general columnist who also wrote about history. He wrote five or six columns a week and there wasn't much he didn't know about local and Texas history. In no way could I hope to match his historical knowledge so each column I wrote had to be well-researched. I learned as I wrote and each column advanced my knowledge of the past. It was made easier by the work of those who came before me, like Walraven and Dan Kilgore, and by contemporary historians like Norman Delaney and Mary Jo O'Rear.

I am not the product of any college history department. From an academic standpoint, I am a non-historian, a reporter who has looked for his stories in the annals of history, the equivalent of interviewing the dead.

I got into journalism because I wasn't smart enough to do anything else. I started at the bottom and worked my way down. Sixty-one years ago, when I was 12, I sold newspapers on street corners. I stayed around the business. I worked as a reporter and copy editor at a time when newsrooms were exciting places, with clattering typewriters and, in composing rooms, clicking linotypes. That tells you how long ago it was. By comparison, the typical newsroom today is as quiet as a morgue at midnight.

As a reporter in Alabama, I covered George Wallace's campaign and once got the worst haircut in my life in Decatur. The barber, who looked like a dead weasel, asked about Wallace and I provided a scathing assessment. I had failed to notice the Wallace sticker on the window when I went in. He gave me a good going-over. I walked out with a bowl-like haircut, the style affected by the Three Stooges, and a pencil-thin Ronald Colman mustache. I kept a low profile for about a month, avoiding mirrors and stooging about. That taught me something about barbers with political opinions, for I never discussed politics in a barbershop again.

I worked on the copy desk at the Flint, Mich., Journal and as a reporter in Mississippi, where I interviewed former Gov. Ross Barnett, who feared that integration would lead to blacks and whites being buried in the same cemeteries. I wrote about a UFO that landed and examined two shipyard workers on the coast. The mother of the younger one told me she warned her son before he left for Pascagoula to stay away from strangers.

I came to Corpus Christi in 1981 and soon joined the editorial page staff. My job was to write editorials which was like shooting arrows into an empty field that would hit no targets or like carrying the same heavy rock up a hill until it rolls down and you start all over again. They could have, just as easily, paid me not to write editorials for about the same effect and the same lack of results.

It turned out that writing about historical topics was more rewarding than writing editorials that nobody wanted to read. Delving into the past was fun, a form of escape like reading mystery novels, and one column led to another.

I compiled two photo history books for the Caller-Times and Jim Moloney and I teamed up to publish several history books, including "Corpus Christi, A History," "1919, The Storm," "Great Tales from the History of South Texas," and several volumes of past columns. It was fun and I was pleased as a dog with two tails.

I retired nine years ago, traded my watch for a calendar, but I was asked to continue to write a weekly column on historical topics. You get used to doing something and you sometimes forget how not to do it. The other day, as I was researching the Walter Timon piece, I realized there comes a time in the age of a writer when he is like the milkman's gray horse. One cold rainy morning he's too old to pull the milk wagon.

This is my second retirement. I knew a weekly newspaper editor in Louisiana who, before taking off for a week, left instructions to republish the previous week's edition with the headline "Reprinted by Popular Demand." As I leave off writing a column each week, the Caller-Times plans to reprint some old ones, whether by popular demand or not.

I wish to offer heartfelt thanks to those who have voiced their encouragement and given me assistance over these twenty years. I put down my notebook and ballpoint pen — the Walter Timon story will have to wait. I'll be around, at least until I'm history myself.   —*May 9, 2018*

Atkinson, Mamie (m. Hawley, Jones) 36, 428
Austin Brothers Bridge Company 467
Austin, Stephen F. 85, 126, 131
Avant, Andrew Jackson 82
Avery Point 116

Baffin Bay 217, 224, 414, 477
Bagdad, Mexico 42, 229, 288
Bagnall, Annie (Schallert) 253
Bagnall, Ernest 27
Baldes, Pete 247
Baldeschwiler, Andrew 292
Baldeschwiler, Blaize M. 292
Baldeschwiler, Peter 288, 292
Banks, Nathaniel P. 391
Banquete 14, 22, 25, 78, 117, 260
Banquete Cemetery 14
Banquete Creek 13
Barlow's Ferry 431
Barnard, E. L. 337
Barnard, John D. 484
Barnes, C. L. 398
Bascule Bridge 1-8, 3 (photo), 211, 401-404, 403 (photo)
Bauerfeind, Pearl 205
Bayside 121
Bayview Cemetery 164, 214, 436, 448

Bay View College 419-426, 421 (photo), 425 (photo), 465
Bean, Roy 476
Beason's Crossing 149
Bedichek, Roy 83, 86
Bee, Hamilton 118, 157, 229
Beeville 178, 247, 248, 423
Behmann, Herman 502
Belden, Frederick 71, 72, 269, 288, 327, 490
Bell, John 179
Benavides, Cristobal 112
Benavides, Placido 140
Benavides, Santos 391-392
Benson, Peter 176
Bernhard, Alva 202-203
Berry, Bob 279
Berry, Henry W. 258, 259, 269, 444-445
Beynon, Rosa 495 (photo), 496, 498
Beynon, Thomas 456, 477
Bickley, George 77-78
Bidwell Hotel 293
Biggio, William 275, 367-368
Billingsley, Walter 323
Bingham, R. H. 297
Black Land Special 481-483, 482 (photo)
Blacknall, J. C. 269
Black Point 116
Blackjack Point 116
Blake, William G. 35
Bliss, W. W. 444
Blossman, R. G. 98, 296

510

Buena Vista Hotel 218
(photo)
Buffalo Bayou 150, 152
Bunk's Café 362 (photo), 363
Burke, Rhoda 496
Burks, Amanda 323
Burleson, Edward 131-132
Burnet, David 149
Burnham's Ferry 149
Burns, Walter 75
Burr, Aaron 320
Burris, Basil 432
Burris, Mary Susanna 93,
360, 432
Burton, Isaac 116
Bush, George W. 180
Busse, Frederick 45
Buttrey's Ladies Wear 350
Byrne & Buckley 272

Cahill, Cornelius 253, 254,
255, 268, 369
Cabaniss Field 416
Cahill, Tom 22
Calallen 192, 193, 194, 203,
397, 423, 424
Caldwell, Ada (Lasater) 343
Caldwell, Edward Harvey 9-
10, 94, 269, 282, 334, 341-
343, 343 (home photo), 461
Caldwell, Julia 342
Caldwell, Sarah 343
Caldwell, William Herbert
341-342
Caller and Caller-Times 18-
19, 20-25, 28-29, 33, 35,

119, 272, 293, 350, 369-
370
Camacho, Manuel Avila 418
Camp Logan 198
Camp Scurry 119, 120, 163,
189-200, 191 (photo), 195
(photo), 199 (photo), 352
Camp Stanley 200
Camp Travis 197
Campion, William
Shakespeare 491-492
Carancahua Creek 241
Carpenter, C. W. 471
Carpenter, J. B., Mr. & Mrs.
332, 494
Carroll, Charles 262, 501
Carroll, Mary 262, 491, 501-
504, 502 (photo)
Carroll, William 491
Carruth, W. E. 475, 483
Carson Association 68
Cart Road 228
Casa Blanca 188, 359
Cass, Lewis 178
Castaneda, Francisco 123-
124
Castleberry, Ed 77
Cayo del Oso 415
Cazneau, Jane (Storm) 319-
320
Cazneau, William 319-320
Central Power & Light 405-
407, 406 (photos)
Central School 498 (photo),
499
Central Wharf 103

Chamberlain, Will 107
Chandler, D. T. 447
Chapman, Helen 233
Chapman, William 332, 355-356
Chatham Ravine 427
Chat 'N Chew 361-363, 362 (photo)
Chihuahua, Mexico 68, 70
Chiltipin Creek 101, 102
Chocolate Bayou 275, 367
Church of the Good Shepherd 164, 284, 341-342, 342 (photo)
City Drug Store 284
City Hall 185
City National Bank 62, 63 (photo)
Clara Ranch 50
Clark, Alice (Yantis) 420-426
Clark, Ellen 498
Clark, George 307
Clark, Jap 278
Clark, Jasper 172
Clark, Thomas Marshall (T. M.) 420-426
Clark, Wallace 420-426, 465
Clark, W. A. (Farmer) 11, 12
Clark, William 324
Clark, Z. H. 398
Clark's Island 324
Clarkwood 398
Clemmer, Marion (Merriman) 35, 257
Coakley, F. M. 236
Coffee, Mrs. Guy 202
Cohn, Herman 286, 333, 373

Cole, E. B. 300
Cole Park 300
Coleman, Charles 504
Coleman, C. N. 206
Coleman-Fulton Pasture Company 28, 101-102, 419
Coleman mansion 101-103, 102 (photo)
Coleman, Robert 128
Coleman, Thomas 101-103, 456
Coles, Solomon 499
Coleto Creek 146
Collier's magazine 416
Collins, L. G. 39
Collins, Warren (Rip) 196
Collinsworth, George 125-126, 129
Company B (Marines) 169-171, 170 (photo)
Concepcion (mission) 126-128, 127 (photo), 132
Conklin, Hannah 494, 496, 498
Constantine Hotel (see Bidwell)
Constitution (ship) 4, 402
Cook, Cora 493
Cooper, J. M. 427, 428
Cooper's Clean Bakery 98, 283, 378
Copanes 84
Copano 121-124, 125, 133, 136, 147, 386
Copano Point 116
Copley, J. J. 115, 314
Corbett, Jim 475-477, 480

Hanna, William 496
Hannibal Point 116
Hannah (ship) 264
Harbor Bridge 6-8, 7 (photo), 404
Harbor Island 103-104
Hardin, John Wesley 368, 478
Harney, John 307-309, 309 (art), 384
Harper, Sharlene (m. Whitley) 170
Harris, B. R. 297
Harrisburg 150
Hart, Elizabeth 256, 257, 386
Hart, James 235
Hatch, Eunice 248-249, 249 (photo)
Hatch, George C. 461
Hatch, Jim 248-249, 249 (photo)
Haverty, Daniel 223-224
Hawley, M. K. 36
Hawley, Priscilla (Stephenson) 300-301
Hayes, Rutherford B. 179
Hays, Jack 68, 69 (photo), 79
Headen, Matthew 278
Headen, William 278, 353-4, 356, 498
Headley, Fred 76
Heaney, Alfred G. 164, 208, 338, 340, 436, 483
Heath, Cheston L. 300
Heath, Cheston L. (school) 300, 503, 504

Heath, Mrs. Cheston L. (Smythe) 39
Heinley, Earl 352
Heinley, V. S. 352
Helena (town) 13, 233
Henrietta (mailboat) 255
Henry, Julius 277
Henry, Thomas J. 168
Henry, W. S. 288, 448
Hernandez, Apolinario 249
Hewitt, Daniel 352, 405
Hickey, Thomas 62
Hidalgo Seminary 44, 426, 491-492, 504
Hidalgo (town) 25
Highway Department 6, 404
Hill, John 35
Hill, Josephine (m. Petzel) 35
Hill, Lon 307
Hill, Zula (m. Blucher) 424
Hinnant, Hattie Mae 433
Hinojosa, Martin 277
Hinton, Harry 249
Hirsch, David 62, 273, 274, 276
Hirsch, David (school) 205-208, 206 (photo), 207 (photo), 424, 502
Hirsch, Joe 333
Hitchcock, Ethan Allen 73-74, 447-450, 449 (photo)
Hobbs, George 300
Hoffman, Prokop 253, 272, 282
Hogg, Jim 369
Holland, Dan 240

McCarthy, Elvira (m. Lozano) 42, 288
McCaughan, A. C. 307-309, 309 (art), 339, 379-380
McClane, John 223-225, 224 (photo), 237, 244, 301-302, 477
McClellan, George B. 355
McClintock, William 326-327
McCracken, Bob 201, 383-384, 486
McCulloch, Samuel Jr. 126
McDonough, Pat 280
McGee Beach 346
McGloin, Ameta 168, 206
McGloin, Gilbert 168
McGovern, George 180
McGregor, Doc 2, 3, 181-182, 185, 215-216, 286, 303-304, 307, 309 (art), 310-311, 377, 385, 393
McKenzie, James 281
McKinney, John 232
McMahon, Margaret (m. Nolan) 299
McManigle, Pat 244, 275, 368
McMullen, F. P. 208
McNeill, Alma 423
McNeill, Oliver 423
McNeill, Peyton 374, 423-424
McNeill, Tol 423
McNelly, Leander 368
McOmber, Professor 494, 496

Magnolia Mansion 14-16, 273
Maharis, George 207
Maher, Peter 476
Maldonado, Jesus 6
Malloy, George 328
Maltby, Henry 256
Maltby, William 256
Mancias, Joe 281
Manhattan Café 381
Mann, William 252, 356, 448
Market Hall 57-60, 59 (photo), 270, 274, 295-296, 296 (photo), 396, 479, 500
Marsden, Louella (m. Jones) 336
Marsh, Jane 168, 493
Marsh, Julia 490
Martin, Freeman 207
Martinez, Maximo 248
Mason, Doc 212, 263, 379, 383
Matagorda City 320
Mathis 28, 87
Mathis News 28
Maverick, Maury 65
Maury, Matthew 157
Maximilian, Emperor 157-158, 208
Mayes, Joe 383
Mayflower Café 283, 377-379
Mazatlan Rangers 68-70
Meade, George 446
Means, William 231
Meansville 236

Murray, Roy 289
Musselman, Nellie (m. Dunn) 30-31
Mussett, Wash 244
Mustang Island 221, 275, 367
Mustang Point 116
Muttera's Federal Bakery 182, 225-226
Muttera, Fred & Mae 225-226
Muttera, William 225-226
Myrtle Club 277, 349

Naval Air Station 55, 66, 186, 201-204, 380, 415-418, 486-487
Neal, Benjamin 232
Neighbors, Robert S. 164, 285
Neill, James 134
Neptune (ship) 68
Nicaragua (ship) 95-97, 96 (photos)
Nillson, O. 3, 402
Nine-Mile Point 116
Nixon Building 53, 321, 346
Nixon Café 346
Nixon, Maston 321, 481
Nixon, Richard 180
Noakes Brothers Machine Shop 272, 484
Noakes' store 28, 72
Noakes, Thomas 216, 229, 244-245, 264, 400, 491
Noble, Mary Ethel 326
Noessel, Felix 171
Noessel, George 271

Noessel, Otto 271
Nolan, Matthew (Mat) 214, 270, 299, 365, 408
Nolan, Thomas (Tom) 270, 408
Nold Academy 426
Nold, Henry & Elizabeth 426
North Beach 4, 211-213, 212 (photo), 216-217, 260, 266, 380, 416, 447, 452, 466, 475-477, 480-481
Northside Junior High 504
Norton, M. P. 490
Norvell, Marcus 202
Nueces Bay 414, 448, 459-470
Nueces Bay Causeway 466-470, 465 (photo), 469 (photo)
Nueces County 75-77, 98, 178-179, 228
Nueces County Courthouse (Hollub) 302, 408-409
Nueces County Courthouse (1914) 302, 409
Nueces County Jail 408-409, 409 (photo)
Nueces County Prohibition Club 21-24
Nueces Hardware 357-358, 358 (photos)
Nueces Hotel 18, 22-23, 32, 182, 191, 258, 261, 335, 381-382, 382 (photo), 385, 416, 455, 467
Nueces River 98, 111
Nueces River ferries 111

Solis, Fray Gaspar Jose 85
Sonora, Mexico 68, 70
South, D. B.22
Southern Alkali 321, 322
(photo)
Sowell, J. L. 269
Spence, B. J. (Bunk) 363
Spohn, Arthur 107, 119, 180,
246, 268, 297, 370, 483,
485 (photo)
Spoonts, Lorene (Jones) 221
Squeeze In Café 364
Stamm, Mr. & Mrs. Fred 298
Staples, W. N. 267, 272-273
Starner, Mrs. Ray 191-192
Starvation Point 116
State Hotel 300-301, 301
(photo)
Stayton, John W. 20, 164,
208
Stedman, Jerry 324
Stedman's Island 324
Steen, Fred 274
Steen Hotel 274
Stevens, Henry 76
Stevenson, Adlai 179
Stevenson, Coke 177
Stever, Jim 298
Stewart, Anna & Leo 397
Stewart, Tom 226
Sticktor, Jim 347
Stillman, Charles 97
Stillman, Cornelius 97
Stroman, Clara 40
Sullivan, Eliza Ann 263
Sun Pharmacy 355

Sunday, Billy 113-114, 114
(photo)
Sundeen Schools 400
Sunshine (community) 397,
400
Superach, John 256
Susser, Mr. and Mrs. Sam
364
Sutherland, H. R. Jr. 355
Sutherland, H. R. (Hugh)
181-182, 282, 353, 467
Sutherland, Mary 163, 214,
224, 301
Sutherland, Nellie (French)
422
Sutherland, W. G. 247, 305-
306, 455
Sutton, James 6
Suviah (ship) 443
Sweetland, Bill 347
Swift, J. T. 257
Swift, Mr. and Mrs. Thad
239-241

Taft (town) 87, 184, 317-318
Taft, Charles 102
Taft, William Howard 263,
290, 329
Tapia, Hypolita 236-237
Tarrant, Eleanor 8
Taylor, Hannah 168
Taylor, Horace 255, 498
Taylor, Shirley 421-422
Taylor, Zachary 13, 67-68,
73, 178-179, 213, 219, 257,
265-266, 275, 288, 290,

531

BOOKS AVAILABLE FROM NUECES PRESS

Corpus Christi – A History

A Soldier's Life

Great Tales from the History of South Texas

Recollections of Other Days

Perilous Trails of Texas

Columns   2009 – 2011

Columns 2 2012 – 2013

Columns 3 2014 – 2015

Columns 4 2016 – 2018

Signed copies are available from

www.nuecespress.com

www.ingramcontent.com/pod-product-compliance
Lightning Source LLC
Chambersburg PA
CBHW060419100426
42812CB00030B/3236/J